Conrad and Nature

> Joseph Conrad is a corner-stone for understanding modern literature and the human condition, and *Conrad and Nature: Essays*, both dramatically reshapes our understanding of his work in his contemporary world, and his legacy and importance in ours.
> —David Mulry, College of Coastal Georgia

Conrad and Nature is the first collection of critical essays examining nature and the environment in Joseph Conrad's writings. Together, these essays by established and emerging scholars reveal both the crucial importance of nature in Conrad's work and the vital, ongoing relevance of Conrad's treatment of the environment in our era of globalization and climate change. No richer subject matter for an environmentally engaged criticism can be found than the Conradian contexts and themes under investigation in this volume: island cultures, colonial occupations, storms at sea, mining and extraction, inconstant weather, ecological collapse and human communities competing for resources. The seventeen essays collected here—thirteen new essays, and four excerpts from classic works of Conradian scholarship—consolidate some of the most important voices and perspectives on Conrad's relation to the natural world, and open new avenues for Conradian and environmental scholarship in the twenty-first century.

Lissa Schneider-Rebozo is Professor of English and Director of Undergraduate Research at the University of Wisconsin-River Falls.

Jeffrey Mathes McCarthy is Director of Environmental Humanities at the University of Utah.

John G. Peters is University Distinguished Research Professor at the University of North Texas, past President of the Joseph Conrad Society of America and current General Editor of *Conradiana*.

Routledge Interdisciplinary Perspectives on Literature

90 **Provincializing the Bible**
Faulkner and Postsecular American Literature
Norman W. Jones

91 **Avant-Garde Pieties**
Aesthetics, Race, and the Renewal of Innovative Poetics
Joel Bettridge

92 **Modern Political Aesthetics from Romantic to Modernist Literature**
Choreographies of Social Performance
Tudor Balinisteanu

93 **Spatial Modernities**
Geography, Narrative, Imaginaries
Edited by Johannes Riquet and Elizabeth Kollmann

94 **God Behind the Screen**
Literary Portraits of Personality Disorders and Religion
Janko Andrijasevic

95 **Journeys Exposed**
Women's Writing, Photography, and Mobility
Giorgia Alù

96 **Conrad and Nature**
Essays
Edited by Lissa Schneider-Rebozo, Jeffrey Mathes McCarthy, and John G. Peters

For more information about this series, please visit: https://www.routledge.com

Conrad and Nature
Essays

Edited by
Lissa Schneider-Rebozo,
Jeffrey Mathes McCarthy and
John G. Peters

NEW YORK AND LONDON

First published 2019
by Routledge
711 Third Avenue, New York, NY 10017

and by Routledge
2 Park Square, Milton Park, Abingdon, Oxon OX14 4RN

Routledge is an imprint of the Taylor & Francis Group, an informa business

© 2019 Taylor & Francis

The right of the editors to be identified as the authors of the editorial material, and of the authors for their individual chapters, has been asserted in accordance with sections 77 and 78 of the Copyright, Designs and Patents Act 1988.

All rights reserved. No part of this book may be reprinted or reproduced or utilised in any form or by any electronic, mechanical, or other means, now known or hereafter invented, including photocopying and recording, or in any information storage or retrieval system, without permission in writing from the publishers.

Trademark notice: Product or corporate names may be trademarks or registered trademarks, and are used only for identification and explanation without intent to infringe.

Library of Congress Cataloging-in-Publication Data
CIP data has been applied for.

ISBN: 978-1-138-71012-2 (hbk)
ISBN: 978-1-315-18111-0 (ebk)

Typeset in Sabon
by codeMantra

Contents

1 Conrad, Nature and Environmental Criticism 1
  LISSA SCHNEIDER-REBOZO AND JEFFREY MATHES MCCARTHY

PART I
Conrad and the Anthropocene 19

2 Wilderness after Nature: Conrad, Empire
  and the Anthropocene 21
  JESSE OAK TAYLOR

3 Conrad in the Anthropocene: Steps to an
  Ecology of Catastrophe 43
  NIDESH LAWTOO

4 The Monstrous and the Secure: Reading
  Conrad in the Anthropocene 68
  ROBERT P. MARZEC

PART II
Conrad's Atmospherics 91

5 Dirty Weather 93
  TROY BOONE

6 The "Breaking-Up of the Monsoon and
  Lord Jim's Atmospherics 113
  BRENDAN KAVANAGH

Contents

  7 Conrad's Ecological Performativity: The Scenography of "Nature" from *An Outcast of the Islands* to *Lord Jim*   146
MARK DEGGAN

PART III
Conrad, Ethics and Ecology   171

  8 Conrad and Nature, 1900–1904   173
HUGH EPSTEIN

  9 "A Paradise of Snakes": Conrad's Ecological Ambivalence   196
J.A. BERNSTEIN

10 "What Could His Object Be?" Form and Materiality in Conrad's "The Tale"   211
JARICA LINN WATTS

PART IV
Nature, Empire and Commerce   233

11 *Nostromo* and World-Ecology   235
JAY PARKER

12 "He Can't Throw Any of His Coal-Dust in My Eyes": Adventurers and Entrepreneurs in *Victory*'s Coal Empire   252
SAMUEL PERKS

13 Guano, Globalization and Ecosystem Change in *Lord Jim*   269
MARK D. LARABEE

PART V
Earlier Commentary   287

14 From *The Challenge of Bewilderment*   289
PAUL ARMSTRONG

15 "Too Beautiful Altogether": Ideologies of Gender and Empire in *Heart of Darkness*   292
JOHANNA M. SMITH

16 From "Beyond Mastery: The Future of Conrad's Beginnings" 299
    GEOFFREY GALT HARPHAM

17 The World of Nature 311
    IAN WATT

    Notes on Contributors 319
    Index 323

1 Conrad, Nature and Environmental Criticism

Lissa Schneider-Rebozo and Jeffrey Mathes McCarthy

This collection asserts nature's centrality to Joseph Conrad's fictional worlds, and argues that nature's role in Conrad's writings is a crucial dynamic for Conrad studies in the twenty-first century. An environmentally engaged criticism in an era of globalization and climate change could hardly find a richer subject than the Conradian contexts and themes under investigation in this volume: island cultures, colonial occupations, storms at sea, mining and extraction, inconstant weather and human communities competing for resources. In Conrad's fictions, nature is not "out there"; nor does it stand in easy contrast to nation, place, society or any social construction. Rather, in Conrad's writings nature is a provocative mix of the material and the symbolic which, together, suffuse his explorations of the human experience in modernity. Contemporary environmental criticism provides the theoretical perspective for our examination of nature as an abiding presence in Conrad that, once noted, is as materially prevalent as the fermenting hippo on board the *Nellie* in "Heart of Darkness,"[1] and as allusive as an Eastern breeze in the closing paragraphs of "Youth."[2] The environmentally informed essays collected here build on the insights of ecocriticism, new materialism, critical race studies, gender and sexuality studies, postcolonial and postindependence studies to show how Conrad's work illuminates the environmental issues of his own time, even as it anticipates contemporary environmental criticism and current global environmental crises. The essays we have selected consolidate some of the most important voices and perspectives on these issues, and open new avenues for Conradian and environmental scholarship.

Thus, our era of intensifying storms, sea level rise, extinctions and climate refugees is a fitting moment to launch a collection exploring Joseph Conrad's relation to the natural world. Modernist Studies has reenergized itself in the last decade, and in that same period ecocriticism has become a major interpretive field within literary studies. Conrad's writings remain central to contemporary debates about modernism, postmodernism and meta-modernisms, and his influence on writers and thinkers around the globe continues to grow even as many others from the modern period find their relevance considerably diminished.

Much of the recent media and scholarly attention to Conrad has emphasized his political fictions about terror bombings, government and police corruptions and covert agents operating amid poor and middle-class citizenries in varying states of oblivion and exhaustion.[3] These more recent analyses of Conrad's writings were preceded by equally vital critiques of his colonial and neocolonial contexts.[4] In advancing a new volume that, for the first time, features Conrad and nature, we point to Conrad's own frame of reference as a writer whose work moves twixt land and sea,[5] and whose concept of "wilderness" encompasses the social and the economic as well as the environmental.

Conrad's fictional "wilderness" ranges from the Congolese forest jungle ravaged by late nineteenth-century Belgian misrule in "Heart of Darkness" and "An Outpost of Progress," to the "wilderness of poor houses" that populated early twentieth-century London in *The Secret Agent* (66), to the spaces occupied by the "wilderness of words" that comprise language itself in *Under Western Eyes* (11).[6] Conrad's true sympathies are notoriously difficult to identify, and yet this writer, prone to complex and deeply ironic expression, invariably privileges wilderness over its familiar binary, civilization.[7] *Wilderness* is a fraught term for environmental critics pushing back against a simplification of unpeopled natural spaces while demonstrating the cultural forces activating wilderness's influence—colonialism, androcentrism, classism.[8] This tension makes it even more important to advance a parallel analysis of wilderness and Conrad. At times, Conrad's evident preference for natural wilderness is clear and unequivocal, albeit tinged with the Romantic:

> You, too, shall taste of that peace and that unrest in a searching intimacy with your own self—obscure as we were and as supreme in the face of all the winds and all the seas, in an immensity that receives no impress, preserves no memories, and keeps no reckoning of lives.
> (*Shadow-Line* 47)

In the Romantic fallacy, nature can become a simplified human testing ground for good or for ill; yet Conrad's complex equivocations still align us with wilderness over civilization. Hence, in "Heart of Darkness," Marlow describes his decision to protect Kurtz's memory over the Company and the petty plottings of its other employees, even though he understands Kurtz's time in the wilderness has corrupted him beyond recovery:

> The wilderness had patted [Kurtz] on the head, and, behold, it was like a ball— an ivory ball; it had caressed him, and—lo!—he had withered; it had… sealed his soul to its own by the inconceivable ceremonies of some devilish initiation.
> (93)

Marlow presents the men aboard the *Nellie* with a version of wilderness that serves as a seductive and malignant force acting on Kurtz, yet he still prefers Kurtz, and wilderness, to a civilization that produces the pilgrims of the Eldorado Exploring Expedition, the petty bureaucrats working for the Belgian trading company and the Intended ensconced within her claustrophobic drawing rooms.

Likewise, in Conrad's other Congo fiction, "An Outpost of Progress," Carlier's future vision of a civilized Congo presents its own form of European seduction and criminal corruption: "In a hundred years, there will be perhaps a town here. Quays, and warehouses, and barracks, and—and—billiard-rooms. Civilization, my boy, and virtue—and all" (83). In late nineteenth-century Congo, the default European counterpoint to wilderness is a civilization structured around the forcible seizure of natural resources: warehouses to store ivory and rubber; quays to dock the ships that will export the raw materials; barracks and billiards halls to house and entertain the soldiers enforcing the new order. Carlier's vision of the Congo's future in a hundred years recasts in exact terms the existing order, and thereby puts to rest the lie that the civilizing mission of the occupying Belgians will ever include hospitals, schools or churches. In all of Conrad's fictions, any notion that a model "civilization" might be found in contemporary nineteenth-century Europe, or that a savage or natural "wilderness" might provide the justification for Europe's colonizing expansion, is stripped away. This is true of Conrad's cities as well as his jungles: for instance, in *The Secret Agent* Conrad depicts London's "wilderness of poor houses"—and the people and domesticated animals inhabiting this "wilderness" provide the moral center for this complex treatment of modern psychology, politics and economy. Thus, Winnie Verloc's brother Stevie—traveling with his mother and sister by cab to the charity almshouse—protests the brutish beating of the aging, half-starved cab horse, and the desperation of the cab man, by stammering: "Bad world for poor people" (132).

The editors initiated this project to show environmental thinkers the ongoing importance of Conrad's writings in comprehending historic and present-day environmental conflicts and global communities, and to emphasize to global modernists and Conradians the powerful insights of environmental criticism for our understanding of Conrad's nature as metaphor and theme. *Conrad and Nature* delivers new readings of Conrad's canonical works by foregrounding nature while, at the same time, testing the relevance and validity of environmental criticism against the fin de siècle conflagrations and conflicts that provided the contexts for many of his best-known stories.

Of the word "nature" Raymond Williams has written that it might be "the most complex word in the language" because we lean on it in so many ways (223). We acknowledge this complexity, and welcome the multiple and interlacing ways our authors define nature, and deploy ecocriticism as an interpretive tool. Since the first publication of Williams' *Keywords* in 1974, scores of ecocritics have reinforced the relevance of nature as a locus for literary analysis and have toiled with increasing care and precision in their application of the interpretive tools this provides. In recent years, ecocriticism and environmental studies have deepened the contrast between Romantic notions of nature as an inspiring realm of more-than-human, ungoverned force and post-structuralist understandings of nature as a set of human constructions sculpted from the cultural experiences and political constellations that frame the world around us.[9] Of course, as Barbara K. Seeber has pointed out in her recent analysis of Jane Austen, "when 19th and early 20th century authors spoke of nature, they usually meant human nature" (1). Not so in Conrad. In this moment of uneasy jostling between post-structuralist and new materialist sensibilities, Conrad allows us to explore definitions of nature as a world separate from humanity or as the ground for Kantian figures of human consciousness.

The essays we have included in this volume map this contested terrain. Recent environmental scholarship pushes beyond the tired ground of wilderness epiphanies, Romantic self-improvement and celebrations of place. This is not to say ecocriticism has lost its green edge, only that ecocritics are contributing to ongoing conversations about gender, race, power and nature's material presence. The new Modernist studies has likewise bloomed beyond its roots. There was a time when studying modernism meant celebrating the heroic words of artists decrying the conformist, commercial culture that oppressed them.[10] Astradur Eysteinsson sums this up nicely: "Modernism is viewed as a kind of aesthetic heroism, which in the face of the chaos of the modern world…sees art as the only dependable reality" (9). But the character of individual resistance via radical art has been unmasked with increasing vehemence. Since the 1980s, cultural critics have challenged some modernists, especially those modernist forerunners associated with the avant-garde, for implicit and explicit collaborations with capitalism, misogyny, imperialism, anti-Semitism and reactionary politics.[11] Only in recent years, with the emergence of revisionist Congo histories and renewed global attention, has the full extent to which all of Conrad's art—not just the sea stories—has been informed by realism begun to impress itself anew on critics. In this vein, Hunt Hawkins has noted the way Conrad "on many topics, including race, offers views that are multiple, ambiguous, ambivalent, conflicting and perhaps even ultimately incoherent" (366). Yet Hawkins goes on to say that in Conrad's "Heart of Darkness," its "lasting political legacy… more than any confirmation of racism, has been its alarm over atrocity.… Far from condoning genocide, Conrad clearly saw humanity's horrific capacity and gave it a name" (375). Adam Hochschild takes this argument even further when he notes Conrad's use of irony, ambiguity and complex framing devices to challenge rather than to concede to the widespread reactionary politics and imperialist logic of the late nineteenth and early twentieth centuries, and create a literary form both new and modern. Across this collection, scholars place Conrad's writings in their historical and cultural contexts; they look closely at the cultural and literary functions nature performs and provide an intentional, systematic examination of nature in the fictions.

Environmental readings can also foreground the significance of material nature in Conrad's work.[12] Whether as vibrant matter, object-oriented ontology or transcorporeality, scholars in this collection unpack the urgent transaction between people and places. The political theorist Jane Bennett says natural things are "vivid entities not entirely reducible to the contexts in which (human) subjects set them" (5). The environmental critic Stacy Alaimo's *Bodily Natures* "explores the interconnections, interchanges and transits between human bodies and non-human natures" (2). The new materialism emphasizes the influence of the more-than-human world. In a similar manner, Conrad's fictions unsettle human confidence in human exceptionalism—regional, national, political—and reinforce the enduring presence of nonhuman natures in a more-than-human world. Thus, while traveling up the tree-lined Congo River in "Heart of Darkness," Marlow remarks on the insignificance of the men and their "begrimed" beetle-like boat in the midst of the jungle:

> Trees, trees, millions of trees, massive, immense, running up high, and at their foot, hugging the bank against the stream, crept the little begrimed steamboat like a sluggish beetle crawling on the floor of a lofty portico. [...] Where the pilgrims imagined it crawled to I don't know. To some place where they expected to get something, I bet!
>
> (78)

Throughout Conrad's writings, we find similar moments that disallow European exceptionalism and confidence in a progress as flawed or futile as that of the European pilgrims on Marlow's steamer. Several essays in this volume push that important work another step forward using new materialist analyses to show the limitations of species-ism and anthropocentrism. In Conrad, the natural world is often presented as an active force integrating with human designs and overlapping with human bodies to reveal other agencies beyond the human.

This collection supplements traditional modernist criticism by uniting treatments of Conrad's fiction with theorizations of the natural world. *Conrad and Nature* delivers new critical work by tilling the common ground of cultural critique, of a material natural world, and of historicism to reveal the limits of our concept of nature, and the grand possibility of nature as an analytic tool. At one time, nature was widely conceptualized as a site of and for Romantic self-improvement; this once near-ubiquitous understanding has given way to new understandings of nature as inseparably entwined with environmental justice, object-oriented ontology, post-wilderness ecology and social construction. The position of Romantic nature is especially significant here. Once, nature was represented as a healing scene of wholeness and harmony, a restorative balm to the afflicted modern subject. The works of poets William Wordsworth, John Clare, and Percy Shelley have often been read as setting a soulless industrial society against redemptive versions of "the natural." The world may be too much with us, but contemporary environmental critics have shown that Romantic simplifications of nature's restorative power obscure the actual uses to which nature is put. From a postcolonial perspective, Ramachandra Guha's "Radical American Environmentalism and Wilderness Preservation: A Third World Critique" challenges the naive application of Romantic nature to the developing world:

> Because India is a long settled and densely populated country in which agrarian populations have a finely balanced relationship with nature, the setting aside of wilderness areas has resulted in a direct transfer of resources from the poor to the rich.
>
> (75)

Here a western idealization of wilderness displaces the vulnerable of India in the service of the powerful. Similarly, William Cronon's "The Trouble with Wilderness" has disrupted American environmentalism's own infatuation with wilderness by locating the frontier and the sublime in a particular cultural moment, and by highlighting this ideology's indigenous victims:

> The myth of the wilderness as 'virgin,' uninhabited land had always been especially cruel when seen from the perspective of the Indians who had once called that land home. Now they were forced to move elsewhere, with the result that tourists could safely enjoy the illusion that they were seeing their nation in its pristine, original state, in the new morning of God's own creation.
>
> (78)

For Cronon (and for other scholars like J. Baird Callicott and Giovanna Di Chiro) the long period dominated by a Romantic narrative of wilderness and transcendence enforced a false dualism between nature and culture while tending to obscure the Eurocentric domination of indigenous groups and working people. In Conrad, the tragedy of this false dualism is most manifest in *Lord Jim*, when Marlow suggests that Jim hide himself away from the world in Patusan, a decision with disastrous consequences for the Bugis people of that region, and ultimately for Jim himself. In "An Outpost of Progress," the nameless narrator reminds us that where Kayerts and Carlier see a dark wilderness, desolate and empty, the jungle is in fact a place of "brilliant sunshine," teeming with the life of a complex multicultural society (81).[13]

This study shows that many of Conrad's European characters have demonstrated the suspicion, articulated by Guha and Cronon, of a virgin and Edenic, redeeming, natural world. From Old Singleton to Mister Kurtz, the promise of pastoral escape has been supplanted by humanity negotiating an unreliable environment through craft, through persistence, and through struggle. Virginia Woolf idealizes nature's import to Conrad in her obituary essay "Joseph Conrad." She writes that Conrad's distinctive characters were

> used to solitude and silence. They were in conflict with Nature, but at peace with man. Nature was their antagonist; she it was who drew forth honour, magnanimity, loyalty, the qualities proper to man; she who in sheltered bays reared to womanhood beautiful girls unfathomable and austere. Above all, it was Nature who turned out such gnarled and tested characters as Captain Whalley and old Singleton, obscure but glorious in their obscurity.
>
> (225)

Here Woolf herself uncharacteristically falls prey to a Romantic fallacy, seeing in Conrad's nature only the testing ground, the foundry from which best selves can be wrought. But Conrad's natural arena, whether in presentations of stormy savagery or of calm, has its casualties too, as evinced by Decoud in *Nostromo*, the deranged second mate in "Typhoon," and Kayerts and Carlier in "An Outpost of Progress." Romantic notions of human refreshment and renewal through wild nature are generally refused by Conrad's tales. As Marlow warns the men aboard the *Nellie*, "Here you all are, each moored with two good addresses, like a hulk with two anchors, a butcher round one corner, a policeman round another, excellent appetites, and temperature normal" (93). How westerners respond when unmoored from their society is Conrad's special terrain.

Conrad's double-edged presentations of nature are important amid the twenty-first century's Anthropocene preoccupations and our unprecedented, ever intensifying series of super storms, fires and tsunamis. Ultimately, works such as "Typhoon," *Lord Jim* or *Nostromo* attend to human kinships under strain. The term "Anthropocene" is often used as shorthand for environmental crises that unfurl from human impacts, and it especially references the gathering catastrophe that we call climate change. Essays in this book emphasize Conrad's importance in understanding the Anthropocene, arguing that his texts come to us both as instruments for reckoning disruption and as models for scripting recovery.

The key insight is that human tools of morality and social organization choreograph social responses to environmental pressures and dwindling resources. From "Youth" to *Victory*, the impacts of an uncertain environment are social—human communities experience the physical reality of environmental change through social frames like ethics and morality. Moreover, after disruption, human communities struggle to recreate themselves with the moral equipment at hand. "Typhoon"—perhaps Conrad's most focused dissection of environmental disruption and social consequences—is a tale that strongly illustrates our claim that the Anthropocene is best understood as a phenomenon of both nature and culture.

"Typhoon" is the story of a human community beset by natural violence. It matters that typhoons are tropical cyclones and that their tight spirals of wind regularly beset the western Pacific Ocean. What matters more, however, is that Conrad delivers a merchant ship into a ferocious storm, and that the men must contend with one another to bring both the physical ship that carries them and the ethical community that sustains them through the danger. Within the *Nan-Shan* the extreme weather event threatens two bifurcated human societies—the European seamen above decks and the homeward-bound Chinese workers siloed below—with social chaos and with the breakdown of moral obligation between people: "This is the disintegrating power of a great wind: it isolates one from one's kind" (40). The threats in "Typhoon" are isolation and social disintegration. Steve Mentz's *Shipwreck Modernity* (2015) makes ships under stress a trope for humanity under ecological strain: "shipwreck stories represent the human experience of natural hostility, narrating humankind's failed attempts to navigate an uncertain world" (xxv). In "Typhoon" this attempt is as much moral as it is physical. The effects of a superstorm on the struggling ship, the *Nan-Shan*, serve to intensify the existing social frictions in ways that anticipate twenty-first-century displacements, disruptions, and racial and national tensions. Conrad's "Typhoon" spotlights first what Mentz calls "an uncertain world," and forces readers to linger on every community's ethical precarity. The Chinese laborers returning home are buffeted and tossed by the *Nan-Shan*'s gyrations, and the hold becomes a chaos of the dispossessed—poor people in a global system uncertain whether to cling to their paltry wages or to their own abused bodies. The view by lantern is a metaphor of climate-induced disaster: "a mass of writhing bodies piled up to port detached itself from the ship's side and skidding, inert and struggling, shifted to starboard with a dull, brutal thump" (58). The moral center of the story is the recognition of their trouble, and Captain MacWhirr's decision to address this misery no matter the ship's physical condition even as, or perhaps, precisely because, in his decision to drive head on into the storm, MacWhirr is its author. What this says is that the shipwreck threatening the *Nan-Shan* is also an ethical threat, and the people who share this frail craft must acknowledge one another's plight in a collapsing climate. "Typhoon" makes its eponymous weather event the perfect vehicle for exploring the ethical imperatives that define a community under stress.

Society itself has long been symbolized as a ship, so the ship remains a useful metaphor for reckoning with climate change. In the writings of Plato, Melville, Conrad and beyond, the ship, beset by storms of dissension or state threat, has occasionally represented a troubled body politic.[14] To write about Conrad and nature, it is worth lingering on theories of the sea and expressions of humanity's posture within the maritime environment. Conrad was by any reckoning far more than just an author of sea tales; and yet in a volume on Conrad and nature, the seas, and the ships upon them, warrant additional attention. Michel Serres insists we must renegotiate a "natural contract" between people and planet. The violence humans press on the planet is now reciprocated by droughts, sea level rise and the countless horsemen of climate change. "Those who share power today have forgotten nature," writes Serres, "which could be said to be taking its revenge but which, more to the point, is reminding us of its existence" (29). For Serres, the natural contract is a constant of shipboard life and necessitates an instructive commitment between crew members:

> on board, social existence never ceases, and no one can retire to his private tent, as the infantry warrior Achilles did long ago. On a boat, there's no refuge on which to pitch a tent, for the collectivity is enclosed by the strict definition of the guardrails: outside the barrier is death by drowning. This total social state ... holds seagoers to the law of politeness, where 'polite' means politic or political. ... They get the social contract directly from nature.
>
> (40)

This social state as described by Serres is never more evident than in Conradian sea tales, which contain the raw materials of social construction and of intense life-or-death relations to nature. It is why, on board Conrad's *Narcissus*, the mate castigates a whinging crew: "Are you a lot of women passengers to be taken care of? We are here to take care of the ship—and some of you ain't up to that" (63). Or again from "Typhoon," the deck officers and the engine-room crew must put aside their frictions to face the storm. The social contract is a recurrent theme in Conrad's sea tales, and it is each ship's relation to a difficult nature that intensifies what Serres calls "this total social state." Within our own twenty-first-century context of superstorms, rising seas and intensifying weather, humanity navigates an unfriendly environment, and the poorest humans—"inert and struggling"—have the fewest resources to negotiate that environment, making shipboard unity all the more vital.

Amid all this, environmental readings of Conrad warn us that while the craft we use matters, the community on board ship is always the most important part. Thus, Conrad's sea stories offer both a warning and a promise about humanity's ongoing encounters with a disrupted climate, and its negative effects—the unequal allocation of shrinking resources and increasingly hostile racial, sociocultural and national divisions.

Conrad and Nature repeatedly returns to Conradian fictions that represent meteorological and social upheaval. If this natural world seems especially disrupted, it is worth noting that Conrad has ever been suspicious of pastoral peace. *Pastoral* is a key term for environmental criticism. From Virgil onward, the pastoral has been posited as a contrived but culturally important retreat into an idealized natural setting. Thus, essays in this volume measure climatological and human disruption of the natural world as key elements of Conrad's fictional achievement.

Conrad's work often deploys an anti-pastoral that raises expectations for green ease and simplicity, only to dash them. Even Conrad's lesser-known tales such as "Amy Foster" and "The Idiots," both set in peacetime European farming villages, are riven by destructive social and environmental forces and an anti-pastoral sensibility. Thus Yanko Goorall, the sole human survivor to reach the English shoreline after a gruesome storm and shipwreck in "Amy Foster," will be beaten, chased and confined by local farmers. Rare kindnesses remain insufficient to sustain him; his death from exposure and neglect resonates painfully with a Hobbesian view of human life as "nasty, brutish, and short." In "The Idiots," green ease on pastoral farmlands is equally illusory: the Bacadou family's genetic tragedy will evoke a murder-suicide followed by a cynical anti-republican plot to leverage control over the community by taking control of the Bacadou farm. In both tales, the vividly rendered tragedy of one human being is made to stand in for the tragedy of the many; hence, Yanko Goorall is placeholder not just for the plight of one in a xenophobic English village, or even for the 200 lost souls of his own ship, but for all the displaced youth of the Carpathian mountains who signed over farmland and livestock to be freighted away in cattle trains and cargo holds seeking American fortunes while falling prey to late nineteenth-century Eastern European land grabs.

Ian Watt also notes the anti-pastoral in Conrad, saying: "Conrad's attitude to nature is in one sense the opposite of Wordsworth's. He does not feel love for the landscape, or try to persuade himself that his feelings are in any way reciprocated" (96–7). In "Heart of Darkness," Kurtz (erstwhile member of the "gang of virtue") could be the Romantic voyager journeying into leafy nature his best self to find. Like Wordsworth or Thoreau, he heads into the jungle—"the lone white man turning his back suddenly on the headquarters, on relief, on thoughts of home" (75). Unlike Wordsworth's poetic speaker who laments, "little we see in nature that is ours," Kurtz immerses himself in a pastoral tableau with green nature and simple living, but instead of improving himself becomes a monstrous and voracious consumer, devouring all in his path. As Marlow tells the men aboard the *Nellie*, "You should have heard him say, 'My ivory.' Oh, yes, I heard him. 'My Intended, my ivory, my station, my river, my—'Everything belonged to him'" (94). Paul Fussell's *The Great War and Modern Memory* catalogues an analogous ironic pastoral between World War I poetry and the Flanders fields plowed by shells and planted with bodies. His chapter "Arcadian Recourses" argues war poets accosted their readers with the bitter irony of exploded pastoral scenes. The point for Fussell is that pastoral expectations intensify the modern reader's shock at trench warfare, and the parallel point for Conrad studies is the way a tradition of English nature-writing primes readers to be stunned by Kurtz's transformation in the wild—not uplifted but undone.

The essays in *Conrad and Nature* offer dramatic counterpoints to the affirmative, even naive, nature-writing tradition Raymond Williams called "the green language." In *The Country and the City*, Williams sought to change that tradition by asserting the centrality of labor, and by showing that stories of a past, Edenic stability always recede into myth. Williams replaces a fantastical vision of an idealized rural stability with a nuanced, historically grounded picture of economic oppression. Conrad's fictions repeatedly subvert an idealized, pastoral tradition of sociocultural and economic stability. Greg Garrard characterizes "pastoral ecology" as a "stable, enduring counterpoint to the disruptive energy and change of human societies" (56). An environmental reading of Conrad participates in ecocriticism's wholesale reappraisal of "green language" and emphasizes, instead, the fundamental entropy and disruption of the natural systems that surround us in the twenty-first century. This is where it is beneficial to change our critical thinking from green to blue, from the land to the sea. Scholars of the "Blue Humanities" argue that environmental criticism has mistakenly accepted the model of the garden for humans in nature when a better model is the rolling, splashing uncertainty of the sea waters that compose 70 percent of planet Earth. Conrad chafed against those who would reduce him to merely a purveyor of sea stories and boys' adventures; however, Conrad's acute depictions of sailors at sea present us with one template for positive human relations to nature. In place of idealized pastoral stability Conrad gives us the tempestuous upheaval of shipboard life and dramatizes the resilience necessary for human communities to subsist.

If Conrad's sea tales push us from land to sea in our thinking about nature and humanity, such a move is matched by recent assertions from environmental critics. Influential scholars like Stephanie Lemenager, Allison Carruth and Paul Outka write that the term "resilience" better captures ecological aspirations under climate change than a word like "sustainability" because the former emphasizes negotiating constant change, while the latter urges us toward an unrealistic stasis.[15] Again, constant change versus a comforting stability is the difference between the sea and the garden. Steve Mentz argues that the sea is a more helpful rendering of humanity's relation to a changing natural environment than the garden, because the sea offers us no false stability; it is forever unstable and disordered: "Imagining earth as ocean rather than garden enables us to escape pastoral nostalgia," and this is crucial because "we need dynamic narratives about our relation to the biosphere" ("After Sustainability" 587). The pastoral's master trope of the garden—tended into order by human hands—is dishonest to the Anthropocene disruptions that surround us, and from the *Narcissus* to the San Tomé mine, Conrad locates his narratives in dynamic fast-changing environments that threaten human and animal health and destabilize sustaining communal structures and bonds.

In 1908, Conrad's close friend, the novelist John Galsworthy, published one of the most astute Conradian commentaries of his day, and was the first to point to nature's primacy in Conrad's writings:

> In the novels of Balzac and Charles Dickens there is the feeling of environment, of the growth of men from men. In the novels of Turgenev the characters are bathed in light. Nature with her many moods is all around them, but man is first. In the novels of Joseph Conrad, Nature is first, Man second.
>
> (628)

We take our cue from Galsworthy and argue that a theoretically informed environmental criticism is the perfect tool for unpacking Conrad's significance to contemporary environmental thought, and vice versa. The scholars in this collection also lay the groundwork for future explorations of a society changing its relation to nature. Much has been written of Conrad's own response to evolution and to nineteenth-century science, and all of it indicates the transformative social power of new understandings of the human place in nature.[16] Galsworthy's argument is that other novelists give us nature as setting or nature as process, but Conrad gives us nature itself. In *Nostromo*, Conrad's Golfo Placido refines human insecurities; aboard the *Narcissus*, storm winds bring human conflicts to crisis; and in "An Outpost of Progress" European removal to the jungle accelerates their moral collapse. The Anthropocene brings us again to a social renegotiation of humanity's place in the global story, and in this fraught transaction Conrad's work offers some firm precedent.

In a sense, the environmental critic is positioned to enhance Conrad's relevance today precisely because, as Galsworthy put it, "Nature is first, Man second." The Anthropocene's vast unsettling obliges us to measure our ethical obligations to "shipmates" in peril—displaced peoples, climate refugees, the tattered remnants of colonialism. Neoliberal globalization and colonial legacies distribute environmental harms and environmental benefits unequally, and the critical insights of slow violence, of shipwreck modernity, of the anti-pastoral all help us discern what is at stake in fiction's relation to reality. Across this volume, scholars examine exactly these issues through the lens of Conrad studies.

So, *Conrad and Nature* rewrites the story of Conrad and nature. These pages scrutinize nature in the modernist imagination, nature in nationalist ideology, nature in cultural appropriation and nature in the global economy. What emerges is a timely confirmation of Conrad's role in connecting contemporary scholarship to the burning issues of this day's environmental change.

Notes

1 In a well-known passage, Marlow tries to explain to the men aboard the *Nellie* what it was really like on his "tin pot steamer" as he traveled up the Congo river with a crew whose principal food supply was hippo meat: "The earth for us is a place to live in, where we must put up with sights, with sounds, with smells too by Jove! — breathe dead hippo, so to speak, and not be contaminated" (94).
2 "We drag at the oars with aching arms, and suddenly a puff of wind, a puff faint and tepid and laden with strange odours of blossoms, of aromatic wood, comes out of the still night—the first sigh of the East on my face. That I can never forget. It was impalpable and enslaving, like a charm, like a whispered promise of mysterious delight" ("Youth" 35–6). For more on anthropomorphism, femininity, and the Eastern breeze in Conrad's "Youth," see Schneider's *Conrad's Narratives of Difference*, Routledge, 2003. pp. 36–38.
3 Houen, Alex. *Terrorism and Modern Literature, From Joseph Conrad to Ciaran Carson*, Oxford University Press, 2002; Reiss, Tom. "The True Classic of Terrorism." *The New York Times*, New York. September 11, 2005; Miller, John J. "The Dawn of the Terror Era." *The National Review*, October 10, 2016; Mulry, David. *Joseph Conrad among the Anarchists: Nineteenth Century Terrorism and the Secret Agent*, Palgrave Macmillan, 2016; Jasanoff, Maya. *The Dawn Watch: Joseph Conrad in a Global World*, William Collins, 2017.
4 See, for just a few examples, Edward Said, *The World, the Text, and the Critic*, Harvard, 1983; Said, *Culture and Imperialism*, Vintage, 1993; Homi K. Bhabha, *Nation and Narration*, Routledge, 1990; Patrick Brantlinger, *Rule of Darkness: British Literature and Imperialism 1830–1940*, Cornell University Press, 1988; Gail Fincham, *Under Postcolonial Eyes: Joseph Conrad after Empire*, University of Cape Town Press, 1996; Adam Hochschild, *King Leopold's Ghost: A Story of Greed, Terror and Heroism in Colonial Africa*, Houghton Mifflin, 1998; Michela Wrong, *Living on the Brink of Disaster in Mobutu's Congo: In the Footsteps of Mr. Kurtz*, Harper Collins, 2000.
5 *Twixt Land and Sea: Tales* (1912).
6 For more on the significance of Conrad's depiction of London's "wilderness of poor houses," see Schneider's "Politics in the House: Genre, Narrative, and the Domestic Drama" in *Conrad's Narratives of Difference*, Routledge, 2003. pp 103–120. For more on language and words as formulas for peace

and as wilderness, see Schneider's "Plots and Performance" in *Conrad's Narratives of Difference,* especially 43–51. In *Under Western Eyes,* the English Instructor of Languages sets words in opposition to imagination:

> To begin with I wish to disclaim the possession of those high gifts of imagination and expression which would have enabled my pen to create for the reader the personality of the man who called himself, after the Russian custom, Cyril son of Isidor—Kirylo Sidorovitch—Razumov.
>
> If I have ever had these gifts in any sort of living form they have been smothered out of existence a long time ago under a wilderness of words. Words, as is well known, are the great foes of reality.
>
> (11)

7 Of Conrad's view on civilization, Ted Billy has said, "Conrad presents civilization as a refinement of primal savagery, capitalism as an evolutionary phase of the struggle for existence, and institutional religion as a haven for hypocrites" (37) in *A Wilderness of Words: Closure and Disclosure in Conrad's Short Fiction,* Texas Tech Press, 1997.

8 See William Cronon's "The Trouble with Wilderness", Timothy Luke's *Ecocritique,* University of Minnesota Press, 1997; and Vera Norwood's *Made from This Earth,* University of North Carolina Press, 1993.

9 Consider, to name a few studies that recast Romantic nature, Timothy Morton's *Ecology Without Nature,* Harvard University Press, 2009; Val Plumwood's *Feminism and the Mastery of Nature,* Routledge Press, 1993; Dana Phillips' *The Truth of Ecology,* Oxford University Press, 2003; David Mazel's *American Literary Environmentalism,* University of Georgia Press, 2000; Stacy Alaimo's *Bodily Natures,* Indiana University Press, 2010; and Ursula Heise's *Sense of Place Sense of Planet,* Oxford University Press, 2010.

10 Influential postwar studies of modernism celebrated its iconoclasm and resistance to modernity. For example, Irving Howe's *Politics and the Novel,* Columbia University Press, 1957; Hugh Kenner's *The Pound Era,* University of California Press, 1971; and *Matei* Calinescu's *Faces of Modernity,* Indiana University Press, 1977.

11 See, for example, Marianne Dekoven's *Rich and Strange,* Princeton University Press, 1991; Charles Ferrall's *Modernism and Reactionary Politics,* Cambridge University Press, 2009; Anthony Julius's *T.S. Eliot, Anti-Semitism and Literary Form,* Thames & Hudson, 2003.

12 See Jeffrey Mathes McCarthy's chapter "Conrad's Weather" in *Green Modernism,* Palgrave Macmillan, 2015; and Bill Brown on Virginia Woolf in "The Secret Life of Things."

13 In describing Carlier and Kayerts in "An Outpost of Progress," Conrad writes,

> They lived like blind men in a large room, aware only of what came in contact with them, (and of that only imperfectly) but unable to see the general aspect of things. The river, the forest, all the great land throbbing with life were like a great emptiness. Even the brilliant sunshine disclosed nothing intelligible.
>
> (*Tales of Unrest* 81)

14 For more on ships and literature read W.H. Auden's *The Enchafed Flood,* University of Virginia Press, 1950; Margaret Cohen's *The Novel and the Sea,* Princeton University Press, 2010; Jerry Allen's *The Sea Years of Joseph Conrad,* Doubleday, 1965; and Steve Mentz's *Shipwreck Modernity,* University of Minnesota Press, 2015.

15 See the journal *Resilience* and its comparative definitions of the term *resilience*.
16 Regarding Conrad and evolutionary science see George Levine's *Darwin and the Novelists*, University of Chicago Press, 1991; Allan Hunter's *Joseph Conrad and the Ethics of Darwinism*, Routledge Press, 1983; and Redmond O'Hanlon's *Joseph Conrad and Charles Darwin*, Salamander, 1984.

Works Cited

Alaimo, Stacy. *Bodily Natures: Science, Environment, and the Material Self*. Indiana University Press, 2010.

Allen, Jerry. *The Sea Years of Joseph Conrad*. Doubleday, 1965.

Auden, W.H. *The Enchafed Flood*, University of Virginia Press, 1950.

Bennett, Jane. *Vibrant Nature: A Political Ecology of Things*. Duke University Press, 2009.

Billy, Theodore. *A Wilderness of Words: Closure and Disclosure in Conrad's Short Fiction*. Texas Tech University Press, 1997.

Brown, Bill. "The Secret Life of Things (Virginia Woolf and the Matter of Modernism)." *Modernism/Modernity*, vol. 6, no. 2, 1999, pp. 1–28.

Calinescu, Matei. *Faces of Modernity: Avant-Garde, Decadence, Kitsch*. Indiana University Press, 1977.

Callicott, J. Baird. *The Great New Wilderness Debate*. University of Georgia Press, 1998.

Cohen, Margaret. *The Novel and the Sea*. Princeton University Press, 2010.

Conrad, Joseph. "Amy Foster," in *Typhoon and Other Stories*. Doubleday, Page, & Co., 1926. pp. 105–144.

———. "An Outpost of Progress," in *Tales of Unrest*. Eds. Allan H. Simmons and J.H. Stape. Cambridge University Press, 2012. pp. 198–206.

———. "Heart of Darkness," in *Youth, Heart of Darkness, "The End of the Tether"*. Ed. Owen Knowles. Cambridge University Press, 2010. pp. 43–126.

———. "The Idiots," in *Tales of Unrest*. Eds. Allan H. Simmons and J.H. Stape. Cambridge University Press, 2012. pp. 51–74.

———. *Nostromo*. Ed. Ian Watt. Cambridge University Press, 1988.

———. *The Secret Agent*. Eds. Bruce Harkness and S.W. Reid. Cambridge University Press, 1990.

———. *The Shadow-Line*. Eds. J.H. Stape et al. Cambridge University Press, 2013.

———. *Twixt Land and Sea*. Eds. J.A Berthoud et al. Cambridge University Press, 2008.

———. "Typhoon," *Typhoon and Other Stories*. Doubleday, Page, & Co., 1926. pp. 3–102.

———. *Under Western Eyes*. Eds. Roger Osborne and Paul Eggert. Cambridge University Press, 2013.

———. *Youth, Heart of Darkness, "The End of the Tether"*. Ed. Owen Knowles. Cambridge University Press, 2010.

Cronon, William. "The Trouble with Wilderness; Or, Getting Back to the Wrong Nature," in *Uncommon Ground*. Ed. William Cronon. Norton, 1996, pp. 69–90.

DeKoven, Marianne. *Rich and Strange: Gender, History, Modernism*. Princeton University Press, 1991.

Di Chiro, Giovanna. "Nature as Community: The Convergence of Environmental and Social Justice," in *Uncommon Ground*. Ed. William Cronon. Norton, 1996. pp. 298–320.
Eysteinsson, Astradur. *The Concept of Modernism*. Cornell University Press, 1992.
Ferrall, Charles. *Modernist Writing and Reactionary Politics*. Cambridge University Press, 2009.
Fussell, Paul. *The Great War and Modern Memory*. Oxford University Press, 1975.
Galsworthy, John. "Joseph Conrad: A Disquisition." *The Fortnightly Review*, vol. LXXXIII (London), 1908, pp. 627–33.
Garrard, Greg. *Ecocriticism*. Routledge Press, 2005.
Guha, Ramachandra. "Radical American Environmentalism and Wilderness Preservation." *Environmental Ethics*, vol. 11, no. 1, 1989, pp. 71–83. *Philosophy Documentation Center*, doi:10.5840/enviroethics198911123.
Hawkins, Hunt. "*Heart of Darkness* and Racism," in *Heart of Darkness: Authoritative Text Backgrounds and Contexts*. 4th edition. Ed. Paul B. Armstrong. Norton Press, 2006. pp. 365–75.
Heise, Ursula K. *Sense of Place and Sense of Planet: The Environmental Imagination of the Global*. Oxford University Press, 2010.
Hochschild, Adam. *King Leopold's Ghost: A Tale of Greed, Terror, and Heroism in Colonial Africa*. Houghton Mifflin Company, 1999.
Houen, Alex. *Terrorism and Modern Literature, From Joseph Conrad to Ciaran Carson*. Oxford University Press, 2002.
Howe, Irving. *Politics and the Novel*. Columbia University Press, 1957.
Hunter, Allan. *Joseph Conrad and the Ethics of Darwinism: The Challenge of Science*. Routledge Press, 1983.
Jasanoff, Maya. *The Dawn Watch: Joseph Conrad in a Global World*. William Collins, 2017.
Julius, Anthony. *T. S. Eliot, Anti-Semitism, and Literary Form*. Thames & Hudson, 2003.
Kenner, Hugh. *The Pound Era*. University of California Press, 1971.
Levine, George Lewis. *Darwin and the Novelists: Patterns of Science in Victorian Fiction*. University of Chicago Press, 1991.
Luke, Timothy. *Ecocritique: Contesting the Politics of Nature, Economy, and Culture*. University of Minnesota Press, 1997.
Mazel, David. *American Literary Environmentalism*. University of Georgia Press, 2000.
McCarthy, Jeffrey. *Green Modernism: Nature and the English Novel, 1900–1930*. Palgrave Macmillan, 2015.
Mentz, Steve. "After Sustainability," *PMLA*, vol. 127, May 2012, pp. 586–92.
———. *Shipwreck Modernity: Ecologies of Globalization, 1550–1719*. University of Minnesota Press, 2015.
Miller, John J. "The Dawn of the Terror Era." *The National Review*. October 10, 2016.
Morton, Timothy. *Ecology without Nature: Rethinking Environmental Aesthetics*. Harvard University Press, 2009.
Mulry, David. *Joseph Conrad among the Anarchists: Nineteenth Century Terrorism and the Secret Agent*. Palgrave Macmillan, 2016.

Norwood, Vera. *Made from This Earth: American Women and Nature.* University of North Carolina Press, 1993.

O'Hanlon, Redmond. *Joseph Conrad and Charles Darwin: The Influence of Scientific Thought on Conrad's Fiction.* Salamander, 1984.

Phillips, Dana. *The Truth of Ecology: Nature, Culture and Literature in America.* Oxford University Press, 2003.

Plumwood, Val. *Feminism and the Mastery of Nature.* Routledge Press, 1993.

Reiss, Tom. "The True Classic of Terrorism." *The New York Times.* September 11, 2005.

Schneider, Lissa. *Conrad's Narratives of Difference.* Routledge Press, 2003.

Seeber, Barbara K. *Jane Austen and Animals.* Ashgate, 2013.

Serres, Michel. *The Natural Contract.* Translated by Elizabeth MacArthur and William Paulson. University of Michigan Press, 2011.

Watt, Ian P. *Conrad in the Nineteenth Century.* University of California Press, 1979.

Williams, Raymond, *The Country and the City.* Oxford University Press, 1973.

———. *Keywords: A Vocabulary of Culture and Society.* Oxford University Press, 1976.

Woolf, Virginia. "Joseph Conrad." *Times Literary Supplement*, August 1924, pp. 490–4.

Part I
Conrad and the Anthropocene

2 Wilderness after Nature
Conrad, Empire and the Anthropocene

Jesse Oak Taylor

"Going up that river," Marlow tells his listeners aboard the Nellie, "was like traveling back to the earliest beginnings of the world, when vegetation rioted upon the earth and the big trees were kings" (77). Unlike the history-saturated Thames where "nothing is easier than to evoke the great spirit of the past," the Congo offers a glimpse of the "prehistoric earth... an earth that wore the aspect of an unknown planet" (44, 79). "The earth seemed unearthly. We are accustomed to look upon the shackled form of a conquered monster, but there—there you could look at a thing monstrous and free" (79). Elements of Marlow's account read like a deep ecological fantasy, a foray into planetary deep time, in which the human intrusion has proven only a momentary disruption. In this view, the Congo appears as wilderness, that sacred ground of the ecological imagination, "the last remaining place where civilization, that all too human disease, has not fully infected the earth" (Cronon 69). But then we get to the heads on stakes.

What is the "wilderness" that finds Kurtz out early? That whispers to him things about himself that he did not know? That tempts him to adorn his dwelling with severed heads, and makes him, in turn, an emblem for "the horror" of empire? One answer to this question would be "darkest Africa," far from the restraining norms of civilized society, a space where his atavistic, primitive, animal being is allowed to run wild—an "unshackled monster" like the "primordial" landscape in which he is immersed. Another (more accurate) answer would be: it is the contact zone between the metropolitan economy and the material resource base on which it feeds. If, as Jason Moore argues, "capitalism is a frontier process" in which "endless accumulation and endless geographical appropriation are joined at the hip" (107), then that frontier provides the setting for much of Conrad's fiction. Kurtz is an agent of extractive industry. When Marlow arrives in Africa, he encounters a landscape of "inhabited devastation," a "waste of excavations" punctuated by explosions ostensibly in service of railway construction (56). Instead of the blank space on the map that captured his imagination as a child, he finds

> Paths, paths, everywhere; a stamped-in network of paths spreading over the empty land, through long grass, through burnt grass, through thickets, down and up chilly ravines, up and down stony hills ablaze with heat; and a solitude, a solitude, nobody, not a hut. The population had cleared out.
>
> (61)

Kurtz's wilderness is the opposite of pristine. It is a landscape of erasure, scorched, exploded, and depopulated—the contact zone in which extractive, imperial–industrial capitalism transforms bodies, machines, animals, fuel, minerals and other elements into economic value while leaving gaping holes, clear-cut forests, smoke, bones and wreckage in its wake. Attending to *Heart of Darkness* as a wilderness narrative provides a way into thinking about such landscapes of conquest and invasion as "novel ecosystems," the scientific term that has been adopted to characterize the distinctive habitats brought into being through human action and ecological disturbance that are the hallmarks of the Anthropocene.

Heart of Darkness unfolds through a series of wilderness encounters set against a backdrop of deep time, in which Roman Britain is only "the other day" and Marlow's steamer glides among prehistoric trees (46). Marlow imagines a Roman captain making his way up the Thames:

> Land in a swamp, march through the woods, and in some inland post feel the savagery, the utter savagery, had closed round him, — all that mysterious life of the wilderness that stirs in the forest, in the jungles, in the hearts of wild men.
>
> (46)

His first image of Kurtz is "a distinct glimpse" of a "dug-out, four paddling savages and the lone white man turning his back suddenly on the headquarters, on relief, on thoughts of home perhaps, setting his face toward the depths of the wilderness, towards his empty and desolate station" (75). The "empty and desolate station" marks the farthest extension of the networks of extraction that feed metropolitan existence, limits that are exposed and tested throughout Conrad's *oeuvre*, beginning with *Almayer's Folly*, which takes its title from Almayer's grand, unfinished, mansion decaying in the Malayan jungle along with his mind and aspirations. To these, we might add Conrad's own journey up the Congo River and the lived experience that he would later transform into one of the most widely discussed pieces of English fiction, and the novella's afterlife (and numerous adaptations) within the expansive literary history of the Anthropocene. Conrad's sea career, which provided the fodder for much of his writing, dovetails with the period, beginning in the 1870s, which Hannah Arendt (an ardent reader of Conrad) identified as a key threshold at which capitalism expanded beyond the bounds of the nation, and placed greater emphasis on speculation and extraction as opposed to industrial production (135; see also Esty 408). As a sailor in the merchant marine, Conrad had a front-row seat to this transition, as well as the material connections necessary to transport natural resources, commodities, people, and ideas around the world. Hence, a shift that might have appeared to de-territorialize the basis of wealth when viewed from a strictly metropolitan perspective became, for Conrad, the tangible, precarious, networks of men and ships that occupy many of his narratives. Marlow's insistence on making his auditors—an accountant, a lawyer, and a director of companies—*see* hinges on precisely this disconnection between lived experience and the abstractions that cross their desks.

Heart of Darkness dramatizes the relationship between literary "world making" and the unmaking of the world through processes of imperial/industrial modernity (Hayot 38–9, 42). In the process, it showcases the direct connection between empire and the Anthropocene. The constitutive power of negation is essential to this dramatization. In the following analysis, I draw on Terrance Deacon's idea of "constitutive absence," the negative presence that, like the hole at the center of a wheel or the emptiness inside a bottle, can enable an object to become an agent because it creates "a specifically constrained range of possibilities, a potential that is created by virtue of something missing" (120). Conrad's reliance on an aesthetic of constitutive absence helps us think through the paradoxical status of the Anthropocene as both the "end of nature," and the concomitant emergence of the human as a "geophysical force" that cannot be experienced directly and thus has "no ontological dimension" (Chakrabarty 2014, 13). According to Chakrabarty,

> we have run up against our own limits as it were. It is true that as beings for whom the question of Being is an eternal question, we will always be concerned about justice. But if we, collectively, have also become a geophysical force, then we also have a collective mode of existence that is justice-blind. Call that mode of being a "species" or something else, but it has no ontology, it is beyond biology, and it acts as a limit to what we also are in the ontological mode.
>
> (2012, 14)

This version of the human demands consideration in quintessentially inhuman terms. The Anthropos takes the shape of what it isn't, by virtue of what is missing, namely those features of morality, justice and intent that constitute human being as distinct from bare force.

If we are looking for an approximation of what such an inhuman being might look like, we could do far worse than Kurtz, who, Marlow tells us, has overstepped the limits of humanity and stepped into the void: "He had kicked himself loose of the earth. Confound the man! he had kicked the very earth to pieces... and I before him did not know whether I stood on the ground or floated in the air" (113). By the end of the novella Kurtz has become the face of extractive industry: his reflection stares back at Marlow out of the polished mahogany of the Intended's door while his voice echoes from the primal forest "with that wide immense stare embracing, condemning, loathing all the universe" (122). What is the "fantastic invasion" for which the wilderness wreaks its "terrible revenge" if not the unsustainable extraction of ivory for profit (104)? When the wilderness finds Kurtz out early and whispers to him things that he doesn't know, it reveals the ecological, human and psychological costs of the effort to "tear treasure out of the bowels of the land" (73). Proposing Kurtz as a model for the Anthropos might appear to align with the universalizing tendencies of Enlightenment humanism for which the Anthropocene concept has been widely critiqued (e.g., Nixon; Moore 448–50). After all, subsuming global inequality and the massive differences in ecological responsibility and vulnerability that arise from it within an undifferentiated mantle of "the human" is dishonest at best. However, I am not turning to Kurtz as a model, not the human as such, but rather as an icon of imperial manhood and its failings, and thus the moment at which "man" as abstract ideal is shown to be a "hollow sham," a mask that serves as the face of an imperial, extractive and exploitative system. In this respect, "Anthropocene", as opposed to alternatives like "Capitalocene" (which Moore prefers) remains more accurate, not only because of its scientific currency, but also because it calls attention to the fiction whereby a particular set of historical processes has masqueraded as inevitable (and incontestably desirable) progress. The idea that humans are an entirely different order of being from the rest of nature is precisely the thing that has led to the emergence of a different order of human being, not as enlightened individual, but rather as devastating, justice-blind "geophysical force."

The Anthropos is not an individual. No single human, no matter how exceptional, acts on a scale capable of altering the Earth System as a whole. It is only collectives and assemblages of numerous humans entwined with technologies and other species that attain such impact. This is the inherent paradox in the term Anthropocene, which apparently refers to the "age of man" but actually depends on redefining the human in terms of massively distributed agency and accountability. Similarly, despite his apparent individuality, reading Kurtz in individual terms is profoundly inaccurate. Marlow implies as much when he tells us, "all Europe contributed to the making of Kurtz" (95). Kurtz's agency cannot be divorced from his status as the agent of an international corporation and is embedded within structures of racism and power that construe white manhood not as the epitome of human being but as the interchangeable currency of empire and extraction. The power that draws Marlow toward Kurtz and advances the narrative is not simply Kurtz's personal magnetism, but rather the imperatives of capitalism at a particular stage of its development, in which the expanding resource frontier led to the "scramble for Africa." Marlow is just doing his job. So is the assistant manager, eager to replace Kurtz for his reliance on "unsound method" in order to secure more ivory (108). Aligning Kurtz with the Anthropocene thus provides a mechanism for distributing responsibility rather than eliding it, locating the geophysical agency of the human in the operations of industrial–imperial modernity at its most violent, rather than in the efficacy of any one individual. Indeed, Kurtz ultimately proves not so much a powerful presence in the novella as a powerful absence: the "hollow sham" that, like the hole at the wheel's hub, provides the constitutive absence around which the rest of the narrative revolves (Deacon 120).

In framing my analysis in terms of the ecological limits of capitalism, I am building on Jason Moore's "world-ecology," an epistemological and ontological framework that seeks to move beyond an expansive conception of Cartesian dualism dividing "nature" and "society" into distinct entities. It is crucial to note here that for Moore, capitalism is not simply an economic system, but rather "a way of organizing nature" around principles of work and value (2). As Moore argues, "If humans are part of nature, historical change… must be understood through dialectical movements of humans making environments, and environments making humans" (28). This nexus of concerns is vividly dramatized in *Heart of Darkness*, as Marlow and Kurtz (and everyone else) are presented as products of the very environments that they participate in bringing into being. For example, Jessica Howell notes that the strained mental states displayed by all the European characters arise out of the pressures of climate and tropical disease, transforming the characters into physiological "barometers" by which the moral limits of empire register as climatological effects, and vice versa (162). Echoing Moore's objection to the Cartesian divide between "society" and "nature," McCarthy suggests that Marlow's struggle to reconcile "exploitation's failings in his experience of imperialism" and "identification's dangers in his dealings with Kurtz" is undergirded by a "Cartesian dualism that separates humans from nature and shapes the interactions between people and the environmental from the Thames to the Congo" (45). Such dualism echoes in the novella's bifurcated structure, in which apparent oppositions are revealed to be co-constitutive mirror images of one another: light/dark, civilized/savage, etc. With this in mind, we might say that the "lie" that the novella exposes is the fiction of infinite growth divorced from its material bases on a finite planet, wherein neither monetary nor aesthetic value can be treated as disembodied abstractions.

> A taint of imbecile rapacity blew through it all, like a whiff from some corpse. By Jove! I've never seen anything so unreal in my life. And outside, the silent wilderness surrounding this cleared speck on the earth struck me as something great and invincible, like evil or truth, waiting patiently for the passing away of this fantastic invasion.
>
> (65)

The "whiff of some corpse" offers an atmospheric reminder of the bodily remainder, the tangible cost of those ecological "externalities" left off the books by the domino-playing accountant on board the *Nellie*, who spends the time elapsed in Marlow's yarn "toying architecturally with the bones" (43).

Among the most telling ecological lessons that *Heart of Darkness* offers is the reminder that invasion is never the end of the story. Narrative, like evolution, persists after the end of nature. McCarthy suggests that *Heart of Darkness* "delivers a parable of modern environmental history: The exploiting force triumphs, but we have learned to regret" (57). The problem with that parable is that regret comes too late—like Jim's realization that the *Patna* didn't sink—making it all too tempting to assume that resistance is futile. If we are to cultivate ecologies of renewal, regret is not enough. Christophe Bonneuil and Jean-Baptiste Fressoz counter this inherently retrospective quality of much environmental history, arguing that "the history of the Anthropocene is not of a frenetic modernism that transforms the world while ignorant of nature, but rather of the scientific and political production of a modernizing unconscious" (199). Given Conrad's profound importance for considerations of how an unconscious might be produced, probed and resisted—from the innumerable psychoanalytic readings of his works to Fredric Jameson's influential reading of *Lord Jim* in *The Political Unconscious*—it is hardly surprising that his work would be fruitful in rendering the modernizing unconscious visible. This is why I am committed to the notion that Conrad's depiction of the ecological limits of empire is not merely a retrospective revelation, but rather an insight that has been present all along. Conrad makes the modernizing unconscious visible, that is to say, conscious. And in so doing, he pulls back the shroud of its inevitability.

In the present context, the key point is that Marlow's tale does not end with the exploitation, nor is the situation depicted in the novel purely one in which human actors remake the world. Instead, we get the promise (or threat) that "wilderness," will outlast the "fantastic invasion." The land has been altered, even devastated, as the as scorched, depopulated earth that Marlow has already witnessed testifies. However, the wilderness remains; it returns with its haunting vastness, its inhumanity, its darkness—and that is why it becomes a useful parable for the Anthropocene. Contemplating the wilderness with Conrad helps think through the Anthropocene as an inherently imperial phenomenon, but it also exceeds and forces us to reevaluate postcolonial perspectives on this much-read novella that has done so much to shape our collective understanding of empire. That *Heart of Darkness* juxtaposes the Thames with the Congo, the "sepulchral city" (Brussels) with the depths of the jungle, and the "gloom brooding" over the "greatest town on earth" (London) with the "dark places of the earth" is well known (118, 44, 45). So is the broad effect of these juxtapositions, which trouble the divide between civilization and barbarism and explode the unnamed narrator's comfortable invocation of imperialist nationalism and the "great spirit of the past," personified by Sir Francis Drake and John Franklin (44). Adding a substantive consideration of "wilderness," the term Marlow uses to characterize each encounter, to the discussions of empire and civilization with which *Heart of Darkness*'s double movement is more commonly aligned can help us rethink the concept of wilderness in a world where human influence has become entwined with ecological processes on a planetary scale.

Given the history of ecocriticism, invoking the idea of wilderness to understand the Anthropocene may seem a strange endeavor. Wilderness was once celebrated as the ideal landscape, defined as pristine, untouched and unsullied: nature in its natural state. The Anthropocene, by definition, marks the point at which no such space exists. The human infection is systemic; it is in the air, the ocean even the rocks. Climate change, ocean acidification, antibiotic resistance and mass extinction seem all-encompassing and might at first glance appear to render the discourse of "wilderness" quaint—the nostalgic concern of a bygone era. However, I argue that the Anthropocene demands a reevaluation of the wilderness concept precisely because it highlights the limits of domestication, demanding in the process a renewed consideration of a radically, irreducibly, inhuman world. As the evermore erratic fluctuations of global climate indicate, the pervasiveness of human influence does not equate to human control. "Inhuman nature," Nigel Clark's phrase for the geophysical processes that force themselves upon us in the form of earthquakes, tsunamis and volcanoes remains indifferent to our presence (2011). Whereas wilderness has always been indebted to the sublime—usually in terms of spectacular landscapes—the wilderness of the Anthropocene smacks of the geological sublime: the way knowledge of a potential earthquake can hover behind an apparently solid landscape, giving even rocks, hills and trees an undercurrent of instability, highlighting the precariousness of existence within the vertiginous depths of planetary time. As Jeffrey Jerome Cohen argues, geological force becomes "evident in the relations that enmesh us over long scales of time and in the 'storied matter' these confederations of the human and inhuman divulge" (20). This investigation places the wilderness movement of the twentieth century within a far more expansive frame and in so doing makes of it a useful conceptual rubric for confronting the dawn of a new geologic age.

Describing anthropogenic climate change as a challenge for the humanities, Dipesh Chakrabarty writes: "the wall between human and natural history has been breached" (2009, 221). This is a condition that I have taken to calling abnatural. "Ab-" means both "away from" and "derived from." It marks a departure without severance. The abnatural refers to everything that flows through that breached and bears the traces of its passage. Decades ahead of the Anthropocene conversation, Raymond Williams recognized this state of affairs in his prescient essay "Ideas of Nature" (1980): "We have mixed our labour with the earth, our forces with its forces too deeply to be able to draw back and separate either out" (83). The abnatural refers to novel derivations of that mixture, to its heady and enticing distillations as well as its toxic brews. *Pace* Timothy Morton (2009), I cannot do away with "nature" entirely, either as an idea or an experience of the world, and thus I turn to the abnatural to capture the felt awareness of everything I encounter: for not just the backyard trees visible from my window or the wood of my desk but also the plastic keys beneath my finders and the flickering images before me on the screen are both "apart from" and "derived from" that inhuman condition once known as nature.[1] As Williams's emphasis on labor indicates, the processes of transformation through which the abnatural arises are inextricable from another "ab-," the abstraction of material substance into monetary value, of the unique object into the fungible commodity. This too is rendered explicit in Conrad. Kurtz's Intended touches bits of the Congo every time she places her hands upon the ivory keys on her piano, unable to hear the ghost behind the music, or to catch the "taint of death" in Marlow's lie (69). Nonetheless, that lie—that Kurtz's last words were "her name"—is haunted by an atmospheric echo: "the dusk was repeating them all around us, in a whisper that seemed to swell menacingly like the first whisper of a rising wind. 'The Horror!' 'The Horror!'" (Conrad 125; McCarthy 74). This climactic moment is thus also climatic. The atmosphere thus becomes a repository for a story, a record in which the "horror" of conquest remains potentially discernible. Such atmospheric testimony has become literalized in the age of ice core analysis and anthropogenic climate change, when atmospheric records attest to the ghostly remnants of fossil fuels, transforming the climate into the ultimate story of unintended consequences. Reading in the Anthropocene always demands attention to the ghostly, atmospheric conditions that hover "outside the tale."

The troubles that flow through the breach between human and natural history are not simply philosophical abstractions. Instead, they recur in debates over whether events such as Hurricane Katrina are "natural" or "man-made" disasters, with social critics and activists arguing for the latter determination since the devastation wrought by such events was exacerbated by ill-advised coastal development, poorly maintained levies, inadequate warning and relief systems, and has furthermore disproportionately heaped upon the poor, a condition that Upamanyu Pablo Mukherjee argues "can be traced back to the fault-lines within the cultures of British imperialism," tracing the Victorian origins of "a common global ideology of disaster" (7–8). Rather than having been ameliorated by the international development efforts in the postcolonial era, the imperial disaster zone has become a definitive global condition of life in the twenty-first century. On the other hand, Clark points out the "radical asymmetry" between earthquakes, tsunamis, and volcanoes and the scale of human influence, noting that despite the pervasiveness of human action, our influence still pales against geologic time and the potential for sudden, radical transformations of the world as we know it by forces beyond our control. "This is the bottom line of human being: we are utterly dependent on an earth and a cosmos that is, to a large degree, indifferent to us" (50). No one would have to remind Conrad on that score. As Marlow puts it when contemplating the "stillness on the face of the immensity…I felt how big, how confoundedly big, was that thing that couldn't talk, and perhaps was deaf as well" (69). In resuscitating the idea of wilderness, then, I am referring not to wilderness as the epitome of nature in its true, untainted state, but rather to an abnatural wilderness, to the persistence of the wild even after the "end of nature." The consequences of doing so include both a cautionary tale about the limits of human mastery on the one hand, and suggest a reevaluation of disturbed, even decimated, landscapes on the other, suggesting that these too might become sites of conservation and ecological renewal.

The Anthropocene cannot be domesticated or contained. Indeed, one of the most dangerous potential effects of the term is the suggestion that it inaugurates a "human age" in the sense of human domination of earth's processes, wherein everything can be geologically, biologically and socially engineered to suit our needs and purposes. As Stuart Brand puts it, "we are as gods, and we have to get good at it" (1). Professing godhood is a trick straight out of Kurtz's playbook. By contrast, an abnatural conception of wilderness provides a way of thinking about what Dana Luciano (2015) calls the "inhuman Anthropocene." The geological and climatological processes within which we now know ourselves to be entangled exceed us in every dimension and are also enfolded with all-too-human histories of violence and conquest. The wildernesses of the Anthropocene are decaying nuclear facilities, superstorm-swept coasts, arctic waters plumbed by deepwater oilrigs, detonated mountaintops and the disease vectors of antibiotic-resistant epidemics. The resurgence of wilderness after nature does not mark a return to the idea of wilderness as an idealized landscape for preservation affiliated with twentieth-century conservation but returns to a much older sense of the term, when its closest synonym was "wasteland": a space of terror and demonic temptation, inhabited by monsters, wolves and witches—a word for the dark spaces of the earth.

"The earth seemed unearthly" (79). No sentence in the English language better encapsulates the predicament of abnatural ecology, in which nature becomes symptomatic of its own removal. As Robert Pogue Harrison argues,

> the unearthing of the earth on a planetary scale—the global assault on the frontiers of nature and non-Western cultures—gives a hollow resonance to all prior rhetoric of the cross, all traditional codes of morality, and all private conceptions about the good and the honorable. The nihilism of a work like *Heart of Darkness* lies in the failure of Marlow's private code of morals to achieve a credible reference to the global future of the new century.
>
> (143)

What Harrison dubs nihilism might be better characterized in terms of the constitutive power of negation. While Marlow's private code of morals may not be up to the challenge of the new century, that failure is itself what enables *Heart of Darkness* to dramatize the implications of a new geological epoch, characterized by both the limits and the excesses of the human imagination. Here, the earth seems unearthly not because it has been disturbed, disrupted or defiled by human presence, but because it hasn't. Earth only seems "unearthly" because Marlow has become accustomed to looking at the "shackled monster." What he thinks of as "the earth" is revealed to be a false impression, possible only after the vanquished monster has been brought home in shackles. The truly earthly earth, then, the one that exists in its natural, preconquest state, is this one that now appears unearthly. The effect is not so much to characterize the African landscape as a pristine wilderness as it is to denaturalize the European conception of both the African and the European landscapes. The latter can no longer appear natural but rather must be understood to be a product of human labor and, as his ruminations on the Roman indicates, of conquest. Marlow is forced to recognize that what he had taken for earthliness isn't so. We inhabitants of the Anthropocene have an urgent need for precisely this recognition, as we reimagine the Earth as a "rambunctious garden," in which disrupted habitats become sites of renewal and biodiversity (Marris 2011).

Part of what is telling about Conrad's wilderness is that he tacks so close to the now familiar definition of wilderness as pristine, untouched nature before charting an alternate course for the Anthropocene. This should not be surprising. Conrad and John Muir were contemporaries. While I have found no indication that either read the other's work (though it is certainly possible), the fact that Conrad wrote from within the same historical juncture that saw the idea of wilderness transformed into an environmentalist ideal is important because thinking about these two, coeval conceptions of wilderness together helps dramatize what each leaves out. In so doing it speaks to McCarthy's injunction that "we must acknowledge the Eurocentric presumption of mislabeling the African homes of African societies 'wilderness,' while at the same time we can recognize that Conrad methodically deploys the contested and unfolding category of 'wilderness' to dramatize his character's transformation" (47). The idea of wilderness as nature's sacred stronghold emerged in the American west during the late nineteenth century, was enshrined in the founding of national parks in Yellowstone and Yosemite and legally codified in the Wilderness Act of 1964, where it is defined explicitly by the lack of human presence: "an area where the earth and its community of life are untrammeled by man, where man himself is a visitor who does not remain" (Sec. 2c). All those who venture into official Wilderness Areas in the United States are enjoined to "leave no trace." In this sense, wilderness is and always has been a constitutive absence within the environmental imagination, defined by the absence of humans.

And yet, as William Cronon explains, this ideal conception of wilderness would once have seemed strange. It emerged out of the aesthetics of the sublime in European and American Romanticism, where the encounter with the wild was tinged with terror, as in the vertigo brought on Wordsworth by the Alps and on Thoreau by Katahdin. Earlier still, the term equated to "waste land"—economically unproductive, dangerous and hostile. In the King James Bible, the "wilderness" is a landscape of spiritual confusion and temptation (Cronon 70–1). As Harrison has argued, the depths of the forest in Medieval and Early Modern Europe were beyond the reach of the law, "in them lived the outcasts, the mad, the lovers, brigands, hermits, saints, lepers, the maquis, fugitives, misfits, the persecuted, the wild men" (61). For early American colonists, the concept of wilderness was a central preoccupation because they saw their mission as pushing back the wilderness in order to spread civilization and Christianity (Abrams 7). They viewed the New World as a wilderness that needed to be subdued, cultivated, converted. Untrammeled land was to be feared, not celebrated. Unsurprisingly, this notion was alien to the continent's indigenous inhabitants. Native Americans did not view the continent as either inhospitable or uncultivated, nor did they view themselves as interlopers on land where their people had been living for thousands of years (Abrams 5; Cronon 79). The idea of uninhabited wilderness as an ecological ideal, then, becomes what Eve Tuck and Wayne Yang (2012) call a "move to innocence," on the part of settler environmentalism seeking to naturalize invasion by erasing even the memory of the genocide that enabled its conditions for concern. This genealogy could be taken as singularly damning for the concept of wilderness—the point at which we are forced to acknowledge that it is by definition a colonial term, one that we must do away with entirely in order to embrace a more ecological mode of thought modeled on the native epistemologies that have no room for the concept. Thoreau, for instance, found himself experiencing the landscape differently as he became acquainted with tribal languages (Abrams 5). However, the problem with giving up on the concept of wilderness is that conquest brought the wilderness into being as a quintessentially new kind of colonial space, in which the fiction of human absence becomes an operative mechanism licensing despoliation and violence. That is why I find it an apt term for apprehending the Anthropocene as an epoch characterized by landscapes that have suffered precisely such degradation.

Cronon critiques the conception of wilderness in part by historicizing it within a larger trajectory that highlights the things it leaves out: prior inhabitation, productive labor and the exploitation of other less-idealized landscapes. However, that critique is in part predicated upon the distinctly American strand of wilderness thinking espoused by John Muir, defended by the Sierra Club and enshrined in the Wilderness Act. Conrad's use of the term, on the other hand, marks an alternate trajectory out of the same history. While Muir's wilderness has been the one celebrated within environmental thought it is dependent on the division between "nature" and "society" that the Anthropocene renders obsolete. It thus provides something of a box canyon to the environmental imagination: an inviting refuge that nonetheless proves to be a dead end. In Conrad, by contrast, wilderness appears wherever and whenever the imperial–industrial world system encounters the limits of its reach. As he writes in *Lord Jim*, "beyond the end of telegraph cables and mailboat lines, the haggard utilitarian lies of our civilisation wither and die" (212). However, the term is deployed only once contact has been made. As Marlow explains when reflecting on the "blank space" on the map that drew his childhood obsession, by the time he arrives "it had ceased to be a blank space of delightful mystery… It had become a place of darkness" (*HD* 48). The "darkness" follows European conquest rather than preceding it. Conrad's "wilderness" fits within an older, more expansive genealogy that also helps contextualize the wilderness movement in the American west within the long history of capitalism's many expanding frontiers. In so doing, it actually helps revitalize and reaffirm aspects of Muir's vision as a mode of counter-discourse that can only be understood as a reaction (and active opposition) to the historical movement within which it is embedded. If Muir's is an affirmative wilderness, Conrad's is a wilderness of negation; if Muir's voice sings the natural splendor enshrined in national parks, Conrad's echoes from within the modernizing unconscious. Neither can be fully understood without its counterpart.

The wilderness concept deployed in the American west is a settler discourse, symptomatic of the historical amnesia that enables settlers to feel at home on someone else's land. It is thus integral to the means by which ecologies of conquest become ecologies of settlement—ecologies both in the sense of mindful dwelling but also multispecies interaction. After all, the conquest of the Americas was, first and foremost, microbial, putting a decidedly sinister slant on the unnamed narrator's celebration of the "germs of empires" flowing out from the Thames (*HD* 45). Conquest brought entire worlds to an end and then, in a final act of desecration, erased them from memory. Imagining the landscape as empty, and as having always been empty, is a "move to innocence" that is actually the ultimate act of extermination (Tuck and Yang 1). In this regard, wilderness areas are all too often memorials to erasure, giving the injunction to "leave no trace" a decidedly unsettling resonance. By contrast, Conrad described writing fiction as

> rescue work carried out in darkness against cross gusts of wind swaying the action of a great multitude. It is rescue work, this snatching of vanishing phrases of turbulence, disguised in fair words, out of the native obscurity into a light where the struggle forms may be seen, seized upon, endowed with the only possible form of permanence in this world of relative values—the permanence of memory.
> (1904, 16)

The question becomes how to bring these two imperatives together: How do we dwell imaginatively, and with care, in a world at once radically indifferent to the human and replete with memory? How do we make wilderness the locus of ecological history rather than amnesia?

The depictions of wilderness in *Heart of Darkness* dovetail with the lineage traced above on many points. Where Theodore Roosevelt and others celebrated the wilderness as a masculine proving ground, Conrad reveals what happens when imperial manhood fails the test, subverting the tropes of imperial adventure fiction (Cronon 77–8; also White 1993; Taylor 2012). Like the American west, Conrad's inscrutable wilderness is not uninhabited: "The steamer toiled along slowly on the edge of a black and incomprehensible frenzy. The prehistoric man was cursing us, praying to us, welcoming us—who could tell?" (*HD* 79). Whether it is the Celts along the banks of the Roman Thames or the unidentified African tribes, the presence of indigenous people becomes an explicit part of what constitutes Conrad's wilderness as such: "that mysterious life of the wilderness that stirs in the forest, in the jungles, in the hearts of wild men" (46). In the jungle, Marlow encounters a world seemingly without time, a world that dwarfs human endeavor and resists interpretation. This replays the persistent colonial trope whereby Africa was depicted as "anachronistic space: prehistoric, atavistic and irrational, inherently out of place in the historical time of modernity" (McClintock 40). Marlow's insistence on the utter incomprehensibility of the "passionate uproar" on the banks un-worlds the Africans' world, robbing it of coherence, and making the villages alongside the shore seems as natural, and thus as ahistorical, as the sunbathing alligators and hippos. This is, fundamentally, the objection that Chinua Achebe (1977) mounts against the novella's racism: that it fails to acknowledge the fact that what Marlow is seeing is not the absence of civilization but simply a different civilization from his own.

This trajectory culminates in Kurtz, of whom Marlow explains:

> the wilderness had found him out early, and taken on him a terrible vengeance for the fantastic invasion. I think it had whispered to him things about himself which he did not know, things of which he had no conception till he took counsel with this great solitude—and the whisper had proved irresistibly fascinating.
>
> (104)

Kurtz's ideals about the "suppression of savage customs" devolve into the savagery of extermination, or the "mimicry by the colonizer of the savagery imputed to the savage" (Taussig 1993, 66). As Michal Taussig has shown, the concept of savagery did not exist except as a product of the colonial encounter that brought it into being as a lived practice predicated on an imagined reflection of that concept. Similarly, the colonial encounter made a wilderness of an inhabited land, violently depopulating the landscape as both prerequisite for and consequence of imagining it as being already empty. In the process, wilderness took shape as a space constituted by palpable absence, arising out of the "space of death where the Indian, African, and white gave birth to a New World" (Taussig 1987, 5).

That "New World" is the one we are only now beginning to recognize as the Anthropocene. Geographers Simon L. Lewis and Mark Maslin have recently proposed that the Anthropocene be dated to 1610 and the "Columbian Exchange" between Old and New World ecologies—as opposed to the more widely cited dates of either the Industrial Revolution, the "Great Acceleration" in fossil fuel use and population growth in the mid-twentieth century, or the isotropic trace left by nuclear testing (Lewis and Maslin 2015; see also Crutzen 2002; Zalasiewicz et al. 2015). Lewis and Maslin explain the conquest of the Americas created a movement of species (intentionally and otherwise) that amounted to "a swift, ongoing, radical reorganization of life on Earth without geological precedent" (174). It also inaugurated a great dying, as war, disease, famine and slavery killed off some 90 percent of the continents' inhabitants, some "50 million" people in one of the most devastating genocides in recorded history. This "decline in human numbers" enters the geologic record as a legible decrease in atmospheric carbon dioxide due to absent cooking fires and inadvertent reforestation (174). Lewis and Maslin

> suggest naming this dip in atmospheric CO^2 the 'Orbis spike' and the suite of changes marking 1610 as the beginning of the Anthropocene the 'Orbis hypothesis', from the Latin for world, because post-1492 humans on the two hemispheres were connected, trade became global, and some prominent social scientists refer to this time as the beginning of the modern 'world-system'.
>
> (174)

The Orbis hypothesis marks the Anthropocene an inherently imperial condition, a landscape of conquest rather than a product of industrialization and entwined with the globalization of capitalism from its inception. In all those missing hearth-fires, it also frames the Anthropocene in terms of the legibility of negation, the felt presence of an absence.

Both dynamics are amply evident in *Heart of Darkness*, a work filled with death, whether in the grove of death where Marlow encounters "black shadows of disease and starvation, lying confusedly in the greenish gloom," the heads on stakes outside Kurtz's station, or the disease that pervades all the European enclaves from the French ship on which the sailors "were dying of fever at the rate of three a day" to the assistant manager distinguished only by his mere survival—the fact "he was never ill" (58, 55, 63). European death rates in Africa were staggering. The west coast, in particular, became known as the "White Man's Grave," a condition that was ascribed largely to the climate and which Conrad dramatizes explicitly (Howell 54, 161–2). Jessica Howell notes that Kurtz's mental breakdown is described in terms that align closely with medical accounts and suggests that the "unsteady hand" with which he scrawls the infamous postscript "Exterminate all the brutes!" indicates the point at which, "shaking with disease, he has transformed lofty, if misguided, intentions into anger towards the Africans around him, who resist the very disease that is killing him" (162). The "wilderness" to which Kurtz succumbs is, in other words, an ecological and microbial contact zone, in which invasive species, bodies and climates intermix with deadly consequences. As such, it is also a "novel ecosystem," brought into being by disruption, and hence among the paradigmatic environments of the Anthropocene.

The wilderness is by definition strange, that which lies beyond the frontier of the familiar, domesticated world, a space of danger and transformation, of visions and temptation and, at least potentially, renewal and new forms of possibility. Perhaps the single greatest problem with the idea of wilderness arises when it is applied to someone else's home; it un-worlds their world both rhetorically and, all too often, literally. But here is the thing: none of us is at home in the Anthropocene. The Anthropocene marks a profound disturbance in the *oikos* of our dwelling; it renders the planet unhomely. We are all strangers here. If the concept of the Anthropocene being articulated by geologists, climatologists and stratigraphers is correct, then whenever we entered it we entered a world where no human (or, for that matter, nonhuman) population had ever inhabited before. If instead of imagining that the wilderness depends on the erasure of history, we reconceive of it as space brought into being by that very history of erasure, then it becomes a way of conceptualizing the Anthropocene as an unprecedented epoch in planetary history. Where the frontier was once geographical, it has now become temporal, as the sites of extraction and dumping grounds extend from below the depths of the sea to the outer atmosphere. The world we have filled now encloses upon us. There is no "outside" left. Thus, the boundary that marks the emergence of the Anthropocene (wherever and whenever it is affixed) will mark the threshold of a new world, abnatural forevermore.

To think about the wilderness with Conrad is to think about race, danger, disease and violence. It is also to think about work. One of the key distinctions between the notion of wilderness critiqued by Cronon and that dramatized by Conrad is that the former is by definition economically unproductive, whereas in Conrad the wilderness is a space that one braves for profit. The landscapes of Conrad's fiction are the contact zones of global capitalism: Conrad's work is rife with sites of extraction—the silver mine in *Nostromo*; the secret river to "inexhaustible" supplies of rattan in the Lingard Trilogy; the assorted guano islands and timber concerns of *Lord Jim* and other works; and of course, the Congo interior and its ivory. Conrad's sea stories trace the networks by which raw materials, commodities and laboring bodies circulate the world: coal shipped from Newcastle to Bangkok in "Youth," coolies aboard the *Nan Shan* in "Typhoon." Thus, Conrad's wilderness is not so much that part of the natural world excised from the economy as the space in which economic networks bump up against the vastness of the nonhuman world—sometimes literally. As Marlow explains, "I don't like work–no man does– but I like what is in the work,–the chance to find yourself. Your own reality . . . " (73). Marlow's "work" is precisely the labor of extraction, transportation and appropriation that make up the capitalist world system at a particular point in the development of its global reach, completing (or at any rate continuing) the expansiveness cited in the frame narrator's celebration of Drake and Franklin. However, rather than being rendered in the abstract terms of value, Marlow's yarn retains its material particularity in ways that open into a genuinely ecological account of both labor and the landscapes in which it takes place. The landscapes of industry and extraction are, for better or for worse, among the definitive ecosystems of the Anthropocene. An Anthropocene environmentalism worthy of the term cannot simply decry wasted lands but must fully incorporate them into our conception of what conservation efforts hope to save.

What Conrad adds to theorizations of the Anthropocene is a vivid cognitive and phenomenological dramatization, not only of the historical forces that have given rise to this new planetary condition, but also of the difficulty of perceiving those forces from the inside out. The wasted landscape that has taken the place of the "blank space" on the map is a scene at once primordial and modern as Marlow sees both Britain and the Congo through a kind of superpositioning, borrowed from Charles Lyell's *Principles of Geology* (1830–33), in which the visible landscape is laid atop its deep history (McCarthy 54–5). Just as we are invited to ask how the modern scramble for Africa both mimics and differs from the Roman conquest of Britain, we might similarly ask how the sacrificial ecologies of modernity both revisit a very old story, one that reaches back to Gilgamesh and Enkidu cutting the cedars of Lebanon, and yet radically exceed all precedents in both scale and speed (Dolph 2015). Conrad's vision of modernity is thus not so much one of "radical rupture" with the past as of acceleration and concentration of forces already in operation (Friedman 2011). In this sense, Marlow's wilderness is an "anachronistic space" not simply because it is old but also because it is new (McClintock 40). It is the landscape of the future, where there are no "bank spaces" left, no pristine "nature" existing apart from human influence. Marlow himself says as much, describing Kurtz as "this grimy fragment of another world, the forerunner of change, of conquest, of trade, of massacres, of blessings"—and, one might add, of the world-transforming power of technological modernity, resting atop and embedded within the networks of extraction (116). Indeed, it is not difficult to imagine a Conradian account of an event like the Exxon Valdez Oil Spill: the captain asleep, drunk, third mate at the helm, a broken radar machine, the sickening crunch of iron on rock, undreamt disaster. It sounds like a Conrad plot already.

The connections between empire, economics and ecological devastation are most evident in the novella's treatment of the ivory trade. Despite never being as central either to the global economy or the Belgian Congo as was rubber, ivory was big business. As McCarthy notes, "from 1875 to 1905, Europeans extracted 70,000 tons of ivory from the Congo every year" (42). Channeling Marx on the "fetishism" of the commodity, Marlow explains: "The word 'ivory' rang in the air, was whispered, was sighed. You would think they were praying to it" (65). And yet the word "elephant" appears only once—in relation to the value of Kurtz's African mistress's adornments: "she must have had the value of several elephant tusks upon her" (107). One might take this omission as a sign that Conrad is fundamentally uninterested in the plight of elephants, or that concern about the impact of their slaughter is anachronistic and beyond the purview of either author or his original audience. Both of those assumptions would be wrong (see Murphy 2013; McCarthy 42–3).

Two months before it ran the first installment of *Heart of Darkness*, *Blackwood's Magazine* published an article by Alfred Sharpe, the Commissioner of the British Central Africa Protectorate and later Governor of Nyasaland (now Malawi), on the question of whether the African elephant was fated with extinction. The article explicitly references public debate and letters to *The Times*, "all united in deploring the fact that the African elephant is being killed for its ivory, and seem to be of the opinion that its slaughter can be prevented by legislation in England" (89). Displaying a frequent pattern in conservation discourse, Sharpe rejects the notion that "elephants are being directly exterminated by Europeans," and with it the idea that expensive hunting licenses and fees would stem the slaughter (89). Instead, he argues,

> the African native throughout the continent, since the introduction of firearms, urged on by the high value of ivory in European markets, has slaughtered elephants wherever he could find them, regardless of size or of sex; and so long as ivory of all descriptions is a valuable trade article, elephants will continue to be indiscriminately killed, until, in many portions of Africa, they will be totally exterminated. (89)

After dismissing the possibility that game preserves will be adequate to maintain a viable population, the article argues that the elephant's future depends on efforts to "regulate the ivory trade in such a manner that it will not eventually become extinct," by banning the sale of tusks under a certain weight and proposing to make it a criminal offense to possess tusks under 14 pounds (91). Read (as it was published) in the wake of Sharpe's proposals for a regulated ivory trade, Kurtz's rapacious appetite for the stuff—"you would think there was not a single tusk left above or below the ground in the whole country"—becomes not merely "unsound" but unsustainable (93). As one manager laments, Kurtz has "done more harm than good to the Company" because "the district is closed to us for a time" (108). Kurtz does not simply embody the logic of extractive capitalism, but also its encounter with the limits that arise directly from its own imperatives. Overexploitation results in exhaustion.

The absence of elephants from *Heart of Darkness* is thus not an oversight but a formal incorporation of the threat of extinction hovering over the species. It is particularly telling that the text's sole mention of "elephant" comes in relation to the adornments on the African woman's body, since it references the animal body as a marker of what appears to be exchange value, "the value of several elephant tusks" which, according to Marx, should be divorced from both use value and the conditions of production (107). The reference makes sense only when taken as the counterpart to the later scene with the Intended, who sits in the sepulchral city surrounded by objects whose origins lie in imperial conquest—mahogany door, the keys of the piano, which is compared to a "sarcophagus"—but which exist for her only as commodities divorced from the ecological and social processes of their production, whether their growth in forests or on an elephant's face. In the Congo, ivory's value is measured in elephants because the raw material is inextricable from its ecological basis. In Europe, that value has been abstracted both conceptually and literally. It is no accident that it is the accountant who toys with a set of (ivory) dominoes—referred to as "bones"—on board the *Nellie*. Elephants are (and were) not merely absent from the text but palpably so, a constitutive absence that makes the conquest ecology dramatized in the novella come into focus just as the animals themselves are the necessary absence at the heart of the ivory trade. The "taint of death" and "whiff of a corpse" that hang in the air along with the word "ivory" thus take on a new materiality as the atmospheric remnants of rotting elephant bodies, much like the stink of dead hippo that nearly drives Marlow out of his mind. As Ryan Francis Murphy argues, "While Conrad has distinct thematic motives for excluding the beast from his novella history provides readers with a second explanation for the elephant's curious absence: men like Kurtz have killed them all" (16). While this is obviously an exaggeration, in that the African elephant survives (at least for the time being) in the world outside the text, *Heart of Darkness* nonetheless offers an intimation of a world in which all that remains of the species are valuable bits of its body, tellingly referred to as "fossil." This term, used for previously buried ivory, nonetheless echoes the formal trace of a dead organism. After all, fossils (in the more familiar sense of the term) lay at the center of nineteenth-century debates over extinction and the preservation of a vanished species. Attending to such linkages demands a reading practice attuned to the aesthetics of negation that inhere in the novella's ironic structure.

Expanding the frame in which we read *Heart of Darkness* from imperialism (or even capitalism) to the Anthropocene demands an extension of the double vision that Edward Said deployed for reading Conrad in the postcolonial era. As Said explains,

> Conrad's tragic limitation is that even though he could see clearly that, on one level imperialism was essentially pure dominance and land-grabbing, he could not then conclude that imperialism had to end so that "natives" could lead lives free from European domination precisely because the dominance of imperialism extends to his own worldview
>
> (30)

Said's contrapuntal reading of Conrad, both "in his own time" and in retrospect, hinges on the fact that we can see what Conrad cannot, namely a future of independent African nations plotting their own destinies and postcolonial authors rereading and rewriting the "colonial masterpieces" (31). As inhabitants of the Anthropocene, we are much closer to Conrad's own position, lodged within a condition whose iniquities we perceive even as we are unable to see the path to an alternative. Rather than simply telling us what we already know, this calls attention to our own limited perception, our own "tragic limitations." As we come to the end of the Holocene, and with it the climatic conditions under which human civilization became possible, we are forced to confront the "darkness" of a genuine unknown, "going at it blind—as is very proper for those who tackle a darkness" (47). In this sense, Conrad's skepticism about our knowledge is precisely what makes his work useful as we contemplate the Anthropocene as an age of unintended consequences and palpable absences, a history still waiting to be rewritten.

The Anthropocene exceeds articulation and presses beyond any conceptual framework that we can construct to apprehend it. We can say with confidence only what it is not. It describes the limit at which thinking and meaning stop—an era that will only come fully into view after humanity itself has exited the stage. The trace of the Anthropocene is, ultimately, the trace of an absence. Whether it is ultimately determined to be the CO_2 from industrialization around 1800, nuclear isotopes in 1945—adding a more sinister valence to Marlow's "we live in the flicker" (46)—or the vanished farms and campfires of 1610, the trace by which the Anthropocene becomes legible is an inscription upon the geological memory of the planet. The Global Stratotype Section and Point that makes the Anthropocene official will not reflect an intended memorial but rather an unintentional impression left by the unintended consequences of our actions as dispersed in the Earth's atmosphere. As such, it will acknowledge the long-term legibility of that which hovers outside the narrative of history, much in the way the unnamed narrator describes what distinguishes Marlow's storytelling from the yarns typical of seamen:

> to him the meaning of an episode was not inside like a kernel but outside, enveloping the tale which brought it out only as a glow brings out a haze, in the likeness of one of these misty halos that sometimes are made visible by the spectral illumination of moonshine.
>
> (45)

This wonderfully atmospheric image is especially apt to the Anthropocene, an epoch defined by the retentive power of the Earth's atmosphere as an archive enveloping human endeavor, in which the residues of history remain suspended, enveloping both the past and the future. Hovering "outside the tale" the atmosphere becomes a space in which both CO_2 and meaning accumulate, the unintended exhalations and bodily traces that accompany our stories, affecting our experience of the narrative that makes it visible "as a glow brings out a haze" (45). This, in turn, suggests a mode of reading for the Anthropocene, in which the meaning of events lies not within but without, in the long-range ecological consequences and atmospheric traces they leave behind.

Note

1 For more on the abnatural, see Timothy Morton *Ecology Without Nature: Rethinking Environmental Aesthetics*. Harvard UP, 2009.

Works Cited

Abrams, Robert E. *Landscape and Ideology in American Renaissance Literature*. Cambridge UP, 2004.
Achebe, Chinua. "An Image of Africa: Racism in Conrad's *Heart of Darkness*." *Massachusetts Review* vol. 18, 1977, pp. 782–794.
Arendt, Hannah. *The Origins of Totalitarianism*. Harcourt, 1968.
Brand, Stewart. *Whole Earth Discipline: An Ecopragmatist Manifesto*. Viking, 2009.
Chakrabarty, Dipesh. "The Climate of History: Four Theses." *Critical Inquiry* vol. 35, no. 2, 2009, pp. 197–222.
———. "Postcolonial Studies and the Challenge of Climate Change." *New Literary History* vol. 43, no. 1, Winter 2012, pp. 1–18.
Clark, Nigel. *Inhuman Nature: Sociable Life on a Dynamic Planet*. Sage, 2011.
Cohen, Jeffrey Jerome. *Stone: An Ecology of the Inhuman*. Minnesota UP, 2015.
Conrad, Joseph. "Henry James: An Appreciation." in *Notes on Life and Letters*. Ed J. H. Stape. Cambridge UP, 2004. pp. 15–20.
———. *Lord Jim*. Edited by J. H. Stape and Earnest W. Sullivan II. Cambridge UP, 2012.
———. *Youth, Heart of Darkness* and "The End of the Tether". Edited by Owen Knowles. Cambridge UP, 2010.
Cronon, William. "The Trouble with Wilderness; or, Getting Back to the Wrong Nature." in *Uncommon Ground: Re-thinking the Human Place in Nature*. Ed. William Cronon, W. W. Norton, 1995, pp. 69–90.
Deacon, Terrance W. "Emergence: The Hole at the Wheel's Hub." in *The Re-Emergence of Emergence: The Emergentist Hypothesis from Science to Religion*. Ed. Philip Clayton and Paul Davies, Oxford UP, 2008, pp. 111–150.
Dolph, Steve. "The Nature of Our Ruin: Part 1." *Penn Program in Environmental Humanities Lab*, 17 December 2015. Web. www.ppehlab.org/blogposts/2015/12/17/the-nature-of-our-ruin-part-1
Esty, Jed. "The Colonial Bildungsroman: The Story of an African Farm and the Ghost of Goethe." *Victorian Studies* vol. 49, no. 3, Spring 2007, pp. 407–430.
Friedman, Susan Stanford. "Definitional Excursions: The Meanings of Modern/Modernity/Modernism." *Modernism/Modernity* vol. 8, no. 3, 2001, pp. 493–513.
Harrison, Robert Pogue. *Forests: The Shadow of Civilization*. Chicago UP, 1992.
Hayot, Eric. *On Literary Worlds*. Oxford UP, 2012.

Howell, Jessica. *Exploring Victorian Travel Literature: Disease, Race, and Climate*. Edinburgh UP, 2014.

Lewis, Simon L. and Mark A. Maslin. "Defining the Anthropocene." *Nature* vol. 519, March 2015, pp. 171–180.

Luciano, Dana. "The Inhuman Anthropocene." *Avidly*, 22 March 2015. Web. http://avidly.lareviewofbooks.org/2015/03/22/the-inhuman-anthropocene/

Marris, Emma. *Rambunctious Garden: Saving Nature in a Post-Wild World*. Bloomsbury, 2011.

McCarthy, Jeffrey Mathes, *Green Modernism: Nature and the English Novel, 1900–1930*. Palgrave Macmillan, 2015.

McClintock, Anne. *Imperial Leather: Race, Gender, and Sexuality in the Colonial Contest*. Routledge, 1995.

Moore, Jason. *Capitalism in the Web of Life: Ecology and the Accumulation of Capital*. Verso, 2015.

Morton, Timothy. *Ecology Without Nature: Rethinking Environmental Aesthetics*. Harvard UP, 2009.

Mukherjee, Upamanyu Pablo. *Natural Disasters and Victorian Empire: Famines, Fevers and the Literary Cultures of South Asia*. Palgrave MacMillan, 2013.

Murphy, Ryan Francis. "Exterminating the Elephant in *Heart of Darkness*." *The Conradian* vol. 38, no. 2, 2013, pp. 1–17.

Nixon, Rob. "The Anthropocene: The Promise and Pitfalls of an Epochal Idea." *EdgeEffects*, 6 November 2014. Web. http://edgeeffects.net/anthropocene-promise-and-pitfalls/

Said, Edward. *Culture and Imperialism*. Verso, 1994.

Sharpe, Alfred. "The Preservation of African Elephants." *Blackwood's Magazine*, January 1899, pp. 89–92.

Taussig, Michael. *Mimesis and Alterity: A Particular History of the Senses*. Routledge, 1993.

———. *Shamanism, Colonialism, and the Wild Man: Studies in Terror and Healing*. Chicago UP, 1987.

Taylor, Jesse Oak. "White Skin, White Masks: Conrad and the Face(s) of Imperial Manhood." *Conradiana* vol. 44, no. 2–3, 2012, pp. 191–210.

Tuck, Eve and Wayne K. Yang. "Decolonization Is Not a Metaphor." *Decolonization: Indigeneity, Education & Society* vol. 1, no. 1, 2012, pp. 1–40.

United States. Cong. Senate. 88th Congress, 2nd Session. 16 U.S. C. 1131–1136. *An Act to Establish a National Wilderness Preservation System for the Permanent Good of the Whole People, and for Other Purposes*. 3 September 1964.

White, Andrea. *Joseph Conrad and the Adventure Tradition: Constructing and Deconstructing the Imperial Subject*. Cambridge UP, 1993.

Williams, Raymond. "Ideas of Nature." in *Problems in Materialism and Culture: Selected Essays*, Verso, 1980, pp. 67–85.

3 Conrad in the Anthropocene
Steps to an Ecology of Catastrophe

Nidesh Lawtoo[1]

> To Bill Connolly and Jane Bennett,
> for vital matters

> Had he been informed by an indisputable authority that the end of the world was to be finally accomplished by a catastrophic disturbance of the atmosphere, he would have assimilated the information under the simple idea of dirty weather....
> —Joseph Conrad, Captain MacWhirr, "Typhoon"

> Wisdom I take to be the knowledge of the larger interactive system—that system which, if disturbed is likely to generate exponential curves of change.
> —Gregory Bateson, *Steps to an Ecology of Mind*

After the Miocene and the Pliocene, the Pleistocene and the Holocene, we are now entering the age of the Anthropocene. As the term suggests, this is a new "geological epoch" (Crutzen and Stoermer 17) in which humans are having a direct impact on the ecosystem of the earth and are thus, quite literally, at the center of this age.[2] But what does it mean to be at the center of an age that is currently decentering us? Is the Anthropos that is the subject of devastating actions on the earth not also simultaneously subjected to a variety of environmental reactions? And, if so, which approach can help us better understand, diagnose and perhaps counter the widening spiral of human and nonhuman forces currently introducing continuities between nature and culture where we previously saw structural discontinuities?

Influential figures in critical theory from Michel Serres to Bruno Latour, Jean-Luc Nancy to Jane Bennett are currently giving theoretical substance to the second wave of ecocriticism and environmental studies and agree on one point: the age of the Anthropocene calls for less, not more, anthropocentric approaches to the environment. It is as if being provisionally placed at the center puts us in a position to see that we might soon be displaced to the periphery, precarious creatures that can easily be washed away by the ecological disasters we generate. This is, indeed, a narcissistic blow to an anthropocentric image of man. If previous decenterings commonly associated with Copernicus, Darwin and Freud, were still based on all-too-human intellectual moves, the decentering of man in the age of the Anthropocene is generated by nonhuman physical movements that have the power to dislocate our superhuman status of "geological agents" (Chakrabarty, "Four Theses" 207). This environmental reflection not only forces us to face the irrationality of conscious human actions on a massive global scale; it also makes us see that evolutionary success as a species cannot be evaluated in an ecological vacuum but must take into consideration the "systemic pathology" (Bateson 438) we are currently spreading that is retroactively infecting us. Indeed, as the shadow of climate change is now cast on the twenty-first century, the suspicion is emerging that the age of human decentering may actually only have begun. After logocentrism and ethnocentrism, phallocentrism and phallogocentrism, anthropocentrism is, paradoxically, the fallacy that must be avoided in the age of Anthropocene. This, at least, is what the interdisciplinary field of environmental studies is currently suggesting as it encourages new generations of critics and theorists to reframe human agency against the wider ecology of (non)human actions and reactions whose spiraling feedback loops still sustain us for the moment but threaten to engulf us in the future.

In search of a local case study to give critical substance to such global theoretical realizations, it might appear misguided to turn to a literary author who has been accused precisely of logocentrism, phallocentrism and, especially, ethnocentrism in the twentieth century. When it comes to reflecting on the shared environmental catastrophes that threaten humans collectively—that is, as a species[3]—Joseph Conrad is well-positioned to represent, diagnose and perhaps even provide some remedies against anthropocentric fallacies that must be avoided in the twenty-first century. Rather than dismissing Conrad's environmental representations of "exotic seas and the last plunge of flaming wrecks" as a simple background for human actions at best and material for "compilers of Prose anthologies" (Leavis 188) at worst, the epoch of the Anthropocene compels us to reread his untimely fictions from a more environmentally aware perspective. I argue that Conrad's nautical tales, which have the microcosm of the ship as a paradigmatic model of the "planet," can help us reframe the place of humans in a wider ecology of catastrophe. At the dawn of ecocriticism, Michel Serres regretted that "those who used to live out in the weather's rain and wind, whose habitual acts brought forth long-lasting cultures out of local experiences—peasants and sailors—have had no say for a long time now" (31). Conrad is exceptional in this respect: as a sailor turned writer he did have a say—and we are now in a position to listen.

In what follows, I begin by placing Conrad's name on the radar of "disaster narratives" (Rigby 214) by reframing the images of catastrophe that haunt so many of his nautical fictions. So far, these images have not received the attention they deserve, perhaps because concerns with identity politics that dominated critical discussions in the last decades of the twentieth century have tended to foreground images of human agents, leaving nonhuman "actants"—a term Bruno Latour borrows from literary studies (Latour, *Reassembling* 54)—in the background. This article offers some steps toward a less human-centered image of Conrad by considering the power of nonhuman forces, such as terrific storms, ocean currents, gigantic waves and contagious epidemics that in-*form* (give form to) what he repeatedly calls "end of the world" scenarios. But please rest assured: it does not intend to dismiss past approaches to Conrad in terms of race, gender, class or sexuality as exemplary cases of thoroughgoing anthropocentrism!

Instead, I would like to tilt critical attention from the human foreground depicted in Conrad's tales of the sea to the nonhuman background that always informs human actions in disaster narratives such as "Typhoon," *The Shadow-Line*, *The Nigger of the "Narcissus"* and "The Secret Sharer."[4] This shift of perspective calls attention to what political theorist William Connolly calls "an enlarged sense of the planetary entanglement of the species" (13), a mimetic sense essential to fully bring Conrad studies in the twenty-first century for it reveals a decentered picture of humans caught in what theorists of the Anthropocene call complex "social-ecological systems" (Glaser 4). These non-anthropocentric systems have the power to generate "systemic pathologies" that, as Bateson recognized, requires careful "diagnostic" of the relations between social and ecological forces before thinking about possible "remedies" (437). Conrad adds a supplement to this diagnostic as he helps us see that these "pathologies" cannot be dissociated from the question of mimesis, which, I have argued elsewhere, is central to modernism in general and his work in particular.[5] Conrad is, in fact, an author who is timelier than ever in the age of the Anthropocene for mimetic reasons that are at least double: On the one hand, he represents systemic pathologies that appear increasingly realistic today (mimesis as realistic representation); on the other hand, he uses the socio-ecological microcosm of the ship to diagnose how humans can be trapped in an ecology of mimetic actions and reactions that require an education in nonlinear thinking in order to be perceived, diagnosed and effectively countered (mimesis as systemic patho-logy). In the process, he also encourages us to rethink agency, (will to) power, and ethics across the human/nonhuman binary along materialist, systemic and relational lines that both echo and supplement recent developments in ecocriticism, environmental studies and new materialism from a mimetic and, thus, literary perspective.[6]

There is significant theoretical potential in Conrad's disaster narratives. Well before the threat of anthropogenic storms, Conrad joins his experiential and aesthetic sensibility as a sailor-turned-writer to make us feel and see that in a catastrophic scenario binary oppositions between nature and culture, human and nonhuman forces no longer hold but must be thought in a relation of mimetic continuity that introduces environmental sameness where we previously saw human differences. Conrad's images of catastrophe, and the diagnostic of pathological actions and reactions they entail (such as madness, affective contagion and epidemic contamination), make him more than ever one of us. He also encourages future-oriented readers to take some active steps to face the ecological challenges the Anthropocene is currently generating.

A Picture of Catastrophe

From typhoons to terrific storms, becalmed seas to infection epidemics, Conrad's "Calm-pieces" as well as "Storm-pieces" (*'Twix Land* 6) are haunted by the shadow of what he repeatedly calls "catastrophe" ("Typhoon" 52; *The Shadow-Line* 52). These nautical catastrophes are local in their narrative representation and are not directly anthropocentric in nature, yet they have global theoretical implications that can be put to productive critical and theoretical use in the age of the Anthropocene. For Conrad, in fact, the ship is not simply a ship; it represents the social macrocosm. At times, the microcosm of the ship metonymically transgresses the nature/culture binary as it expands to include what he calls the "planet" as a whole. Conrad is insistent on this point. In *The Nigger of the "Narcissus,"* for instance, he compares the ship to a "small planet" (29). In *Lord Jim*, we read, "When your ship fails you, your whole world seems to fail you" (95). And in *The Shadow-Line*, Conrad compares an epidemically infected ship to the disastrous (*dis-astro*, under the influence of a bad star) image of a "planet flying vertiginously on its appointed path" (62). It is true that such phrases could be read as metaphors meant to add an exotic touch to anthropocentric narratives concerned with solidarity in the lives of few individuals onboard the ship, but it is equally true that as the crew is collectively embarked on this "appointed path," these narratives consistently show how the "small planet" of the ship is quite literally exposed to the agentic forces of the planet, binding not only "men to each other," but also, as Conrad says in his famous Preface to *The Nigger of the "Narcissus,"* "all mankind to the visible world" (xiv). From the October gale depicted in *Youth* to the storm at center of *The Nigger of the "Narcissus,"* from Jim's infamous leap from the *Patna* in *Lord Jim* to the end of the world storm in "The Secret Sharer," time and again, Conrad's account of the ship as a "small planet" lends support to Michel Serres' theoretical insight in *The Natural Contract* that "the ship provides a model of globality" (41).

Conrad and Serres could not have agreed more, perhaps because they shared a formation that is at least double: they both went through a nautical training in their lives which, in turn, provided them with the experiential foundation to reflect (on) the image of the ship qua globe in their writings.[7] Since classical antiquity, the image of the ship has continued to serve as a privileged model to think about the body politic. There is thus plenty at stake in such seemingly past-oriented nautical tales to justify future-oriented, environmental, and less anthropocentric approaches to most of Conrad's narratives of the sea.

But it is probably in "Typhoon" that Conrad's picture of catastrophe, and the diagnostic of the contagious ecology of action and reaction it entails, is most clearly foregrounded. "Typhoon" tells the story of Captain MacWhirr and his crew navigating a steamer called the *Nan-Shan* across the Pacific Ocean. Often read as an unimaginative, stupid and even comic figure, in the past MacWhirr has been treated with "ironic" distance by modernist readers concerned with the "introspective" aspects of the tale. But is such a distance still timely today? Bruno Latour does not seem to think so. He reminds us that "If modernism claimed to be detached from the constraints of the world, ecology for its part gets attached to everything" (*Politics* 21). This sticky, immanent and rather stubborn attachment to the world is precisely what fictional characters like MacWhirr, and real sailors like Conrad, never let go of. It is in fact important to stress that in the Author's Note to "Typhoon" *and Other Stories* Conrad immediately brackets skeptical views as he reminds readers that MacWhirr is "the product of twenty years of life" (viii). And he immediately adds, in a mimetic mood, "My own life" (viii). Conrad, then, makes clear at the outset that his nautical "experience" in-*forms* this fictional character. He goes even further as he says that his life as a sailor provides what he calls "the canvas of the attempted picture" (ix), a striking phrase suggesting that art (the picture) rests on the immanence of his life-experiences for its material foundations (the canvas). This is an important aspect of Conrad's poetics which, in the age of modernist suspicion about material referents, has not received much attention. Yet, as the French philosopher Philippe Lacoue-Labarthe reminds us, a referent is already inscribed in the etymology of the term "experience" itself. As he puts it, thinking of Ulysses but with Conrad not far from his mind, "experience is a nautical term": "ex-perience: to traverse, in the maritime sense of a sea passage [*traversée maritime*]" (110).[8] Quite literally, for Conrad, his life-experience is not simply in the background of his tales; it also serves as the very material substratum on which his artistic representations of sea passages rest. Consequently, his nautical experience and the human and nonhuman forces they entail (bodily reactions, affective states, communal bonds, racial discrimination, nautical training, epidemic infections, on the side of humans; ocean currents, winds, temperature, epidemic infections, storms, waves on the side of nature) cannot be peeled off from Conrad's fictions, lest the fictions lose the very subject matter that gives them substance, density and form.

Still, when it comes to representations of "end of the world" scenarios some initial caution is in order to avoid projecting contemporary apocalyptic anxieties onto the text from the outside-in. The third-person anonymous narrator, for instance, immediately informs us that MacWhirr had "no experience of cataclysms" (20). And he adds, in a skeptical mood:

> Had he been informed by an indisputable authority that *the end of the world was to be finally accomplished by a catastrophic disturbance of the atmosphere*, he would have assimilated the information under the simple idea of dirty weather, and no other, for *he had no experience of cataclysms, and belief does not necessarily imply comprehension*.
>
> (20; my italics)

For contemporary readers attentive to the experiential canvas behind the aesthetic picture, this image of catastrophe has the uncanny ring of contemporary climate change denial. Within the attempted picture, MacWhirr posits the test of "experience" over and against an "indisputable authority," "comprehension" over "belief" as the empirical foundation to evaluate possible "end of the world" catastrophes. He thus seems to operate on rational, empirical grounds most readers would have found quite reasonable a few years ago. Lest some empirical evidence about a "catastrophic disturbance of the atmosphere" be provided, the logic goes, down-to-earth characters like MacWhirr will dismiss such an apocalyptic environmental possibility as "dirty weather."

Unsurprisingly, however, in a novella titled "Typhoon" the experience of such an "end of the world" scenario is precisely what the picture itself will eventually represent from the inside out. Caught in the midst of a circular storm MacWhirr initially refuses to believe in and, as belief gives way to experience, stubbornly refuses to circumnavigate, he is soon confronted with the following, even more haunting picture:

> a white line of foam [was] coming on at such a height that he couldn't believe his eyes—nobody was to know the steepness of that sea and the awful depth of the hollow the hurricane had scooped out behind the running wall of water.
>
> (74)

MacWhirr can't believe his eyes, for this fictional character has had no experience of such "mountains of water" (64). In the age of the Anthropocene, however, we now know that such "running wall[s] of water" are not only fictional; they can spill over into the real world as well—with devastating consequences. Hence, ecocritics have started promoting a return to what Timothy Clark calls a "'realist' or mimetic aesthetics" (47). This re-turn of attention from the literary text to the material referents reflects contemporary preoccupations. Yet, Conrad's image of catastrophe is not inferred from the context of the tale; it is already internal to the text itself. Failure to acknowledge the catastrophic implications of the nonhuman forces Conrad experienced as a seaman and subsequently re-presented as a writer does not only injustice to the texture of the text (critical reasons); it also prevents readers from seeing Conrad as an untimely writer who depicts scenarios we are now familiar with in the age of the Anthropocene (theoretical reasons).

While Nobel prize-winning atmospheric chemist Paul J. Crutzen dates the beginning of the Anthropocene "in the latter part of the eighteenth century" ("Geology" 23)—a period that coincides with the invention of the steam engine, which already had a direct effect on Conrad's nautical career—it is important to stress that Conrad's images of catastrophe are not explicitly anthropogenic in nature. Nor are they transparently realistic in the narrow sense that they faithfully represent storms that actually took place during the particular sea passage Conrad dramatizes in this fiction. Mimesis is thus not synonymous with a restricted conception of homogeneous realism. As we shall see shortly, mimesis stretches to include heterogeneous forms of imitation that are as literary as they are behavioral, as human as they are nonhuman. From this perspective, Conrad's disaster narratives offer timely case studies to think about the interplay between nonhuman and human forces in catastrophic contexts. They also dramatize current non-anthropocentric realizations about the agentic power of nature, our radical dependency on the environment and the fragility and precariousness of life. Such theoretical insights sound new in an age that is slowly awakening to the threat of climate change, yet they must have sounded obvious to Conrad: They were not only part of his local experience as sailor; they also served as a canvas for the attempted picture.

Having reframed the picture of catastrophe Conrad makes us see, I now turn to consider the materiality of the canvas he makes us feel. This subject matter is less visible at the level of mimetic representation, yet continues to sustain the picture and operates at the imperceptible but tangible level of affective contagion Conrad encourages us to diagnose.

Contagious Pathologies/Systemic Patho-logies

The pictures of catastrophe that haunt Conrad's nautical fictions generate a type of horror that can no longer be confined to the depth of psychic profundities or to the surface of aesthetic forms. Instead, they cast a physical shadow on the real world along mimetic lines that transgress the shadow-line between surface and depth, text and context, thereby giving contemporary readers an aesthetic and experiential insight into the terror of catastrophic scenarios. But there is another, less visible and no less mimetic side to Conrad's pictures that we need to face if we want to turn these critical reflections to theoretical and thus practical use in the age of the Anthropocene. Conrad encourages us to supplement a realistic, mimetic aesthetics concerned with external representations of catastrophes by urging us to reflect on the contagious, mimetic pathologies that link exterior natural forces to interior human forces in end of the world scenarios generating a system of relations between human and nonhuman actors qua actants.[9]

As Conrad had made clear in the Author's Note to "Typhoon" *and Other Stories*, he is not interested in "bad weather" (vii) as such—i.e. natural forces. Instead, he is interested in what he calls "the extraordinary complication brought into the ship's life at a moment of exceptional stress by the human element below her deck" (vii)—i.e. the interplay of nonhuman and human forces. Unlike contemporary Hollywood disaster movies that focus on heroic, spectacular and ultimately solipsistic actions on deck (Wolfgang Petersen's *The Perfect Storm* is just an example), Conrad is not especially concerned with triggering sensational pathos. Instead, he pays close diagnostic attention to the "systemic pathologies" (Bateson's term) generated by the interplay of natural actions and human reactions on the microcosm of the ship. This is a significant contribution to environmental criticism. As Bateson already put it in his groundbreaking *Steps to an Ecology of Mind*, "man commits the error of purposive thinking and disregards the systemic nature of the world with which he must deal" (436), whereas "in creative art, man must experience himself—his total self—as cybernetic model" (438). Joining his nautical experience with his artistic sensibility, the canvas and the picture, Conrad is directly concerned with the patho(-)logical view of total self in the double sense of systemic sickness that infects humans (or pathology) on the one hand, and of critical discourse, or *logos*, on the *pathos* this contagious sickness generates (or patho-logy), on the other. In so doing, Conrad takes some important steps to an ecology of catastrophe attentive to the patho(-)logical feedback loops that tie environmental actions to human reactions—and back. Let us diagnose these loops more closely.

Loaded with a cargo of 200 Chinese workers who start a row as the mountainous waves hit the ship, Conrad zeroes in on the agentic effect of the typhoon on human behavior, suggesting that the threat of catastrophe does not lie in environmental forces alone, nor in human forces alone but, rather, on the spiraling interplay between human and nonhuman systemic pathologies. Conrad is here recognizing what contemporary environmental theorists have also recognized: namely, that humans are implicated, interpenetrated or entangled in a web of connections that generate vibrations across the human/nonhuman divide. As Jane Bennett puts it in *Vibrant Matter*, "receptivity to the impersonal life that surrounds and infuses us, will generate a more subtle awareness of the complicated web of dissonant connections between bodies and will enable wiser interventions into that ecology" (4). Conrad is very receptive to what he calls, in the "Preface" of *The Nigger of the "Narcissus,"* the "vibration" (xv) of the impersonal life of his surroundings. In particular, his aesthetic representations of storms, contribute to contemporary ecological debates by making us see that the circulation of power during a catastrophic scenario is fundamentally mimetic in the specific sense that it introduces a relational and contagious continuity between the vibrations of the storms outside and the vibration of men inside. Thus, the narrative specifies that "the wrath and fury of the passionate sea" (19) threatening the ship from without also generates a violent riot among the "crazed" Chinese coolies, whose frenzy threatens to overhaul the ship from within.

To be sure, wrath, fury and a passionate, mad sea, are anthropomorphic representations of nature. They can thus be read as metaphorical depictions of a human pathos let loose and projected onto the environment along lines we have become accustomed to dismissing in terms of pathetic fallacies. According to this anthropocentric vector of analysis, which originates in humans and moves toward the nonhuman, the exterior, natural image is only a narcissistic mirror of the interior, human world; the passionate sea simply reflects an irrational human pathos; the systemic pathology is a mirror of a human, all too human pathology. An ecocritical reading of Conrad can bring to the fore theoretical associations that have remained in the shadow of postcolonial critiques of racist images in the past, but must be brought to the fore in the age of the Anthropocene in the future. And what we see reflected in what Conrad also calls the "mirror of the sea" is, indeed, a racist image of China that should still be critiqued today for the irrational, dehumanizing frenzy it depicts. The ideological diagnostic is clear: As the coolies "charged in, stamping on breasts, on fingers, on faces," etc. (77), we are given to see a contagious, mimetic behavior that is violently projected onto the subaltern other, confining the pathologies of mimetic actions and reactions on the side of the "other." Such critiques are more in order than ever in an age in which ecological catastrophes cannot be dissociated from the plague of social inequality. The confinement of the workers below the deck, deprived of agency, basic human rights and a narrative perspective that would give individuals a singular voice to tell their stories, reminds us that the lives of the "wretched of the earth" are always the first to be exposed to precarious situations and the last to be protected and dignified. This remains true in the twenty-first century as perilous crossings and violent dislocations continue to end in catastrophic scenarios. Postcolonial criticism is thus not at all opposed to ecocriticism but rather supplements it, for these approaches address two aspects of the same problem (or pathology).[10]

If we take seriously the "end of the world" scenario Conrad is depicting, we notice that he articulates the mimetic continuities between the material force of typhoon outside and the pathos of humans inside. He does so via a less visible, yet no less powerful narrative vector that goes from nature to human nature, not the other way round. It is in fact crucial to realize that, as a seaman turned writer, Conrad treats the disastrous typhoon literally, not metaphorically, as an agentic power in its own right. The storm's "wrath and fury" is thus not simply an anthropocentric projection of a psychic human pathos onto the environment. Rather, it entails a patho-logical recognition of the real "force" or "power" of the typhoon—what he also calls "the disintegrating power of a great wind" (40) or "the force of the hurricane which made the very source of action utterly vain" (51). And setting up a distinction between different natural forces at work in catastrophic contexts, Conrad gives material substance to his aesthetic personification of the storm's power as follows:

> An earthquake, a landslip, and avalanche, overtake a man incidentally, as it were—without passion. A furious gale attacks him like a personal enemy, tries to grasp his limbs, fastens upon his mind, seeks to rout the very spirit out of him.
>
> (40)

Human passion or pathos, is clearly at work in the systemic pathology triggered by the gale, yet the vector of Conrad's patho-*logical* narrative trajectory is not naively anthropocentric insofar as agency is located in a natural force which has the power to attack, grasp and paralyze human agency and the spirit that animates it. In short, agency, for Conrad, is clearly not limited to human agency. On the contrary, human actions in catastrophic contexts are radically affected by the power of nonhuman actants, whose mimetic interplay with human actors the novel encourages us to delineate.

As we follow these entangled associations we notice that mimetic terms usually attributed to crowd behavior in general and native cultures in particular in Conrad's fictions now appear to define the qualities of environmental actions on the ship qua planet. For instance, the narrator says that the ship "was like a living creature thrown to the rage of a mob" (47); he proceeds by diagnosing the hypnotic "spell of the storm" (53) on the first mate, Jukes, who finds himself "possessed" by a state of "frenzy" (76); and when speaking of "the clamour" of the winds, he compares it to "the throb as of many drums ... like the chant of a tramping multitude" (90). Conrad is here relying on an animistic perception of nature as a living force that was still dominant in the late nineteenth century and is powerfully at work in his most influential text, *Heart of Darkness*.[11] In "Typhoon," however, Conrad puts the anthropological language of mimetic (dis)possession (ritual spells, chanting, drums, crowd behavior, etc.) to a different and less anthropocentric theoretical use. He makes us see that mimesis captures not only the irrational behavior of human groups qua "mob" but also the hypnotic power of natural forces qua "catastrophe." Thus, the chanting and drumming characteristic of animistic rituals in the jungle is here re-presented onboard ship in order to register and mediate the "multitude" of material vibrations at the heart of the storm. There is a significant shift of perspective at work in this narrative move: Conrad relies on the language of animism characteristic of mimetic rituals that endow life to nonhuman forces among native cultures; and he does so in order to give aesthetic, affective and conceptual form to the experience of natural forces he himself felt as a sailor. For Conrad, mimesis is no longer only a human experience; it can be used to understand the contagion at work in nonhuman powers as well. Natural power is mimetic power in the sense that it is animated by contagious, affective and hypnotic storm power.

Tracing mimetic associations across the human/nonhuman divide demonstrates that far from being a primitive form of thought, animism can be productively recuperated for a political theory attentive to the multiplicity of forces animating the nonhuman. This is what Jane Bennett also suggests as she convokes animism in order to make the point that "an anthropomorphic element in perception can uncover a whole world of resonances and resemblances" (99) between vibrant matter. Latour makes a similar point as he says that there is much to learn from non-Western actors who "did not seem to make any sharp distinction between things and people" and instead, established "correspondences between the order of nature and the social order" (*Politics* 44).[12] Conrad fundamentally agrees with these claims. He also furthers them by stressing that resemblances, correspondences and entanglements rest on mimetic principles. More precisely, in his anthropological experiences, Conrad develops an anthropomorphic language that captures the life that flows from natural to human pathos, and back; and in his experiential writings he re-presents the vibrant power of catastrophic storms to generate human and nonhuman entanglements caught in a the spiraling feedback loops of mimetic patho(-)logies. If anthropomorphism, and the mimetic associations it relies on, can be put to regressive uses concerning identity politics, Conrad also teaches us to see that it can be put to progressive use in the politics of nature. Neither good nor evil in itself, mimesis can both be the source of ideological pathologies and ecological patho-logies insofar as eco-patho(-)logies have the paradoxical structure of poison and remedy.[13]

There is a subtle diagnostic reflected in Conrad's mimetic resemblances between nature and human nature. The linguistic continuity between natural and human "clamour," the "passions" of the sea and the "crazed" men, suggests that in catastrophic scenarios, a contagious continuity—what Jean-Luc Nancy calls the "contagion" generated by the "equivalence of catastrophe" (56)—exists between the physical, natural actions outside (the planet) and the psychosomatic human actions inside (the ship). In *The Equivalence of Catastrophe*, Nancy speaks of a type of "circulation," "interaction" or "intercommunication" generating a "generalized transformability" (48–9) which, in catastrophic contexts, produces "equivalence" in place of difference. Conrad, as a writer who consistently in his work shows a profound awareness of the ancient lesson that humans are thoroughly imitative creatures who are vulnerable to mimetic pathos (be it frenzy, violence, compassion, horror or panic), extends this all-too-human capacity of being mimetically affected to include nonhuman forms of power, or better, will to power. This is, after all, how Nietzsche, a writer whose mimetic affinities with Conrad run deep, defines "will to power": that is, as "dynamic quanta" that are "not a being, not a becoming, but a *pathos*—the most elemental fact from which a becoming and effecting first emerge" (637). Conrad knew about these quanta of power from personal experience; in the age of the Anthropocene he helps us imagine this nonhuman power of nature to affect us before we shall experience it.

We are now in a position to reframe Conrad's image of catastrophe from a less anthropocentric, more ecocentric perspective. Conrad is not simply depicting a racist image of irrational humans without agency; nor is he only dramatizing the agentic power of nature—though he is doing both these things. Rather, as he says that the "hurricane...had set all these bodies whirling like dust" (77), he is depicting the complex, spiraling interplay between human and nonhuman forces, using oxymoronic phrases like the "passion" of the sea, or conversely, humans "whirling like dust," in order to break free of ossified subject/object, culture/nature dichotomies and stress how matter and humans interpenetrate, vibrate, and affect one another, generating a mimetic continuity where there previously was discontinuity. In short, a major theoretical message of Conrad's fictions of disaster is that mimetic contagion is the medium of catastrophic eco-pathologies. The horror in "end of the world" scenarios is no longer the horror of leaders' will to power alone; it also triggers an equivalence characteristic of the horror of environmental mimesis.

Furthermore, this patho-logical diagnostic, understood as a critical *logos* on mimetic *pathos*, makes us see the contagious effects of environmental forces on human behavior along lines that transgress the binary that divides nature from culture, environmental actions from human reactions. Making visible the spiraling movement of patho(-)logy requires a skill that is double and joins a love of close reading, on the one hand, with a perspectival approach that includes different *logoi* (ecology, anthropology, psychology, materialist ontology, political theory and as we shall soon see, ethics), on the other. If we adopt both principles to radically slow down this movement, we notice that the "maddened sea" generates a "crazed" human behavior, and this crazed behavior, in turn, retroacts via a feedback loop on the small planet of the ship, accentuating the possibility of disaster. Such a systemic patho(-)logy, it is important to realize, runs like an undercurrent throughout Conrad's narratives of catastrophe. It is at the center of *The Nigger of the "Narcissus"* as the "invisible violence of the winds" (49), we are told, "tossed about [the ship] shaken furiously, like a toy in the hands of a lunatic" (53) generating "darkness, clamour, fury" (54), and this lunatic and frenzied behavior soon affects the crew as well. It resurfaces in "The Secret Sharer" in the context of yet another "end of the world" (*'Twix Land* 105) storm in which, we are told, a "sea gone mad" (124) induces, by mimetic contagion, a psychological madness in the mutinous sailor who becomes "crazed with funk" (102), and this madness spreads to infect the rest of the crew, which, in turn, accentuates the possibility of catastrophe.

With an additional complication, a contagious eco-patho(-)logy reappears in *The Shadow-Line*'s ship infected by malaria and stuck in a becalmed river, and environmental and epidemiological factors act and retroact on human behavior in a spiraling logic that has the power to paralyze human action—while at the same time distributing agency in a multiplicity of nonhuman factors. This is how Conrad renders us perceptively attentive to the agency of nonhuman forces:

> The fact was that disease played with us capriciously very much as the winds did. It would go from one man to another with a lighter or heavier touch, which always left its mark behind, staggering some, knocking others over for a time, leaving this one, returning to another, so that all of them had now an invalidish aspect and a hunted, apprehensive look in their eyes. …It was a double fight. The adverse weather held us in front; and the disease pressed on our rear.
>
> (70)

Human action, for Conrad is clearly squeezed in-between nonhuman fronts which press in on the subjects assembled on the ship in the middle. This fight is thus at least double for it confronts both epidemic and climatic factors at once. Yet it does not simply pitch two antagonist forces against each other in a human versus nonhuman dialectical struggle against death. On the contrary, a nonhuman infection has already contaminated humans, generating a contagious circulation that is quite effective in dramatizing Latour's insight that "ecology dissolves nature's contours and redistributes its agents" (*Politics* 21). The absence of wind, the infected river, the mosquitos, the infectious protozoa outside and inside humans, the ship and its social structure, the climate and finally the affected and infected sailors, are all caught up in the same continuum of heterogeneous forces that prevent the microcosm of the ship to set out toward its intended human destination. In this sense, Conrad's fictions contribute to training our ability to disentangle the process of mimetic contagion as it generates agentic continuities between nonhuman and human forces. His literary diagnostic of this systemic pathology is specific: it depicts a spiral of emerging and mutually reinforcing problems whereby nature affects culture, which affects nature, in a never-ending turbulence of environmental/epidemiological pathological actions and human reactions that introduce nonhuman sameness in place of human difference.

And yet, this environmental sameness does not prevent Conrad from affirming some human differences that attempt to reintroduce discontinuities to counter catastrophic continuities. In particular, Conrad sets out to reframe the ethical value of immoral actions performed by unique individuals, who, by training and profession, have the responsibility to intervene in the system of eco-pathology—in order to make a difference.

Toward an Ethics of Immoral Actions

Conrad repeatedly stresses that in catastrophic scenarios human behavior is complicit with the natural forces it attempts to keep at bay and that ethical choices need to be placed within the context of natural actions and human reactions in order to be properly evaluated. This lesson is ancient and is as old as the birth of ethical theory itself. Since classical antiquity, the image of the ship's hierarchic social structure and radical dependency on nonhuman forces has served as a metaphor of the ethical and political challenge to govern the body politic. This analogy first appears in Book 6 of Plato's *Republic*, which is also the founding text of mimetic theory. There Socrates famously compares the body politic to a ship that has been beset by irrational sailors from within "wrangling with one another for control of the helm" (724). And in this all-too-human situation concerned with sociopolitical power, Socrates urges the "shipmaster" to pay attention to the nonhuman forces on which the ship as a social body fundamentally depends, such as "the time of the year, the seasons, the sky, the winds, the stars" (725). Conrad is thus not only true to his experience as a sailor in paying attention to both human and nonhuman forces; he is also true to a philosophical tradition that taught him to consider the ship "the moral symbol of our lives" (*Notes* 149).

This moral symbol has not lost any of its power in the Anthropocene. On the contrary, it is at the center of critical reflections on the interplay between ethical and natural contracts in times of precarity and vulnerability. Michel Serres is probably the philosopher who has done most to revitalize this ancient Platonic symbol for the present times. As he puts it in *The Natural Contract*, elaborating on his image of the ship qua globe:

> Since remotest antiquity, sailors (and doubtless they alone) have been familiar with the proximity and connection between subjective wars and objective violence, because they know that, if they come to fighting among themselves, they will condemn their craft to shipwreck before they can defeat their internal adversary. They get the social contract directly from nature.
>
> (40)

For Serres there is a mimetic relation between the social and the natural contract. If the former is a copy of laws that are implicitly inscribed in nature, it is because nature in general, and the microcosm of the ship in particular, reveals a type of violence, which, as René Girard would say, is mimetic, "reciprocal" and has the potential to "escalate to extremes" (11). And thinking of the outbreaks of violent frenzy among the mob that already preoccupied Plato, Serres continues his diagnostic as follows:

> Unable to have any private life, they [sailors] live in ceaseless danger of anger. A single unwritten law thus reigns on board, the divine courtesy that defines the sailor, a nonaggression pact among seagoers, who are at the mercy of their fragility. The ocean threatens them continuously with its inanimate but fearful strength, seeing to it that they keep the peace.
>
> (40)

The affinities between Conrad and Serres are numerous and profound. Conrad relentlessly interrogates the mimetic power of violence and is severe with characters that disseminate aggression and asocial feelings aboard ship (Donkin in *The Nigger of the "Narcissus"* is but one example). He could thus not have agreed more with Serres in theory. And yet, in his fictional practice, he often transgresses this natural contract by aligning his narrative perspective with violent, brutal and at times even murderous actions carried out during highly catastrophic nautical scenarios.

Time and again, Conrad posits extremely violent human actions at the heart of catastrophic storms, posing ethical dilemmas that have cast a long shadow on the reception of some of his tales in the twentieth century. In order to reevaluate Conrad's notorious representations of violent human actions onboard ship for our present times, it is important to supplement past anthropocentric approaches and situate ethical actions in a more general ecology of actions and reactions. For instance, in "Typhoon," we see MacWhirr violently knocking down a sailor, thus patently transgressing the "single law" of "nonaggression" Serres derives from nature. But what if nature, in catastrophic contexts, does not propose single, homogeneous laws but calls for the diagnostic of multiple, heterogeneous forces instead? More precisely, what if MacWhirr's violent human transgression continues to be motivated by a deep systemic understanding of patho(-)logies we have been carefully tracing in the preceding section?

The scene is eminently Platonic and in line with Serres' concern with an "internal adversary;" and yet, Conrad adds the threat of an external adversary to this scene: namely, the typhoon. MacWhirr retrospectively tells us that in the midst of the storm, the second mate, "lost his nerve"; and the captain gives an account of what he calls an "awkward circumstance" in loose, disconnected sentences: "'Gone crazy'…'Rushed at me…Just now. Had to knock him down….'" (68). This is a moral transgression of the maritime code as well as of Serres' natural contract. Yet, for Conrad, this violent solution is not deprived of ethical value; at least if we understand ethics not as a set of general, transcendental norms based on an idea of Justice (Plato), nor as contract based on the imitation of the homogeneous law of nature (Serres) but, rather, as a critical interrogation of what a just action may be in an imminent, heterogeneous and potentially catastrophic situation that generates systemic eco-patho(-)logies (Conrad).

The complexity of the scenario urges critics to slow down and situate MacWhirr's moral transgression in the system of mimetic correspondences we have previously disentangled. Notice, in fact, that the adjective "crazy" is used again in the context of this particular storm. For the reader who has been carefully following the contagious effects of the "madness" of the sea across human and nonhuman actants, this repetition does not simply designate the actions of a single human individual considered in isolation. On the contrary, the systemic sets of association in the novella call attention to the invisible yet nonetheless mimetic circulation of madness initially located in the typhoon, which, as we have seen, triggers the madness of the Chinese workers. And as both human and nonhuman madness gains momentum during the typhoon, Conrad's narrative zooms in on a figure in a position of authority, such as a second mate, whose "crazy" actions have the power to change the destiny of the whole ship qua "state" or "planet." MacWhirr violently counters this pathological escalation of human and nonhuman madness when he uses his nautical experience and ethical judgment to intervene at a decisive turning point in the narrative.

This is a return of human agency—with a vengeance. But we are now in a position to see that the source of this intervention is not located in an individual considered in isolation but, rather, stems from what Bateson calls "the total network system" (433) on which the ship qua planet rests. Put differently, Conrad suggests that ethical actions must always be considered as part of the complex ecology of (non) human (re)actions on which the ship's survival depends. And if it is true that violence, as René Girard and Michel Serres insist, spreads mimetically onboard ship and must be avoided at all costs in normal homogeneous circumstances, it is equally true that in a catastrophic, heterogeneous situation, a violent but carefully calibrated action from a competent actant such as the captain can be the only effective antidote to put an end to a systemic eco-pathology that threatens to overturn the microcosm of the ship. In sum, Conrad, *with* Serres, claims that ethics is rooted in an understanding of the *natural* contract between the human and the nonhuman world; yet, contra Serres, he specifies that natural contracts are relative rather than absolute, immanent rather than transcendent, based on singular experiences rather than on single laws.

Now, the violent episode in "Typhoon" makes us wonder: How far can such moral transgressions be pushed and still be ethically justified? Does an ethic of catastrophe urge us to go beyond good and evil, as Nietzsche famously suggested?[14] Conrad seems to have asked himself such questions. Thus, nearly a decade later, in one of the best short stories he ever wrote, "The Secret Sharer," he returns to depict a "sea gone mad" (105) that threatens to destroy the ship in order to ask a problematic ethical question in the context of the ecology of catastrophe he had already depicted in "Typhoon." This alignment between what appear to be radically different tales might initially surprise. Given its symbolic density, narrative indeterminacy and linguistic compression, "The Secret Sharer" has been read from a variety of anthropocentric perspectives that played no role in "Typhoon," such as split selves, unconscious secrets, imaginary projections and homoerotic desires.[15] Still, from an ecocentric perspective that considers the natural background as an indispensable canvas for the human picture in the foreground, the continuities between "Typhoon" and "The Secret Sharer" turn out to be revealing. For instance, at the end of "Typhoon," we are left with an image of "The hurricane, with its power to madden the seas, to sink ships, to uproot trees, to overturn strong walls and dash the very birds of the air to the ground" (90). This environmental picture of disaster whereby "Typhoon" ends sounds like a warning for readers of Conrad in the Anthropocene; and this warning is represented at the beginning of "The Secret Sharer." At the opening of the tale, we are in fact told that the soil is left "barren," there is "no sign of human habitation as far as the eye could reach" (*'Twixt Land* 81) and there is "not a bird in the air" (82). There is thus a secret sense in which "The Secret Sharer" starts where "Typhoon" ends. It re-presents, for the second time, a hypothetical posthuman scenario in which we are left to reflect on the devastating effects of what Conrad called "catastrophic disturbance of the atmosphere" (20) on humans, animals and the geology of the earth. Both tales are indeed a welcome to the storms of the Anthropocene!

But it is actually by reloading the problematic of extreme violent actions in a disastrous nautical situation that "The Secret Sharer" takes a further step toward the ecology of catastrophe initiated in "Typhoon." That the storm has catastrophic implications is clear. This point is, in fact, made by two characters who otherwise offer two antithetical perspectives on the events. Captain Archbold of the *Sephora* says, in an echo of MacWhirr: the "mountainous seas...seemed ready every moment to swallow up the ship herself and the terrified lives on board of her" (101). And Leggatt, the first mate of the *Sephora*, confirms this point as he says that "'It wasn't a heavy sea—it was a sea gone mad!'" (105). And he adds, in an apocalyptic mood, "I suppose the end of the world will be something like that" (105).

"The Secret Sharer" is thus situated in a relation of direct continuity with the "end of the world" scenario we have discussed in "Typhoon"; yet this time the social structure of the conflict has been radically inverted, and the violence accentuated. The key passage in question reads, once again, as the opposite of Serres' call for a contract of nonaggression and urges us to reevaluate the value of violent actions in an emerging situation of catastrophe from a less normative perspective. Leggatt is responsible for setting a storm sail and is confronted with a systemic disturbance which emerges from the interplay between natural and human forces as follows:

> It was when setting a reefed foresail, at dusk. Reefed foresail—you understand the sort of weather—the only sail we had left to keep her running, so you may guess what it had been like for days. Anxious sort of job that. He gave me some of his cursed insolence at the sheet. I tell you I was overdone with this terrific weather that seemed to have no end to it. Terrific I tell you—and a deep ship. I believe the fellow himself was half crazed with funk. That was no time for gentlemanly reproof, so I turned around and felled him like an ox.
>
> (89)

Anthropocentric approaches to Leggatt have often represented him as a brutal, irrational ruffian representative of "unconscious" forces characteristic of the Freudian id buried within a solipsistic conception of the ego,[16] rather than of a first mate ethically concerned with the external fate of the ship caught in "mountainous seas" (101). And yet, Freudian decentering of man in the solipsistic privacy of the unconscious should not lead us to center the analysis of human actions taken in isolation. It is plain from the passage quoted that Leggatt, just like MacWhirr, is far from "unconscious." On the contrary, he is hyperconsciously attentive to the ecology of actions that surrounds him, broadening his visual and affective sensorium to list nautical details of vital importance—such as the time of the day ("dusk"), the kind of weather ("terrific"), the duration of the storm ("days"), the type of ship ("deep") and the specific sail needed ("reefed foresail")—to save the ship, and by metonymic association, the body politic and, perhaps the small planet it represents.

Now, since the "end of the world" context could have been the one of "Typhoon," the ethical evaluation of Leggatt's action could have been the same as MacWhirr's: felling a man who has been contaminated by a "sea gone mad" and, as a consequence of this mimetic correspondence is "crazed with funk," acts pathologically, and thus dangerously, seems the adequate thing to do in the context of this ecology of catastrophe. And yet, Conrad never sails through the same storm twice. It is in fact no longer the captain who intervenes but the first mate (against the Captain's will) and the agentic intervention is pushed to a violent extreme:

> He up and at me....I had him by the throat and went on shaking him like a rat, the men above us yelling 'Look out! look out!' Then a crash as if the sky had fallen....It was a miracle that they found us jammed together behind the forebits. Not a pretty miracle either. It's clear that I meant business because I was holding him by the throat still. He was black in the face. It was too much for them; it seems they rushed us aft together gripped as we were screaming Murder! Like a lot of lunatics and broke into the cuddy.
>
> (89)

This is an extremely violent scene that reminds us of what Serres calls the "danger of anger" onboard ship. Yet, surprisingly, via the medium of an internal narrator who sides unconditionally with Leggatt, Conrad aligns the reader's sympathy with the murderer. We are in fact encouraged to think that Leggatt's murderous action did not lead to shipwreck but saved the ship instead. Bluntly put, then, the last and most difficult ethical step Conrad's tale urges us to consider as he sails, like Nietzsche before him, "straight over morality and past it" (*Beyond* 54), is whether a catastrophic nautical scenario can ever justify murder.

Over the years, such a question has generated strikingly contradictory responses that evaluated Leggatt as a murder or as a hero, but the catastrophic systemic implications of the scene have not received the attention they deserve. If I reopen the case of Leggatt at the closure of this turbulent essay on the Anthropocene, it is because the decentering of man we have been exploring in Conrad's narratives of disaster taught us to situate human actions in their proper ecology of actions and reactions the artist takes the trouble to represent before attempting any ethical reevaluation of values. If we take a last look at this scene we notice that Leggatt, for one, is clearly "anxious" because of the "terrific weather," and his duty is hoisting the vital storm sail. But the narrative implies a more general, systemic lesson as well. Namely, that the physical, exterior turmoil of "a sea gone mad" induces a pathological madness in a member of the crew, so that, we are told, "the fellow himself [not only the sea] was half crazed with funk." At the heart of this storm there is thus, once again, an infective pathology that is "pestiferous" and has the potential to spread contagiously—via what Conrad calls in *Lord Jim*, "the contagion of example" (38)—infecting the system of this ship as a whole, from the "lunatic" sailors to the shipmaster responsible for the ship qua body politic. Thus, Leggatt specifies: "I understand that the skipper too started raving, like the rest of them" (89). It is this systemic socio-eco-pathology that infects the entire social structure of the ship; it deprives the social body of its head, and generates a contagious madness, which as Nancy also recognized, is responsible for a "general equivalence" (54) that dissolves differential relations and triggers horror. In short, it is the horror of (non)human mimesis that Leggatt is countering with such a horrific human action.

So, is Conrad suggesting that a murderous action can be justified in situations of catastrophe? That extreme violence can serve as a possible antidote to systemic socio-eco-pathologies? Rather than answering in moral terms of good and evil Conrad urges us to trace the specific system of relations between human actors in the foreground and nonhuman actants in the background that frame ethical actions in the first place. If such ethical dilemmas have tended to make readers "uncomfortable" in the past, the uncomfortable age we're about to enter calls for such a systemic education. Once the system is accurately diagnosed, practical ethical conclusions should naturally follow. Catastrophe theorists like Jean-Pierre Dupuy, for instance, urge us to move away from normative conceptions of morality based on imperatives or laws in order to consider ethics as part of systemic scenario that evaluates the consequence of actions along lines Conrad had been depicting in his tales all along. Dupuy puts it in quasi-Conradian terms as he says: "in exceptional cases, which constitute a dilemma for ethical reflection, the maximization of global good, prescribes a transgression of moral prohibitions" (42). And he specifies:

> What if, by killing an innocent, I avoid that other twenty-two innocents are killed? If I really think that the murder of an innocent is an abominable action, then the prohibition of murder, in this case, appears contrary to reason.
>
> (42)

Ethical reflections like these benefit from Conrad's pictures, just like aesthetic pictures benefit from lived experiences. In the end, readers will have to appeal to their own practical reason when it comes to ethical decisions, but such difficult reflections need not be done in a vacuum. Conrad's profound lesson in the age of the Anthropocene is not so much that in one of his narratives of disaster he proposes an ethics that goes beyond good and evil and justifies the murder of a systemically pathological individual in order to save the greatest number; contemporary theorists who are rethinking ethics in a broader ecology are currently coming to similar conclusions. Rather, Conrad is essential for us today because he provides complex experiential and aesthetic case studies of catastrophic scenarios that not only Conrad critics but each of us must learn to diagnose, evaluate and reevaluate in the age of the Anthropocene. This also means that for future-oriented readers, new critical interpretations of Conrad's fictions could perhaps be mirrored by theoretical reflections on how these fictions can help us read the real world. In sum Conrad's fictions make us feel in order to make us see, which is what theory means (from *theorein*, to see). They provide pictures of catastrophic scenarios that trigger literary, ethical, political and environmental reflections relevant for literary scholars, social theorists and ultimately, one would hope, each one of us.

While the sea change the Anthropocene is currently generating is likely to be for the worse, a sailor turned writer who has a say suggests that the decentering of man in the Anthropocene might also motivate a change for the better. We know that Conrad's images of otherness divided human groups in the past. We can now only hope that his steps to an ecological understanding of catastrophe will contribute to reuniting us in the future.

Notes

1 I am grateful to the Swiss National Science Foundation which funded my research at Johns Hopkins University and made time to write this article; many thanks to fellow Conradians for their feedback at the 2015 MLA conference in Vancouver, where I presented a first version of this paper, and to Lissa Schneider-Rebozo and Jeff McCarthy in particular for their helpful editorial suggestions. I feel privileged that political theorist William Connolly assigned this article in a graduate seminar on the Anthropocene, here at Hopkins. I have benefited enormously from Bill's thought-provoking Nietzschean insights into our dicey future and from the students' penetrating comments on the political importance of reading Conrad's fictions today. Last but not least, I am very grateful to both Jane Bennett and Bill Connolly for their numerous, friendly and vibrant conversations that—among other things—encouraged me to revitalize an immanent materialist tradition whose roots run deep in mimetic theory. This paper is dedicated to them.

2 Geologists have not yet officially declared our entrance in this new geological age, but there is little doubt that humans now operate as geological agents on the earth, and that the Anthropocene is here to stay, as the growing literature on this concept clearly indicates. For the official scientific articulation of "the term 'anthropocene' for the current geological epoch," see Crutzen and Stoermer 17; for an historically informed framing of the Anthropocene see Chakrabarti, "Four Theses" 207–12; on the relation between human and nonhuman agency in the Anthropocene see Glaser et al.; for special theoretical issues devoted to climate change in the Anthropocene in leading journals in the humanities, see

Oxford Literary Review 34 (2012), *Symplokē* 21.1–2 (2013), *Diacritics* 41.3 (2013); for a sociological lecture on the Anthropocene, see Latour, "The Anthropocene."

3 While the species *Homo Sapiens* is obviously not equally responsible for the horror of the Anthropocene (its origins are firmly located in a Western techne that culminated in the Industrial Revolution in capitalist societies), and humans will be affected differently by its consequences, Chakrabarti is right in stressing that this is "a shared catastrophe we have fallen into" ("Four Theses" 218).

4 Initial departures to anthropocentric tendencies in Conrad studies have so far tended to strategically focus on *Heart of Darkness*. See for instance McCarthy and Weilin.

5 On the relation between mimesis and pathology in literary and philosophical modernism in general, and Conrad in particular, see Lawtoo, *Phantom of the Ego*. In this book I argued that experiential writers like Conrad (but also Nietzsche, Lawrence, Bataille among others) who experienced and suffered from mimetic pathologies (madness, vulnerability to affect, hysterical symptoms and other affects that generate *pathos*) are in an ideal position give a clinical account (*logos*) of how mimetic *pathos* spreads (patho-*logy*). The concept of "patho(-)logy" thus designates the duplicity of affective mimesis as both the source of contagion (or pathology) and of a diagnostic, experiential method (patho-*logy*). See Lawtoo, *Phantom*, 6–8. More recently, I have pursed the exploration of mimetic patho(-)logies in Conrad's corpus as a whole in *Conrad's Shadow*. This article builds on these books and extends the loops of mimetic patho(-)logy beyond human contagion in order to include forms of nonhuman contagion that generate what I will call "eco-patho(-)logies."

6 In the wake of the reality of climate change, there is now a growing consensus that "Everybody should have an understanding of system thinking" (Glaser et al. 16). And what better introduction to learning to understand how parts relate to the whole while the whole informs our understanding of the parts than a literary education in general, and reading an author who describes systemic catastrophic scenarios in particular? As Latour also recognized: "Because they deal with fiction, literary theorists have been much freer in their inquiries about figuration than any social scientist...Novels, plays and films from classical tragedy to comics provide vast playground to rehearse accounts of what makes us act" (*Reassembling* 54–5). And in an interview, he specifies, "to think that you have mastered actor-network theory just because there will be actants, non-humans, no context and so on—this is a very simplified version. I mean, you really need to be able to write it" (Latour qtd. in Blok and Jensen 163). Conrad is so-far unrecognized master of this type of writing.

7 More recently, environmental theorists have joined efforts to "conceptualize the earth and its people as an increasingly integrated SES [social-ecological system] that is characterized by surprise, non-linear behavior and unpredictable changes of trajectory" (Glaser et al. 8), a condition that is, once again, best exemplified by life onboard ship.

8 My transl. Lacoue-Labarthe's *La Réponse d'Ulysse* includes, among other essays on the West, his philosophical reading of *Heart of Darkness*, "The Horror of the West." For the English translation and critical reception of this important essay, see my edited collection, *Conrad's Heart of Darkness and Contemporary Thought*.

9 If "actant" is a term Latour borrows from literary studies to articulate relational associations between humans and nonhumans central to

Actor-Network-Theory (ANT), literary studies can contribute to ANT by reminding these actors of what social psychologist Gabriel Tarde called "the laws of imitation." It is well known that Latour has done much to revitalize interest in Tarde, whose theory of mimetic contagion in *The Laws of Imitation* has, I have shown elsewhere, many affinities with Conrad, see Lawtoo, *Phantom* 94–5, 104–13. Yet, Latour is strangely silent on the literary/sociological concept of imitation (which for Tarde, as for Conrad, include contagion, suggestion and unconscious reflexes) that informs the movement of association between actors: that is, eminently *mimetic* creatures. What follows is thus not an attempt to apply ANT to Conrad's fiction (i.e., a contradiction in terms for Latour, see *Reassembling* 140). Rather, it provides a mimetic supplement to ANT by showing that imitation is a privileged link that associates nonhuman and humans in catastrophic scenarios.

10 For an account that shows how postcolonial concerns with "difference" must be productively supplemented with a view of humans as a single "species" in the age of the Anthropocene, see Chakrabarti, "Postcolonial."
11 On the mimetic link between animism, frenzy and the clamor of possession trance in *Heart of Darkness*, see Lawtoo's "A Picture of Europe."
12 Latour specifies: "Among these peoples, it was said, nothing happens to the order of the world that does not happen to humans, and vice versa." And taking this principle one step further he adds: "the other cultures under consideration did not blend the social and the natural order at all; *they were unconcerned by the distinction*" (*Politics* 44–5).
13 Srinivas Aravamudan puts it in classical pharmacological parlance as he argues that "Anthropomorphization appears to be both the problem and the solution" (14).
14 In order to affirm an imminent, consequentialist ethics that goes beyond good and evil, Nietzsche also relies on the image of the ship caught in a storm: "[I]f your ship *has* been driven into these seas, very well! Now clench your teeth! Keep your eyes open! Keep a firm hand on the helm! — We sail straight over morality and *past* it..." Nietzsche, *Beyond Good and Evil*, 54. On the continuities between Conrad's and Nietzsche's account of ethics see Lawtoo, *Conrad's Shadow*, Part I.
15 For a collection of theoretical essays on "The Secret Sharer," see Schwarz.
16 See Johnson and Garber 631.

Works Cited

Aravamudan, Srinivas. "The Cathacronism of Climate Change." *Diacritics*, vol. 41, no. 3, 2013, pp. 6–30.

Bateson, Gregory. *Steps to an Ecology of Mind: A Revolutionary Approach to Man's Understanding of Himself*. Ballantine Books, 1972.

Bennett, Jane. *Vibrant Matter: A Political Ecology of Things*. Duke UP, 2010.

Blok, Anders, Torben Elgaard Jensen. "'We Would Like to Do a Bit of Science Studies on You': An Interview with Bruno Latour." *Bruno Latour: Hybrid Thoughts in a Hybrid World*. Ed. Andres Blok and Torben Elgaard Jensen. Routledge, 2011, pp. 151–166.

Chakrabarti, Dipesh. "The Climate of History: Four Theses." *Critical Inquiry*, vol. 35, no. 2, 2009, pp. 197–222.

———. "Postcolonial Studies and the Challenge of Climate Change." *New Literary History*, vol. 43, no. 1, 2012, pp. 1–18.

Clark, Timothy. *The Cambridge Introduction to Literature and the Environment*. Cambridge UP, 2011.
Connolly, William. *The Fragility of Things: Self-Organizing Processes, Neoliberal Fantasies and Democratic Activism*. Duke UP, 2013.
Conrad, Joseph. *Lord Jim*. Edited by J. H. Stape and Ernest W. Sullivan II. Cambridge UP, 2012.
———. *The Nigger of the "Narcissus."* Doubleday, Page & Company, 1924.
———. *Notes on Life and Letters*, Edited by J. H. Stape. Cambridge UP, 2004.
———. "The Secret Sharer." *'Twix Land and Sea*. Ed. J. A. Berthoud, Laura L. Davis and S. W. Reid. Cambridge UP, 2008. pp 205–24
———. *The Shadow-Line: A Confession*. Edited by J. H. Stape and Allan Simmons. Cambridge UP, 2013.
———. *Typhoon*. Doubleday, Page & Company, 1925.
Crutzen, Paul J. "Geology of Mankind: The Anthropocene." *Nature*, vol. 415, 2002, p. 23.
Crutzen, Paul J. and Stoermer Eugene F. "The 'Anthropocene.'" *Global Change Newsletter*, vol. 41, 2000, pp. 17–18.
Dupuy, Jean-Pierre. *Pour un catastrophisme éclairé: Quand l'impossible est certain*. Seuil, 2002.
Girard, René. *Battling to the End: Conversations with Benoît Chantre*. Translated by Mary Baker. Michigan State UP, 2010.
Glaser, Marion, Krause Gesche, Ratter M. W. Beate, and Martin Welp, eds. *Human-Nature Interactions in the Anthropocene: Potential of Socio-Ecological Systems Analysis*. Routledge, 2012. Print.
Kavanagh, Brendan. "Dirty Weather: Typhoon's Meterology and MacWhirr's Point of View." *Conradian*, vol. 41, no. 1, 2016, pp. 1–19. Print.
Lacoue-Labarthe, Philippe. *La Réponse d'Ulysse: et autres textes sur L'Occident*. Edited by Aristide Bianchi and Leonid Kharlamov. Lignes/Imec, 2012, Print.
Latour, Bruno. "The Anthropocene and the Destruction of the Image of the Globe." *Gifford Lecture* 4. Web. www.youtube.com/watch?v=4-l6FQN4P1c.
———. *Politics of Nature: How to Bring the Sciences into Democracy*. Translated by Catherine Porter. Harvard UP, 2004.
———. *Reassembling the Social: An Introduction to Actor-Network-Theory*. Oxford UP, 2005.
Lawtoo, Nidesh. *Conrad's Shadow: Mimesis, Catastrophe, Theory*. Michigan State UP, 2016.
———. *The Phantom of the Ego: Modernism and the Mimetic Unconscious*. Michigan State UP, 2013.
———. "A Picture of Europe: Possession Trance in *Heart of Darkness*." *Novel*, vol. 45, no. 3, 2012, pp. 409–432.
Leavis, F. R. *The Great Tradition: George Eliot, Henry James, Joseph Conrad*. New York UP, 1964.
McCarthy, Jeffrey. "A Choice of Nightmares: The Ecology of *Heart of Darkness*." *Modern Fiction Studies*, vol. 55, no. 3, 2009, pp. 620–648.
Nancy, Jean-Luc. *L'Équivalence des catastrophes (après Fukushima)*. Galilée, 2012.
Nietzsche, Friedrich. *The Will to Power*. Translated by Walter Kaufmann and R. J. Hollingdale. Vintage Books, 1967.

Plato, *The Republic*. Translated by Paul Shorey in *The Collected Dialogues of Plato*, Edited by Edith Hamilton and Huntington Cairns, Translated by Lane Cooper et al. Princeton UP, 1963. pp. 575–844.

Rigby, Kate. "Confronting Catastrophe: Ecocriticism in a Warming World." *The Cambridge Companion to Literature and the Environment*. Ed. Louise Westling. Cambridge UP, 2013. pp. 212–225.

Schwarz, Daniel R., ed. *The Secret Sharer: Case Studies in Contemporary Criticism*. Bedford Books, 1997.

Serres, Michel. *The Natural Contract*. Translated by Elizabeth MacArthur and William Paulson. The U of Michigan P, 1995.

Weilin, Li. "An Ecological Analysis: The Sense of Loss from *Heart of Darkness*." *Studies in Literature and Language*, vol. 2, no. 3, 2011, pp. 153–160.

4 The Monstrous and the Secure
Reading Conrad in the Anthropocene

Robert P. Marzec

> [A]ll round him, on and on, even to the limits of the horizon hidden by the enormous piles of bricks, he felt the mass of mankind mighty in its numbers.
>
> Joseph Conrad, *Victory*

In 2012 Dipesh Chakrabarty challenged postcolonial scholars to stretch their thinking to "adjust...to the reality of global warming" (Chakrabarty 1). His argument specifically focused on the concept of the "Anthropocene"—that is, the "era when humans act as a geological force on the planet," changing the earth's ecosystem on a global scale for centuries to come (2). Chakrabarty is not the first scholar in the humanities to draw our attention toward the consequential transformation of humans from local to planetary actors. But his appeal focalizes the need to expand disciplinary limits as the ecological impact of humanity expands in ways unanticipated by previous postcolonial theories of the human. Humans acting as a geological force pose two problems for the kind of ideological or postcolonial critique optimized by literary studies. First, postcolonial theory, which is well honed at decentering, human-constituted structures of meaning, has little experience confronting multi- and planetary-scale conceptions and compositions of the human. Its current critical jurisdiction in the Anthropocene is thus limited. Second, the disciplines that do study and thus have authority to speak about the nature of large-scale forces have little experience understanding the influence that ideological, human-constituted structures of meaning have on these forces. These disciplines are generally techno-scientific, treat the Anthropocene empirically, and, if they venture into the domain of history at all, understand the past as a process of technological advancement. Joseph Conrad's novels expose the violence of this techno-scientific worldview, and, at the same time, link its rationale to an existentialist critique of what it means to be human.

In this essay I focalize Conrad's interrogation of colonial technological expansions at the turn of the twentieth century, in which, I argue, Conrad anticipates the kinds of large-scale energies now acutely apparent in the twenty-first-century era of climate change. More specifically, Conrad foregrounds the essential role of security in the historical development of the technologies that have enabled the transition of the human from ecological species to geological force. It is precisely the colonial concern for security, and its connection to the large-scale character of the human, that Conrad confronts with increasing intensity in his novels. It is in and through the growth of a securitized form of techno-scientific development and environmental exploitation (techne) that he locates the origin of the anthropogenic human. In the movement from the African context of *Heart of Darkness* to the South American context of *Nostromo*, and eventually to the London and European context of *The Secret Agent*, Conrad articulates a concern for the rising global nature of security as coterminous with the expansion of human subjectivity. These novels trace the attempt to securitize and administer the ecosystems (physis) of the earth and direct them isomorphically toward Western capitalist development. They envisage the human transition to a new historical epoch, in which humans begin to maneuver increasingly toward the dead-end ecologies of the Anthropocene.

Postcolonial theory and literary studies have a long history of exploring the tensions between techne ("revealing," "practice," "technology," "engineering,") and physis ("nature," "habitation," "environment," "ecosystem"). As I will trace in this essay, the movement from *Heart of Darkness* to *The Secret Agent* reveals that Conrad understands modern colonial and environmental developments as indissolubly centered on the metamorphosis of techne into security. One of the most significant considerations of Conrad's analysis of Western techne is Lacoue-Labarthe's 1995 essay on *Heart of Darkness*. Humans have always fabricated relationships with nature through some form of technology, modern or otherwise. But for Lacoue-Labarthe, techne in the modern world names an essentially violent comportment with nature (physis). According to Lacoue-Labarthe, *Heart of Darkness* takes up this relation unlike any other modern novel. The novel reveals that no ontological guarantee lies at the heart of the relation between techne and physis, and Lacoue-Labarthe argues that the "horror" is "the nothingness" at the center of human subjectivity and human technologies (Lacoue-Labarthe 117). In this sense, Kurtz's particular "revealing" of and attempt to control physis, which is founded on the civilizing program of Western-European colonialism, is ultimately self-destructive.

But Lacoue-Labarthe also gives a second definition to "the horror," one more widespread in its significance and weight. This appears in his critical confrontation with the modern human comportment to techne. Techne manifests itself in Lacoue-Labarthe's essay through many definitions: as art (the artifice manufactured by the human that transforms physis into a work of art), as "limitation" (115), as "voice" and "language" (116), as "knowledge" (117), and as "literature" itself (120).

None of these human endeavors and the work/worlds they build can be justified by any recourse to a transcendent truth, by anything metaphysical, in other words. Nature (physis) carries nothing innate within itself that would justify the particular techne generated. The problem—the "horror"—arises when the human subject attempts to deny this emptiness, to fill in the void of the Nothing. This is precisely the core of the Western imperial project, according to Lacoue-Labarthe. Warding off this emptiness transforms techne into a violent activity: "ivory trafficking and colonial royalty" (117). When the essential emptiness of techne is occluded, human formations of physis become increasingly aggressive and violent: "The response to the vertigo of techne is technical agitation" (117). Conrad's novel thus shows that the West's destruction of the African ecosystem in the form of colonial rule is a symptom of the coming-to-rule of modern technologization.

Lacoue-Labarthe engages this tension between physis and techne more fully in *Heidegger, Art and Politics*. There he lays out the stakes in the human historical constitution of techne. We find the most significant definition of the term in the chapter that confronts the dangers of aestheticizing politics: "techne can be defined as the sur-plus of physis, through which physis 'deciphers' and presents itself" (69). Lacoue-Labarthe reads the act of techne as essentially an act of "revealing"—in other words, as an act of creation that keeps alive the singular, open-ended character of the artifact created. Its createdness is not reduced or constrained by a set of demands arising from outside its immanent domain. There's a fundamental difference, for instance, between steering a boat up a river carefully (so as not to plow through or pollute the river's many ecosystems) and widening a river with heavy machinery in order to make way for a fleet of oil tankers. Language, art and technology can thus be ways of relating to physis that do their best not to disturb the character of ecological communities. Furthermore, physis does not "self-reveal"; our access to and understanding of physis is mediated by and through human forms of representation and understanding (in other words, techne).

As such, technologies and representations cannot be disconnected from an entire series of ethical questions because physis only appears as meaningful in relation to the particular manner in which it is brought forth. If it were of the essence of physis to do its own revealing, then there would be no need for techne. Physis/Nature would speak for itself, and all the various forms of techne—from language through all forms of art and technology—would be reduced to mere description, to transparency. At such a moment technology "oversteps the limits" of nature and becomes lethal (69). The (impossible) rejection of the Nothing produces the symptomatic results of a "massive unleashing of techne," to use Lacoue-Labarthe's apt phrase, which constitutes the basis for techne's "radical transmutation into excrescence" (69). This very reduction—the transformation of techne into mere transparency, and the simultaneous overstepping of limits and creation of unwanted side effects—lies at the heart of the supplanting of techne by security. What strikes one immediately about *Heart of Darkness* (and what Lacoue-Labarthe does not consider) is Conrad's awareness of the global character of technological expansion and agitation—of, that is, the growing scale of Western humanity's influence on the planet. This magnification of the human, supported by technological transparency, is framed throughout the novel in terms of environmental destruction. London, as represented in the opening pages, was once the wild environment that stood at the limit of the Roman Empire. The reference to England's primordial past, as many Conrad scholars have suggested, links the civilized British citizen with the presumably savage indigenous inhabitants of the Congo:

> It was unearthly, and the men were—No, they were not inhuman.... They howled and leaped, and spun, and made horrid faces; but what thrilled you was just the thought of their humanity—like yours—the thought of your remote kinship with this wild and passionate uproar.
>
> (Conrad, *Heart of Darkness* 51)

Yet this image of "first nature" (to invoke Lawrence Buell's important reformulation of Karl Marx's term) is set against the image of London as an ecological ruin. Marlow appears to have little enthusiasm for the modern ecosystem of London; it is described as little more than graveyard devastated by the processes of "cultivation/civilization." When he moves his attention to another European capital, Brussels, the city is a "whited sepulchre," a "city of the dead" with "grass sprouting between the stones," not unlike the African "grass growing through" the remains of one of the Company's captains, the Danish Fresleven who was killed in the act of beating an African to death (*Heart of Darkness* 23, 26). When Marlow searches the city for the Company Offices, they are easy to find because the Company takes dominion over everything: "It was the biggest thing in the town, and everybody I met was full of it" (24). Marlow's jaded sense of empire's enlightenment evangelism—the "rot let loose in print"—indicates his marginal relation to the social system, unlike his Aunt, who happily ingests the view that the West is "'weaning those ignorant millions from their horrid ways'" (27). What's left of the environment, the impression we're given, is a Europe in a "sepulchral" state, with first nature reduced to a residuum of its former self: all we see is "grass sprouting between...stones" (25). The built human ecosystem allows for very little first nature; the streets are overtaken by "high houses, innumerable windows with venetian blinds, a dead silence" (25), and the interior of the city's structures are "arid," like "deserts" (24). Of the environment in the Congo, critics such as Nidesh

Lawtoo, Jeffrey Mathes McCarthy, J. Hillis Miller and Greg Winston have highlighted the environmentally destructive nature of the colonial order in *Heart of Darkness*. Jeffrey Mathes McCarthy's nuanced reading of the role of ivory in the novel paves the way for critics to see the significance of Conrad's attunement to humanity's late-colonial penchant for environmental destruction. McCarthy argues that Conrad's novel shows the "ecological limits of imperialism" (621). Imperialism depends on the Congo ecosystem, but its ruthless pursuit of resources, paradoxically embodied in disembodied "heaps of" ivory, reveal the self-destructive nature of the enterprise: the lack of elephants in the novella, in the face of a surfeit of the treasured resource itself, "describes an economy whose fructifying power is extinct,...thereby [rendering] an environment tipping towards collapse" (621) As McCarthy emphasizes even the word elephant "appears to have been hunted to extinction" (621). The distinct lack of elephants matches the equal lack of any other animal life, which provokes the ecocritic to wonder why a text so obsessed with the "wildness" of nature and its supposed effect on the human would actually offer us so little of nature itself in the end. The more we read the more we realize that nature comes to presence as a lacuna, and Marlow's relationship to nature is equally plagued by ideological assumptions now sheared by years of perturbing experience. Our access to nature is measured through a character whose original understanding of nature depended on ideologies of colonial romance and travel adventures stories: the Congo was "a blank space of delightful mystery—a white patch for a boy to dream gloriously over" (*Heart of Darkness* 22). When this imaginary is demystified, the result is not a more complex understanding of the environment, but a decentering plummet to nihilism: "It had ceased to be a blank space of delightful mystery.... It had become a place of darkness" (22). This abyssal relation to nature is curiously redeemed by a doubled metaphor of a colonial imaging of foreign land, and a capitalist-influenced return to a quasi-boyhood enthusiasm for shopping:

> But there was in [the darkness] one river especially, a mighty big river, that you could see on the map, resembling an immense snake uncoiled, with its head in the sea, its body at rest curving afar over a vast country, and its tail lost in the depths of the land. And as I looked at the map of it in a shop-window it fascinated me as a snake would a bird—a silly little bird. Then I remembered there was a big concern, a Company for trade on that river. Dash it all! I thought to myself, they can't trade without using some kind of craft on that lot of fresh water—steamboats! Why shouldn't I try to get charge of one? I went on along Fleet Street, but could not shake off the idea. The snake had charmed me.
>
> (22–3)

This boyhood conceptualization of the Congo is quickly dispelled, but the use of animal imagery is nowhere else clearer than in this "shop-window" framework. The aestheticization of the nature of the Congo, then—a nature as imaged by colonial-childhood fantasies—is the dominant cultural framework the novella challenges and de-structures. What replaces this vision is the violence of the technological utopia of the early (European) Anthropocene and its securitizing praxis.

Marlow witnesses the first stages of the human unleashing of techne before he steps on land, as he watches the French "man-of-war" "incomprehensibly" shell the continent while anchored off the coast:

> Pop, would go one of the six-inch guns; a small flame would dart and vanish, a little white smoke would disappear, a tiny projectile would give a feeble screech—and nothing happened. Nothing could happen. There was a touch of insanity in the proceeding.
> (28–9)

Everywhere nature is overtaken by "scene[s] of inhabited devastation" (30); boilers "wallow in the grass"; the land is strewn with "decaying machinery" and "rusty nails" (30); and the predominant metaphors of the enlightenment project are recoded into their opposites: "A blinding sunlight drowned all this at times in a sudden recrudescence of glare" (30). The romance of human (colonial) expansion is quickly dispelled by the horror of a technology agitated by its own lack of control. The desire for technological control is so pervasive, and its transparency so unquestioned, that alternative forms of relating to nature become impossible. Such forms are outside the narrowly framed windows of both boyhood and adulthood. Hence nature's "appearance" as a lacuna in the novel—precisely because commodity culture and techno-imperialism are not in the business of considering alternatives to their forms of techne.

Against Marlow's clear objections to the madness of colonial technological aggression stands his contradictory thematization of the environment. At times his representations of nature are of a piece with colonial renditions of the land as empty and chaotic: "an untouched expanse," "a God-forsaken wilderness," "a monotonous grimness," "a mournful and senseless delusion" and an "empty land" (28, 34). Such depictions suggest a well-worn intelligibility that extends at least as far back as *Robinson Crusoe*, which understands non-Western lands as devoid of populations and ripe for the taking. Marlow, for instance, gives us no indication of the multiplicity of languages, cultures and histories of indigenous tribes that inhabit the spaces through which he and the other characters navigate. Nonetheless he also offers a very different engagement with the environment, one more closely related to the kinds of nonaggressive and non-commanding representations characterizing Heidegger's descriptions of the "concealed" and "withholding" earth

(174, 181). We see this in Marlow's description of the ecosystem immediately outside the Central Station:

> Beyond the fence the forest stood up spectrally in the moonlight, and through the dim stir, through the faint sounds of that lamentable courtyard, the silence of the land went home to one's very heart—its mystery, its greatness, the amazing reality of its concealed life.
>
> (*Heart of Darkness* 41)

Here the land is not captured in assignations arising from the metaphysical imperatives of the civilizing project but considered as an entity that Marlow understands to be fully outside his mode of intelligibility. It speaks not of its own "emptiness," a form of meaning summoning cultivation. Rather Marlow gives the land the gift of "silence," which is more suggestive of an ethical, open-ended use of language that considers the limitations of its own prefigured frame. There's much that could be drawn from these nonaggressive representational moments in *Heart of Darkness*, and much that can be asked as well. Are we to see these failures to "image" the environment as an inefficiency in Marlow? Or are they indicative of an ethical relation to the limits of one's knowledge and the absolute nature of the Other that lies beyond? Are these admissions of limited knowledge to be praised or are we to fault Marlow for possibly lacking any desire whatsoever to attempt an encounter with the Other (he is, after all, mainly concerned about finding and talking to Kurtz). I would argue they reveal a stage in Conrad's developing understanding of human globality and influence, one in which the stakes of the techno-colonial "affair" already reveal its widespread capacity for destruction.

These adversarial discursive constitutions tend to disappear in *Nostromo*, and make even less of an appearance in *The Secret Agent*. Conrad's concerns shift to a more concerted interrogation of the expanding scale of the anthropogenic human. In *Nostromo* the imperial order bearing down on the environment of a South American province is of a much larger proportion than that controlling the production of ivory in *Heart of Darkness*. The global initiative of England, Europe and America express an impulse to secure the Global South (emblematized in the form of the Sulaco silver mine) by ideologically transforming the complex heterogeneity of an ecosystem into a single "raw materiality" in need of technological "improvement." Conrad makes clear in the opening pages that the environment of Sulaco constitutes an ecological dilemma to those seeking to capture its natural resources. Here we see Marlow's Heideggerian moments of characterization more fully pronounced. Sheltered from exploitation the earth appears as an "inviolable sanctuary," one resisting "the temptations of a trading world," and actively "withdrawing" from human encroachment and technological progress; its "antiquity" is preserved from the "worlding" of the anthropocentric forces that would seek to transform its nonhuman nature into a "resource" (3).

"Resource," like "ivory" in *Heart of Darkness*, is an allotrope for reterritorializing an ecosystem for the purposes of capitalist production and development in *Nostromo*. *Nostromo* echoes *Heart of Darkness* again where "resource" names the tension surrounding the modern technological attempt to erase the Nothing at the heart of existence—on both a cultural and an environmental register. Culturally the reduction of indigenous diversity to a single "resource" constitutes an obvious erasure of that diversity, and the transformation of human inhabitants themselves into a raw labor resource. The reification that occurs in this transformation of nature in the Anthropocene, however, involves more than the kinds of processes of extraction that defined previous human harvestings of nature. The coalition of forces involved in colonial, and neocolonial, technologies of extraction operate through what I have called elsewhere a principle of targeting (Marzec 47). The "resource" targeted is not understood to be "within" nature, in the sense of being an integral part of a system. Rather, it is decoded along the lines similar to a mathematical cypher—seen as a "discovered" element entrapped by nature. Technology is thus the productive force that extracts the elements "true potential," securing it to itself, thus making it capable to be inserted as if it were a prosthetic extension of the human-gone-global.

In *Nostromo* the self-destructive efforts to securitize resources from the environment are situated against the background of a more complex global occasion. On a cultural register we first read about the "violent," mottled heterogeneity of the population through the English superintendent Captain Mitchell. In Mitchell Conrad introduces us to the ideological imperatives of the security society. Sulaco is seen geopolitically as not only a politically unstable region but as a locality in need of a strong military presence capable of controlling the "crazy mob" of native Indians, former African slaves, Spanish and Europeans: "We were infested—infested, overrun, sir…by ladrones and matreros, thieves and murderers from the whole province…flocking into Sulaco" (Conrad, *Nostromo* 14). In fact the tragic character of Nostromo is first introduced in all his mysterious grandeur precisely as a kind of "natural security officer": "This Nostromo, sir, a man absolutely above reproach, became the terror of all the thieves in the town" (14). Before we even begin the narrative proper we learn from Mitchell that Nostromo's securitizing efforts are decisive to the area's future: The South American republic of Costaguana has had to endure a seemingly endless history of revolutionary and military violence. The novel opens roughly in the wake of the dictatorship of Señor Ribiera. Overthrown at the Battle of Socorro Ribiera has had to flee. Mitchell is charged with managing his escape, but Nostromo is the key figure endowed with the natural ability to ensure security on the ground: "Nostromo, a fellow in a thousand,...[who holds] the jetty against the rabble, thus giving the fugitives time" (13).

This revolutionary "multitude" is presented as part of the chaotic tissue of nature—a part that needs to be cleansed in order that the entrepreneur Charles Gould can successfully access his ancestral "concession": the San Tomé silver mines. In the complex economic and political forces necessary for the mining of silver we see the already immense scale of the early Anthropocene and its attendant ecological security industry, dreamed of by the American banker Holroyd who backs Gould's scheme. Holroyd's characterization of his participatory claim to the silver mine, like Marlow's foregrounding of the principle existential power of language (the "voice"), grounds itself in the imperial logos and its power to function as a global apparatus of capture:

> We shall be giving the word for everything—industry, trade, law, journalism, art, politics and religion, from Cape Horn clear over to Smith's Sound, and beyond too, if anything worth taking hold of turns up at the North Pole. And then we shall have the leisure to take in hand the outlying islands and continents of the earth. We shall run the world's business whether the world likes it or not. The world can't help it—and neither can we, I guess.
>
> (85)

This "giving" of "the word"—extended in size to a global scale—reveals Conrad's attunement to a fundamental shift in the quality of the imperial-sovereign subject. The exploitation of an ecosystem is not solely, nor even mainly, for the colonial control of natural resources. Holroyd's explanation of his decision to financially support Gould's mine reveals a much greater venture, indicating the desire to incorporate nature within a total system of control. His "giving of the word for everything" encompasses not only the exploitative cultivation of raw resources ("industry" and "trade") but acts as a pathogen that spreads across all sites of human cultural production: "journalism, art, politics and religion." His cultural "giving" of the "word" names the co-constitutive action of a "taking hold of" ("if anything worth taking hold of turns up at the North Pole") that presages in an uncanny fashion Heidegger's characterizations of techne's modern metamorphosis into monstrous forms of technology that "set upon," "take hold of" and "order" nature as a set of discreet and isolated elements useful only for developmental projects (Heidegger, "The Question Concerning Technology" 17).

Conrad's problematizes through the term "resource." The collapse of nature under the sign of "resource" constitutes an act of "targeting" and "unlocking" an element in nature, lacerating it from its unique, immanent set of relations and inserting into a new, non-ecological, anthropocentric-oriented system of "distribution" that sets it upon a new "course" ("The Question Concerning Technology" 16). It is within this act of unlocking and setting upon a new course that Heidegger tellingly begins to use metaphors of security to define the specific technological mode operative in modern, human-centered systems of production: "This regulating itself is, for its part, everywhere secured. Regulating and securing even become the chief characteristics of the challenging revealing" (16). Security is named as one of the "chief characteristics" of modern technology. In the German verb "to secure" [*sicherstellen*] Heidegger means to invoke the key concept found in the stem-word associated with linguistic "representation"—*stellen*—which means "to set up" and "to supply." More importantly *stellen* is ontologically connected to the two crucial forms of production peculiar to *techne* in the modern world: *vorstellen* (to represent) and *Ge-stell* (Enframing). *Vorstellen* names a use of language that understands words to be merely descriptive tools, secondary devices for describing a more essential and primary reality. In the well-known poststructuralist terms, *vorstellen* as representation is the belief in language as "transparent." *Ge-stell*, or *Enframing*, is of course Heidegger's term for the essence of modern technology—that is, a militarized "grabbing hold of," "challenging" and "engaging" that "furnishes" and "supplies." *Vorstellen* and *Ge-stell* therefore define the primary cultural and cultivation activities of *techne* in the modern era.

Holroyd's logocentric "giving of the word for everything" is at one and the same time a form of monstrous-scale "worlding" of all the ecosystems of the planet (the "outlying islands and continents of the earth"). His simultaneous "wording/worlding" constitutes a re-presenting of nature on the colonial basis of pursuing and trapping nature as a set or resources made to "stand on reserve": "anything worth taking hold of." For Holroyd this extension of his subjectivity to the ends of the earth—the simultaneous coupling of cultivation and culturation—is an implicit realization of his "destiny" (*Nostromo* 85). But for Gould, a more complex man, this destiny (which he accepts "with no objection") extends this commanding language to the nexus between a society increasingly concerned with security, and the environment—where the environment enters the security society's frame of intelligibility through the technological improvement of the land in terms of economic production, or "material interests." Gould argues:

> What is wanted here is law, good faith, order, security...[and] I pin my faith to material interests. Only let the material interests get a firm footing, and they are bound to impose the conditions on which alone they can continue to exist. That's how your moneymaking is justified here in the face of lawlessness and disorder. It is justified because the security which it demands must be shared with an

oppressed people. A better justice will come afterwards....And who knows whether in that sense the San Tomé mine may not become that little rift in the darkness.

(92–3)

"Justice" here is based on and arising out of the ecological plunder of nature's "material interests." As such Gould's enterprise is of a piece with Holroyd's imperial project. The extraction of nature's resources is the first step in a battle to overcome "lawlessness and disorder": the San Tomé mine will be a "little rift in the darkness." The technological extraction of the silver will then bring the demand for "security," without which civilization would be impossible. Most critics have read this as a political critique; if we, instead, recognize nature's centrality to Conrad's analysis we find a Heideggerian distrust for technology and domination. Everything hinges on the securing of resources, which clears the way for the constitution of law and order and the subsequent extraction of the local "oppressed" population from its "darkness" into a "better justice." All this is made possible through the simultaneous co-constitution of imperialism, security and the reformation of ecological complexity as standing-reserve. The existence of one depends in a reciprocal relation to the other. "Moneymaking" and its ecological grounding in "material interests" inaugurate an apparatus of justice because the extraction of a natural resource requires an immense commitment to security in the face of immense social and environmental risk.

These securitizing actions indicative of the essence of globalized techne in the Anthropocene reach their idealized form in the character of Emilia Gould—the "flame," to invoke Robert Penn Warren's monumental interpretation of her essence, around which "the other characters gather to warm their hands" (Warren xii). Against Warren's apolitical identification of Emilia Gould as the character who "sets up the human community" "against abstractions," and who exudes a "sense of human solidarity in understanding and warmth and kindness outside the historical process," we should situate her in the context of her portentous initial appearance in Sulaco. Despite her supposed distance from the world of the technological (not unlike Kurtz's "Intended" at the end of *Heart of Darkness*), Emilia Gould's arrival is highly staged. Her entrance is purposely framed as a "prospect view" that oversees the situation. I have in mind the scene in which she accompanies her husband as he meticulously surveys the land on horseback soon after their initial arrival from England. Though she is meant to be a passive presence as he searches for future laborers for the mine, we experience the event primarily through her eyes. Her description of the Sulaco Valley is rich and detailed:

> It unrolled itself, with green young crops, plains, woodland, and gleams of water, parklike, from the blue vapour of the distant sierra

to an immense quivering horizon of grass and sky, where big white clouds seemed to fall slowly into the darkness of their own shadows.

Men ploughed with wooden ploughs and yoked oxen, small on a boundless expanse, as if attacking immensity itself. The mounted figures of vaqueros galloped in the distance, and the great herds fed with all their horned heads one way, in one single wavering line as far as eye could reach across the broad potreros. A spreading cotton-wood tree shaded a thatched ranche by the road; the trudging files of burdened Indians taking off their hats, would lift sad, mute eyes to the cavalcade raising the dust of the crumbling Camino Real made by the hands of their enslaved forefathers. And Mrs. Gould, with each day's journey, seemed to come nearer to the soul of the land in the tremendous disclosure of this interior unaffected by the slight European veneer of the coast towns, a great land of plain and mountain and people, suffering and mute, waiting for the future in a pathetic immobility of patience.

(*Nostromo* 96–7)

This passage speaks of the Nothingness of the environment (*physis*) and of an ideological supplementation of that Nothingness within an apocalyptic system of re-presentation. In her vision of the land from on high Emilia Gould immediately glimpses its *physis*—the land's "immensity" that withholds its potential from the futile "attacks" of the workers. As such the "first nature" of the land is in need of saving for it is grounded in a Nothing that offers no stability. Hence this vision of *physis* is already an "insight" serving to justify colonial expansion and the demand for security that expansion requires: The farmers have yet to tame the land, and their "small," "wavering" and "mute" attempts to control the land are "waiting" for the "different future" of a more (technologically) advanced order capable of systematically taking it in hand.

This is the novel's version of the "night of first ages" Marlow presents from Africa. It is an encounter with a raw nature still to be domesticated. Resituated in the geographical context of Latin America, the premodern human in this scene is depicted not in the chaos of an unleashed energy but in the equally uncivilized "drudgery" of a labor that leads nowhere. Despite the efforts of indigenous peoples and the Spanish descendants of slaveholders, the "soul of the land" still "patiently" awaits the revelation of true cultivation. This representation of the premodern human in a condition of "servitude" to the land is part of the discourse of enclosure, which historically characterizes itself as an escape (through the technological advances brought about by an act of enclosure) from the feudal world in which serfs were "chained to the land" and unable to escape its pull. In this sense the humans inhabiting this land have yet to achieve their "full potential." Their preformed subjectivity is caught within a kind of limbo in which they stand alongside nature's concealed and withdrawn status (*physis*): "a great land of plain and mountain and people, suffering and mute, waiting for the future in a pathetic immobility of patience." These apocalyptic representations, to refer back to Lacoue-Labarthe's discussion of "technical agitation," are indicative of a political aestheticization of *physis* as a lacuna in need of technological permeation. The "immensity" of undomesticated nature is, in the final instance, not an open, accommodating relationship to *physis* but a problematic overshadowing of nature for characterizing it as a threat to anthropogenic sovereignty.

Again, Conrad's nature is the key to Conrad's politics. This depiction of nature and the premodern human is related to the depiction of the region's political instability. The land and inhabitants of Sulaco are each in need of development. Because the inhabitants lack proper development they also lack the political knowhow and will to lift themselves out of the prepolitical chaos of their existence. Conrad's preparatory stagings of the political in the first half of the novel are not mere foreshadowings of events to come; they are of the same piece in their use of *physis* as an "insecurity" yet to be properly taken in hand. Again it is through Emilia Gould's "understanding and warmth" that we view these truths:

> In all these households she could hear stories of political outrage; friends, relatives, ruined, imprisoned, killed in the battles of senseless civil wars, barbarously executed in ferocious proscriptions, as though the government of the country had been a struggle of lust between bands of absurd devils let loose upon the land…. And on all the lips she found a weary desire for peace, the dread of officialdom with its nightmarish parody of administration without law, without security, and without justice.
>
> (97–8)

Here Emilia Gould reveals the essential technological relation taken up toward *physis*: The proper imposition of a legitimate system of law that would bring security and in turn justify its presence in the colony. Without the proper supplementation of *techne* by a securitizing apparatus, the "land" will continue, in its essential unruliness, to support the "lustful" hostility of quasi-political factions. Security thus constitutes a kind of missing link to the political—the key that transforms governance from a "nightmarish parody" into a genuine system of administration that would finally transform the essential instability of the ecosystem and satisfy the "weary desire for peace."

Curiously, the character Nostromo appears to lack, or not need, this desire for peace throughout the majority of the novel—up until the point when the narrative turns tragic. As we've seen, the peace brought to Sulaco by this security administration leads humanity and nature into the revelation of the post-political end of political struggle—in other words, the messianic moment of the "end of history" that supposedly defines the ultimate stage of human development in the Anthropocene. This concept of the post-political is a significant aspect of the generalized human–nature nexus in the late modern and postmodern era. The belief that the colonial West has reached the end point of human sociopolitical development (espoused by conservatives like Francis Fukuyama and Samuel Huntington and critiqued by contemporary theorists and scholars such as Edward W. Said, Judith Butler and Slavoj Žižek) is part and parcel of the transformation of the human into an anthropogenic force. Being unchained from politics and technologically unchaining from nature (by transforming nature into a "resource" for "development") are pieces of the same puzzle. Nostromo is tellingly equated with a version of this post-political neutrality. His ability to maintain order in the town, to serve as the vehicle of security, is emphatically presented alongside his nonpolitical intellectual character.

Previous critics have sensed this post-political neutrality but have attributed it to traditionally psychological factors such as human narcissism. Avrom Fleishman treats Nostromo as a character study in the embodiment of personal and egocentric motives (176); Michael John DiSanto extends this reading and sees Nostromo as motivated by self-preservation when he and Decoud turn against Hirsch (126). But Conrad himself said in his Foreword that he "needed…a man of the People" who did "not want to raise himself above the mass." Being a "man of the people" can be read in a number of ways, but in the post-political order, the man of the people is precisely the self-reliant and rugged individual who maintains his distance from politics. In other words, Nostromo does not stand apart as a political figure with an agenda, and it is this lack of agenda that makes him the ideal, individualized warrior. His loss of this political neutrality is precisely what leads to his "tragic downfall." His absence of belief is a double-edged sword. It has been the very blindness that makes him powerful, admired and famous. But after taking the silver and returning, he can no longer hold his former position as a member of the post-political-natural order that Gould attempts to establish. Unlike his previous neutral stance, he now clings to a new anger, which arises from his enlightenment that he has been exploited by the imperial order. Instead of turning away from this order, he flings himself into it, fully entering it for the first time by waging war against it as a kind of proto-ideological commitment. His obsession with the silver, which comes to be in the wake of his awareness of being exploited by the Gould-Holroyd corporate industry, is the prime symptom of this commitment. We are told repeatedly that he cannot "let it go," that the "specter of the treasure…claim[s] his allegiance," and makes him its "slave" (*Nostromo* 593, 595). Yet his attempt to confront his own exploitation fails to move beyond the established relationship to nature as a "treasure." The post-political ideological commitment to "material interests"—to a *physis* captured by technology—is transformed here into the treasure of "being free" that is taken from him by the system exploiting his life. The irony, then, is that Nostromo is unable to let go of the very passion—the violation of nature through its transformation into a resource—that defined Gould's existence.

Ultimately, Nostromo the character points readers toward the novel as a tragedy. After all, the corporate attempt to obscure the emptiness of resource extraction through a political system of security ends in a great fall. Put differently, the self-destructive enterprise of colonial development is incorporated into the traditional narrative structure of the genre of tragedy. One could read this conclusion of the novel as a reticence to fully confront the violence of colonial humanity, as the reluctance to confront the conceit of humanity's geological-scale pretensions. The clear foregrounding of the contradictions inherent in the "massing unleashing" of *techne*, and the single-minded hubris on the part of Gould in the majority of the novel come to be subsumed with the struggles of a (anti)heroic man. In this sense one could even go so far as to accuse Conrad himself of a certain "Marlowism." In failing to reveal Kurtz's last words to his Intended, Marlow ensures that the myth of the colonial civilizing project maintains its hold on the home front. In blanketing the Nothing with the tragedy of the heroic individual—by supplementing, that is, the novel's interrogation of a globalized *techne* grown increasingly violent in its attempts to transform the decentered complexity of *physis* into standing-reserve—Conrad humanizes the anthropogenic refusal to be answerable to nature's essential groundlessness. The downfall of Nostromo might also be interpreted differently and seen as a realization that this securitizing of nature is a dead-end pursuit. Regardless, when we set these observations against *The Secret Agent* we encounter a Conrad extremely pessimistic about the growth of faith and interest in "human potential."

In *The Secret Agent* we enter a scenario in which this technological agitation in the absence of any secure and foundational meaning is turned inside out. In a sense the novel picks up where *Nostromo* left off but in a manner distinctly less hopeful in its appraisal of contemporary humanity. As Martin Seymour-Smith argues in his introduction to the novel, *The Secret Agent* "is a kind of sardonic sequel to *Nostromo*," and London "a cruel and mocking elaboration" of how "Sulaco would 'evolve'" (9). The instability at the center of the imperial project is brought out into the light of day, so to speak; it becomes a presence in the novel. This "appearance" of instability marks what we might mark as the maturation or full development of technical agitation—a development that signals the shift from the colonial order to the post-World War II security society. That is, Conrad's shifting of "the Horror" back to the center of empire restages in an uncanny fashion the securitizing imperatives of the Anthropocene that were only a vestigial component of the earlier novel. As security becomes the dominant paradigm of existence, it deploys the principle technological tactic of paradoxically admitting the Nothing through the representative act of giving it an identity. The identity of the Nothing comes to be seen and known as a daily feature of existence; its "presence" is constantly a threat at every moment. This positivized instability of the Nothing comes to constitute the main problematized object of the post-political—the transcendent nonpolitical order that escapes the agendas of all ideologies by taking on the Nothing as its enemy. Put differently the Nothing is universalized in the form of a pure insecurity that renders the necessity of security—and its globalization—permanent.

Nature (resource) is never mentioned openly in the novel, but its presence is felt nonetheless in the political and economic intensity of an increasingly self-conscious and distressed imperialism. The secret agent Verloc, planted in the midst of a central London anarchist bloc (but working without the anarchists' knowledge in the service of an unnamed foreign government), expresses the essential connection between the new capitalism and security:

> He surveyed the town's opulence and luxury....All these people had to be protected. Protection is the first necessity of opulence and luxury....[T]heir horses, carriages, houses, servants had to be protected, and the source of their wealth had to be protected in the heart of the city and the heart of the country; the whole social order favourable to their idleness had to be protected against the shallow enviousness of unhygienic labour.
>
> (Conrad, *The Secret Agent* 51–2)

Verloc's view, however, is not like Emilia Gould's; he is not the "flame" around which others can build a community. In fact in this novel there are no daring characters endowed with substantive agency, as we find in *Nostromo* and *Heart of Darkness*, and no charismatic persona in and through which one might construct a tragic figure. There is only the raw essence of the void of meaning lying at the center of the colonial order—staged in the form of great despondency and bleak comic irony by a third-person narrator. The third-person narration eliminates the safety net of critical distance made possible in *Heart of Darkness* by Marlow's play with voices. Our attention toward the critical work of emphasizing the importance of the "linguistic turn" is refocused on a more difficult problem: The adoption of a conceptual anarchy as a mandate of modern politics. Conrad uses *The Secret Agent* to confront politics as a policing of the growing presence and subsequent naturalization of anarchism.

As an agent Verloc's beliefs are neither reactionary nor idealistic. We are told that Verloc's "mission in life [is] the protection of the social mechanism, not its perfectionism nor even its criticism" (*The Secret

Agent 54). Privy Councillor Wurmt, Verloc's supervisor, operates under similar assumptions, despite his criticisms of Verloc as not active enough for the new regime. He desires no radical change in the order but seeks instead for an increase in its essential operations: "What is desired...is the occurrence of something definite which would stimulate their vigilance" (55). London, he feels, is falling behind the rest of the European community: The "leniency" of its "repressive [security] measures" are a "scandal to Europe." His aim is to "accentuate the unrest" teeming at the heart of the global economic order (55). This "accentuation" does not take the usual form of an attack against British values. Neither religion nor the Crown will serve as meaningful sites of confrontation. This strategic attitude is further emphasized by Wurmt's colleague, First Secretary Vladimir, who sees little need to concern himself with the essential Western value of individualism that lies at the heart of the social contract. Rather it is science—the custodian of *techne*—that he targets as the site in need of "accentuation." He reasons that science is in "some mysterious way...the source of material prosperity" (67). In this sense the "terrorist act" around which the novel hinges cannot be identified according to the forms of intelligibility that make up the West, nor can it be associated either with how the West is typically understood and confronted in the political offensives waged against its cultural forms and systems of meaning.

The attempted bombing of Greenwich constitutes an entirely different political problem, for it highlights a new stage of development in humanity's attempt to technologize nature. Conrad's restaging of the historical bombing in the novel cannot be comprehended in-line with the customary postmodern critique as powerfully identified by Lacoue-Labarthe in his reading of "the Horror." In other words, the characterization of the periphery as a threat to the center of the empire, a maneuver designed to cover the empire's internal lack of an ontological guarantee, reveals the very impossibility of this guarantee in the violence (the "technical agitation") inflicted on peripheral cultures (what Lacoue-Labarthe's names as the "horror"). Yet in *The Secret Agent* the instability at the heart of empire has come to saturate the imperial metropolis. Science, according to Vladimir, has become the "sacrosanct fetish" "of the hour" (65). This talismanic elevation of science, and Vladimir's simultaneous desire to attack science, reveals a kind of "evolution" in "technical agitation." It is no accident that it is no longer religion, the Crown, the commodity fetish suturing the socioeconomic, nor even the great historical edifice of art itself (Vladimir claims that even a bomb exploding the National Gallery "would not be serious enough") (65–7). Nonetheless, what precisely is it about science that transcends each of all these other ideological commitments?

The key seems to lie in a radical quality found in the presumably non-ideological character of science and scientific inquiry. Vladimir indicates that science is a form of "organic intelligibility." He states that a bomb directed at science would transcend "vengeance" and constitute an act of "pure destruction" that could not even be classified as an act of "terrorism" (66). It would constitute an act of "ultimate senselessness," an autonomous event having a rationality only unto itself. Bombing "pure mathematics" would be the ideal, but the untouchability of this ideality necessitates that the attack settle for a supplement. Greenwich serves that function because it names the conjunction of pure mathematics (the mathematical measuring of the physical world) and physical world itself (the physical clock itself).

More importantly, the targeting of "pure mathematics" is symptomatic of a larger problem foregrounded first by *Nostromo* and now by *The Secret Agent*: the extension of human forces beyond their previous nationalist and cultural scale. The spread of the West, and of capitalism, has come to stretch beyond national geographies. Consequently, the ability to attack the growing immensity and complexity of humanity as a species has become increasingly difficult and cannot be waged along the traditional lines of warfare. The event of an ecological predominance of the human is imaged profoundly in the character of the Professor:

> Lost in the crowd, miserable and undersized, [the Professor] meditated confidently on his power....[B]ut after a while he became disagreeably affected by the sight of the roadway thronged with vehicles and of the pavement crowded with men and women. He was in a long, straight street, peopled by a mere fraction of an immense multitude; but all round him, on and on, even to the limits of the horizon hidden by the enormous piles of bricks, he felt the mass of mankind mighty in its numbers. They swarmed numerous like locusts, industrious like ants, thoughtless like a natural force, pushing on blind and orderly and absorbed, impervious to sentiment, to logic, to terror, too, perhaps.
>
> (102–3)

One could replace the immensity of humanity in this passage with the immensity of the jungle of *Heart of Darkness*. The parallels are striking and made more so by the fact that this essential transformation in the constitution of the "immensity" announces the completion of nature's cultivation/colonization. It is no longer the jungle that poses a threat to the anthropocentric progress; it is the saturation of the environment by the human that now threatens progress. The Professor's mind offers a paralyzing image of the human pressure now defining the temporality and ecosystems of the Anthropocene. The "night of first ages" that Marlow indicates as the original provenance of London at the opening of *Heart of Darkness* comes back to haunt the economic and political reality of modern London in *The Secret Agent*. Twentieth-century humanity itself is now that animalistic "first age." The binary of the African jungle and the civility of London that we saw operative in *Heart of Darkness* has been turned on its head. Marlow's highly suggestive "first age" comment, and the subsequent associations of this "age" with the violence at the heart of the European colonial order ("All of Europe went into the making of Kurtz" [*Heart of Darkness* 66]) unfolds as a kind of pervasive immensity in *The Secret Agent*. The act of "recoiling from the horror" that Lacoue-Labarthe names as the central act of "Western barbarity" is no longer the act of supplementation designed to conceal the emptiness of the colonial act. It has become fully postmodernized. That is, the internal antagonism of an absent ontological certainty is no longer concealed in a displacement to the margin of culture but instead fully adopted as the animalization-humanization of the ecosystem. The "horror" has become the incapacity of any single force to affect the direction of human expansion and supremacy: "That was the form of doubt he feared most....[H]e had such moments of dreadful and sane mistrust of mankind. What if nothing could move them?" (*The Secret Agent* 103).

A number of critics have interpreted *The Secret Agent* as a political struggle between anarchism and liberalism and recently, in the wake of 9/11, as an exploration of terrorism and its mentalities. The struggle between anarchy and liberalism is certainly a significant aspect of the novel. However this approach hinges on an act of isolating the novel from the larger continuum of Conrad's fiction, through which we can see his developing interrogation of human socioeconomic structures at the turn of the century.[1] Reading the three works developmentally, we can see Conrad starting to identify the phenomenon of insecurity as central to understanding humanity's changing relationship to nature. By situating this novel against the larger geopolitical background of the colonial struggle with nature, we notice increasingly suffocating humanity in Conrad's portrayal of social systems.[2]

The trajectory of this portrayal ends bleakly in *The Secret Agent*. We encounter very little excitement of discovery, as we did with Marlow, very little idealism or hope for the future, as we did with Emilia and Charles Gould, and, with no heroic figure such as Nostromo, very little to be tragic about. In the end the Professor offers us limited alternatives for the future, to say the least. Against the animalistic and mindless throng of human movement the Professor insists that the "weak should be taken in hand for utter extermination" (263). He walks out into the "odious multitude of mankind," and we watch as he imagines himself "caressing...images of ruin and destruction"—his vision of the only force strong enough to "regenerate" humankind (268). But even this embrace of a totalizing violence is not accorded the kind of momentousness that we see given to Kurtz in *Heart of Darkness*. The perverse magnificence of Kurtz that we encounter in Marlow's narrative is absent when the Professor walks off into the multitude "like a pest in the street full of men" (268). His use of *techne* against the mindless expanse of humanity and its technological order is not even worthy of reformation within a tragic aesthetic form. Reading these three works in terms of nature shows that the evolution of *techne* in the modern world can only reach its conclusion in "madness and despair." For the Professor *techne* is a resolution that forms the basis of his "force"—that is, his claim to world transformation through the destruction of the odious and boundless throng of humanity. His veneration for the strong and his commitment to violence reflects the very releasing of insecurity that the security society paradoxically chases after with every instrument at its disposal. In this sense he shares more with deployed forms of insecurity than with any single or actual terrorist. His threat is of a different order, one that arises from the encounter with the human in all its disinterested and boundless anthropogenic energy. Even more pessimistic than the Professor's ineffectual resolution is Conrad's lack of any alternative to this planetary order of anti-ecological, technologized Man.

From *Heart of Darkness* to *Nostromo* to *The Secret Agent*, the evolving technological colonization of nature marks Conrad's intuitive apprehension of the Anthropocene as the looming state of planetary existence. In *Heart of Darkness* the core of the Western imperial project appears in terms of the transformation of nature into ivory. Already that transformation is staged as immense in scale—experienced ultimately by Marlow as both the violence and void of Europe. In its exegesis of European supremacy, the novella reveals the arrant emptiness of the human attempt to technologically control and exploit ecosystems. In *Nostromo* the technological transformation appears in the reification of nature as the resource of the silver mine. The seduction of that resource, and its kinship to the post-political order, proves too overpowering for Nostromo, who cannot delink this resourcing of nature from his anger at being exploited, and from his attempts to resist the colonial order. But what we encounter in *The Secret Agent* is the ultimate consequence of this historical trajectory: the effacement of nature and its supplementation by a technologized human writ large. This end point was suggested, even sounded, as a warning, in *Heart of Darkness*—a novella, as we've seen, so obsessed with nature yet symptomatically sustaining so little of nature within its pages. In *The Secret Agent* the prized objects of the first two novels—ivory then silver—are tellingly replaced by the only element left visible to a humanity seeking to confront the limitations of its own existence: science. In the battle with nature the prized possession that must be captured and (in the case of the anarchist) destroyed thus ends up being not *physis* but *techne* itself. In the world of *The Secret Agent* technology stands as the ultimate form of (in)security; its acceptance as a commonplace, raw fact of existence so thoroughly colonizes humanity's visible affiliation and violation of nature that the distinction between the two is no longer visible. It is thus no longer the void of humanity's technological triumphs that ultimately concerns our author but the crudeness of a large-scale technological humanity taking dominion over existence.

Notes

1 The struggle between liberalism and anarchism dates back several decades. See Hay, and Fleishman, esp. pages 185–215. For an example of the novel as an exploration of terrorism see Reiss. The two analyses that come close to my own are Alex Houen's theorization of what he calls "entropolitics," and Carey James Mickalites's theorization of the abject as an anxiety-ridden desire defining the public unconscious. For a recent rethinking of these political tensions see Haines.
2 Alex Houen, for instance, points toward this connection between insecurity, nature and the human social order. In his analysis of the entropic social decay that threatens to dissolve the human political order into a state of unorganized energy, Houen raises what has now become a defining question of the twenty-first century: "what if the stability of social fabric, its very energy, depends on a sun which, according to the scientists, is living on borrowed capital?" Theorizing the physics of thermodynamic theory Houen uses the sun as a metaphor for the novel's exploration of social energy and its unavoidable dissipation, which threatens the "security of the body-politic." Houen confines this entropic approach to the individual characters of the novel and their specific historical occasion. Houen, 1006.

I am greatly indebted to the editors for their excellent comments on this essay. Their suggestions throughout the revision process have made it a far stronger work. Any errors found here are my own.

Works Cited

Chakrabarty, Dipesh. "Postcolonial Studies and the Challenge of Climate Change," *New Literary History*, vol. 43, no. 1, Winter 2012, pp. 1–18. Print.
Conrad, Joseph. *Heart of Darkness*. Ed. by Ross C. Murfin. Bedford Books, 1996.
———. *Nostromo*. Random House, 1951.
———. *The Secret Agent*. Penguin Books, 1984.
DiSanto, Michael John. *Under Conrad's Eyes: The Novel as Criticism*. McGill-Queen's University Press, 2009.
Fleishman, Avrom. *Conrad's Politics: Community and Anarchy in the Fiction of Joseph Conrad*. Johns Hopkins University Press, 1967.
Haines, Christian. "Life in Crisis: The Biopolitical Ambivalence of Joseph Conrad's *The Secret Agent*." *Criticism*, vol. 54, no. 1, Winter 2012, pp. 85–115.
Hay, Eloise Knapp. *The Political Novels of Joseph Conrad: A Critical Study*. University of Chicago Press, 1963.
Heidegger, Martin. "The Origin of the Work of Art," in *Basic Writings*. Ed. by David Farrell Krell. Tr. By Albert Hofstadter, HarperCollins, 1977, pp. 139–212.
———. "The Question Concerning Technology," in *The Question Concerning Technology*. Translated by William Lovitt. Harper and Row, 1977, pp. 3–35.

Houen, Alex. "*The Secret Agent*: Anarchism and the Thermodynamics of Law." *English Literary History*, vol. 65, no. 4, 1998, pp. 995–1016.

Marzec, Robert. *Militarizing the Environment: Climate Change and the Security Society*. University of Minnesota Press, 2015.

McCarthy, Jeffrey Mathes. "'A Choice of Nightmares': The Ecology of *Heart of Darkness*." *Modern Fiction Studies*, vol. 55, no. 3, Fall 2009, pp. 620–648.

Mickalites, James. "The Abject Textuality of *The Secret Agent*." *Criticism*, vol. 50, no. 3, Summer 2008, pp. 501–526.

Reiss, Tom. "The True Classic of Terrorism," *The New York Times*, September 11, 2005. Web.

Seymour-Smith, Martin. "Introduction," in *The Secret Agent*. By Joseph Conrad. Penguin Books, 1984, pp. 9–36.

Warren, Robert Penn. "Introduction," in *Nostromo*. By Joseph Conrad. Modern Library, 1951. xii.

Part II
Conrad's Atmospherics

5 Dirty Weather
Troy Boone

Studying literary representations of past weather can do much to advance our understanding of environmental history and our place in it. This essay contributes to studies of weather in literature by focusing on how Joseph Conrad's writing—in particular "Typhoon" (1902) and, to a lesser degree, *The Nigger of the "Narcissus"* (1897)—represents the ecology of storms at sea. As readers have long noted, many of Conrad's works are centrally concerned with the ethical issues raised by the life of the mariner; and most critics have addressed these ethical issues in humanist terms, concentrating on how Conrad examines the imperatives of a moral code involving fidelity to an ideal of self, to concepts of work and profession and to one's fellow humans in the microcosm of the ship at sea.[1] Although critics have tended to focus much more intently on Conrad's representation of the human condition, particularly with respect to matters raised by empire and race, the fact that Conrad's human dramas so often play out at sea—in contrast to, say, the drawing room—means that Conrad needs to be read as a nature writer.[2] The life of the mariner in Conrad is one in which ethical tests are conducted when the human is challenged by the nonhuman element of the ocean, particularly in the form of storms at sea—or, in seafarer parlance, "dirty weather." This essay will consider how Conrad represents the stormy sea as a living entity with which the mariner must cohabitate. In his depictions of dirty weather, Conrad offers a non-humanist examination of the interrelation between the human and nature that arises elsewhere in his works, for instance in his comments regarding how seamanship has changed in the industrial period.

In a well-known analysis of Romantic-era weather, Jonathan Bate states: "The weather is the primary sign of the inextricability of culture and nature" (102). Noting how we have, to a great extent, treated the two as separate and have treated culture as having the upper hand over nature, Bate reads the depiction of bad and good weather in certain romantic poems as a corrective to such anthropocentric notions of the human ability to control the biosphere: "nature is not stable. Weather is the primary sign of its mutability" (100). Thus, we "have to learn to attend once more to the weather: to read the signs of the times in the signs of the skies, as our ancestors did" (102). Of course, a keen weather eye has not led to ecological humility for all of our ancestors, many of whom share with currently living consumers and polluters a blithe disregard for the ecological effects of human actions, and it is important that any such comparison of present and past views of the weather not succumb to nostalgia. For his part, Bate shows how an analysis of the apocalyptic weather depicted in Byron's "Darkness" (1816) renders it both contemporary, rooted in the ecological conditions surrounding its writing, and also intimately related to our own increasingly actualized "vision of a world seasonless, herbless, treeless, the rivers, lakes and oceans silent" (Bate 98). Because Byron—in defiance of the humanist worldview common in his period as in ours—"does not set culture apart from nature," he "may be reclaimed as a prophet of [...] ecocide" (Bate 98).[3]

For Bate, a reading of weather in literary works such as Byron's reveals powerfully that "we cannot master nature [...] The earth has its way of striking back, most dramatically with earthquakes and volcanic eruptions, but more often with plain old bad weather" (100). However, most ecocritics working in the field of what one might call the meteorological humanities have focused on instances of dramatic striking back rather than plain old bad weather.[4] For example, discussions of historical weather have prominently centered on the April 1815 eruption of the volcano Mount Tambora in what is now Indonesia, the ashfall from which brought about low temperatures and harsh weather from Europe to Asia, resulted in "the year without a summer" in 1816, and, in a manner foreshadowing the climatic events we increasingly face, affected crop production and caused economic and political instability for three years. Tambora has become the classic cataclysm in the meteorological humanities, perhaps because ecocritics working on these materials are understandably invested in finding historical analogues for the alarming weather we experience and anticipate as a result of more recent and anthropogenic climate change. For instance, Adeline Johns-Putra examines how the Tambora eruption caused a "global climatic instability," one effect of which was "an unprecedented degree of polar ice-melt" enabling the proliferation of Arctic exploration that characterizes the era (28).[5] Johns-Putra treats this climatic history as offering "valuable lessons about how all such encounters" with natural events like Tambora "are mediated" by cultural representations, although the history she presents, she admits, "may not offer us any lessons about how to live with 'nature'" (30) since Tambora is an instance of how "[c]limate change had happened as the result of a very dramatic and specific episode" (36). Similarly, in his studies of the eruption, Gillen D'Arcy Wood offers a cultural history of what he calls "the Tambora climate emergency of 1815–18" (Wood, *Tambora* 8), an event he locates very particularly in a brief period after which the way of the world returned, "just as suddenly, to its prior relative equilibrium" (Wood, "1816" 2). For Bate, too, romantic poetry offers a history of abnormal eruption and return to normalcy: Bate follows his analysis of the Tambora eruption and Byron's "Darkness" with a reading of John Keats's "To Autumn" (1820) that shows how it, like Byron's poem, rejects "the Cartesian constitution which splits apart thinking mind and embodied substance" (107); but Bate's reading comfortably aims to show how in Keats's ode the "world of the poem [...] comes to resemble a well-regulated ecosystem" (106), the climatic stability that returns once the 1816 Tambora catastrophe obliquely depicted in Byron's "Darkness" has passed. Keats's 1820 poem thus signals with relief the "good summer and clear autumn of 1819" that gave "a new lease of life" to the tubercular Keats ("very literally") and to those who suffered through "the bad weather of the immediate post-Tambora years" (105).

As valuable as these studies of the weather of the past have been, focusing on singular climatic events such as Tambora runs the risk of reinforcing a humanist understanding of the weather whereby extreme weather is identified as a cataclysmic happening erupting against a background of climatic regularity. Conrad offers us a contrasting insight into the ways in which we might understand the relations between human action, climate and dramatic, significant weather events (typhoons, for instance), the experience of which is not extraordinary (like the Tambora eruption) but instead common, at least for sailors such as Conrad and the seafarers who populate his works. In order to find "lessons about how to live with 'nature,'" as Johns-Putra puts it (30), and ones that will be useful to us in our age of advanced climate change, we should perhaps attend not so much to historical representations of climate emergencies that come and go but to depictions of how humans must respond, intellectually and ethically, to routine experiences of bad weather. Such a lesson about living with the weather is provided by the maritime writings of Joseph Conrad, particularly his depictions of "dirty weather."

Conrad once wrote that "a wrestle with wind and weather has a moral value like the primitive acts of faith on which may be built a doctrine of salvation and a rule of life" (qtd. in Watt 32). When such a wrestle happens aboard a ship, that moral value is heightened just as the human's vulnerability is. As Conrad puts it in his autobiographical work *The Mirror of the Sea: Memories and Impressions* (1906), a ship is thus "a creature which we have brought into the world, as it were on purpose to keep us up to the mark" (28). Conrad identifies the sailor's life as one that has ethical value because the sailor necessarily engages with nature. As his narrator puts it in "Typhoon," the China seas are "full of every-day, eloquent facts, such as islands, sand-banks, reefs, swift and changeable currents—tangled facts that nevertheless speak to a seaman in clear and definite language" (11). Conrad anticipates the arguments of a philosopher who links environmental ethics with sailing. In *The Natural Contract*, Michel Serres writes:

> In days gone by, two men lived out in the often intemperate weather: the peasant and the sailor. How they spent their time, hour by hour, depended on the state of the sky and on the seasons. We've lost all memory of what we owe these two types of men [...] In the West, these two populations are gradually disappearing from the face of the earth; agricultural surpluses and high-tonnage vessels are turning the sea and the land into deserts.
>
> (28)

By contrast to the sailor and peasant, Serres argues, most people in the West now are "[i]ndifferent to the climate [...] they naively pollute what they don't know, which rarely harms them and never concerns them" (28), a tendency that reinforces a relationship to nature based on "[m]astery and possession: these are the master words launched by Descartes at the dawn of the scientific and technological age, when our Western reason went off to conquer the universe" (32). Serres's primary argument is that we must counter this tendency by adding

> to the exclusively social contract a natural contract of symbiosis and reciprocity in which our relationship to things [in nature] would set aside mastery and possession in favor of admiring attention, reciprocity, contemplation, and respect; where knowledge would no longer imply property, nor action mastery.
>
> (38)

And for Serres, the life of sailors aboard ship constitutes a "seagoing pact" that "is in fact equivalent to what I'm calling a natural contract," because "here the collectivity, if sundered, immediately exposes itself to the destruction of its fragile niche, with no possible recourse or retreat" (40). Because life at sea "is enclosed by the strict definition of the guardrails" and "outside the barrier is death by drowning," sailors "know that, if they come to fight among themselves, they will condemn their craft to shipwreck" (40). The seaman thus gets "the social contract directly from nature" (40) and adheres to "a natural contract, concluded silently out of fear or respect, between the rumbling ire of the great social beast and the noise, sound, and fury of the sea" (41). The following discussion will show that Conrad's novellas exemplify how the life of the sailor depends upon just such a natural contract and its ethical implications.[6]

In "Typhoon," Conrad represents the storm at sea as an agent with the intent to harm humans, as in the following description: "A furious gale attacks him like a personal enemy, tries to grasp his limbs, fastens upon his mind, seeks to rout his very spirit out of him" (30). Such passages might seem to make Conrad's text an instance of what Simon C. Estok calls ecophobia, "the contempt and fear we feel for the agency of the natural environment" (207). Estok argues that this "contempt for the natural world" constitutes "a definable and recognizable discourse" (204) dating from early modern "changes in humanity's relationship with the natural world"—including "the crossing of the seas in the fifteenth century" (210)—and in particular from the industrial period, when nature came to be seen as "predictable" (210) and was redefined "from participative subject and organism in an organic community to the status of pure object" (211). "Representations of nature as an opponent that hurts, hinders, threatens, or kills us [...] are ecophobic" (209), Estok claims, and he offers as his primary example "profound storms" (209) such as the one in *King Lear*, as well as the news media's depictions of weather events such as Hurricane Katrina: like Shakespeare, CNN "writes nature as a hostile opponent who is responding angrily to our incursions and actions, an opponent to be feared and, with any luck, controlled" by "first imagining agency and intent in nature and then quashing that imagined agency and intent" (210). Ecophobia, according to Estok, "is rooted in and dependent on anthropocentric arrogance and speciesism, on the ethical position that humanity is outside of and exempt from the laws of nature" (216–17).

Although Conrad does represent "nature as an opponent that hurts, hinders, threatens or kills us," these representations do not constitute ecophobia, specifically because those in peril on the sea do not treat dirty weather with contempt or hold the "ethical position that humanity is outside of and exempt from the laws of nature." As we will see, Conrad emphasizes "the agency of the natural environment," yet he never suggests that humans can succeed in "quashing" the "agency and intent" of the ocean (210). Indeed, Conrad specifically seems to counter ecophobia, as Estok defines it, by emphasizing how the storm is a "participative subject" interacting with humans. Conrad's representation of the typhoon comes close to Jane Bennett's description of a lively material world defined by "the capacity of things"—including storms and hurricanes—"not only to impede or block the will and designs of humans but also to act as quasi agents or forces with trajectories, propensities, or tendencies of their own" (viii), including "a potentially violent vitality intrinsic to matter" (61). In representing the stormy sea as a motivated character within his tale, Conrad is, in Stacy Alaimo's terms, "[g]rappling with what it means to understand [...] the material world as agential, rather than as passive, inert, and malleable" (193). In order to see how Conrad's representation of an agential ocean attacking humans can teach us "lessons about how to live with 'nature'" (Johns-Putra 30) in an age of climate change fueled by industrialization, we need to resist normative critical readings of nature striking back, such as that of Kate Rigby, who follows Estok in seeing the attribution of "weather-borne disasters to a violent, amoral, and frequently feminized Nature" as having "the potential to fuel ecophobia, shoring up nature-culture dualism" (213–14). In "Typhoon" Conrad treats the storm as a character with a motive for violence, and thus imagines the sea not as "amoral [...] Nature" but as bound with the human in a profoundly ethical relationship. "Typhoon" perpetuates a movement in post-Enlightenment culture that opposes humanist norms and anticipates contemporary concerns about climate change by perceiving, as Fabien Locher and Jean-Baptiste Fressoz put it, "humanity [...] as a planetary force and the planet as a fragile being to care about" (586).

At the start of "Typhoon," the narrator informs us that Captain MacWhirr, commander of the steamship *Nan-Shan*, "had had an experience of moderately dirty weather—the term dirty as applied to the weather implying only moderate discomfort to the seaman" (15). But MacWhirr has not experienced the very dirty weather that he will encounter when he steams his ship into the typhoon:

> The sea itself [...] had never put itself out to startle the silent man, who seldom looked up, and wandered innocently over the waters with the only visible purpose of getting food, raiment, and house-room for three people ashore [his family]. Dirty weather he had known, of course. He had been made wet, uncomfortable, tired in the usual way, felt at the time and presently forgotten. [...] But he had never been given a glimpse of immeasurable strength and of immoderate wrath, the wrath that passes exhausted but never appeased—the wrath and fury of the passionate sea. He knew it existed, as we know that crime and abominations exist; he had heard of it as a peaceable citizen in a town hears of battles, famines, and floods, and yet knows nothing of what these things mean—though, indeed, he may have been mixed up in a street row, have gone without his dinner once, or been soaked to the skin in a shower. Captain MacWhirr had sailed over the surface of the oceans as some men go skimming over the years of existence to sink gently into a placid grave, ignorant of life to the last, without ever having been made to see all it may contain of perfidy, of violence, and of terror. There are on sea and land such men thus fortunate—or thus disdained by destiny or by the sea.
> (14)

Although Conrad's metaphors here seem negative to the point of phobia—the typhoon is associated with "crime" and "abominations," for instance—one must remember that this passage is reflecting the viewpoint of the complacent, untested Captain MacWhirr: from "He knew it existed" to "in a shower," the passage is close to free indirect discourse, in that these are the comparisons that would arise to Captain MacWhirr's easily shocked mind (he is deeply offended by "a defective lock on the cabin door" [7], for instance). MacWhirr's relation to extremely dirty weather (as opposed to the sort that merely makes one "wet, uncomfortable, tired in the usual way") parallels the relation of an untroubled provincial person (a suburban watcher of CNN, perhaps) to battles, famines and floods. From such a perspective—and Conrad clearly finds it "disdained by destiny" and "by the sea" rather than "fortunate"—the wrath and fury of the sea seem like a "crime," an "abomination," "perfidy," "violence," "terror." From the perspective of the sailor who has not merely gone "skimming" over the sea or existence, Conrad implies, such heavy weather is a professional inevitability that the wise mariner meets with dislike, no doubt, but also respect. Conrad imagines and endorses what Margaret Cohen calls "the compleat mariner, [...] whose professional persona projects prudence toward the mighty and treacherous ocean" (109).[7] Indeed, Conrad writes that the sea has a "fascination" (*Mirror* 142) for him specifically because, "[u]nlike the earth, it cannot be subjugated at any cost of patience and toil" (*Mirror* 136). Although one should not minimize the frequency with which Conrad makes claims about the hostility of the sea—the "most amazing wonder of the deep is its unfathomable cruelty" (*Mirror* 137), for instance—his complementary statements that it must be approached with humility rather than desire for conquest means that we much examine Conrad in ecological terms and as opposed to a culture of anthropocentrism.[8]

In "Typhoon," Conrad offers detailed depictions of the storm as a living creature confronting the ship, her captain and her crew—if one likes, using one of Estok's terms, as an organism sharing an ecosystem with them. Similarly, in *The Mirror of the Sea*, Conrad asserts,

> Gales have their personalities, and, after all, perhaps it is not strange; for, when all is said and done, they are adversaries whose wiles you must defeat, whose violence you must resist, and yet with whom you must live in the intimacies of nights and days.
>
> (71)

Thus Conrad speaks as a seaman for whom "the sea is not a navigable element, but an intimate companion" (*Mirror* 71). In his autobiographical writings as in his novels, however, the sea often confronts the human with hostility, and nature plays none of the roles ascribed to it according to humanist thinking (resource, helpmeet, stage or backdrop). Conrad's works exemplify how, as Christopher Connery puts it, the ocean's "very elemental character" and its "inability to be categorized as place or space, its unboundedness, make it fundamentally incompatible with a range of importations from land-based thinking, among them dominion itself" (687). Thus in "Typhoon" we learn that there

> was hate in the way she [the *Nan-Shan*] was handled, and a ferocity in the blows that fell. She was like a living creature thrown to the

rage of a mob; hustled terribly, struck at, borne up, flung down, leaped upon.

(35)

One might simply label Conrad's characterization of the storm as a creature with intelligence, agency and emotion an extended form of pathetic fallacy and be done with it. Yet, as Scott Knickerbocker persuasively argues, because "metaphor structures the very way we think and perceive, such figurative devices as personification [...] should not be dismissed as anthropocentric pathetic fallacies with which we merely project the human onto the nonhuman" (5). For Knickerbocker, figurative language such as personification "can help us experience the world as more than inert, unresponsive matter" and at the same time recognize "nature's alterity" (6): personifications of nature "overtly claim that we take note of the nonhuman world; yet they also imply the possibility that the nonhuman world takes note of us, as they rhetorically place the nonhuman in the position of interlocutor, even if silent" (6).[9] Sea storms in Conrad certainly take note of humans and their nautical technologies; moreover, the typhoon does so anything but silently, and it was "tumultuous and very loud [...] with that prolonged deep vibration of the air, like the roll of an immense and remote drum beating the charge of the gale" (27). Conrad's depiction of the stormy sea in "Typhoon" as an agential subject might mean that Conrad's "aesthetics are simultaneously an ethics" in which "metaphorical language encourages wonder and the ensuing respect toward nature," as Knickerbocker describes (13) Emily Dickinson's depiction of the bird in her poem "A Bird, came down the Walk" (written 1862; published 1891). However, because Conrad depicts the stormy sea as an agent that is inimical in its relation to the human, the ecologically minded reader of "Typhoon" faces a challenge more difficult than the reader of Dickinson's poem about a little bird hopping down a path: "Typhoon" asks us to acknowledge an ethical relation, wondering and respectful, toward a natural entity that comes at the human with wrath, passion and fury, with ferocity and hate, as a massed, corporate adversary with the power of a mob or, as suggested by the repeated imagery of battles, war drums and charges, a military opponent.[10]

Crucially, Conrad balances such passages emphasizing the sea's wrath toward the human with passages emphasizing the sea's fragility, as in this paragraph from "Typhoon":

> The mutter of the winds drew near apace. In the forefront could be distinguished a drowsy waking plaint passing on, and far off the growth of a multiple clamour, marching and expanding. There was the throb as of many drums in it, a vicious rushing note, and like the chant of a tramping multitude.

(65)

The very first structure of this paragraph constitutes an environmentally ethical aesthetics for depicting the storm at sea: the word "mutter" in the first sentence represents the natural world as distant but also seemingly diminutive, disempowered, harboring a complaint. The second sentence shows how "a drowsy waking plaint" can grow into "a multiple clamour" that, "marching and expanding," becomes the militarized "tramping multitude" that meets the ship at sea with chants and the beats of warlike drums. Conrad's paragraph, read ecocritically, indicates that the full-on attack of the typhoon is not merely unmotivated hate—much less a natural vicissitude put there for humans or their technologies to control—but rather the final result of a preexisting complaint about some wrong, a complaint on the part of a motivated and premeditating agent. The narrator of Conrad's *The Nigger of the "Narcissus"* describes the storm in that novella similarly: "Outside the night moaned and sobbed to the accompaniment of a continuous loud tremor as of innumerable drums beating far off" (33). And in *The Mirror of the Sea* Conrad remarks "the peculiar, terrible, and mysterious moaning that may be heard sometimes passing through the roar of a hurricane [...] that unforgettable sound, as if the soul of the universe had been goaded into a mournful groan" (79). In "Typhoon," the narrator explains that a "ring of dense vapours, gyrating madly round the calm of the centre, encompassed the ship like a motionless and unbroken wall of an aspect inconceivably sinister," and "a low moaning sound, the infinite plaint of the storm's fury, came from beyond the limits of the menacing calm" (59). Thus the narrator tells us that the storm's "howls and shrieks seemed to take on, in the emptiness of the bunker, something of the human character, of human rage and pain—being not vast but infinitely poignant" (41).[11] Here menace, fury and the sinister are bound together with moaning and plaint, just as gyration and calm are both essential parts of a hurricane.

Why does the sea become so passionate, wrathful, furious? The hostile but sympathetic dirty weather in "Typhoon," to adapt Serres's terms, "could be said to be taking its revenge" but, "more to the point, is reminding us of its existence" (29). Although it might be going too far to suggest that Conrad in "Typhoon" is anticipating global climate change (as Bate argues that Byron does in "Darkness"), it is nevertheless significant how Conrad's metaphoric descriptions of the angry sea enjamb with his criticisms of industrialization. The period of Conrad's professional life as a seaman (1879–93) coincides with one of the most profound technological transformations of the industrial era, the displacement of sail by steam in commercial and military vessels in the nineteenth century. As Robert Foulke notes, "No year served as a decisive turning point, and no single development was the prime cause of the sailing ship's demise; the technological perfection of sailing ships and the development of steamships occurred more or less simultaneously"; yet by the 1880s steam technology had managed to "depress sailing-ship freights permanently" (139). The rise of steam not only limited the sailor Joseph Conrad's chances for advancement in the merchant marine but also resulted in a degradation of the seafaring life, as Ian Watt notes:

> Another result of the fierce competition with steam was that sailing ships increasingly carried too few men and too much canvas—often to a dangerous degree; and this was in addition to a general deterioration of conditions under sail and steam alike, in which safety precautions, nautical training, and rates of pay all suffered.
>
> (17)

Conrad's writings frequently denounce this transformation of seafaring in the age of steam, perhaps most dramatically in his writings on the sinking of the *Titanic*.[12] In *The Mirror of the Sea*, Conrad asserts that the "taking of a modern steamship about the world [...] has not the same quality of intimacy with nature" (30) but, rather, reflects a humanist desire to dominate nature: "It is [...] simply the skilled use of a captured force, merely another step forward upon the way of universal conquest" (31). The steamship is "fed on fire and water, breathing black smoke into the air, pulsating, throbbing, shouldering its arrogant way against the great rollers in blind disdain of wind and sea" (*Mirror* 65), whereas the sailing ship is "sustained by the inspiration of the life-giving and death-dealing winds" (*Mirror* 64). Working on a steamship, Conrad says with an acid critique that applies precisely to men like Captain MacWhirr, "is an occupation which a man not desperately subject to sea-sickness can be imagined to follow with content, without enthusiasm, with industry, without affection" (*Mirror* 30). Thus the narrator of *The Nigger of the "Narcissus"* looks back in time when he tells his tale of mariners who plied their trade exclusively under sail: such men now "were gone [...] They were the everlasting children of the mysterious sea" (15). Of his fellow sailors on the *Narcissus* the narrator says: "I never saw them again. The sea took some, the steamers took others, the graveyards of the earth will account for the rest" (107). "Their successors"—mariners taken by the steamers in the age of industrial seafaring—"are the grown-up children of a discontented earth" (15). As Conrad bluntly sums up his view of the transformation of seamanship by steam power in *A Personal Record* (1909), "I have no use for engines" (11).[13]

The ship that Captain MacWhirr commands, the *Nan-Shan*, is every bit a steamship,[14] and compared to the sailing vessel moved by the wind the steamer is a thoroughly artificial being: "the pulsation of the engines" sounds "like the beat of the ship's heart" (48), and the mechanisms that propel the *Nan-Shan* "would slow down simultaneously, as if they had been the functions of a living organism, stricken suddenly by the blight of languor" (50). Just as Conrad critiques the steamship by blurring natural and mechanical images, his metaphors in turn show that the industrialization of seafaring dehumanizes seamen: in the boiler room of the ship there are "angry clangs and scrapes of metal, as if men with limbs of iron and throats of bronze had been quarrelling down there" (17). When the narrator remarks that "lumps of coal skipped to and fro, from end to end, rattling like an avalanche of peddles on a slope of iron" (51), the fact that the ship is powered by the burning of fossil fuels is depicted as unnatural ("slope of iron") and is connected to destructive natural events ("an avalanche"). In fact, the most negative description of the ship's steam-driven technology specifically comments on its creation of pollution: "The smoke struggled with difficulty out of the funnel, and instead of streaming away spread itself out like an infernal sort of cloud, smelling of sulphur and raining soot all over the decks" (15–16). Similarly, in *The Nigger of the "Narcissus"* Conrad's narrator describes a steam-powered tug as resembling

> an enormous and aquatic black beetle, surprised by the light, overwhelmed by the sunshine, trying to escape with ineffectual effort into the distant gloom of the land. She left a lingering smudge of smoke on the sky, and two vanishing trails of foam on the water. On the place where she had stopped a round patch of soot remained, undulating on the swell—an unclean mark of the creature's rest.
> (16)

When the *Narcissus* reaches England, she encounters "a string of smoking steamboats" that "waddled, hugging the coast, like migrating and amphibious monsters, distrustful of the restless waves" (100), and these steamboats are related to the broader degradation caused by industrialization: "Farther on, the tall factory chimneys appeared in insolent bands and watched her [the *Narcissus*] go by, like a straggling crowd of slim giants, swaggering and upright under the black plummets of smoke, cavalierly aslant" (101). By contrast to the *Nan-Shan* and these other steam-driven vessels and their relatives the factory chimneys, the sailing ship *Narcissus* is an image of purity and nature: "The loose upper canvas blew out in the breeze with soft round contours, resembling small white clouds snared in the maze of ropes" (16), and elsewhere the narrator describes her sails as "the glory of her white wings" (101). Perhaps significantly, the stormy sea that attacks the *Narcissus* is described as having less reason for its antagonism toward the sailing vessel than the typhoon that attacks the *Nan-Shan*: the *Narcissus* was "tossed about, shaken furiously, like a toy in the hand of a lunatic" (32), and a "big, foaming sea came out of the mist; it made for the ship, roaring wildly, and in its rush it looked as mischievous and discomposing as a madman with an axe" (35). The sailing ship *Narcissus* rather than the sea is meant to be the object of readerly sympathy: she is

> obstinate and yielding. She drove to and fro in the unceasing endeavour to fight her way through the invisible violence of the winds: [...] she rolled, restless, from side to side, like a thing in pain. Enduring and valiant, she answered to the call of men; and her slim spars waving for ever in abrupt semicircles, seemed to beckon in vain for help towards the stormy sky.
>
> (30)

By contrast, later on in the ecological disaster we call the industrial period, the steamer *Nan-Shan* confronts a wrathful sea with cause. Although I would not argue that "Typhoon" specifically prefigures our awareness of, for instance, the way in which global climate change results in "superstorms" such as Hurricane Sandy, the novella nevertheless clearly represents the hurricane as attacking the polluting product of human industry (here, the steamship) and represents that attack as motivated not merely by hate but also by a justified complaint. In other words, I would argue that "Typhoon" is a stage in the environmental critique that has, as its later stage, writings by our contemporaries about global climate change and its relation to the very dirty weather that has become increasingly common and increasingly dirty.

Critics have long been divided on how to assess Captain MacWhirr. For F. R. Leavis—the humanist reader par excellence—MacWhirr "stands there the embodiment of a tradition," the "crowning triumph of the spirit" (214). By contrast, Margaret Cohen condemns "the stupid, steadfast Captain MacWhirr, who inexplicably decides to sail through rather than around a terrible storm" and thus demonstrates that he "lacks imagination," which is "essential to the creative improvisations of" seamanship, or the practice of "craft amidst uncertainty" (33).[15] Stubbornly steaming into a hurricane might represent triumph over nature in the humanist tradition, but it represents no example of the tradition of seamanship and opposes the sailor's ethical relation to the environment of the sea as put forth by thinkers such as Conrad and Serres. The ecocritical reader must side with critics such as Cohen and treat the comments on MacWhirr's seamanship in "Typhoon" with heavy irony:

> The hurricane, with its power to madden the seas, to sink ships, to uproot trees, to overturn strong walls and dash the very birds of the air to the ground, had found this taciturn man in its path, and, doing its utmost, had managed to wring out a few words. Before the

renewed wrath of winds swooped on his ship, Captain MacWhirr was moved to declare, in a tone of vexation, as it were: "I wouldn't like to lose her [the *Nan-Shan*]."

(65)

As the narrator puts it, "The experience of the last six hours had enlarged his conception of what heavy weather could be like" (61). Faint praise indeed.

Throughout, in fact, the narrative subtly critiques MacWhirr and his chief mate, Jukes, for their faith in steam. When Jukes suggests changing their course to avoid heavy seas, MacWhirr asks ("with dawning astonishment"), "What put it into your head that I would start to tack a steamer as if she were a sailing-ship?" (23). To which Jukes replies ("with bitter readiness"), "Jolly good thing she isn't [...] She would have rolled every blessed stick out of her this afternoon" (23). Captain and chief mate are both, unlike Conrad the retired sailor, men of the age of steam. Thus MacWhirr dispenses with generations of sailing knowledge to lecture Jukes on the way to power a steamship through a typhoon:

> you don't find everything in books. All these rules for dodging breezes and circumventing the winds of heaven, Mr. Jukes, seem to me the maddest thing, when you come to look at it sensibly [...] A gale is a gale, Mr. Jukes [...] and a full-powered steam-ship has got to face it. There's just so much dirty weather knocking about the world, and the proper thing to do is to go through it.
>
> (25)

Captain MacWhirr "had indeed been making his confession of faith, had he only known it" (26).[16] Jukes in turn sees the steam produced by the *Nan-Shan* not in the way that the narrator does—as a polluting sign of the industrial present—but as making the ship heroic in its battle with nature: adopting his viewpoint, the narrative shows Jukes observing the ship

> battered and solitary, laboring heavily in a wild scene of mountainous black waters lit by the gleams of distant worlds. She moved slowly, breathing into the still core of the hurricane the excess of her strength in a white cloud of steam—and the deep-toned vibration of the escape was like the defiant trumpeting of a living creature of the sea impatient for the renewal of the contest.
>
> (60)

Jukes's view of the steamship here is close to the humanist view of nature, as there for our technological conquest, which is at the heart of ecophobia. In *A Personal Record*, Conrad reports that the examiner for his master's certificate informed him simply, "You will go into steam presently. Everybody goes into steam" (105). Yet, Conrad insists, the examiner

> was wrong. I never went into steam—not really. If I only live long enough I shall become a bizarre relic of a dead barbarism, a sort of monstrous antiquity, the only seaman of the dark ages who had never gone into steam—not really.
>
> (105)

Seafaring in the age of the *Nan-Shan* is committed to industrial technology and has irrevocably left the more ecocentric technology of the sailing ship behind, as Conrad's "Typhoon" points out in even the smallest details: on first coming aboard the *Nan Shan*, MacWhirr nonchalantly hangs his coat "on the end of a steam windlass embodying all the latest improvements" (6).

Through his representation of the angry and injured stormy sea, Conrad actively critiques the reliance on steam and its associated evils—including both pollution and a declining quality of seamanship. Although it would be going too far to say that Conrad specifically predicts the long-term effects of the reliance on fossil fuels, he is nevertheless particularly aware of his place in the history of human relations with the environment and with the industrial technologies that damage both those relations and the environment. For one small but telling instance, in *The Mirror of the Sea* Conrad remarks with prescience that Southend is "where petroleum ships discharge their dangerous cargoes" (105). Indeed, "Typhoon" links with Byron's poem in the past and with our dire present when the novella has recourse to apocalyptic imagery to describe the dirty weather that lashes out at the humans who pollute nature:

> At its setting the sun had a diminished diameter and an expiring brown, rayless glow, as if millions of centuries elapsing since the morning had brought it near its end. A dense bank of cloud became visible to the northward; it had a sinister dark olive tint, and lay low and motionless upon the sea, resembling a solid obstacle in the path of the ship. She went floundering towards it like an exhausted creature driven to its death. The coppery twilight retired slowly, and the darkness brought out overhead a swarm of unsteady, big stars, that, as if blown upon, flickered exceedingly and seemed to hang very near the earth.
>
> (19)

Conrad's image of the sun coming to its end in the distant future and of the stars flickering uncertainly is quite close to the dream vision depicted in Byron's "Darkness," which Jonathan Bate reads as prophetic of our ecocidal position 200 years further on in the Anthropocene:

> I had a dream, which was not all a dream.
> The bright sun was extinguish'd, and the stars
> Did wander darkling in the eternal space,
> Rayless, and pathless; and the icy earth
> Swung blind and blackening in the moonless air [...].
> (Byron 40)

Similarly, in *The Nigger of the "Narcissus"* the narrator describes how "the sun, as if put out, disappeared" (46). And the *Nan-Shan* signifies not the power of steam which MacWhirr celebrates; rather, the ship represents a fragile living creature, like the men on board her and all of us as we face the consequences of the industrial era Conrad criticizes, "floundering towards" the threat of the destruction of the natural world.

Conrad's depictions of dirty weather challenge normative readings of Conrad and of literary weather, in several ways. Such depictions move away from the concern with human relations that critics have characteristically seen as the basis of Conrad's ethics; and his depictions of dirty weather challenge the ecocritical tendency to focus on climate emergency rather than the routine experience of bad weather with which the professional sailor was familiar and from which we can learn in an era of dirtier weather caused by human action. Conrad's representation of the typhoon as an agent whose violence toward the human has discernable motivations—and is even sympathetic—is braided together with his critique of the industrialization of seafaring and the hubristic faith in a massively polluting steam technology that characterize his era. Particularly in his stormier fictions, Conrad reveals an ethical stance focused on our relations with the nonhuman world understood as a material force and as an agent that may respond to our neglect or violence and that will certainly expose as folly the hubristic desire to conquer nature.

Notes

1 For a well-known instance, Ian Watt states that "individual loyalty and group cohesion" are the themes that "dominate Conrad's fiction; fidelity is the supreme value in Conrad's ethic" (6). James Phelan has analyzed the ethics of Conrad's narration, where ethics similarly involves exclusively human matters such as "the captain's responsibility to his crew" (120). More recently, critics have addressed Conrad's ethics in similarly human-centered terms. David Prickett argues that Conrad's "sailing ship embodies a collective and coherent social world [...] that is being eroded and fragmented by individualism" (4). Rachel Hollander examines how, although many of Conrad's works "are anchored by the ideal of a shared understanding among sailors of the moral codes of life at sea," *Under Western Eyes* (1911) lacks such an ideal and "becomes the occasion for new representations of

the relationship between morality and justice" (2)—although both of those concepts are defined in terms of human politics. In a subtle analysis—borrowing, like many recent ethical readings of Conrad, from the work of Emmanuel Levinas—Andrew Roberts distinguishes between "older moral criticism," focusing on the humanist values that have interested Watt and later readers, and "newer ethical criticism," works that "challenge questions of ethical value in a way that goes beyond [...] codes of behavior" (134), yet his examples are all drawn from the human realm of politics, and he makes no mention of the ethics of our relations with the nonhuman world.

Of course, Conrad himself went to some lengths to enable such readings of his ethics in humanist terms, as when he has the young captain-narrator of *The Secret Sharer: An Episode from the Coast* (1912) remark, "I wondered how far I should turn out faithful to that ideal conception of one's own personality every man sets up for himself secretly" (181). Thus I am not arguing that readings of the humanist ethics in Conrad's texts are wrong but rather that we need to attend to how his works involve an ethical relation to the nonhuman as well.

2 As Geoffrey Galt Harpham succinctly puts it, "'Ethical' readings of Conrad underestimate the spectacular force of the sea in his work" (136).

3 Wood, *Tambora* 67 similarly credits Byron's "classic meditation on the human impacts of climate change."

4 Historical weather has engaged several literature scholars, working outside the field of ecocriticism, who tend to focus on representations of everyday weather. See for instance Reed; Sweeting; and Lewis. The best history of Victorian meteorology is Anderson.

5 A similar study is presented in Carroll.

6 In focusing an ecocritical reading on the ways in which mariners in the ages of sail and steam contended with storms at sea, my essay seeks to participate in what Heather Blum calls "a practice of oceanic studies that is attentive to the material conditions and praxis of the maritime world" (670).

7 Cohen (106–31) offers an excellent discussion of the interrelations of the sublime and the everyday in depictions of the sea, including the angry sea. Representations of dirty weather such as Conrad's "make descriptions of craft and sublime landscape coexist," showing "not only the dangerous conditions at sea that occasion sublime terror, but also the mariner's work struggling to overcome them" (122–3).

8 Such observations about the hostility of the sea occur frequently in Conrad's works, even those that are not "storm-pieces." For instance, in *Lord Jim: A Tale* (1900) we are told that the title character had only once had a "glimpse of the earnestness in the anger of the sea," the awareness that "these elemental furies are coming at him with a purpose of malice" (14). Nautical writers other than Conrad make similar remarks commonly enough that the literature of the sea constitutes a record of respect for its dangerous agency: for example, in Herman Melville's *Moby-Dick; or, The Whale* (1851), Ishmael remarks that when one is on a calm sea one is only "beholding the tranquil beauty and brilliancy of the ocean's skin" and not "the tiger heart that pants beneath it"; one "would not willingly remember, that this velvet paw but conceals a remorseless fang" (534). Indeed, according to Ishmael, the "warmest climes but nurse the cruellest fangs," and in the "resplendent" south seas which the *Pequod* shares with the *Nan-Shan* the mariner "encounters the direst of all storms, the Typhoon. It will sometimes burst from out that cloudless sky, like an exploding bomb upon a dazed and sleepy town" (546).

9 For an incisive discussion of anthropomorphism as a specifically ethical practice in Victorian literature, see also Cosslett 181–3. Jane Bennett argues

that "[w]e need to cultivate a bit of anthropomorphism—the idea that human agency has some echoes in nonhuman nature—to counter the narcissism of humans in charge of the world" (xvi). Similarly, Alaimo 198–202 examines how the use of the pathetic fallacy in Charles Moore's *Plastic Ocean* operates as a form of ecocentric ethics critiquing the pollution of the oceans with plastic. In the earliest years of the field of ecocriticism, some of its practitioners sought to reclaim the pathetic fallacy: see, for instance, Neil Evernden's memorable 1978 statement that "the Pathetic Fallacy is a fallacy only to the ego clencher" (101).

10 Rebecca Raglon and Marian Scholtmeijer argue that the most valuable writings about nature "are those that have sensed the power of nature to resist, or question, or evade the meanings we attempt to impose on the natural world" (252).

11 In a provocative analysis of the storm in "Typhoon," Amar Acheraïou argues for Conrad's close and admiring identification with the storm. It is an "emblem of Conrad's love of paradox and irresolution" (29) and "challenges the Enlightenment concept of man through the storm motif" (33), but Conrad also uses the storm to represent his own experimental art: he "intimates through the raging storm an attack on the polished and policed surface of life and language, in an effort to bring to light the irrational and hidden depths that realistic representation has refined away" (36).

12 For a discussion of this critique of technology in Conrad's writings on the *Titanic* sinking, see Boone 5–20.

13 Critics have long taken note of Conrad's negative depiction of industrialism but have not addressed this depiction as an ecological concern about the effect of steam on the sea and life at sea. For instance, in a well-known reading of *Lord Jim*, Fredric Jameson argues that the sea is in Conrad's works the "privileged place of the strategy of containment" (210) whereby "a world of work and history" is "displaced" (207) through "repression" (214). Thus for Jameson the clang of a furnace-door below decks in the *Patna* is the only remaining trace of industry in a work that seeks to offer instead a highly stylized impressionist "moral story" (217) about "the absurdity of human existence in the face of a malevolent Nature" (216). Similarly, Lillian Nayder argues that Conrad's criticism of industrialism is really about class issues, which he displaces onto gender issues: "Conrad resolves his fears by imagining class relations as marital relations […] displacing the dangers of working-class resentment with the threat of female insubordination" (192). While both of these readings offer some subtle insights, an ecocritical analysis of Conrad must acknowledge that his concern about new human interactions with the sea in the industrial age is not only (or even primarily) about his latent class and gender anxieties but, rather, is manifestly about a global history of environmental damage and climate change that we are still working to understand.

14 Pearson 30–1 offers an excellent discussion of how the *Nan-Shan* is "a forceful symbol of industry and capitalist modernity" (30).

15 For another such pair of contrasting critical opinions, Byron Caminero-Santangelo examines in detail (271–84) how MacWhirr's fitness to command is tested by the storm, and he fails; Gail Fraser correctly notes that "Typhoon" "is concerned with the manifold ways in which a steamer's ordeal differs from that of a sailing ship" (38) but follows Leavis in admiring how "MacWhirr's simple practicality and humane instincts take on mythic significance" (39).

16 Compare MacWhirr's disdain for books on seamanship with Marlow's response, in *Heart of Darkness* (1899), to "*An Inquiry into some Points of*

Seamanship by a man Towzer, Towson—some such name": the book by the "simple old sailor" has "a singleness of intention, an honest concern for the right way of going to work which made these humble pages thought out so many years ago luminous with another than a professional light" (141).

Works Cited

Acheraïou, Amar. "Floating Words: Sea as Metaphor of Style in 'Typhoon.'" *Conradian: Journal of the Joseph Conrad Society* 29.1 (2004): 27–38.

Alaimo, Stacy. "Oceanic Origins, Plastic Activism, and New Materialism at Sea." *Material Ecocriticism*. Eds. Serenella Iovino and Serpil Oppermann. Indiana UP, 2014. 186–203.

Anderson, Katharine. *Predicting the Weather: Victorians and the Science of Meteorology*. U of Chicago P, 2005.

Bate, Jonathan. *The Song of the Earth*. Harvard UP, 2000.

Bennett, Jane. *Vibrant Matter: A Political Ecology of Things*. Duke UP, 2010.

Blum, Hester. "The Prospect of Oceanic Studies." *PMLA* 125.3 (2010): 670–677.

Boone, Troy. "The *Titanic* Century: Mourning and Modernity." *Interdisciplinary Literary Studies: A Journal of Criticism and Theory* 5.1 (2003): 5–20.

Byron, George Gordon Byron Baron. "Darkness." 1816. *The Complete Poetical Works*. Ed. Jerome J. McGann. 7 vols. Clarendon P, 1986. 4:40–43.

Caminero-Santangelo, Byron. "Testing for Truth: Joseph Conrad and the Ideology of the Examination." *CLIO* 23.3 (1994): 271–284.

Carroll, Siobhan. "Crusades against Frost: *Frankenstein*, Polar Ice, and Climate Change in 1818." *European Romantic Review* 24.2 (2013): 211–230.

Cohen, Margaret. *The Novel and the Sea*. Princeton UP, 2010.

Connery, Christopher. "Sea Power." *PMLA* 125.3 (2010): 685–692.

Conrad, Joseph. *Heart of Darkness*. 1899. *Youth, Heart of Darkness, "The End of the Tether"*. Ed. Owen Knowles. Cambridge UP, 2010. 43–126.

———. *Lord Jim*. 1900. Eds. J. H. Stape and Ernest W. Sullivan II. Cambridge UP, 2012.

———. *The Mirror of the Sea*. 1906. Doubleday, 1924.

———. *The Nigger of the "Narcissus."* 1897. Ed. Robert Kimbrough. Norton Critical Editions, 1979.

———. *A Personal Record*. 1909. Eds. Zdzisław Najder and J. H. Stape. Cambridge UP, 2008.

———. *The Secret Sharer: An Episode from the Coast*. 1912. Conrad, *Typhoon and Other Tales*. 177–217.

———. "Typhoon." Conrad, *Typhoon and Other Tales*. 1–74.

———. *Typhoon and Other Tales*. Ed. Cedric Watts. Oxford UP, 2002.

Cosslett, Tess. *Talking Animals in British Children's Fiction, 1786–1914*. Ashgate, 2006.

Estok, Simon C. "Theorizing in a Space of Ambivalent Openness: Ecocriticism and Ecophobia." *Interdisciplinary Studies in Literature and Environment* 16.2 (2009): 203–225.

Evernden, Neil. "Beyond Ecology: Self, Place, and the Pathetic Fallacy." 1978. *The Ecocriticism Reader: Landmarks in Literary Ecology*. Eds. Cheryll Glotfelty and Harold Fromm. U of Georgia P, 1996. 92–104.

Foulke, Robert. *The Sea Voyage Narrative.* Studies in Literary Themes and Genres 14. Twayne, 1997.

Fraser, Gail. "The Short Fiction." *The Cambridge Companion to Joseph Conrad.* Ed. J. H. Stape. Cambridge UP, 1996. 25–44.

Harpham, Geoffrey Galt. *One of Us: The Mastery of Joseph Conrad.* U of Chicago P, 1996.

Hollander, Rachel. "Thinking Otherwise: Ethics and Politics in Joseph Conrad's *Under Western Eyes.*" *Journal of Modern Literature* 38.3 (2015): 1–19.

Jameson, Fredric. *The Political Unconscious: Narrative as a Socially Symbolic Act.* Cornell UP, 1981.

Johns-Putra, Adeline. "Historicizing the Networks of Ecology and Culture: Eleanor Anne Porden and Nineteenth-Century Climate Change." *Interdisciplinary Studies in Literature and Environment* 22.1 (2015): 27–46.

Knickerbocker, Scott. *Ecopoetics: The Language of Nature, the Nature of Language.* U of Massachusetts P, 2012.

Leavis, F. R. *The Great Tradition: George Eliot, Henry James, Joseph Conrad.* 1948. Penguin, 1962.

Lewis, Jayne Elizabeth. *Air's Appearance: Literary Atmosphere in British Fiction, 1660–1794.* U of Chicago P, 2012.

Locher, Fabien, and Jean-Baptiste Fressoz. "Modernity's Frail Climate: A Climate History of Environmental Reflexivity." *Critical Inquiry* 38.3 (2012): 579–598.

Melville, Herman. *Moby-Dick; or, the Whale.* 1851. Ed. Tom Quirk. Penguin, 1992.

Nayder, Lillian. "Sailing Ships and Steamers, Angels and Whores: History and Gender in Conrad's Maritime Fiction." *Iron Men, Wooden Women: Gender and Seafaring in the Atlantic World, 1700–1920.* Eds. Margaret S. Creighton and Lisa Norling. Johns Hopkins UP, 1996. 189–203.

Pearson, Nels C. "'Whirr' Is King: International Capital and the Paradox of Consciousness in *Typhoon.*" *Conradiana: A Journal of Joseph Conrad Studies* 39.1 (2007): 29–37.

Phelan, James. *Narrative as Rhetoric: Technique, Audiences, Ethics, Ideology.* Ohio State UP, 1996.

Prickett, David. "Art Out of Bread-Winning: Conrad and the Question of the Plimsoll Man." *Conradian: Journal of the Joseph Conrad Society* 39.2 (2014): 1–18.

Raglon, Rebecca, and Marian Scholtmeijer. "Heading off the Trail: Language, Literature, and Nature's Resistance to Narrative." *Beyond Nature Writing: Expanding the Boundaries of Ecocriticism.* Eds. Karla Armbruster and Kathleen R. Wallace. UP of Virginia, 2001. 248–262.

Reed, Arden. *Romantic Weather: The Climates of Coleridge and Baudelaire.* UP of New England, 1983.

Rigby, Kate. "Confronting Catastrophe: Ecocriticism in a Warming World." *The Cambridge Companion to Literature and the Environment.* Ed. Louise Westling. Cambridge UP, 2014. 212–225.

Roberts, Andrew Michael. "Conrad and the Territory of Ethics." *Conradiana: A Journal of Joseph Conrad Studies* 37.1–2 (2005): 133–146.

Serres, Michel. *The Natural Contract.* 1992. Trans. Elizabeth MacArthur and William Paulson. U of Michigan P, 1995.

Sweeting, Adam. *Beneath the Second Sun: A Cultural History of Indian Summer.* UP of New England, 2003.

Watt, Ian. *Conrad in the Nineteenth Century.* U of California P, 1979.

Wood, Gillen D'Arcy. "1816: The Year without a Summer." *BRANCH: Britain, Representation and Nineteenth-Century History.* Ed. Dino Franco Felluga. Extension of *Romanticism and Victorianism on the Net.* Web. 10 July 2015.

———. *Tambora: The Eruption That Changed the World.* Princeton UP, 2014.

# 6 The "Breaking-Up" of the Monsoon and *Lord Jim*'s Atmospherics

Brendan Kavanagh

"The monsoon breaks up early this year" (*Lord Jim* 136), Jim "remark[s] conversationally" to Marlow, as a "perfect deluge" (138) falls outside the "bit of shelter" (137) of Marlow's room, in the Malabar Hotel, Bombay. Amid the raging storm, Jim invokes a common phrase of nautical parlance, dating back at least to the seventeenth century, used to describe the tempests that precede the biannual shifts in direction of India's monsoon winds. As English astronomer and meteorologist Edmund Halley writes, in a late seventeenth-century account of India's monsoons:

> [...] the last two months of the southerly monsoon [...] are very subject to be tempestuous. The violence of these storms is such that they seem to be of the nature of the West India hurricanes, and render the navigation of these parts very unsafe about that time of the year. These tempests are by our seamen usually termed *the breaking-up of the monsoons*.
>
> (Halley 160–1)

Lord Jim's depiction of the "breaking-up" of the monsoon indeed suggests such violence, in its description of the "heavy uninterrupted rush of a sweeping flood, with a sound of unchecked overwhelming fury" (138). But more significantly, Jim's remark recognizes that the "bit of shelter" (137) of Marlow's room is situated within the climatology of the breaking-up of the monsoon, as a circular storm rages, with a "colossal and headlong stream that seem[s] to break and *swirl*" (138; emphasis added).[1] Much of nineteenth-century British nautical meteorology absorbed German meteorologist Heinrich Dove's account of storm circulation in hurricanes, cyclones and typhoons (Kavanagh 4–5). In his 1861 second edition of *The Law of Storms* (the English translation of which was financed by the British Board of Trade), Dove presented the "breaking-up of the monsoon" as a particularly violent class of cyclonic storm, with meteorological dynamics involving the "many agencies always at work disturbing the equilibrium of the atmosphere," in an atmospherics "eternally striving to attain equilibrium without ever succeeding" (Dove 275, 318).[2] Using nineteenth-century accounts of meteorological theory (such as that of Dove), this essay contextualizes *Lord Jim*'s depiction of the nonequilibrium weather dynamics of the breaking-up of the monsoon, and reads *Lord Jim* as a narrative of the propagation of disturbances to "equilibrium of the atmosphere" (Dove 318). In examining *Lord Jim*'s writing of atmospheric disturbances, this essay explicates the text's portrayal of the imbrication of human habitation within the workings of nonhuman atmospheric agencies and processes, which work alongside human agencies.

This study thereby responds to Nidesh Lawtoo's compelling call for less anthropocentric approaches to Conrad, and carries further Lawtoo's imperative to "tilt critical attention" from the "human foreground" to the "nonhuman background" depicted in Conrad's narratives (Lawtoo). In the following reading of *Lord Jim*, background becomes foreground, as this essay analyzes Conrad's climatological foregrounding of a narrative of human stammering and stuttering. The conclusion to this essay demonstrates that *Lord Jim*'s writing of the parallel disequilibria of the weather and the stammer constitutes a carefully negotiated engagement with a particular problem—that of portraying a weather dynamic beyond human construction, while weaving a narrative texture composed of human language. Using insight drawn from present-day object-oriented ontology, Jeffrey McCarthy recently has argued that Conrad's weather is "an element of epistemological construction" "at the level of artistic production," yet is "always beyond" "human construction," as "nature [for Conrad] is simultaneously the constructed ground for discourse and the brute reality behind representation" (83, 82). In further considering Conrad's writing of weather beyond human construction, we would do well to formulate a reading which draws on fields of thought that were readily accessible at Conrad's time of writing. Nineteenth-century meteorology provides one such field of thought; the next section of this essay addresses *Lord Jim*'s implicit refutation of a mid- to late nineteenth-century conception of an atmospherics of "general equilibrium" (Humboldt, *Essay on the Geography* 79).

"Humboldtian Science" and India's Meteorology

As Katharine Anderson acknowledges, one influential strain of late nineteenth-century British meteorology represented the subcontinent of India as a scaled model of the whole planet, in which the relations between global weather patterns and local weather disturbances could be studied within the limits of a more manageable geographical area (258–9). In an 1883 article in *Nature*, British meteorologist Douglas Archibald emphasized the problematics of carrying out meteorological study in this manner; he highlighted the difficulty of "confining attention to the atmospheric conditions of one small political division of the earth's surface and attempt[ing] to educe from data collected within that region alone the laws which regulate them" (405). Yet as Archibald recognized, leading British meteorologists had found a solution to this problem, in the subcontinent of India, which offered "rare facilities for the study, not merely of climate and weather, but of what is acknowledged to be the 'highest branch of meteorology,' viz. *atmospheric physics*" (406). In *The Indian Meteorologist's Vade-Mecum* (1877), British meteorologist Henry Blanford likewise stressed the need to carry out "systematic observation" of the atmospheric "conditions, prevailing at one and the same time, over a considerable tract of the earth's surface," in order to trace "certain uniformities" of global atmospherics, "amid the immense vicissitudes of local climate" (98). Blanford suggested that India provided such a tract of the planet's surface, with "a secluded and independent area of atmospheric action" (99). He wrote of India as "an epitome of atmospheric physics," and noted that atmospheric patterns (in India) could be studied over a vast range of terrain including "all those contrasts of desert and forest, of plain, plateau and mountain ridge, of continent and sea, that we meet with on the earth's surface" (99, 145).[3] Moreover, Blanford emphasized that "order and regularity" were "prominent characteristics of [India's] atmospheric phenomena," and cited as evidence the periodic patterns of India's monsoons (144). In portraying the weather of the summer monsoon in Chapters XVI and XVII, *Lord Jim* thus invokes a climatology which late nineteenth-century British meteorology regarded as central to a planetary atmospherics of order, regularity and periodic patterns. However, as this study will show, *Lord Jim*'s depiction of the monsoon's weather emphasizes disturbance and disruption; the text's writing of the breaking-up of the monsoon acts as a means of focalizing an account of planetary atmospherics, yet one which unsettles a "sheltering conception" (*Lord Jim* 236) of "order and regularity" (Blanford 144).

In its postulation of a climatology of order and regularity, the above British meteorology was influenced by the work of German Romantic naturalist Alexander von Humboldt; a few decades earlier, Humboldt had suggested that the study of the climate of the torrid zone would provide a means of determining meteorological laws (Anderson 260). As Humboldt argued in his 1845 *Cosmos: A Sketch of a Physical Description of the Universe* (1845–62), the "regions of the torrid zone" (including India) would "afford the inestimable advantage of revealing to man, by the uniformity of the variations of the atmosphere […] the invariability of the laws" of atmospherics (*Cosmos* 13 [1849]). Humboldt wrote of "important weather changes" as "the consequence of a disturbance in the equilibrium" of global "aerial currents" (*Cosmos* 347 [1849]). Moreover, he hypothesized that such disturbances to atmospheric equilibrium would be uniform and "of periodic occurrence" within the torrid zone, the study of which therefore would provide a "foundation" for the "progress" of meteorology (*Cosmos* 347 [1849]). Thirty-one years after Humboldt, Blanford discussed atmospheric equilibrium (and its restoration) in a Humboldtian fashion; he wrote that "every storm is the result of a great disturbance of atmospheric equilibrium," and highlighted the "compensating" air currents which would "restore" equilibrium following disturbance (Blanford 226, 168). Blanford's Indian meteorology thus constituted a "Humboldtian science" (Anderson 260). "Humboldtian science" is a history of science term used to describe a major current of mid- to late-Victorian scientific thought.[4] As Michael Dettelbach points out, "Humboldtian science" emphasized the ideas of "reciprocal balance," "general equilibrium," and an "all-embracing concept of Nature's lawfulness and progressiveness" (290, 304). According to the *OED*, equilibrium is a "state of equal balance" or "condition of equal balance between opposing forces." "Humboldtian science" specifically postulated that atmospheric disturbances (and variations or fluctuations) would average themselves out, around a state of "general equilibrium," which Humboldt first formulated in his *Essay on the Geography of Plants* (1807): "The general equilibrium obtaining in the midst of these disturbances and apparent disorder is the result of an infinite number of mechanical forces and chemical attractions which balance each other" (*Essay on the Geography* 79). Humboldt postulated a global atmospherics always in the process of stabilizing itself; his conception of "general equilibrium" stressed that "lawfulness emerged gradually and progressively," as it stressed that equilibrium would eternally restore itself, amid the apparent proliferation of atmospheric disorder (Dettelbach 300).

With its principle of "general equilibrium," "Humboldtian science" strived after lawful order, balance and stability—the very concepts displaced by certain strains of late nineteenth-century British science, such as thermodynamics (which emphasized a physical universe in which order declines).[5] Allen MacDuffie recently has highlighted Conrad's writing of the thermodynamic concept of entropy (the decline of order in the physical universe). For MacDuffie, Conrad's depiction of entropic decay acts as a critique of an "imperial machinery" that generates "monumental forms of waste and inefficiency" in its exploitation of the "natural world" (94, 90). MacDuffie suggests that "entropy is a crucial concept in Conrad's critique" because it "represents the grit in the imperial machinery, the scientific principle that undoes from within scientific pretensions to total mastery" over the natural world (94). Through the work of MacDuffie, Alex Houen and Michael Whitworth, Conrad's writing of thermodynamic entropy has been well established.[6] However, Conrad's writing of atmospherics thus far has gone unnoticed. The following discussion explicates *Lord Jim*'s implicit formulation of a productive contrast, between a Humboldtian atmospherics of "general equilibrium" and a Conradian atmospherics of non-equilibrium dynamics—which emphasizes the continual propagation of atmospheric disturbances, rather than the restoration of a balanced equilibrium state. As we shall see, *Lord Jim*'s portrayal of atmospherics of nonequilibrium dynamics likewise undoes any notion of a nonhuman "natural world" amenable to what MacDuffie refers to as "scientific pretensions to total mastery" (MacDuffie 94). But more significantly, *Lord Jim*'s depiction of atmospherics also demonstrates Conrad's writing of an ecological consciousness of planetary entanglement between the human and the nonhuman; the later stages of this essay address the close link between *Lord Jim*'s writing of entanglement and its critique of a "metanarrative of progressive modernization" (Esty 95).

The text of *Lord Jim* indeed engages with Humboldtian ideas, particularly in Stein's description of the "perfect equilibrium" and "balance" of a Humboldtian "Kosmos":

> Look! The beauty—but that is nothing—look at the accuracy, the harmony [...] And so exact! This is Nature—the balance of colossal forces. Every star is so—and every blade of grass stands so—and the mighty Kosmos in perfect equilibrium produces—this. This wonder; this masterpiece of Nature—the great artist.
>
> (158)

In reading the above passage, Con Coroneos recognizes that "Conrad gives his most Humboldtian comment to Stein in *Lord Jim*," when Stein contemplates the butterfly (54). However, as Coroneos goes on to suggest, "these tempting parallels can be pursued only so far," for Stein "has long given up on nature's power to redeem imperfect humanity" (54–5). Coroneos cites as evidence Stein's statement to Marlow: "Man is amazing, but he is not a masterpiece [...] Sometimes it seems to me that man is come where he is not wanted, where there is no place for him" (158). In order to add to Coroneos's insight, this essay further articulates the limits of Humboldtian thought, as it applies to *Lord Jim*, through examining *Lord Jim*'s portrayal of the atmospherics of human habitation.

Lord Jim's Malabar Hotel monsoon scene provides a useful starting point for an account of the text's writing of human habitation within atmospherics of nonequilibrium dynamics, in which balance is unstable, dynamic and subject to change. Amid the breaking-up of the monsoon, the "bit of shelter" (137) inside the Malabar Hotel provides an island of sheltered buoyancy; as Marlow describes his conversation with Jim: "I became extremely buoyant" (136). This allusion to buoyancy anticipates the buoyant balance and equilibrium of Stein's swimmer, evoked in Stein's imperative of "to the destructive element submit yourself, and with the exertions of your hands and feet in the water make the deep, deep sea keep you up" (162). However, amid the swirling of the "colossal and headlong stream" of the storm, which "no man could breast," any buoyancy within the fluidic medium is lost, as the leakage of the "perforated pipe" splashes in "odious ridicule" of Stein's swimmer:

> The downpour fell with the heavy uninterrupted rush of a sweeping flood, with a sound of unchecked overwhelming fury that called to one's mind the images of collapsing bridges, of uprooted trees, of undermined mountains. No man could breast the colossal and headlong stream that seemed to break and swirl against the dim stillness in which we were precariously sheltered as if on an island. The perforated pipe gurgled, choked, spat, and splashed in odious ridicule of a swimmer fighting for his life.
> (138)

When applied to the atmospherics of human habitation, within the breaking-up of the monsoon, Stein's Humboldtian "perfect equilibrium" or "balance of *colossal* forces" (158; emphasis added) becomes a fallacy, as the "*colossal* and headlong stream" (138; emphasis added) surrounds the "dim stillness" of Marlow and Jim's "bit of shelter" (137). Any stable ground for Marlow and Jim's "bit of shelter" is threatened, as the "sound of unchecked overwhelming fury" evokes images of collapsing grounds and structures. The buoyant equilibrium provided by Marlow and Jim's "bit of shelter" constitutes a delicate balance, as Marlow alludes to the "way one dares not move for fear of losing a slippery hold" (137). Critics such as Mark Wollaeger and Jed Esty have analyzed *Lord Jim* as a narrative which invokes a series of "sheltering conceptions," which are continually eroded; in Esty's reading, such "sheltering conceptions" include "racial solidarity, masculine honor, and the Protestant work ethic" (Esty 89), while Wollaeger's reading emphasizes the "refuge of romantic art," "which Conrad proposes in response to the potential corrosiveness of total skepticism" (Wollaeger 79). Yet these critical accounts of metaphorical shelters seem to undervalue *Lord Jim*'s climatological foregrounding of a more basic refuge—that of protection from weather and the "destructive element" (162). As the "colossal and headlong stream" (138) encloses and threatens to erode Marlow and Jim's "bit of shelter" (137), *Lord Jim* displaces the "sheltering conception" (236) offered by a Humboldtian scheme of "perfect equilibrium" (158). In other words, *Lord Jim*'s depiction of weather unsettles and dismantles the insulative framework of a Humboldtian portrait of "Kosmos" (158), in which the principle of equilibrium informs a comforting, sheltered vision of human habitation, situated within an atmospherics in cosmic balance.

Dettelbach stresses that Humboldtian cosmology and atmospherics "made natural philosophy the privileged custodian and anchor of order," and thereby provided a natural backdrop of "lawfulness and progressiveness" for the advancement of Europe's "civilizing mission" (300, 304). We have become accustomed to reading Conrad's narratives as critiques of the Victorian discourse of "progress" attached to the new imperialism; a number of critics have recognized that Conrad's narratives expose contradictions "between the ideals of progress and enlightenment and the rapacity of an imperialism tied to them" (Peters 183). A comprehensive review of the vast critical literature on Conrad and colonialism, imperialism and empire is well beyond the scope of this essay.[7] However, it is important to point out that in implicitly refuting the principles of "Humboldtian science," *Lord Jim*'s depiction of atmospherics writes the displacement of a scientific perspective linked to both the new imperialism and a Victorian discourse of "progress."[8] The third section of this essay returns to this thought, in reinterpreting *Lord Jim*'s engagement with what Esty refers to as a "metanarrative of progressive modernization" (Esty 95).

Additional consideration of the Humboldtian concepts of cosmos and equilibrium is necessary here, in order to elucidate further the Humboldtian perspective that *Lord Jim* displaces. Humboldt begins his *Cosmos* with an exposition of cosmic phenomena in the depths of space, then descends to consideration of Earth and its atmosphere and finishes with an account of the "fullness of organic life" (*Cosmos* 63 [1849]), including humanity; as Humboldt writes: "I propose to begin with the depths of space and the remotest nebulae, and thence gradually to descend [...] as the sphere of contemplation contracts in dimension [...] we descend to our own planet" (*Cosmos* 62–3). Peter Sloterdijk points out that this contracting "sphere of contemplation" traces a return from the astral and oceanic depths of space to the dimensions of human habitation (*World Interior* 24). Humboldt's portrait of "cosmos" thereby centers itself around the earth, as "aesthetic observation of the whole" (of an Earth-centered cosmos) compensates for a "sense of lost safety in the vaulted universe," which dates all the way back to a post-Copernican loss of Earth's privileged place, as the planet at the center of the universe (Sloterdijk, *World Interior* 22). Humboldt's contracting "sphere of contemplation" thus formulates an anthropocentric "return from cosmic exteriority to the self-reflexive world" of human habitation, as Earth becomes the planet "to which one returns," and European "humanity" "preserve[s] its distinction as the intelligent nerve cell in the cosmos that must be a point of reference under all circumstances and in all situations" (Sloterdijk, *World Interior* 23, 24). In this formulation of an anthropocentric, self-reflexive return from cosmic exteriority, "modernized dwelling" becomes the "condition of possibility for modern cognition," as "humans are left to reflect on their situation" from the shelters of their inhabited spaces (Sloterdijk, *World Interior* 25). The exterior space of the outside thus is conceived as an extension of a "regionally confined," sheltered, *human* imagination (Sloterdijk, *World Interior* 23). To use the words of Quentin Meillassoux, such a formulation of the outside conceives of the "space of exteriority" as "merely the space of what faces us, of what exists only as a correlate of our own [human] existence" (Meillassoux 7). Humboldt's conception of "general equilibrium" (*Essay on the Geography* 79) superimposes principles of stability and cosmic balance onto the atmospherics of the outside, and thereby informs his sheltered, anthropocentric scheme of human habitation within a cosmos of "one harmoniously ordered whole" (*Cosmos* 3 [1849]). As the "colossal and headlong stream[ing]" (*Lord Jim* 138) of the storm evokes an atmospherics which "no man could breast" (138), *Lord Jim*'s portrayal of the breaking-up of the monsoon unsettles such sheltered, anthropocentric perspective. In Conrad's atmospherics, the balanced calm of equilibrium is not a stable state that eternally restores itself, but is rather an unstable, temporary state which is "startlingly tense and unsafe" ("Typhoon" 86). Calm in *Lord Jim* appears "formidably insecure," as it does just before the *Patna* incident: "[...] suddenly the calm sea, the sky without a cloud, appeared formidably insecure in their immobility" (25). The next section of this essay further considers Conrad's portrayal of human habitation in atmospherics of nonequilibrium dynamics. In doing so, the following discussion shows that Conrad's depiction of atmospheric circulation works against the perpetuation of that which Sloterdijk terms a "backdrop ontology," in which "the human being plays the dramatic animal on stage before the backdrop of a mountain of nature," which is merely a "scenery behind human operations" ("Anthropocene" 334).

Atmospheric Circulation in *Lord Jim* and "Typhoon"

In the above depiction of the "colossal and headlong stream that seemed to break and *swirl*" (138; emphasis added), *Lord Jim* highlights the circulation of a far-from-equilibrium rotary storm system; moreover, the swirling systematicity of the breaking-up of the monsoon seems to absorb Jim into its eddying circulation, as Marlow compares Jim's agitation to that of "a dry leaf imprisoned in an eddy of wind" (141). This image of eddying circulation recalls the air of Jim's hearing, in which the "wind of the punkahs eddied down" (30). Redundant forms of systematic disturbances (such as eddies, whirls and hurricanes) proliferate throughout additional locales: In "the tall whirls of dust" (111) of Sydney, when Marlow speaks with the French lieutenant; in the "hurricane" (134) which passes through the Walpole reefs; and in the gale which surrounds Jim's training boat, which blows with "the strength of a hurricane in fitful bursts" (11).

In order to develop further an account of *Lord Jim*'s depiction of human habitation within atmospheric circulation, we would do well to turn to Conrad's writing of the weather and rotary storm system of "Typhoon," the story of which Conrad began to conceive in February 1899, eighteen months before the completion of *Lord Jim*. "Typhoon" alludes to a certain "Act of Parliament" (20), which presumably has mandated that the

Nan-Shan's Captain MacWhirr "should be able to answer certain simple questions on the subject of circular storms such as hurricanes, cyclones, typhoons" (20). The Act of Parliament at issue was the Mercantile Act of 1850, which added questions regarding the "law of storms" and storm theory to the Board of Trade certification exams for British merchant marine captains and first mates.[9] MacWhirr indeed does grapple with the "terminology of the subject" (32) of nineteenth-century storm theory, as he reads his book with the "chapter on storms" (32), but is unable to come to terms with its "headwork and supposition" (32). Elsewhere I have demonstrated the relevance of nineteenth-century storm theory to the texture of "Typhoon" (Kavanagh 1–10); it bears re-mentioning here that certain strains of the science behind such storm theory stressed the problem of treating meteorology as a science of equilibrium and its restoration. In his important work on circular storm theory in *The Law of Storms* (1861; English translation 1862),[10] German meteorologist Heinrich Dove pointed out "the error of the idea that all atmospheric phenomena may be discussed according to any one cut-and-dry pattern" of disturbance to equilibrium and subsequent "restoration" (317–8). Moreover, Dove emphasized the many (nonhuman) agencies of atmospheric disturbance:

> There are so many agencies always at work disturbing the equilibrium of the atmosphere – the radiation, whose extent varies from day to day – the infinite variety in the surface of the ground – the ocean currents, and the different forms in which aqueous vapour presents itself – that the calms ought to excite our astonishment in a much higher degree than the Wind. The atmosphere is eternally striving to attain equilibrium without ever succeeding. The character of the disturbance itself, and the process of restoration of the equilibrium, exhibits in each case a distinct type; so that the problem which presents itself to the meteorologist is to discover the typical form of the phenomenon, which presents in each several case of its occurrence variations of more or less extent from the original type.
>
> (318)

Observation of the "many agencies" of atmospheric disturbance here problematizes a meteorology based on the concept of equilibrium and its "restoration," as equilibrium becomes a state which is never quite reached in an atmosphere "eternally striving to attain equilibrium without ever succeeding." The allusion in "Typhoon" to the "headwork and supposition" in MacWhirr's book with the "chapter on storms" (32)—which is "without a glimmer of certitude" (32)—subtly points to the very problematics which nineteenth-century meteorology encountered in formulating an account of the nonequilibrium dynamics of atmospheric disturbance. As Ilya Prigogine and Isabelle Stengers point out, nonequilibrium dynamics apply to a physical system which is "far-from-equilibrium"—in which equilibrium is a temporary state that is unstable, dynamic and constantly subject to change, due to the system's exchanges of energy and matter with other systems (5–6). Sciences of nonequilibrium dynamics emphasize fluctuations, instability, disturbance and uncertainty, as opposed to the order, stable equilibrium and certainty of classical science and Newtonian mechanics (Prigogine and Stengers 4).[11]

Lord Jim prefigures "Typhoon" in that both texts depict atmospherics of nonequilibrium dynamics, in which equilibrium constitutes merely a "comparative steadiness": "The ship, after a pause of comparative steadiness, started upon a series of rolls, one worse than the other, and for a time Jukes, preserving his equilibrium, was too busy to open his mouth" ("Typhoon" 30). From one point of view, this "series of rolls" disturbs or interrupts the steadiness of the ship, and strains the stability of the equilibrium of human habitation on board. However, from another point of view, equilibrium is a state which is only temporarily attained, and the calm "ought to excite our astonishment in a much higher degree than the Wind" (Dove 318). The "comparative steadiness" (30) of equilibrium is itself merely a "pause" which inversely interrupts the redundant rolling of the ship, and thereby anticipates the "awful pause" (86) of the calm at the end of Chapter V: "But the quietude of the air was startlingly tense and unsafe, like a slender hair holding a sword suspended over his head" (86). "Typhoon" thus depicts the instability of atmospheric equilibrium, which is "startlingly tense and unsafe." But more significantly, "Typhoon" embeds its above portrayal of an unstable equilibrium of human habitation within its depiction of the atmospheric circulation of a far-from-equilibrium weather system: "[...] the *Nan-Shan* wallowed heavily at the bottom of a circular cistern of clouds. This ring of dense vapours, gyrating madly round the calm of the centre, encompassed the ship" ("Typhoon" 82). The gyrating "ring of dense vapours" recalls the swirling of the breaking-up of the monsoon, which encloses itself around Marlow and Jim's "bit of shelter" (*Lord Jim* 137); rotating air currents of systematic storm circulation surround both the "precariously sheltered" "stillness" (138) of Marlow's hotel room in *Lord Jim* and the "menacing" "calm of the centre" (82) of the storm in "Typhoon." Through situating an unstable equilibrium of human habitation within the circulation of the far-from-equilibrium weather system—so that humans are precariously circumscribed within it—both "Typhoon" and *Lord Jim*'s Malabar Hotel scene emphasize the entanglement of humans in atmospherics of nonequilibrium dynamics. The third and fourth sections of this essay further address *Lord Jim*'s portrayal of this entanglement, through examining the text's climatological foregrounding of a narrative of "all our stammerings" (178).[12]

The Monsoon and Lord Jim's Atmospherics 123

Robert Marzec's important work on modernist inhabitancy articulates a land-based account of Conrad's writing of human habitation, and thereby provides a useful counterpoint to the current study of Conrad's portrayal of the atmospherics of human habitation. Marzec elaborates a modernist "inhabitancy" crisis—one which emphasizes human displacement and dislocation as a result of a "long war against inhabitancy," initiated by the British land enclosure movement, which brought about the enclosure and privatization of lands which previously had been public or communal ("Speaking" 435).[13] Marzec argues that through the workings of privatization and land enclosure, a Cartesian "human subject sets up the land, territorializes it," and thereby enframes it within the scopic gaze (*Ecological* 13). For Marzec, this development "sets the subject-object split firmly in place, with the human [subject] standing over the land as an object," which "need[s] to be comprehended by being made totally visible to the subject's gaze" ("Speaking" 425). Marzec argues that the discourse of land enclosure informed and rationalized the privatization of colonized land in imperial territories, where "the reterritorialization of land" was "accomplished through increasing degrees of surveillance" ("Speaking" 423), as "open fields were erased in favour of a normalizing panoptic representation of the land, making the land conform to the larger imperial design" (*Ecological* 83). Marzec applies these thoughts to a brief discussion of Conrad's narratives, and argues that Conrad's environments of "unenclosed land" come to "serve as the key vehicle" for the foregrounding of a problem of representation, in which "unenclosed land at the edge of empire" becomes the unrepresentable, or the "aesthetically and mentally unthinkable" (*Ecological* 6). In support of his argument, Marzec quotes *Heart of Darkness*, in which Marlow describes the Congo landscape as "featureless" (54) and "an empty land" (61).

Such an emphasis on territorialization and enframed enclosure implicitly relies on a conception of habitation as primarily a land- or earth-based mode of dwelling. As Luce Irigaray reminds us, much of Western philosophy (including that of the Cartesian subject, which Marzec's discussion invokes) presupposes "a solid crust from which to raise a construction," and thereby forgets that "dwelling" involves living not just on land, but also within air (2).[14] Marzec's discussion of modernist human dislocation (from the "land as an object" ["Speaking" 425]) may be usefully applied to *Lord Jim*'s depiction of human dislocation, particularly to Stein's description of "man" as he who "disturb[s] the blades of grass" (158). However, it runs the risk of relegating to the background the workings of atmospheric agencies and processes, including that of the "colossal and headlong stream that seemed to break and swirl," which "no man could breast" (138). Even a land-based study of Conrad's environmental writing needs to take into account Conrad's depictions of weather and climatology—which emphasize the imbrication of human habitation within the workings of nonhuman atmospheric systems, which have the capacity to unsettle human equilibrium. In its portrayal of atmospheric circulation, *Lord Jim* certainly does not forget the materiality and turbulence of air, nor does it presuppose the existence of a "solid crust" (Irigaray 2). Moreover, Conrad's writing of human habitation as immersion in air—within the circulation of far-from-equilibrium weather systems, such as the breaking-up of the monsoon—emphasizes an equilibrium of human habitation which is inherently unstable, always already on the brink of disturbance and dislocation.

Furthermore, Conrad's portrayal of human habitation as immersion in atmospheric circulation highlights the workings of nonhuman atmospheric agencies and processes, which work alongside human agencies, as in the gyration of the typhoon's "ring of dense vapours" ("Typhoon" 82). As Jeffrey McCarthy recognizes, "Conrad's weather runs contrary to the anthropocentric commonplace of human agents affecting inert objects," and Conrad's storms "demonstrate the natural world as a parallel and overlapping realm, an active presence with its own ontological priority" (McCarthy 82, 110). To extend McCarthy's insight, we might only reinforce that Conrad's weather constitutes a multiplicity of atmospheric constellations and meteorological systems, such as the cyclonic breaking-up of the monsoon in *Lord Jim*, the rotary storm of "Typhoon," the polluted atmospherics of London in *The Secret Agent* and the snow of *Under Western Eyes* (and these are only a few examples).[15] Moreover, Conrad's writings of rotary storms recognize the limits of enframing atmospheric agencies using circular models. Conrad writes rotary storm systems as both redundancy and noise, as both circular pattern and noisy variation from circular pattern (Kavanagh 6–7); Conrad's depictions of such storms thereby emphasize that the redundant form of the circle cannot quite enclose or enframe the action of wind gyration and other atmospheric agencies in rotary storms. While "Typhoon" alludes to the circulation of air currents at "certain moments" (43), in which "the air streamed against the ship as if sucked through a tunnel" (43), it also stresses the "howl[ing] and scuffl[ing]" (43) noise of the currents of the gale. *Lord Jim*'s "colossal and headlong stream[ing]" of the breaking-up of the monsoon only "seem[s] to" "swirl" (138); it is not fully circumscribed into the text's redundant vocabulary of circular forms (the implications of which this essay will revisit, in the conclusion).

Because Marzec's argument highlights situations in which a Cartesian "human subject sets up the land" and thereby "territorializes it" (Marzec, *Ecological* 13), it may be usefully applied to Henry Blanford's account of India's meteorology. Blanford's discussion of India's atmospheric physics advocated the systematic observation of territorialized, enclosed tracts of atmosphere. His scheme suggested dividing India's atmosphere into various sections, corresponding to "contrasts of desert and forest, of plain, plateau and mountain ridge, of continent and sea"—each of which could be placed "under a meteorological blockade" of ordered observation, in order to obtain "a bird's eye view of the conditions, prevailing at one and the same time, over a considerable tract of the earth's surface" (Blanford 98). Blanford thereby aimed to "place knowledge of meteorological laws on a very advanced footing" (Blanford 99); as Anderson argues, "India was Britain's continent, an ideal laboratory in which to develop a scientific command of the unruly forces of the atmosphere" (Anderson 282). Blanford's attribution of "order and regularity" (Blanford 144) to India's atmospherics (and his account of meteorology as a science of empirical laws) amounted to an "imposition of Western conceptions of order" upon the "chaos" of a "vast, confusing subject" (Anderson 261-2).

Blanford's discussion of India's meteorology informs this study precisely because it frames this confrontation, between "Western conceptions of order" and the so-called "chaos" of meteorological disturbance—which is the very confrontation which Conrad's writing of atmospherics effectively recasts. At times, Conrad's depictions of weather systems do point to an opposition between the apparent disorder of weather disturbances and the schemes of order (and geometric enclosure) which are superimposed onto them, through the workings of systematic observation. For example, "Typhoon" alludes to MacWhirr's failed attempt to use the geometric models of "advancing semi-circles, left- and right-hand quadrants" (32) to grasp the systematicity of the rotary storm. However, Conrad's writing of atmospherics stresses less this opposition or confrontation, and more the *sheltering aspect* of certain conceptions of order, as in Marlow's invocation of "that sheltering conception of light and order which is our refuge" (*Lord Jim* 236). "Typhoon" embeds MacWhirr's placement of the matchbox—as MacWhirr's source of light and regularity, "in its corner of the shelf [...] by his order" (85)—within the shelter of his chartroom, where things have "their safe appointed places" (85). This placement of the matchbox implicates MacWhirr's simpler, human conception of order, which structures the chartroom's shelter, within the atmospherics of far-from-equilibrium weather dynamics.[16] One significant "sheltering conception" relevant to *Lord Jim* is Humboldtian equilibrium, which informs the anthropocentric scheme which the text displaces—that of human habitation in a balanced cosmos of "one harmoniously ordered whole" (Humboldt, *Cosmos* 3 [1849]).

Lord Jim effectively precludes a concept of "Nature" (134) that overemphasizes such harmonious order. If human habitation is conceived against the "backdrop ontology" (Sloterdjik, "Anthropocene" 334) of a balanced "Nature" or a Humboldtian "Kosmos" (*Lord Jim* 158), the disequilibrium of human life brings itself out of balance with such a backdrop. Stein states about "man": "Why should he run about here and there making a great noise about himself, talking about the stars, disturbing the blades of grass?" (158). Humanity acts as a disturbing agent which disrupts the "perfect equilibrium" of Humboldtian portraiture, in which "there is no place" for "man" (158). While emphasizing humanity's removal from a displaced Humboldtian atmospherics of "perfect equilibrium," *Lord Jim* re-embeds humanity within an ecology of atmospheric disturbance, which the second half of this essay addresses.

The Propagation of Atmospheric Disturbance in *Lord Jim*

One could describe *Lord Jim* as a narrative of the propagation of disturbances to various equilibria; such disturbances manifest themselves atmospherically, as in the "quiver" which brings about the *Patna* incident:

> What had happened? The wheezy thump of the engines went on. Had the earth been checked in her course? [...] A faint noise as of thunder, of thunder infinitely remote, less than a sound, hardly more than a vibration, passed slowly, and the ship quivered in response, as if the thunder had growled deep down in the water [...] Its quivering stopped, and the faint noise of thunder ceased all at once, as though the ship had steamed across a narrow belt of vibrating water and of humming air.
>
> (25–6)

Here the text represents the "quiver" as a perceivable disturbance to the equilibrium and regularity of the ship's previously smoothed out, "unceasing vibration" (20). The manifestation of this disturbance unsettles the security of the earlier description of the ship's balanced, vibrating mechanism, the "beat" of which seems to be "part of the scheme of a safe universe": "The propeller turned without a check, as though its beat had been part of the scheme of a safe universe; and on each side of the *Patna* two deep folds of water [...] enclosed within their straight and diverging ridges a few white swirls of foam" (19). In transfiguring the mechanical vibration of the "quiver" into a form of atmospheric vibration—as the "faint noise as of thunder, of thunder infinitely remote"—the text foreshadows its depictions of an atmospheric equilibrium which is unstable and subject to agitation, as in the breaking-up of the monsoon, where the "swirl[ing]" of the "colossal and headlong stream" (138) amplifies that of the "few white swirls of foam" (19) of the *Patna*'s wake. Steven Connor provides a helpful account of unstable equilibrium:

> There are two kinds of equilibrium, the first inert, the second dynamic. In the first kind of equilibrium, the two sides are completely and exactly balanced [...] The scales stand still, locked in the exactitude of their equilibrium [...] There is another kind of equilibrium,

the kind signalled when we speak of a "delicate balance," in which the equilibrium is unstable, inhabited and defined by tremor.
(Book of Skin 269)

In opposition to the stabilized equilibrium suggested by the *Patna*'s wake—in which the disturbance to the water is balanced, with "two deep folds of water" "*on each side*" (19; emphasis added), an image of the "even and scrupulous balance" (241) to which Marlow later alludes—*Lord Jim* depicts an atmospheric equilibrium which is unstable and dynamic. The "dim stillness" of Marlow's hotel room provides merely a temporary refuge, in which Marlow and Jim are "precariously sheltered as if on an island" (138). As in the pause of calm during the storm of "Typhoon" (in which the "quietude of the air" is "startlingly tense and unsafe" [86]), calm in *Lord Jim* is a delicate balance, subject to agitation, within an atmospherics that is "inhabited and defined by tremor" (Connor, *Book of Skin* 269). Disturbances to this unstable equilibrium propagate and modulate, in recurrent references to tremors, quivers and shocks, such as the "splashing shock" (88) of the *Patna*, or the "sort of preparatory tremor" (112) of the French lieutenant in Sydney, where "tall whirls of dust" (111) circulate. The "humming air" (26) of the *Patna* incident and the tremor particularly recur in Marlow's description of Gentleman Brown's camp in Patusan, following Brown's crew's intrusion—a disturbance which manifests itself as an "increasing tremor that might have been the stamping of a multitude of feet, the hum of many voices, or the fall of an immensely distant waterfall" (281). Atmospheric disturbances also amplify, as in the "swirl[ing]" (138) of the breaking-up of the monsoon. Within *Lord Jim*'s ecology of atmospheric disturbance, the "faint noise as of thunder" (25) acts as a remote, reverberating anticipation of the amplifying "growl of thunder," which strikes during the breaking-up of the monsoon: "The growl of the thunder increased steadily while I looked at him, distinct and black, planted solidly upon the shores of a sea of light" (136).

Regarding vibration in *Lord Jim*, Julie Beth Napolin recently has analyzed Conrad's writing of "sympathetic vibration" as a "site of working through" of Conrad's "project of solidarity," as outlined in his famous "Preface" to *The Nigger of the "Narcissus"* (Napolin 60, 73). Napolin points out that Conrad's vibration registers a "material continuity between trembling and quivering bodies," and "poses a physical impact across distance that both unites and disrupts" (Napolin 69, 63).[17] To add to Napolin's insight, truly sympathetic, harmonious vibration between human bodies and nonhuman surroundings occurs only in the "different atmosphere" (250) of Patusan—which, as Robert Hampson recognizes, is the "exotic space" made impossible by the text's "systematic overturning of romantic conventions" (Hampson 129). Marlow describes:

I breathed deeply, I revelled in the vastness of the opened horizon, in the different atmosphere that seemed to vibrate with the toil of life, with the energy of an impeccable world. This sky and this sea were open to me. The girl was right—there was a sign, a call in them—something to which I responded with every fibre of my being.

(250)

At the beginning of the Malabar Hotel monsoon scene, Marlow briefly alludes to this "different atmosphere" (250) of Patusan, where Jim is "in close touch with Nature, that keeps faith on such easy terms with her lovers" (134). Marlow suggests that it is only in Patusan that a "complete accord" is found with one's "surroundings," "with the life of the forests and with the life of men" (134). Marlow's invocation of "Nature" in Patusan points to Stein's Humboldtian discussion, where "the mighty Kosmos in perfect equilibrium produces" a "masterpiece of Nature—the great artist" (158). With its "complete accord," Patusan's "different atmosphere" likewise functions as an illusory production of a harmonious figuration of "Nature." "Three hundred miles beyond the end of telegraph cables and mail-boat lines" (213), Patusan provides the figuration of an atmospheric balance existing prior to modernization. But such premodern atmospheric balance of course is a fallacy; if an idea of stabilized balance is only a "sheltering conception" (236), then equilibrium is (and *always* has been) only a temporary balance, in atmospherics "eternally striving to attain equilibrium without ever succeeding" (Dove 318).

Outside of the "different atmosphere" of Patusan, human tremorings and quiverings manifest not a sense of harmonious vibration between human bodies and nonhuman surroundings, but rather a sense of jarring vibration, of dislocation and agitation, within atmospherics of disturbance. For example, the text highlights the agitation of the "accident case" (45), whose body trembles with "jerks as of galvanic shocks," inside the Bombay hospital: "Quick jerks as of galvanic shocks disclosed under the flat coverlet the outlines of meagre and agitated legs [...] his body trembled tensely like a released harp-string" (45). As an additional form of agitation, jumps proliferate throughout *Lord Jim*, not only in Jim's recurrent jumps and in Captain Brierly's suicide, but also in Captain Robinson's "submissive little jump" (129), the "jumps" (159) of Stein's hat, the "snort, jump, and stand" of Stein's pony (159), the Patusan mats which "jumped and flew" (226) and the figurative "jump into the unknown" (174).[18] The text writes the agitation of the jump into its description of the convulsive pronunciation of the word itself, the stress of which imparts a slight tremor into Marlow's body: "[Jim] shivered as if about to swallow some nauseous drug... 'jumped,' he pronounced with a convulsive effort, whose stress, as if propagated by the waves of the air, made my body stir a little in the chair" (102). As that which highlights tremorings, quiverings and tremblings, the text's writing of vibration and agitation contributes to the text's further depiction of atmospherics of unstable equilibrium, and manifests human dislocation within such atmospherics. At the same time the text systematically overturns romantic conventions and conceptions, such as one of "complete accord" (134) between human beings and their surroundings, within harmonious "Nature" (Hampson 129), the text evokes its ecology of atmospheric disturbance. The explication of this ecology further demonstrates the text's displacement of an anthropocentric, Humboldtian scheme of human habitation (in which humans reside within an atmospherics of "perfect equilibrium" [*Lord Jim* 158], in a cosmos of "one harmoniously ordered whole" [Humboldt, *Cosmos* 3]).

Jed Esty recently has extended the well-established critical study of *Lord Jim* and imperialism to a compelling analysis of *Lord Jim* as a "laying bare" of the "facts of radically uneven development" in the late nineteenth-century "colonial world-system" (97). For Esty, *Lord Jim*'s "sites of stasis" (such as the merchant ship of the *Patna* and the colonial outpost of Patusan) constitute "pocketed worlds" of "stalled development" at the imperial periphery (85, 87). In acting as pockets of "bounded space and stopped time," these sites of stasis exist in tension with the "radically open and unbounded space-time of empire and globalization" (90). Such sites of "stalled development" "temporarily resist the forces of modernity/historicization," yet are finally "swept into" a "metanarrative of progressive modernization," as they are unsettled by "violent accident or intrusion," such as the *Patna* incident and Brown's arrival in Patusan (87, 95, 98–9). Esty stresses that *Lord Jim*'s writing of these sites of stasis or "stalled development" reveals a "central contradiction" in "the civilizational discourse of progress attached to the new imperialism" (85, 92). This "central contradiction" is that such a discourse of progress "seeks to underdevelop and develop at the same time," through linking itself to the authorization of a conventional imperial romance narrative—in which the "colonial romance of Patusan" as "stalled development" fundamentally contradicts "the imperial reality of Patusan as raw material" for "progressive modernization" (96). In Esty's reading of *Lord Jim*, the text's atmospherics and weather remain in the background. My reading shows that Esty's "sites of stasis" are also pockets of atmospheric balance that are ultimately disrupted, as previously stable equilibria are disturbed. *Lord Jim* atmospherically mediates what Esty identifies as "violent accident or intrusion" (Esty 87); as shown above, *Lord Jim* renders both the *Patna* incident and Brown's intrusion as the tremor and humming air of atmospheric disturbances, which propagate throughout the narrative. To add to Esty's thought, a Humboldtian conception of atmospherics (which presents equilibrium as a stabilized state that restores itself) is effaced or swept away, at the same time *Lord Jim*'s sites of stasis and "stalled development" are "swept into" Esty's "metanarrative of progressive modernization" (Esty 95). This essay shows that *Lord Jim*'s effacement of this Humboldtian paradigm entails the dissolution of a scheme of human habitation within an anthropocentric cosmos of "perfect equilibrium" (*Lord Jim* 158)—the "sheltering conception" (*Lord Jim* 236) of which insulates humans from awareness of the actual extent of their entanglement in the complex, destabilizing nonequilibrium dynamics of atmospheric agencies and processes.

Bruno Latour articulates a "completely different great narrative" of entanglement, which runs alongside the more critically established "great narrative" of "Progress" (Latour 4–5), and thereby provides a means of reinterpreting *Lord Jim*'s relation to a "metanarrative of progressive modernization" (Esty 95). As Latour explains, a traditional metanarrative of the "Progress" of modernization highlights the means by which human beings work to remove or "emancipate" themselves from their attachment with a background of nonhuman "nature" (5). In this traditional metanarrative, so-called "emancipation" is achieved as humans continue to develop complex networks of commercial exchange and engineer technologies and systems that make space more inhabitable (such as advanced climate control systems and artificial environments, which provide insulation and separation from the outdoor elements). An alternative metanarrative of modernization is one of entanglement. Latour points out that developments in various interrelated markets, sciences and technologies (such as those of biotechnology and pharmacology, or those of climate control and meteorology) "have amplified, for at least the last two centuries" both the scale and the "intimacy" of attachment or entanglement between the human and the nonhuman (5). Latour writes: "What distinguishes the second [metanarrative] is that we constantly move from a superficial to a deeper interpretation of what it is to be entangled" (5). This metanarrative of entanglement traces "a continuous movement toward a greater and greater" awareness of the "level of attachments" between the human and the nonhuman (5). In conversation with Latour's insight, Sloterdijk emphasizes that air and the atmosphere especially have come under a "pressure of explication" from the late nineteenth century onward, as sciences such as microbiology, toxicology, climatology and meteorology have worked to make explicit the extent of the entanglement of human beings in the atmospheric conditions which they inhabit (*Foams* 178). This metanarrative of entanglement is more precisely a counter-metanarrative, in that it contests the metanarrative or "grand narrative" of the "progress" of European humanity's mastery over (and removal from attachment with) a background of nonhuman "nature."

Both *Lord Jim* and "Typhoon" engage with this counter-metanarrative of entanglement. In effacing a Humboldtian conception of atmospherics and recasting equilibrium as a temporary state which never quite maintains itself, *Lord Jim* writes an ecological consciousness of human imbrication in atmospherics of nonequilibrium dynamics. Through writing human immersion in the far-from-equilibrium weather dynamics of atmospheric circulation, "Typhoon" further develops this ecological consciousness, and additionally depicts the entanglement of humans in the "dirty weather" (20) generated by machinery of modernization, such as the internal combustion engine of the steamship: "The air seemed thick [...] The smoke struggled with difficulty out of the funnel, and instead of streaming away spread itself out like an infernal sort of cloud, smelling of sulphur and raining soot all over the decks" (21). In *The Mirror of the Sea*, Conrad suggests that "the taking of a modern steamship about the world" "has not the same quality of intimacy with nature" as the "absorbing practice" of the "art" of sailing "any vessel afloat" (30). However, if the steamship's use of technologically "captured force" (*Mirror* 31) to some extent removes the sailor from "intimacy with nature" (*Mirror* 30), it also immerses and entangles him in a weather of the steamship's own production; Jukes breathes the sooty cloud of the *Nan-Shan*'s smoke pollution, which "rain[s] soot all over the decks" ("Typhoon" 21). The *Nan-Shan*'s crew survives its encounter with the "dirty weather" of the typhoon through maintaining the ship's production of its own "dirty weather" of particulate pollution, amid the far-from-equilibrium weather dynamics of the storm system. The inhalation of smoke pollution registers the survival of the ship: "The smoke tossed out of the funnel was settling down upon her deck. [Jukes] breathed it as he passed forward. He felt the deliberate throb of the engines, and heard small sounds that seemed to have survived the great uproar" (81). In "Typhoon," weathering the storm becomes a matter of climate control, of keeping the engine going and ensuring the ship's production of regulated smoke pollution with proper ventilation (through "trimming properly the stokehold ventilators" [23]).[19]

Moreover, through writing human habitation in atmospherics of nonequilibrium dynamics, *Lord Jim* displaces a mid- to late nineteenth-century scheme of Nature's lawfulness and progressiveness—a Humboldtian climatological perspective linked to a European metanarrative of "progress" (Dettelbach 300, 304). In the introduction to a revised and expanded edition of his *Cosmos*, Humboldt directly ties his science of the "order of nature" to a discourse of "progressive development" (*Cosmos* 17 [1864]). Humboldt then connects the development of human knowledge of this natural order to the progress of human industry: "[S]o ought we [...] to strive after a knowledge of the laws and principles of unity that pervade the vital forces of the universe; and it is by such a course that physical studies may be made subservient to the progress of industry, which is a conquest of mind over matter" (*Cosmos* 34 [1864]). For Humboldt, human ingenuity works in pursuit of a "more intimate knowledge" of the "order of nature," which "ever unfold[s] itself" to the human observer (*Cosmos* 20, 21 [1864]). In Humboldtian perspective, the revelation of this order contributes to the "progress" of human industry (which brings about the mastery of human "mind over matter"), and also "increases" human "sense of the calm of nature," through "dispel[ling]" "belief in a 'discord of the elements'" (*Cosmos* 22 [1864]). *Lord Jim* discloses a contradiction in the linking of Humboldtian perspective to a metanarrative of "progressive development." If a "Nature" of "one harmoniously ordered whole" (Humboldt, *Cosmos* 3 [1849]) is conceived as a backdrop—which unfolds its cosmic balance, in the background of such a metanarrative—the anthropogenic agencies of European humanity and its machinery of "progressive development" act as a collective disturbance to such a backdrop. This collective disturbance unsettles and contradicts Humboldtian balance. As the steamship *Patna* "pound[s] in the dusk the calm water of the Strait" (18), it troubles the calm of the equilibrium atmospherics of Chapters II and III, and the "black smoke pouring heavily" (20) from its funnel pollutes and "shadow[s]" the "serenity of the sky" (20). In *Lord Jim*, the observation of anthropogenic agency reinforces a sense of European humanity's removal from Humboldtian portraiture—in which, as Stein observes, "there is no place" for "man," as "man" is he who "mak[es] a great noise" and "disturb[s] the blades of grass" (158). The mechanical "quiver" of the *Patna* marks this very removal. When the *Patna* "quiver[s]" "as though" it were "steam[ing] across a narrow belt of vibrating water and of humming air" (26), the text highlights anthropogenic disturbance, and transfigures it into a vibrational anticipation of the tremulous air of the wider narrative's ecology of atmospheric disturbance. Within this ecology, human habitation is entangled with the workings of both atmospheric agencies and anthropogenic agencies, which generate propagating tremors, quivers and shocks.

It is important to note that quivering, tremoring and jerking refer to a number of forms of agitation in *Lord Jim*, including those of atmospheric disturbance, mechanical shaking, hydraulic convulsing, bodily shaking and tremulous human communication. Some important examples are the "preparatory tremor" (112) of the French lieutenant, the "quiver[ing]" (104) of Jim's lips during his narration of the *Patna* incident, the "jerky agitation" (140) of Jim's movements, the "empty sky and empty ocean all a-quiver" (128), the "increasing tremor" (281) of the air of Patusan, the "quivering" (26) of the *Patna*, and the "jerky spasms" of the perforated "water-pipe" (136). In *Lord Jim*'s depiction of human habitation within an ecology of atmospheric disturbance, recurrent words such as "tremor" and "quiver" point to both the disequilibria of agitated human communication and the disequilibria of atmospheric disturbances, which parallel each other. Human communication trembles amid the disturbances that propagate throughout *Lord Jim*'s atmospherics, as the text's writing of atmospheric tremorings and quiverings foregrounds a narrative of human stammering and stuttering, which the final section of this essay considers. The following discussion addresses *Lord Jim*'s careful negotiation of the interrelation the text introduces between these parallel disequilibria, and the conclusion to this essay reinforces McCarthy's point that Conrad writes a natural world "overlapping with human being" but "existing in itself" (McCarthy 226, no. 11, 105).

"The Perforated Pipe": Convulsive Hydraulics and Stammering in *Lord Jim*

Through alluding to an early breaking-up of the monsoon—as in Jim's statement of "[t]he monsoon breaks up early this year" (136)—*Lord Jim* specifically draws attention to a variation in the periodicity of atmospheric disturbance. In other words, the text highlights a further disturbance to a preestablished pattern of atmospheric disturbance, in that it marks an early occurrence of the cyclonic storms preceding the biannual shift in direction of India's monsoon winds. Because India receives nearly all of its yearly rainfall during the months of the monsoons, an early breaking-up of the monsoon often resulted in drought and famine during the nineteenth century. By the late nineteenth century, it had long been recognized that the limitations of India's irrigation systems were to blame for the severity of famines; an 1874 article in *The Times* noted: "Famines in India [...] form the natural penalty for inadequate means of internal transit and for an unhusbanded and uncontrolled water supply" (Hunter 10; qtd. in Anderson 271). As Daniel R. Headrick points out, nineteenth-century British imperial engineers vastly expanded India's irrigation systems, under the auspices of public works (after the 1858 transfer of India from the East India Company to the Crown), in order to provide measures for dealing with famine-causing droughts (see Headrick 171–208). After the severe drought of 1876–78, which caused one of the worst famines in India's history, the 1881 Report of the Indian Famine Commission recommended the further development of "protective" irrigation works, such as canals and water storage tanks, in order to mitigate the impact of such droughts. Water storage tanks and systems were built particularly in the North West Provinces, including Bombay, where canal construction was deemed possible but not profitable (Headrick 188–9).[20]

Through its reference to the convulsive overflow of "the perforated pipe" (138), *Lord Jim*'s allusion to Bombay's hydraulic systems subtly points to the "unwearied efforts" (236) of imperial hydraulic engineering to stabilize an equilibrium of human habitation, through making it less vulnerable to the impact of variations in periodic cycles of rainfall (within an atmospherics in which equilibrium is unstable, dynamic and subject to agitation). At the same time that the "colossal and headlong stream[ing]" (138) of the breaking-up of the monsoon evokes a fluidic immersion which "no man could breast" (138), it also generates an overflow which overwhelms the hydraulic system of the "perforated pipe": "The perforated pipe gurgled, choked, spat, and splashed in odious ridicule of a swimmer fighting for his life" (138). The pipe fails to retain water and channel it efficiently, so its leakage demonstrates the limits of the functioning of imperial hydraulic systems, which work to stabilize an equilibrium of human habitation (and, as we have seen, the evoked image of the drowning swimmer provides an antitype to the image of the buoyant equilibrium of Stein's swimmer, who does breast the "destructive element" [162] in which he is immersed). The leakage of the pipe continues amid the rain, while Jim stammers:

> "Thank you, though—your room—jolly convenient—for a chap—badly hipped..." The rain pattered and swished in the garden; a water pipe (it must have had a hole in it) performed just outside the window a parody of blubbering woe with funny sobs and gurgling lamentations interrupted by jerky spasms of silence.... "A bit of shelter," [Jim] mumbled and ceased.
>
> (136)

The convulsive agitation of the "perforated pipe" thereby mimics Jim's stammering and stuttering, which continues throughout the scene: "'You've been—er—uncommonly—really there's no word to... Uncommonly! [...] Because at bottom... you, yourself...' He stuttered" (137). After the rain "passe[s] away," the leakage of the "water-pipe" continues its "drip, drip outside the window" (140), alongside Jim's stammering: "'Why! this is what I—you—I...' he stammered" (141). As Gilles Deleuze argues, a language of the stutter or stammer does not "extract" itself as that of "a homogeneous system, in equilibrium, or close to equilibrium, defined by constant terms and relations," but rather "appears in perpetual disequilibrium" (108). Deleuze draws a parallel between the disequilibrium of the stammer and the reverberation of atmospheric disturbance; Deleuze insists a narrative account of stuttering or stammering that depends solely on an "external marker" (such as "he stuttered...") will be severely limited and poorly conveyed, "unless there is a corresponding form of content—an atmospheric quality, a milieu that acts as the conductor of words—that brings together within itself the quiver, the murmur, the stutter, the tremolo, or the vibrato, and makes the indicated affect reverberate through the words" (108). During the breaking-up of the monsoon in *Lord Jim*, the weather and the stammer both appear to be in perpetual disequilibrium. Whereas Deleuze's account of the stammer posits a more direct relation between atmospheric reverberation and the "indicated affect" of the stammer—which generate parallel disequilibria—*Lord Jim* emphasizes the convulsiveness of Jim's stammer using the intermediary image of the perforated pipe, as if to suggest that the disequilibrium of human communication is not quite commensurate with the disequilibrium of atmospheric disturbance within the milieu. In *Lord Jim*, the vibration within the milieu does not passively reflect or mirror the form of expression of the stammer; rather, the language of the stammer shakes with the convulsion of human agitation, as tremors propagate within an ecology of atmospheric disturbance.

Jim's stammer implicates the limits of language Deleuze identifies: "When a language is so strained that it starts to stutter, or to murmur or stammer... *then language in its entirety reaches the limit* that marks its outside" (Deleuze 113). Following Deleuze, in a discussion of the shaking or tremoring of language, Connor argues:

> Language can be considered as a universal frame or container, that is capable of getting outside, containing and holding together everything with which it has dealings. But when language is made to stammer or shake, the frame itself is threatened [...] Shaking is the actualization of the possibility of stepping outside the skin or envelope of precedence and predictable forms.
> ("The Shakes" 214–5)

Connor's discussion of the stammer—as a form of expression which shakes language's "envelope of precedence and predictable forms"—provides a means of interpreting the dramatic function of Jim's stammering during the storm. The "breaking-up of the monsoon" is a standard sailor's term for a specific series of cyclonic storms; its terminology therefore is part of the frame or container of a conventional nautical language. Meteorological texts absorbed this nautical convention into schemes of storm classification.[21] The symbolic redundancy of the term—which the term accrues, through its conventional usage—highlights a cyclic redundancy and regularity of meteorological occurrence, of a specific class of rotary storm, for which precedent has long been established. Yet Jim's allusion to the breaking-up of the monsoon highlights disruption to such regularity and precedent, for Jim notes that "[t]he monsoon breaks up *early* this year" (138; emphasis added). The Malabar Hotel monsoon scene's depiction of disruption to climatological regularity foregrounds Jim's disjointed utterance, which reduces language's "sheltering conception of light and order" (236) to a "*bit of* shelter" (137; emphasis added). Like the "iron shell" (19) of the *Patna*'s hull, this fragmentary shelter is threatened and made to shake, as the convulsiveness of Jim's stammer registers the dislocating vibration of the storm. Jim's "stammerings" (171) tremble with the "nonhuman" atmospheric disturbances that shake language's "bit of shelter" (136)—a contracted envelope of precedence and predictable forms, which provides merely a limited zone of habitability, a "refuge" (236) within a wider ecology of atmospheric disturbance.

One should note that the jerky convulsiveness of Jim's stammer recalls both his "convulsive jerk" (94) at the dinner table and his "convulsive" pronunciation of the word "jumped," the "stress" of which makes Marlow's body "stir a little in the chair," "as if propagated by the waves of the air" (102). When Jim's utterance of "jumped" imparts a slight "stir" into Marlow's body, what is transmitted is not so much the resonance of a human voice, but rather the dislocating "stress" of Jim's "convulsive" pronunciation. Especially during the breaking-up of the monsoon, the text's emphasis of the jarring vibration of atmospheric disturbance—which Jim's stammer manifests—displaces the sympathetic vibration of human vocal resonance. Marlow later reinforces the limits of vocal resonance, when he suggests the sum total of human articulation amounts to a form of collective stammer:

> Are not our lives too short for that full utterance which through all our stammerings is of course our only and abiding intention? I have given up expecting those last words, whose ring, if they could only be pronounced, would shake both heaven and earth [...] The heaven and the earth must not be shaken, I suppose [...].
>
> (171)

This collective stammer of human communication (of "all our stammerings") is "fragmentary" (260) and fails to add up to a "full utterance" capable of shaking "both heaven and earth." A conception of a "full utterance" that would fully shake a frame of "both heaven and earth" would need to presuppose the prior formulation of a scheme of order capable of generating such a framing, of completely containing "both heaven and earth" within *one* all-encompassing envelope. As a totalization of one whole, such a framing of "both heaven and earth"—with the earth embedded within a surrounding "heaven," fully resonating with *human* communication—constitutes a version of the anthropocentric cosmos that the narrative displaces and disallows.

An April 1900 letter to David Meldrum indicates Conrad was frustrated with the serialization of *Lord Jim* in *Blackwood's*, which separated the two chapters of the Malabar Hotel monsoon scene (Chapter XVI appeared in the April 1900 issue, and Chapter XVII in the May 1900 issue): "I've been horribly disappointed by the shortness of the inst[allment] in the Ap. No the more so that the break there just destroyed an effect. If one could only do without serial publication!" (*Collected Letters* 2: 260). The effect which is lost is that of Jim walking outside the hotel room, after standing in the "very doorway" (138), and then returning. Jim walks outside the hotel room at the close of Chapter XVI, and Marlow entreats him to come back inside: "I lost no time in entreating him [...] to come in and shut the door" (138). Jim returns to the hotel room's refuge at the very beginning of Chapter XVII: "He came in at last; but I believe it was mostly the rain that did it" (139). Jim's walk outside thus occurs during the ellipsis between chapters, and points back to an image which Marlow's narration previously has emphasized, only five pages earlier: "But I cannot fix before my eyes the image of [Jim's] safety. I shall always remember him as seen through the open door of my room, taking, perhaps, too much to heart the consequences of his failure" (134). Through the ellipsis between chapters, Marlow's narrative abstains from further description of Jim standing outside the open hotel room door (and dwelling on his failure), at the very edge of the hotel room's refuge. This ellipsis acts as the point at which Jim walks just beyond the limits of the narrative envelope or "shelter" Marlow "makes for himself" (236). Moving outside of this shelter and describing human immersion in the storm becomes a problem for Marlow; the ellipsis in Marlow's narrative is a telling one (no pun intended). Marlow later alludes to being driven outside of this envelope, as he narrates his experience of listening to Jewel's story. However, he points out that he remains outside its refuge only momentarily, for "one *must*" withdraw back into "that shelter each of us makes for himself to creep under [...] as a tortoise withdraws within its shell" (236):

> For a moment I had a view of a world that seemed to wear a vast and dismal aspect of disorder, while, in truth, thanks to our unwearied efforts, it is as sunny an arrangement of small conveniences as the mind of man can conceive. But still—it was only a moment: I went back into my shell directly. One *must*—don't you know? —though I seemed to have lost all my words in the chaos of dark thoughts I had contemplated for a second or two beyond the pale. These came back, too, very soon, for words also belong to the sheltering conception of light and order which is our refuge.
>
> (236)

Mark Wollaeger suggests that "language itself" here "comes to seem, in Marlow's defensively ironic phrase, a false order" (Wollaeger 109). In the wider text of *Lord Jim*, words perhaps more precisely contribute to the "bit of shelter" (136) of a "fragmentary" (260) order, which shakes amid the "galvanic shocks" (45) of atmospheric disturbance. Marlow's "defensively ironic" (Wollaeger 109) allusion to words as "our refuge" points to the shaking of Jim's stammering, which trembles during the breaking-up of the monsoon. Throughout *Lord Jim*, human utterance quivers with the vibration of atmospheric agitation, as in the "electric rattle" (91) of the teeth of the *Patna*'s second engineer, who stutters "g-g-glad" (91) amid the "squall" (91) of the *Patna* incident. Just as weather induces "strain on the bulkhead" (108) of the *Patna*, atmospheric disturbance strains human communication, while the convulsions of the stammer register the agitation of dislocating vibration. After emphasizing his own momentary dislocation from "that shelter each of us makes for himself" (236), Marlow stresses the necessity of stepping back inside, into the fragmentary shelters provided by language and certain schemes of order, and thereby acknowledges the difficulty of maintaining a vantage point outside of their refuge. In the Malabar Hotel monsoon scene, Marlow highlights his and Jim's residence indoors, behind the glass window: "'Perfect deluge,' Jim muttered after a while: he leaned his forehead on the glass" (138). In describing the storm, Marlow must remain behind the glass, within the shelter of his "tortoise shell" (236). He translates the storm's fury and disintegrative force into descriptions of images that he can narrate (and that his human mind can process), through making recourse to "images of collapsing bridges, of uprooted trees, of undermined mountains"—which the "sound of unchecked overwhelming fury" "call[s] to one's mind" (138).

Recently Jeffrey McCarthy has argued that Conrad's depictions of storms "demonstrate the natural world as a parallel and overlapping realm [to the realm of human actors], an active presence with its own ontological priority," which is "beyond human structuring" (110, 39). McCarthy makes use of insight drawn from Quentin Meillassoux's critique of "correlationism"—a critique of the argument "that the things of the world can exist only in relation to human thinking or human language" (McCarthy 37). If the organization of nonhuman forms of atmospheric disturbance is conceived as following a logic derived from anthropocentric models (such as Humboldt's cosmos of general equilibrium), the space of the atmosphere likewise becomes merely the "space of what faces us, of what exists only as a correlate of our own existence" (Meillassoux 7). However, as Conrad's Marlow suggests, an exterior vantage point cannot be maintained, outside of human sheltering conceptions—such a vantage point can be attained for "only a moment," as "one *must*" go back into one's shell "directly" (236). The question therefore remains, as to how *Lord Jim* addresses the particular narrative problem of how to write an ecology of atmospheric disturbances, while working with the sheltered envelope provided by human language, without artificially superimposing anthropocentric schemes of order onto the workings of such disturbances (as Henry Blanford does, in his Humboldtian account of India's meteorology).

This study has shown that the greater text of *Lord Jim* evokes its ecology of nonequilibrium atmospheric dynamics through writing two parallel series of recurrent forms of disturbance—a series of atmospheric circulations (including eddies, whirls and swirls) and a series of vibrational disruptions (including tremors, quivers and shocks). As references to such disturbances continually recur throughout the narrative, the text translates the noise of atmospheric disruption into patterned redundancy. The form of the swirling rotary storm system—as an image of the deflection of noisy air currents into *circular* patterns—provides *Lord Jim* with a means of reflexively representing its own media practice of pattern formation, which writes the noise of atmospheric disturbances into redundant forms (such as the tremor, quiver and shock). Here it is helpful to recall J. Hillis Miller's canonical reading of *Lord Jim*'s repetition: "[...] one word refers the reader to another word which refers him to another and then back to the first word again, in an endless circling" (39). Through the workings of such "endless circling" of repeated references (to tremors, quivers and shocks), atmospheric disturbance is rendered systematic. In other words, the endless circling of *Lord Jim*'s texture of word repetition parallels the swirling systematicity of Conrad's weather systems (such as the cyclonic breaking-up of the monsoon in *Lord Jim*, or the rotary storm of "Typhoon").[22] Moreover, while writing the entanglement of humans in atmospherics of nonequilibrium dynamics, *Lord Jim*'s texture weaves the agitated utterance of individual human voices into its systematic patterning. Using dashes and ellipses, the text typographically inscribes Jim's stuttering and stammering: "'Why! this is what I—you—I...' he stammered" (141). Jim's "jerky agitation" (141) becomes that of "a dry leaf imprisoned in an eddy of wind" (141), as *Lord Jim* more precisely circumscribes Jim's agitated stammer into the endless circling of the narrative's systematic texture. At the same time *Lord Jim* writes the circumscription of humans within the eddying circulation of weather disturbances, the text reflexively composes itself as a "piec[ing] together" (260) of fragmentary bits of a collective utterance of human "stammerings" (171).[23] These "stammerings" tremble in perpetual disequilibrium, but the parallel disequilibria of human stammering and atmospheric disturbance ultimately are not quite commensurate. *Lord Jim* more aptly places the convulsions of human stammering alongside the "jerky spasms" of the perforated "water-pipe" (136), which is part of the faulty hydraulic system that works to engineer a sheltered space for human habitation. Rather than imposing a form of human structuring onto the workings of weather disturbances, *Lord Jim*'s narrative of "all our stammerings" (171) re-implicates human efforts to generate a "precarious refuge" (204) for human habitation, which is embedded within an ecology of atmospheric disturbance.

When the "growl of thunder" (136) increases, the "colossal and headlong stream" of the breaking-up of the monsoon only "seem[s] to" "swirl" (138); the systematic patterning of the text does not quite absorb the streaming fury of the storm into its redundant vocabulary (of recurrent forms of circulation such as whirls, swirls and eddies). The circulation of the storm system parallels the endless circling of *Lord Jim*'s systematic texture, but ultimately remains beyond it—beyond what Marshall McLuhan, seventy years after Conrad's *Lord Jim*, would refer to as the "form of organized stutter" (Yorke) of language.[24] In other words, the weather of the breaking-up of the monsoon retains its ontological priority. Through emphasizing parallel disequilibria, *Lord Jim*'s writing of stammerings and weather disturbances thereby addresses the particular narrative problem of how to depict human imbrication within the workings of nonhuman atmospheric systems, while weaving a narrative texture composed of human language, without impinging upon the ontological priority of nonhuman agencies and processes.

Notes

1 J.E. Tanner's chronology of *Lord Jim* shows that Jim's inquiry occurs during August of some unspecified year (Tanner 371). Jim's conversation with Marlow at the Malabar Hotel therefore takes place during the breaking-up of the "southerly" or southwest monsoon.
2 In the case of the breaking-up of the southwest or southerly monsoon, Dove emphasized that the cause of such cyclonic storms (as in other circular storms) was not a true rotary action, but rather a displacement of air currents, in which the "heavy air of the Trade-wind region" would force its way "laterally into the rarefied air" of the southwest monsoon wind, generating an air flow that would deflect or turn back on itself (275).
3 As the director of the Indian Meteorological Service, Blanford oversaw an extensive compiling of India's meteorological data, which was written into the *Memoirs of the Indian Meteorological Department* (the publication of which continued after Blanford's death, in 1893). An 1897 editorial in *Nature* highlighted the lasting importance of Blanford's research, emphasized its "evident growth of certainty and breadth of view" and concluded that "Mr. Blanford's prediction is being fulfilled even more satisfactorily than he could have anticipated" ("Twenty Years of Indian Meteorology" 226).
4 As Dettelbach points out, "Humboldtian science" refers to multiple strains of Victorian imperial science, including Edward Sabine's British Magnetic Crusade (the mid-nineteenth-century geophysical project dedicated to carrying out a global survey of magnetic variation) (287). For a discussion of the influence of Humboldt's ideas on the work of nineteenth-century British scientists (including Charles Darwin), see Brock.
5 See Brock, and also Wise and Smith. As Norton Wise and Crosbie Smith point out, a "balancing model" of equilibrium (as an "eternal stability of systems ruled by natural law") had provided a means of mediating eighteenth- and early nineteenth-century crosscurrents of thought, between strains of British political economy (of economists such as Thomas Malthus, David Ricardo and Adam Smith) and strains of British natural philosophy (of scientists such as John Herschel and William Whewell) ("Work and Waste (I)" 293–4). By the late nineteenth century (through the work of Charles Babbage on engines, and the work of William Thomson and James Clerk Maxwell on thermodynamics), this balancing model had been displaced in favor of the "cultural mediator" of the steam engine, which emphasized a "temporal dynamics" of "perpetual disequilibrium," in which "disturbance and variation" became "primary phenomena" of the workings of both natural and economic systems ("Work and Waste (II)" 397). However, within strains of mid- to late nineteenth century "Humboldtian" imperial science, such as Blanford's Indian meteorology, a variation of a balancing model persisted, and stressed order, regularity and periodic patterns.
6 On the social influence of thermodynamic thought in late Victorian Britain, see especially Myers, and also Beer. On Conrad's response to thermodynamic thought, see Whitworth, Houen and MacDuffie.

The Monsoon and Lord Jim's *Atmospherics* 141

7 For a thorough summary of contemporary critical literature on this topic, see Peters 199–207. Esty provides perhaps the most compelling recent treatment of this line of inquiry; see also Ross. On Conrad's subversion of the conventions of imperial romance narrative, see esp. Hampson, Dryden and Parry.
8 For further discussion of the relation between "Humboldtian science" and Victorian progress, see Dettelbach, and also Brock. In discussing the influence and popularity of English translations of Humboldt's works in Victorian Britain, Brock emphasizes that Humboldt's writings offered the promise of "unification, order and simplicity" during "a period of growing cultural fragmentation" (372).
9 The "law of storms" was first formulated in 1827, by the German meteorologist Heinrich Dove, and its application to maritime meteorology was further developed by British sailors such as Henry Piddington. As Piddington wrote in his *The Sailor's Horn-Book for the Law of Storms* (1848), the "law of storms" holds that the "wind in hurricanes [...] turns or blows *round* a focus or *centre* in a more or less circular form" (6). For a more extensive discussion, see Kavanagh 1–5.
10 Dove dedicated this text to Admiral Robert FitzRoy, the British sailor and meteorologist who coined the term "weather forecast" (and who also captained the HMS *Beagle* for Charles Darwin's well-known voyage). Moreover, Robert H. Scott's 1862 English translation of Dove's text was partly financed by the Meteorological Department of the British Board of Trade; see Dove x. According to Macnab, the 1862 English translation of Dove's *The Law of Storms* was recommended reading for British merchant marine captains and first mates (Macnab 6).
11 One present-day model of a hurricane analyzes it as a "far-from-equilibrium" system that converts heat (absorbed at the ocean's surface) into the mechanical energy of the circulating hurricane wind (Kondepudi and Prigogine 117). Though nineteenth-century meteorology lacked the mathematical language of nonlinear thermodynamics necessary to model a hurricane in this way, it alluded to a significant problem that would be addressed by later sciences of nonequilibrium dynamics—that of accounting for the non-equilibrium dynamics of physical systems in which equilibrium is only a temporary state.
12 Some material from the preceding two paragraphs previously appeared in Kavanagh. This material has been revisited and modified here, with the permission of the editors of *The Conradian*.
13 As Marzec points out, the British Land Enclosure movement began with the erasure of the term "inhabitant" from the British legal system, in the 1603 legal proceeding of Gateward's Case. Gateward's Case ruled that only a landowner, laborer working for a landowner or tenant (and not a squatter or so-called "inhabitant") could invoke rights of use for an enclosed, privatized tract of land ("Speaking" 435).
14 As Irigaray asks, "Is there a dwelling more vast, more spacious, or even more generally peaceful than that of air?"; Irigaray especially faults Martin Heidegger's well-known essay "Building, Dwelling, Thinking" for its "forgetting of air" (2). However, as Steven Connor points out, Irigaray herself perhaps "forgets too much of the air," for "in seeing the air only as abundance," Irigaray "radically and risibly omits the materiality of air" ("Modernism in Midair"). Connor emphasizes that certain strains of literary modernism (including the work of Conrad) "stay in touch with a palpable air," and thereby resist such forgetting of the atmospheric dimension of human habitation, within the materiality and finitude of air ("Modernism in Midair").

15 For a discussion of the snow and weather of *Under Western Eyes*, see McCarthy 77–113.
16 It is important to note that the rotary storm of "Typhoon" is not chaos, but rather follows higher level patterns of order that are beyond MacWhirr's comprehension, and which cannot quite be grasped using abstract geometrical models. See Kavanagh 1–17.
17 For Napolin, Conrad's writing of vibration "locates the hidden, connective fibres of physical space," registers a "material continuity between trembling and quivering bodies," and thereby works through the "explicit problem" of transforming the "literary work of art" into "a materialist basis" of "solidarity among men" (69, 59). As Napolin recognizes, this "material continuity between trembling and quivering bodies" also exists between human bodies and nonhuman bodies, which vibrate, tremor, tremble and quiver (65).
18 A number of critical accounts have addressed the proliferation of jumps in *Lord Jim*. For example, see Miller 22–41 or Coroneos 130–54.
19 For further discussion, see Kavanagh 6–14.
20 For an account of the inadequacy of Victorian imperial measures for dealing with India's famines, see Mukherjee 29–60. For a discussion of Victorian studies of the correlations between India's famines and meteorological disturbances, see Anderson 235–84.
21 For example, see the texts of Halley and Dove, which are quoted in this essay's introduction.
22 For a more extensive account of similar dynamics and textual patterning in Conrad's "Typhoon," see Kavanagh 6–8.
23 *Lord Jim*'s gathering together of a composite narrative of human "stammerings" is of course a partial one, which the Marlovian narrative assembles from the words of a finite group of narrators. Moreover, one might object that the omniscient frame narrative of the first few chapters (and which returns in Chapter XXXVI, to depict the scene of the "privileged man" [254] receiving Marlow's letter) presents a problem for the interpretation of *Lord Jim* as a narrative composite of human stammerings. However, in response, one should note that the frame narrative of Chapter XXXVI alludes to the "confused and unceasing mutter" (254), which "ascend[s]" from the "depths of the town" underneath the "privileged" man's "highest flat of a lofty building" (254). Even when the narrative temporarily invokes the vantage point of an omniscient frame narrator, the narrative does not wholly mute the collective stammering of human utterance. This "confused and unceasing mutter" recalls both Marlow's reference to "our hurried mutters" (239) and Marlow's "confused" stammer in response to Jim's narrative: "'It must be awfully hard,' I stammered, confused by this display of speechless feeling" (64). The stammer, stutter and mutter are closely connected in the narrative, as in Jim's utterance during the breaking-up of the monsoon: "'I want—I want tobacco,' [Jim] muttered" (136).
24 With his suggestion that the sum total of human utterance constitutes a form of collective speech impediment, Conrad's Marlow anticipates media and communication theorist Marshall McLuhan's statement (in a 1970 interview with John Lennon) that "language is a form of organized stutter." See Yorke.

Works Cited

Anderson, Katharine. *Predicting the Weather: Victorians and the Science of Meteorology*. U of Chicago P, 2005.

Archibald, Douglas. "Indian Meteorology." *Nature*, vol. 23, Aug. 1883, pp. 405–407.
Beer, Gillian. *Open Fields: Science in Cultural Encounter*. Oxford UP, 1996.
Blanford, Henry Francis. *The Indian Meteorologist's Vade-Mecum*. Thacker, Spink and Co., 1877.
Brock, W.H. "Humboldt and the British: A Note on the Character of British Science." *Annals of Science*, vol. 50, no. 4, 1993, pp. 365–372.
Connor, Steven. *The Book of Skin*. Cornell UP, 2004.
———. "Modernism in Midair." *stevenconnor.com*. 25 Sep. 2003. Web. 30 Mar. 2017. <www.stevenconnor.com/midair>.
———. "The Shakes: Conditions of Tremor." *Senses and Society*, vol. 3, no. 2, 2008, pp. 205–220.
Conrad, Joseph. *The Collected Letters of Joseph Conrad*. Edited by Frederick R. Karl and Laurence Davies. Vol. 2, Cambridge UP, 1986.
———. *Heart of Darkness*. Edited by Owen Knowles. Cambridge UP, 2012.
———. *Lord Jim*. Edited by J.H. Stape and Ernest W. Sullivan. Cambridge UP, 2008. Print.
———. *The Mirror of the Sea*. Doubleday, Page & Company, 1928.
———. *The Nigger of the "Narcissus."* Doubleday, Page & Company, 1924.
———. *Typhoon*. Doubleday, Page & Company, 1925.
Coroneos, Con. *Conrad, Space, and Modernity*. Oxford UP, 2002.
Deleuze, Gilles. *Essays Critical and Clinical*. Translated by Daniel W. Smith and Michael A. Greco. Verso, 1998.
Dettelbach, Michael. "Humboldtian Science." *Cultures of Natural History*. Edited by Nicholas Jardine, J.A. Secord, and E.C. Spary. Cambridge UP, 1996. 287–304.
Dove, Heinrich. *The Law of Storms Considered in Connection with the Ordinary Movements of the Atmosphere*. 2nd Ed. Translated by Robert H. Scott. Longman, 1862.
Dryden, Linda. *Joseph Conrad and the Imperial Romance*. Macmillan, 2000.
Esty, Jed. *Unseasonable Youth: Modernism, Colonialism, and the Fiction of Development*. Oxford UP, 2012.
Halley, Edmund. "An Historical Account of the Trade Winds, and Monsoons, Observable in the Seas between and Near the Tropics, with an Attempt to Assign to the Physical Cause of the Said Winds." *Philosophical Transactions of the Royal Society of London*, vol. 16, no. 1686, pp. 153–168.
Hampson, Robert. *Cross-Cultural Encounters in Joseph Conrad's Malay Fiction*. Palgrave Macmillan, 2000.
Headrick, Daniel R. *The Tentacles of Progress: Technology Transfer in the Age of Imperialism, 1850–1940*. Oxford UP, 1988.
Heidegger, Martin. "Building Dwelling Thinking." *Poetry, Language, Thought*. Translated by Albert Hofstadter. Harper and Row, 1971. 141–160.
Home, R.W. "Humboldtian Science Revisited: An Australian Case Study." *History of Science*, vol. 33, 1995, pp. 1–22.
Houen, Alex. *Terrorism in Modern Literature, from Joseph Conrad to Ciaran Carson*. Oxford UP, 2002.
Humboldt, Alexander von. *Cosmos: A Sketch of a Physical Description of the Universe*. Vol. 1. Translated by E.C. Otté. Henry G. Bohn, 1849.

———. *Cosmos: A Sketch of a Physical Description of the Universe*. Vol. 1. Translated by E.C. Otté. Henry G. Bohn, 1864.

———. *Essay on the Geography of Plants*. Edited by Stephen T. Jackson. Translated by Sylvie Romanowski. U of Chicago P, 2009.

Hunter, W.W. "The Bengal Famine." *The Times*, 17 Mar. 1874, 10. Print.

Irigaray, Luce. *The Forgetting of Air in Martin Heidegger*. Translated by Mary Beth Mader. Athlone, 1999.

Kavanagh, Brendan. "'Dirty weather': *Typhoon*'s Meteorology and MacWhirr's Point of View." *The Conradian*, vol. 41, no. 1, 2016, pp. 1–19.

Kondepudi, Dilip and Ilya Prigogine. *Modern Thermodynamics: From Heat Engines to Dissipative Structures*. Wiley, 2015.

Latour, Bruno. "'It's Development, Stupid!' or: How to Modernize Modernization." 2011. Web. 30 Mar. 2017. <www.bruno-latour.fr/sites/default/files/107-NORDHAUS&SHELLENBERGER.pdf>.

Lawtoo, Nidesh. "Conrad in the Anthropocene: Steps to an Ecology of Catastrophe." *Conrad and Nature: A Collection of Essays*. Edited by Lissa Schneider-Rebozo, Jeffrey Mathes McCarthy, and John G. Peters. Routledge, 2018.

MacDuffie, Allan. "Joseph Conrad's Geographies of Energy." *ELH*, vol. 76, no. 1, 2009, pp. 75–98.

Macnab, John. *Catechism of the Law of Storms for the Use of Sea Officers*. George Philip and Son, 1884.

Marzec, Robert. *An Ecological and Postcolonial Study of Literature: From Daniel Defoe to Salman Rushdie*. Palgrave Macmillan, 2007.

———. "Speaking before the Environment: Modern Fiction and the Ecological." *Modern Fiction Studies*, vol. 55, no. 3, pp. 419–442.

McCarthy, Jeffrey Mathes. *Green Modernism: Nature and the English Novel, 1900 to 1930*. Palgrave Macmillan, 2015.

Meillassoux, Quentin. *After Finitude: An Essay on the Necessity of Contingency*. Continuum, 2008.

Miller, J. Hillis. *Fiction and Repetition*. Basil Blackwell, 1985.

Mukherjee, Upamanyu Pablo. *Natural Disasters and Victorian Empire: Famines, Fevers and the Literary Cultures of South Asia*. Palgrave MacMillan, 2013.

Myers, Greg. "Nineteenth-Century Popularizations of Thermodynamics and the Rhetoric of Social Prophecy." *Victorian Studies*, vol. 29, no. 1, 1985, pp. 35–66.

Napolin, Julie Beth. "'A Sinister Resonance': Vibration, Sound, and the Birth of Conrad's Marlow." *Vibratory Modernism*. Edited by Anthony Enns and Shelley Trower. Palgrave Macmillan, 2013. 53–79.

Parry, Benita. *Conrad and Imperialism: Ideological Boundaries and Visionary Frontiers*. Macmillan, 1983.

Peters, John G. *Joseph Conrad's Critical Reception*. Cambridge UP, 2013.

Piddington, Henry. *The Sailor's Horn-book for the Law of Storms*. Williams and Norgate, 1848.

Prigogine, Ilya and Isabelle Stengers. *The End of Certainty*. The Free Press, 1996.

Ross, Stephen. *Conrad and Empire*. U of Missouri P, 2004.

Sloterdijk, Peter. "The Anthropocene: A Process-State at the Edge of Geohistory." Translated by Anna-Sophie Springer. *Art in the Anthropocene*. Edited by Heather Davis and Etienne Turpin. Open Humanities Press, 2014. 327–340.

———. *Foams: Plural Spherology*. Translated by Wieland Hoban. Semiotext(e), 2016.

———. *In the World Interior of Capital: For a Philosophical Theory of Globalization*. Translated by Wieland Hoban. Polity, 2013.

Tanner, J.E. "The Chronology and Enigmatic End of *Lord Jim*." *Nineteenth Century Fiction*, vol. 21, no. 4, 1967, pp. 369–380.

Trower, Shelley. *Senses of Vibration*. Continuum, 2012.

———. "Twenty Years of Indian Meteorology." *Nature*, vol. 8, July 1897, pp. 226–228.

Whitworth, Michael. *Einstein's Wake: Relativity, Metaphor, and Modernist Literature*. Oxford UP, 2001.

Wise, M. Norton and Crosbie Smith. "Work and Waste: Political Economy and Natural Philosophy in Nineteenth Century Britain (I)." *History of Science*, vol. 27, no. 3, 1989, pp. 263–300.

———. "Work and Waste: Political Economy and Natural Philosophy in Nineteenth Century Britain (II)." *History of Science*, vol. 27, no. 4, 1989, pp. 391–448.

———. "Work and Waste: Political Economy and Natural Philosophy in Nineteenth Century Britain (III)." *History of Science*, vol. 28, no. 3, 1990, pp. 221–261.

Wollaeger, Mark. *Joseph Conrad and the Fictions of Skepticism*. Stanford UP, 1990.

Yorke, Ritchie. "John Lennon Talks with Marshall McLuhan." 28 June 1970. *Life of the Beatles*. 20 Aug. 2009. Web. 30 Mar. 2017. <http://lifeofthebeatles.blogspot.co.uk/2009/08/john-lennon-talks-with-marshall-mcluhan.html>.

7 Conrad's Ecological Performativity
The Scenography of "Nature" from *An Outcast of the Islands* to *Lord Jim*

Mark Deggan

> There is a vastness, a solemnity, a gloom, a sense of solitude and of human insignificance which for a time overwhelm him; and it is only when the novelty of these feelings have passed away that he is able to turn his attention to the separate constituents that combine to produce these emotions, and examine the varied and beautiful forms of life which, in inexhaustible profusion, are spread around him.
> Alfred Wallace. "Equatorial Vegetation,"
> *Tropical Nature & Other Essays* (1878)

> It is impossible to meditate on time and the mystery of the creative passage of nature without an overwhelming emotion at the limitations of human intelligence.
> Alfred North Whitehead. *The Concept of Nature* (1920)

> We live in the midst of man-made objects, among tools, in houses, streets, cities, and most of the time we see them only through the human actions which put them to use. We become used to thinking that all of this exists necessarily and unshakably. Cézanne's painting suspends these habits of thought and reveals the base of inhuman nature upon which man has installed himself. This is why Cézanne's people are strange, as if viewed by a creature of another species. Nature itself is stripped of the attributes which make it ready for animistic communions [...] It is an unfamiliar world in which one is uncomfortable and which forbids all human effusiveness.
> Maurice Merleau-Ponty. "Cézanne's Doubt" (1945)

Many of Joseph Conrad's fictions are built upon his textual exploitation of literary and environmental atmospherics. The early Malay texts are particularly evocative in their representations of natural environments. In these formative works nature is overwhelming—omnipresent, louche, mockingly sublime. Moreover, the coastal and riverine landscapes in which Conrad's characters appear are often as thematically productive in their ambient aspects as the fevered impressions of his protagonists. Such environments may be aloof to the concerns of individual characters, yet they share important connective features with human interiority. At key junctures, nature is seen to act back, not simply as the expected phenomena of a tropical ecosystem, but as a locus of psychosomatic engagements and interactions at work not only under the skin or in consciousness, but as a central dynamic of Conrad's literary art. More pointedly, recognizing what I would term the theatrical performativity of such scenes allows us to read his engagements with natural phenomena not only as extended tropes of contested being, but as symbiotic interleavings of mind and world.

Given their focus on immediate sensory impressions, Conrad's Malay texts can also seem overwritten.[1] Conrad appears complicit with his helplessness to reign in the hothouse aspects of his prose. Writing nearly a quarter century after the composition of his second novel, *An Outcast of the Islands*, he allows that "[i]t is certainly the most tropical of my eastern tales. The mere scenery got a great hold on me as I went on, perhaps because (I may just as well confess that) the story itself was never very near my heart" (xi). Conrad's eponymous "outcast" has not this luxury of separating the wilderness scenery of his exile from matters of the heart. Rather, the novel's environment sets upon him as "the passing, warm touch of an immense breath coming from beyond the forest, like the short panting of an oppressed world" (282). As we shall see, Conrad imagines his absconding commercial trader being overwhelmed by the chiaroscuro atmospherics and misty occlusions of this tropical setting, hence the shared phenomenal realm Conrad constructs in order to depict Peter Willems's absorption into the wilderness at the level of embodied consciousness.

A yet bolder claim can be made concerning the performative aspects of Conrad's fictional engagements with an Eastern locale. In this reading, the natural scene depicted in Conrad's early fiction is neither backdrop nor symbol, nor even the otherwise indifferent locus of a protagonist's interior conflicts; rather, the "scene" of interaction between the self and his or her surroundings produces the drama. As Conrad comes close to conceding, the tropical scenery is the story in the sense that the ambient dynamics given of nature are no less crucial to the forward motion of *Outcast*'s narrative than its human element. Conrad's wilderness poetics might be designed to situate the reader in the midst of his scenarios, but his treatment of nature simultaneously enacts, figuratively and phenomenally, the profound interactions connecting embodied consciousness with a particular environment.

I have used the term, the "natural scene." This notion is itself performative, intending not just the place wherein events occur, but the interactive medium of that presentation. As with Jim's shameful leap into the Arabian Sea in *Lord Jim*, the state of nature into which Willems is inserted in *Outcast* has both concrete and poetic fallouts. The sea or jungle might continue to stand for existential erasure in a symbolic or allegorical manner, but such settings have a more provocatively productive status as arenas wherein the symbiosis of embodied consciousness and nature is textually actualized. Since the flux of nature underscores each protagonist's disillusioning confrontation with a reality that is as bereft of human comfort as it is existentially threatening, we should not be surprised, then, that the author's 1919 note to *Outcast* should evoke the drama of that text via a theatrical conceit, or that this process is largely filtered through the depiction of a powerfully ambient natural scenery.[2] While critical works on the early fiction have yet to remark the means by which the "scenic" mode of presentation has become a central artistic device, commentators have certainly noted Conrad's atmospheric productivity. Thus we find Ian Watt calling attention to the famous 1897 "Preface" to *The Nigger of the 'Narcissus'* wherein, as Watt writes, the "sincere mood" referred to by Conrad "is presumably the condition of the temperament when it is most deeply responsive to 'the moral, the emotional atmosphere of the place and time'" (84).[3] Jakob Lothe makes a similar observation on *Lord Jim*, describing the "distinctly lyrical quality" of Conrad's "descriptive interludes" as deriving from the "subtly contrived evocation of atmosphere" (141, 148).

To such commentaries I would add that in reifying the human response to the phenomena of the natural scene, Conrad underwrites the symbiosis of the human and the ecological as a zone of tensions linking their material and transcendent possibilities—a dynamic which I see extending from *Outcast* to *Lord Jim*, and then on through *The Shadow-Line* to its late flourishing in *The Rescue*. Indeed, Conrad's poetics of interaction is also extended to inanimate things, as where Jim's fears come to be reified through the flaking metal of the *Patna*'s rusted bulkhead in *Lord Jim*, wherein "[t]he thing stirred and jumped off like something alive while I was looking at it" (68). As here, Conrad's ambient scenes teach us to recognize the degree to which that author and his human creations do not just respond to nature's atmospherics in the midst of each respective narrative situation, but *think* it through what the aesthetic philosopher, Martin Seel, has come to call the "synaesthetic play of appearances." In describing the processes wherein place-specific phenomena partake in our being, Seel sets out the "sensuous-emotional awareness of existential correspondences" (93), as when we are "surrounded by the atmosphere of a room and sense it even if we do not know anything about it" (92). Conrad appears sensitive to this sort of dynamic. Writing of the presence of Jim's consort, Jewel, as a particular kind of ambience, Conrad goes on to note how human affects create correspondences in place through the shared performativity of atmosphere and mood:

> Her vigilant affection had an intensity that made it almost perceptible to the senses; it seemed actually to exist in the ambient matter

of space, to envelop him like a peculiar fragrance, to dwell in the sunshine like a tremulous, subdued, and impassioned note.

(*LJ* 213)

In essence, where fictional consciousness finds itself integrated with its surroundings, the natural environment ceases to provide a mere backdrop or symbolic screen to the narration but offers a frame of engagement in which places and the human begin to aesthetically and ecologically co-perform. To borrow a line from Derek Gregory, just as the performative "produces the effects that it names" (18; original emphasis), so "nature"—like consciousness—infers the scene of poiesis by which nature "produces" its own being along with the effects which constitute it. As Gregory states, "performance here as elsewhere resides in the spacing between what happens and what does not happen, between what is seen and what is not seen" (140).[4] This last point of Gregory's may be underlined via another Conradian story. Completed almost exactly a year after *Outcast*, "The Lagoon" (1896) demonstrates the process wherein human affects change the reception of natural phenomena. There, a character is sufficiently agitated such that "[i]n that fleeting and powerful disturbance of his being the earth enfolded in the starlight peace became [an] unquiet and mysterious country of inextinguishable desires and fears" (*TU* 193–4). It is in this basic sense that we find human presences altering the environment in a proactive manner. Yet if it is one thing to note how "Arsat's voice vibrated loudly in the profound peace" (201), it is another to discover natural phenomena channeled toward human affects as where a "breath of warm air touched the two men's faces and passed on with a mournful sound [...] like an uneasy sigh of the dreaming earth" (199). Such atmospherics do not imply a negotiatory third space of interactions, but the involvement of places with embodied consciousness. More broadly, these observations jibe with the outlook of the environmental philosopher, Simon James, for whom the presence of nature is not some sort of between phenomenon linking the human and the numinous (that which Conrad's "dreaming earth" dreams); rather,

> Nature is [...] not something that we perceive; it is at work in our perception. It is not something we can capture in understanding, but something into which we are always already, and for the most part unknowingly, taken up.
>
> (155)

Still, coming to grips with the representation of nature in the early fiction can seem as slippery a task as trying to tie down Conrad's conceptions of "reality." Despite his attention to the minutiae of the archipelago's natural scene, Conrad will sometimes approximate a more mind-centered outlook. At such moments he appears congruent with the idealism later voiced by the pioneering sociologist Karl Mannheim, whereby "the world as 'world' exists only with reference to the knowing mind", from which "the mental activity of the subject determines the form in which it appears" (58–9). Indeed, where notions of world are concerned, Conrad tends to align his usages with the social rather than the "natural" realm, a distinction that the Malay fictions often seem to press against.[5] With *Outcast*, however, the novel's Dutch antihero drifts back and forth between exalted surety "in his genius and in his knowledge of the world" (6) and submersion in his tropical environment, a wavering made critical with his exile to an abandoned wilderness village wherein "[t]he world seemed to end there. The forests of the other bank appeared unattainable, enigmatical, for ever beyond reach like the stars of heaven—and as indifferent" (329). Moreover, in order to guard against the dangers of solipsism at the edge of his "world," Willems must struggle to stave off "the elusive, the distorted and menacing shadows of existence" (320). Here Conrad appears to stand with the naturalist, Alfred Wallace, who, in his own travels in the archipelago, battles against an isolating environment of "solemnity" and "gloom." All the same, unlike so many of Conrad's protagonists, Wallace is at last able to direct one's "attention" to the discrete phenomena "that combine to produce" that affective response—thus expanding the notion of "world" into the natural realm (67–8). Wallace's wording is exact, for we too are to turn our "attention" to the "inexhaustible" dynamics of the production of affective states through the same "great dark place" wherein Conrad's outcast finds only "lofty indifference" and "merciless and mysterious purpose" (O 337). This is not to say that Conrad's idea of "nature" is itself singular or inimical to the human: in the "solitary exile of the forests" in *Outcast*, even birds are "strangled in the dense mass of unstirring leaves" (154). The scene of nature may be indicative of an uncaring universe, but it does not necessarily conspire. As Conrad observes in his retroactive author's note to the novel, nature might simply be there as an "immensity [...] ready to swallow up anything," yet his aesthetic practices argue for a more sophisticated acknowledgment of the "inexhaustible profusion" of the human encounter with nature (xii). At this early stage, then, several factors suggest themselves concerning the affective status of Conrad's depictions of environments: They produce responses in the human, and, as shown below, the environment is thereby altered both at the concrete phenomenal level and, now with regard to representation, in relation to the figurative potential of their author's aesthetic strategies. First, however, we need to pause over Conrad's outlook on nature with regard to the world as a whole.

Paul Armstrong reminds us that there are important interpretative fallouts to Conrad's representations of nature. In *The Challenge of Bewilderment: Understanding and Representation in James, Conrad, and Ford*, Armstrong notes that his target writers do not evince a

Wordsworthian "primordial unity of humanity and nature." Instead, their fictions suggest that the "world's preestablished harmony" is itself a fiction wherein "bewilderment typically undermines a character's assumption that his or her mind is at one with the external world" (3). Accordingly, it is because we are not united with nature that a text such as *Lord Jim* "defies the expectation that coherence is the natural state of things" (122). By extension, and "as with many of Conrad's landscapes, the immanent presence of the natural world seems to point to forces and meaning beyond it" (137)—from which assertion we are free to conclude that the natural universe is finally both separate from, and unconcerned with, human concerns. Indeed, just as the imagination is forced to intervene in Kant's analysis of the sublime, Armstrong goes on to observe that it is at the moment of cognitive blockage that the "chain of figures" of our symbol-making faculty steps in with its "realms of ghosts, echoes, and shadows," or, as is often argued, the affective fallacy as applied to a wilderness setting (ibid.). A second of Armstrong's observations underscores this last point, for where another of Conrad's texts, *Nostromo*, "introduces nature as the mute, indifferent background to the doings of man" (157), we are thereby forced to conceive and structure human society around "the separation of nature and culture" (156). Similarly, it follows that such divisions are presumably negotiated via our propensity to "invent myths, metaphors, or personifications [...] that divide and structure linguistically what cannot be more effectively controlled" (157). In essence, Armstrong deftly articulates what has become a received view of Conrad's depictions of nature: because the natural Malay realm is both endlessly contingent and unswayed by human concerns, integration is dangerous or impossible, hence Conrad's overwhelming tendency to treat nature symbolically while deferring to the necessary fellowship of those individuals capable of navigating its pitfalls.

Before the chapter moves toward a more obviously theatricalized understanding of Conrad's articulations of the land and seascapes of the archipelago—what they give rise to as affectively and thematically charged poetic structures—I need to deepen another of Armstrong's points, this to the effect that not only do the authors he investigates "lay bare the epistemological preconditions that make representation possible, but as 'literary impressionists' they take the novel beyond 'representation' by pursuing its epistemological principles so radically that *they make them thematic*" (16, my emphasis). Notwithstanding the worrisome claim of an impossible to substantiate "beyond" or excess to representation that is not somehow encoded into the form and content of literary works, the idea that Conrad's foregrounding of the flux of nature communicates thematic substance gains much in Armstrong's wording. The suggestion here is that natural processes are akin to poetic forms, and that the latter's communicative apparatus, impressionistic as this may be, remains both atmospherically and thematically active.

But we can go further, too, for where the scene of nature, including its human subjects, produces meanings from its ambient qualities, then we can begin to draw lines between Conrad's art of the scene and more obviously theatrical understanding of the performative. At this point, however, it is enough to recognize how the term "atmospheric" intends the collusion of that word's dual denotations, the actual airy realm in which life proceeds, and the not entirely human mood or tone pervading such locales. As Seel's translator rather archaically sets out, "[a]t the centre of this awareness is the perceptive sensing of how something in this situation – or of how this situation – corresponds or could correspond (positively or negatively) with my weal and woe" (94). Regardless of whatever supposed reality one infers of the performative nexus I have been describing, attention to the ambient effects of particular places corresponds, in a transformative way, with the human interiorities of fictional characters. In short, and as we are about to see, Conrad's poetics and his fictional places jointly constitute a new realm of ecological symbiosis.

It is no great leap to observe how Conrad's no less atmospheric (or impressionistic) prose maps out its own performative actualities. If, in *Outcast*, proximity to the natural scene provides a portal from which one might stare "through and past the illusion of the material world" (291), even that most forward looking character, Lingard, aligns his outlook with the belief that beyond the "last acquaintance" of our social realm "there lies only a vast chaos" (198). Significantly, this abyssal construct finds itself accommodated to the natural realm where one looks (not necessarily with wisdom or understanding) "at the misty valleys, at the distant peaks, at cliffs and morasses, at the dark forests and the hazy plains where other human beings grope their days painfully away" (197). In fact, we know that the phenomenal and numinous aspects of "nature" are conflated in Conrad's cosmology because, at the existential crisis of the novel, Willems confronts the gleaming abyss of his moral failings in the "the ghostly and impalpable sea" of misted treetops, an occluded foreground having both the "appearance of a fantastic and unattainable shore" and the actual substance of a tropical forest emerging from the mist (339). Describing a moment of existential dissolution ("I am a lost man" 340), this particular passage is doubly suggestive in the sense that the colluded world it intends simultaneously maps the figurative victory of darkness over the soul, and the ecological and atmospheric actuality of the natural setting underwriting that dissolution. Indeed, the moment centers upon the simultaneous transaction by which the figurative wealth of Conrad's discourse is united with the ecological phenomena subtending it: here is not the tenor and vehicle of a literary trope involving a tropical surroundings, but an atmospheric co-occasioning.

Second, as with the play of the worlds of illusion and geographic actuality, Conrad's joint enactment of places and interior states of being can be read as a theatrical one, a process of shifting sceneries and orders of reality waiting in the wings—of nature made simultaneously material and "impalpable" through the ambience features of their textual presentation. To this extent, Conrad's conception of nature in the early fiction is more performative than hitherto understood. By analyzing his articulations of the wilderness scene through a theatrical lens, the "scenographic" nature of Conrad's aesthetic practices (his atmospheric art of the scene) allows us to see that author as a modern pioneer of ecological interiority. Moreover, reading Conrad in this vein suggests a way to posit an environmental hermeneutics by which the themes and modernity of his works may be more fully mapped as attempts to animate the natural scene within consciousness. To restate this last point in a larger frame, the representation of the Malay settings in the early fiction provides that scenic point of perspective onto the *Nederlands-Indië* wilderness as a space of encounter between various key thematic tensions in his oeuvre. So, too, given Conrad's awareness of how nature and the human appear, by turns, integrated or separate, the theatrical tone of my analysis infers the play of perspectives by which social or cultural realities may be conceived in their true artifice, hence the natural setting produces the means by which the social realms of his characters may be viewed in relief.[6]

Before seeing how Conrad's fictional discourses bear out the above observations, it might be helpful to collect the chapter's theoretical basis into a more direct statement. The move toward a performative reading of nature in the Malay fiction requires three key terms: "*performative space*", focusing on the interplay between selves and their environments; "scenography" or the art of orchestrating the qualities of the performance arena, dynamic or otherwise; and "literary atmosphere," the shared ambient qualities or phenomena of inferred places and fictional selves.[7] More foundationally, while there will not be enough space to reflect fully upon the mature case of *Lord Jim*, that text will be cited not only because Peter Willems is the prototype of Jim (as he is of Kurtz from "Heart of Darkness"), but because *Lord Jim* remains a fundamental exemplar of the veiling and unveiling of nature in Conrad's works. The play of representational modes in that later novel is of course more developed than that of *Outcast*, but the earlier work has the advantage of showing us Conrad in the midst of working out how to dramatize the blending of tropes of nature with metaphysical categories. For this reason, *An Outcast of the Islands* is the key transitional text by which Conrad's Malay oeuvre emerges around a performative collusion of nature and aesthetics. Further, that work suggests a new way of reading Conrad not just as an observer of the collision of East and West at an imperial fringe, or the cultural effacements of modernity before oceanic nature, but of the helplessly immersive quality of human interactions within a natural surrounding. The present chapter's scenographic apparatus thus offers a powerful means of comprehending the representations of nature produced by an author whose immersive poetics are not merely the imaginings of one alert to the exterior realm of his character's involvements within a particular wilderness environment, but an aesthetic mediation of the phenomenal performativity and thematic excess of those engagements.

There is, of course, a developing discourse of performativity at work at the nexus of theatre and literary studies which helps us to link the consciousness of Conrad's characters on the page to the effusions of nature. As the narratologist, Ute Berns, tells us, the term *performativity* is not only theatrically directed, but sets out a zone of tensions between "the concept of the speech act [and] the concept of performance," that is to say, between language and the transitive dynamics of phenomena (§35).[8] While this chapter will not employ narratological formulae, Berns's vocabulary is evocative when set against the performativity of natural spaces—the "scene" of nature—and especially where it speaks to the levels of "immediacy" or "force" produced via the narrative representation of space (respectively, §3, §23). Preeminently, narrative tensions "introduce a relation of partial congruity between live performances and evocations of the illusion of performativity in purely verbal narrative" (§8). Citing the fictions of Henry James, Berns describes narratives as giving "explicit priority to modes of immediacy [...] in order to achieve empathy," the very process through which James's works create "a 'scenic' impression of life" (§23).[9] Moreover, performativity results wherever "narrative discourse as a whole is treated as a speech act," including, presumably, what Berns describes as the "textual illusion of scenic presentation" (ibid.). Although Berns does not find room to unpack these statements in detail, her speculations on performativity do suggest a "scenic" framework by which the dynamism of Conrad's representations of the Malay habitat might be analyzed, and, by extension, a route by which to explore the tensions his scenarios exploit between "actors" and natural environments. Take, for example, Conrad's theatricalized dramatization of Willems's fear of death. Figuratively transferred onto his surroundings, the energy of that character's dread is read back as an atmospheric fact of the forest scene in a more interactively ambient manner than might be captured, say, via a more traditional projection of human affects onto the surrounding scene:

> He saw it so close that he was always on the point of throwing out his arms to keep it off. It poisoned all he saw, all he did; the miserable food he ate, the muddy water he drank; it gave a frightful aspect to sunrises and sunsets, to the brightness of hot noon, to the cooling shadows of the evenings. He saw the horrible form among the big trees, in the network of creepers in the fantastic outlines of leaves.
> (331)

The idea that texts bridge the human and the natural worlds is of course central to ecocritical perspectives. Lawrence Buell, for instance, sees the "interior" aspects of environmental representation as crucial to discussions concerning the nexus of environments and consciousness. Defending ecocriticism from those too quick to rope the production of fictional landscapes into other discursive realms (as Armstrong intimates above), Buell "focuses on the recuperation of natural objects and the relation between inner and outer landscapes as *primary* projects" (88, emphasis added). Where Buell goes on to sum up such recuperation via what he calls a "thick description of the external world" (90), Conrad's representations of nature do not always provide readers with phenomenal purchase but are as often aligned with tropes of incommensurability. While Buell's wording foregrounds the aesthetic over the natural, we should not be kept from simultaneously allowing that the "contours of human subjectivity" are no less "molded by the configurations of the landscapes" (92), let alone the mist in which, to quote one of *Lord Jim*'s grander pronouncements, Conrad's protagonist "moved and had his being" (100). More directly, the atmospherics of the interactions between selves and settings are themselves "thick" enough to become the dynamic objects of enquiry.

Something of Buell's relational "project" can be discerned in that longer passage from *Outcast* alluded to above, in which Willems, exiled to Sambir, reaches the nadir of his existential crisis. At the critical point of Willems's self-questionings, we see the nexus of environment and interior reflection in a profoundly negative way, not least where Willems's supporting illusions are seen dissolving into the spectral atmospherics of a dawn in which his previous sensibility gives way to a less welcoming comprehension of reality. Further, the moment of dissolution is both a meteorological effect and the product of his mental and emotional exhaustion, one in which the "light" of day quite literally illuminates Willems's moment of personal dissolution through the ghostly ambience of a misted sea of trees:

> He was exhausted, done up; fancied himself hardly alive. He had a disgusted horror of himself that, as he looked at the level sea of mist at his feet, faded quickly into dull indifference. It was like a sudden and final decrepitude of his senses, of his body, of his thoughts. Standing on the high platform, he looked over the expanse of low night fog above which, here and there, stood out the feathery heads of tall bamboo clumps and the round tops of single trees, resembling small islets emerging black and solid from a ghostly and impalpable sea. Upon the luminous background of the eastern sky, the sombre line of the great forests bounded that smooth sea of white vapours with an appearance of a fantastic and unattainable shore.
>
> (339–40)

That Willems immediately declares his sense of personal annihilation before walking "down into the mist that closed above him in shining undulations" atmospherically underwrites the collapsing of his state of mind into the effusions of a natural setting. The end of this climatic chapter of *Outcast* may not be restorative in personal terms, but it does point to Buell's "recuperation" of natural processes—here transposed onto a misted riverine landscape—and the ambient play of interiority and environment through which Conrad stages Willems's crisis (op. cit. 92). More overtly, nature is not just both phenomenal "and" a figure for Willems's existential difficulties but performs an instance of rupture in which both realms collapse into a literally atmospheric juncture through which, to recall Berns's phrasing, appearances and actualities are united within "a 'scenic' impression of life" (op. cit. §23). Indeed, we are not far here from Buell's point of departure in *The Environmental Imagination*, where he quotes Barry Lopez's thoughts on "interior" landscape as "a kind of projection within a person of a part of the exterior landscape" (3).[10] Buell declares himself finally skeptical of this sort of shuttling between interior and exterior landscapes, calling their interplay "mystical" (103), yet such is the collusion I see Conrad animating via his poetics of place. By noting the atmospherics linking subjects and environments, what Buell calls the "thick description of the external world" becomes internalized in Conrad's texts such that Willems's isolation within nature is figuratively performed via the actual conditions through which he moves. In Conrad's handling, embodied consciousness is now, itself, phenomenal—or as Marlow says of Jim at sea, "*in touch* with immensity" (LJ 132, emphasis added).[11]

More broadly, we might claim that nature's meteorological and performative force rehearses the *event* of "reality" in Conrad. Event is a provocative word in this sense; yet as the philosopher Alfred North Whitehead would write in *The Concept of Nature* (1920), "the immediate fact for awareness is the whole occurrence of nature. It is nature as an *event* present for sense-awareness, and *essentially passing*. There is no holding nature still and looking at it" (14–15, emphasis added). Whitehead brings nature's endlessly dynamic aspect into focus not as an object of human attention, but as an experiential continuum that is akin to an event but cannot be adequately bookended into discreet human occasions: "The passage of nature which is only another name for the creative force of existence has no narrow ledge of definite instantaneous present within which to operate" (73). But such a passage would appear to be Willems's experience. For him, natural processes might be akin to fate in a manner according with the affective fallacy, hence, "the voice of the thunder was heard, speaking in a sustained, emphatic and vibrating roll, with violent louder bursts of crashing sound, like a wrathful and threatening discourse of an angry god" (*Outcast* 283); yet the gusts of wind accompanying the storm are not merely figurative, but "*woke him up* from his numbness" just as the rain "streaming over his head, clinging to him, running down his body" leads to an "insane dread" which "*took possession* of him" in an agentive manner (283, emphasis added). As Conrad states in his reflections on Eastern settings in *A Personal Record*, his authorial beginnings were launched through an "hallucinated vision of forests and rivers and seas," but there continues to be a powerfully interiorized phenomenal aspect to his descriptions of the natural scene. Similarly, too, Conrad writes of the "exhilarated atmosphere" of his decision to go to sea as akin to sounds "outside the scale to which men's ears are attuned," and which "remain inaudible to our sense of hearing" (41 *APR*). If such phrasings return us to Seel's observation from above, in which we sense a surrounding atmosphere "even if we do not know anything about it" (92, emphasis added), Conrad's fictional characters can also be seen partaking in the natural scene in a more helplessly automatic way.

Crucially, such characters can appear cognizant of their situation. Even at his most introspective, and therefore liable to project affective states onto actuality, Willems is aware of nature not as some sort of literary conceit or hallucination, but a concrete continuum. In this sense, the moods of that character and of the natural spaces are both ongoing, and liable, in Conrad's handling, to cross-pollination. This is to say, Willems might be given to note how "[r]ound him, ceaselessly, there went on without a sound the mad turmoil of tropical life" (331), yet we see him simultaneously processing such turmoil within consciousness:

> ceaseless, unresting, in widening circles, in zigzagging paths that led to no issue, [Willems] struggled on wearily with a set, distressed face behind which, in his tired brain, seethed his thoughts: restless, sombre, tangled, chilling, horrible and venomous.
>
> (328)

Where the natural world remains "unattainable" for Willems (329), Conrad's circular discourse yet achieves a startling degree of association between nature and the human. Once one begins to notice such moments in his oeuvre, the evidence quickly accumulates. As with *Lord Jim* thereafter, nature in *Outcast* is not just a theatricalized environment, but one in which the conditions of particular places are represented as interactive processes.[12] This does not mean, of course, that we should guard ourselves from "symbolic" readings of the Malay wilderness. The forum created through the joint presencing of self and environment might be performative in the way I am describing, but it still infers the kinds of aesthetic projections undergirding, say, the affective fallacy— as where "the spreading nipa palms nodded their broad leaves over his head as if in contemptuous pity of the wandering outcast" (67). Still, the point remains that in addition to such traditional usages, Willems yet spends much of the novel beset by real-enough phenomena in which "everything stirred, moved, swept by in a rush" (65). These actual conditions do figuratively press him "outside the scheme of creation in a hopeless immobility filled with tormenting anger and with ever-stinging regret" (ibid.), but Conrad's tropes remain tied to the phenomenal scene from which they spring. For example, in approaching his place of exile, Willems is beset by a sudden storm in which his own chaotic sense of loss is underscored via

> a white mist which filled the space with a cloud of waterdust that hid suddenly from Willems the canoe, the forests, the river itself; that woke him up from his numbness in a forlorn shiver, that made him look round despairingly to see nothing but the whirling drift of rain spray before the freshening breeze.
>
> (283)

At this juncture, the "nothing" Willems's fears in a more psychologized existential way is made active at more objective narrative levels, hence "[f]rom under his feet a great vapour of broken water floated up, he felt the ground become soft—melt under him—and saw the water spring out from the dry earth to meet the water that fell from the sombre heaven" (ibid.). At such junctures, the rain is rainy even where its force simultaneously tropes the chaotic falling or submerging of Willems's social aspirations and existence:

> the dread of all that water around him, of the water that ran down the courtyard towards him, of the water that pressed him on every side, of the slanting water that drove across his face in wavering sheets which gleamed pale red with the flicker of lightning streaming through them, as if fire and water were falling together.
>
> (283–4)

While any attempt to grapple with these larger issues of environmentally substantiated "reality" and the evocation of the unseen or of nature's "contemptuous pity" (67) can only be speculative in a chapter on Conrad's early representations of nature, the question concerning what it is to find oneself "moving in a visible world" (*CL II*: 418) bears reiterating, especially when coupled to the process by which the atmospheric effusiveness of nature in the Malay fiction appears to stand in for the performative if still "obscure" spaces of the real.[13] The key, then, recalling Whitehead's process philosophy, is to see where the natural scene in the Malay fiction is both "present for sense-awareness" and available for the passing "occurrence" of figurative transformations (op. cit. 14).[14] Indeed, wherever moods of introspection share dynamic features with a natural scene, Conrad's ecological usages can be addressed via theatrical understandings of the ways in which one's surroundings not only affect individuals in a symbiotic manner, but do so as dynamic environments. It is precisely this sort of symbiosis with nature that I have termed scenographic. Through her researches into the interrelations of settings and characters, the theater theorist Erika Fischer-Lichte underlines how the psychosomatic qualities of performative spaces can point us toward a more ecologically nuanced understanding of fiction.

> By "performative space" I mean a space as it comes into being, when people— or animals—move in and through it. While the architectural-geometrical space in which a performance takes place is more or less stable, the performative space changes with each movement of an actor, an animal, an object, the light, with each change of the light, with each sound ringing out. The performative space is unstable, fluid, ever changing. It is the different spaces that come into being in the course of the performance.
> (180)

An overtly theatrical example of "performative space" can be seen in Conrad's 1897 short story, "Karain: A Memory," in which the title character "presented himself essentially as an actor," and whose "stage" included a "scenic landscape that intruded upon the reality of our lives by its motionless fantasy of outline and colour" (10).[15] The theatrical aspects of this Malay tale have been described elsewhere, notably by Linda Dryden, who suggests that Conrad's use of such tropes critiques "the traditional stereotyping of the East" (11), and by Robert Hampson, for whom that author's "theatrical metaphors register the estranged Western perspective on this Eastern world at the same time as they attempt to normalize and appropriate that world" (122). If, as Hampson asks, the imperial imaginary tends to foreground the "reality that pertains to [a] spectacular Otherness" (ibid.), we might yet wonder where Conrad's "motionless fantasy" lurches free of our conception to link up with the intruding scene of atmospheric phenomena. Indeed, Conrad shows us that this theatricalized poetics is transferable to all environments, as where "it seemed to me, during that moment of waiting, that the cabin of the schooner was becoming filled with a stir invisible and living as of subtle breaths" (48). Through a scenographic reading of the ambient setting, the story's readers are better able to pinpoint the poetics by which the natural scene becomes dynamic both to Karain's troubled interiority and the awareness of his interlocutors (and readers) in the fluid manner delineated above. Hence it is that the natural scene is sometimes a "stage" (6) or, in certain lights had "the suspicious immobility of a painted scene" (7), yet refuses the fixity of a constrained event. Moreover, where such theatricalization appears to offer a means of capturing the illusions of a particular personage while allowing its observers to partake in an ambient natural "reality," the poetics of the process are extendable to other kinds of "ecosystems." Conrad appears to make just this move at the end of "Karain," illuminating London's The Strand with the "watery gleam of sunshine" (54) and thereby presenting that city as "resigned and sullen under the falling gloom" or beset by "a rumour vast, faint, pulsating" in a manner no less forceful than the psychic pressures undergirding Karain's bay earlier in the story (55). Tellingly, too, the purpose of the story's ending is to allow the presumably fluid aspects of the underworld of Karain's experience to illuminate a like ambience in an urbanized Western realm such that "[i]t is there; it pants, it runs, it rolls; it is strong and alive; it would smash you if you didn't look out" (ibid.).

Fischer-Lichte's analysis is also helpful in responding to Hampson's question concerning what performance might be serving to obscure in Conrad's fiction. In her book, *The Transformative Power of Performance: A New Aesthetics*, Fischer-Lichte describes how the theatrical scene is created via "the autopoietic feedback loop, consisting of the mutual interaction between actors and spectators" (163). Behind this phrasing, we are led to recognize that the orchestration of bodies, images, atmospheres and sounds not only changes the way in which each "scene" is understood—or in which the *real* is thereby obscured—but denotes a dynamic process in which changes in the performance environment reify new possibilities of meaning and interpretation. Autopoiesis, or the self-generation of meaning and response, thereby marks the performative aspect of human figures and their environments as a thematically generative process. The effects of such generation remain mobile: they might serve to initiate the emergence of "the surplus of the real" as Slavoj Zizek sees of cinema (116), or, now closer to Hampson, to dissolve, via nature, the categories of imperial alterity—yet such effects are nearly always affectively charged. As Fischer-Lichte notes, the "actor's presence, the ecstasy of things, atmospheres, and the circulation of energy 'occur' in the same way as the meanings brought forth as perceptions or the emotions, ideas, or thoughts resulting from them" (162). This theoretical discourse might rocket toward the poiesis of the ecstatic, but from that theatrical process the audience, like the reader, is led toward a phenomenally activated evocation of particular "imagined spaces" through the actor's encounter with an interactive surrounding. With a nod to Marshall McLuhan, in Fischer-Lichte's performative discourse the "scene" is the message as we saw of "Karain," wherein the departure of that prince's haunting spirit is exorcized via a now responsive scenery: "A shaft of bright hot rays darted into the bay between the summits of two hills, and the water all round broke out as if by magic into a dazzling sparkle" (51). Indeed, it is in this overt manner that a scenographic reading of Conrad's fictions becomes essential to understanding the subtleties of his art and, more specifically, how this author's treatments of natural settings assume thematic force.

Denoting the art by which performance environments are devised and orchestrated as a communicative medium, scenography therefore offers a powerful means of incorporating Conrad's depictions of natural settings with the affectively charged experiences of his characters. But how are such scenes orchestrated in narrative? *The Cambridge Introduction to Scenography* (2009) provides basic concepts for this move where its authors point out how the term intends the arena in which "the space of the performance and the bodies of the performers can interact" (3) and they set out how the scene's "inhabitable spaces" are "determined by the circumstances and purposes of the action in question and by the movement of the bodies within the space." Further, where such interactions "create a formally coherent and dramatically functional system," we come closer to the modus I wish to extend to Conrad's Malay fictions (5). Applying these terms to *Outcast* aids us in comprehending the dynamics whereby Conrad learns to link the atmospheric descriptions of the natural "scene" to the ambient qualities of his scenarios. Such linkage is especially important where Conrad's imagining of the wilderness scene is animated by the moral degeneration of an antihero caught up in the flux of an indifferent physical surroundings—the "immense and impenetrable silence that swallows up without echo the murmur of regret and the cry of revolt" (327). Indeed, the jungle scene of Willem's most stiflingly embodied engagements with his surroundings provides a site for a dynamic framing of that character's consciousness. The landscape might be throbbing with ambience, or bewildering in a recognizably *unheimlich* manner due to its misty effusions or aural confusions, but such phenomena are also interiorized to the extent that the scene as a whole becomes transitive. So, too, by thinking of Conrad's settings as interactive ecosystems, readers become alert to the ways in which the "the bitter peace of the abandoned clearings entered [Willems's] heart" in a more environmentally activated manner than that character's disillusionments might otherwise indicate (ibid.). Marlow's responses to Patusan in *Lord Jim* are no less profound. In a much cited passage concerning the moon rising between Patusan's twin peaks, we read how the nocturnal scene "robs all forms of matter […] of their substance, and gives a sinister reality to shadows alone" (LJ 187). That this statement is immediately followed by the observation that "the shadows were very real around us" upholds Fischer-Licht's assertion that the "actor's presence" is caught up with "the ecstasy of things" and "atmospheres" in a concrete manner (162). However, figurative Conrad's usages remain, the ambient states he draws for us are no less phenomenal than they are potentially ecstatic.

The aesthetic representation of the environment at the core of this chapter can now be restated. Conrad's depictions of nature depend for

162 *Mark Deggan*

their impact on his scenographic approach to the representation and animation of natural phenomena. As such, his depictions employ a theatrical dynamic not as a means of dividing and bridging humans and environments, but of performatively staging the atmospheric collusion of embodied consciousness with particular ecologies. This line of analysis does not imply, of course, that Conrad's fictional characters are made somehow rescuable through such openness. Willems's and Jim's problems remain acute regardless of their relationship to the various natural settings in either novel, but neither does this mean that the wildernesses they traverse, coastal or oceanic, are merely figurative screens for personal alienation. Rather, a character's immersion into the scene of nature produces an environmentally rich forum for thinking through the human situation via natural phenomena. This is a broad claim, yet it speaks to an ecocritical reading of scenography's communicative agency. Indeed, for the theatrical theorist Pamela Howard, "[o]bjects and figures become, as in theatre, emblematic, the carriers of the myth, heightened by darkness and light, and adding value to the empty space" (129).[16] Such are the valuations I see Conrad engaging via his own use of natural space.

But other sorts of spaces are no less open to the ecological poetics I have been describing. Stein's advice to Marlow in the twentieth chapter of *Lord Jim* suggests a like performative apparatus. As Stein famously puts it in that much-cited scene, the "way is to the destructive element submit yourself, and with the exertions of your hands and feet in the water make the deep, deep sea keep you up" (162). If that "element" or "water" offers man an arena of authentic being, so much the better that the immediate setting of Stein's environmental lesson is immediately theatricalized as a house, an ocean deep or a stage—a scenographic occasioning in which the two interlocutors are imagined "stealing silently across the depths of a crystalline void" or "stealing with flickering flames within unfathomable and pellucid depths" (164). This domestic "scene" not only reflects the human dislocation of Jim's situation but performs a number of figurative locations just as Conrad's representations of nature are seen to do across the novel.[17] The theatrical gestures of Marlow's encounter with Stein might take place in a colonial house, yet they point powerfully toward those moments in *Lord Jim* wherein nature and human existence coalesce in a more overtly performative manner. For instance, where Jim and the other officers of the *Patna* spend a night in a small boat following their abandonment of their ship, the tensions of the human drama are theatrically evoked out of the natural scene just as Jim's co-conspirators appear ("became") from the natural play of atmospheric phenomena.

> Can you imagine him, silent and on his feet half the night, his face to the gusts of rain, staring at sombre forms watchful of vague

movements, straining his ears to catch rare low murmurs in the stern-sheets! [...] six hours of alert immobility while the boat drove slowly or floated arrested, according to the caprice of the wind; while the sea, calmed, slept at last; while the clouds passed above his head; while the sky from an immensity lustreless and black, diminished to a sombre and lustrous vault, scintillated with a greater brilliance, faded to the east, paled at the zenith; *while the dark shapes blotting the low stars astern got outlines*, relief became shoulders, heads, faces, features,—confronted him with dreary stares, had dishevelled hair, torn clothes, blinked red eyelids at the white dawn.

(96, emphasis added)

The theatricalized atmospheres of *Outcast* might be less developed, but they are equally prevalent, ranging from the erotic underpinnings of the plot wherein "the monotonous song of praise and desire that, commencing at creation, wraps up the world like an atmosphere and shall end only in the end of all things" (76) to "the stifling gloom of the courtyard" wherein the abandoned lovers "stood colourless and shadowy, as if surrounded by a black and superheated mist" (277).[18]

An important theorization of the aesthetic potential of atmospheres has been undertaken by the German philosopher, Gernot Böhme, whose work underlines the subjective and somatic qualities of atmospheric states alongside objective recognition of the "qualities possessed by things" including their chromatic, ambient or ambulant aspects (1993: 122). As Böhme writes, an atmosphere is a coexistence where "[s]ensual perception means participating in the articulate presence of things" (187).[19] While Böhme's thinking is not always directed toward the study of how environments impinge on embodied consciousness, his works are translatable into the sort of ecological phenomenologies one associates with ecocritical discourse, where the theory of atmospheres remains evocative of the shared synergies of humans with nature's ambient actuality:

[the] space of moods is physical expanse, in so far as it involves me affectively. The space of moods is atmospheric space, that is, a certain mental or emotive tone permeating a particular environment, and it is also the atmosphere spreading spatially around me, in which I participate through my mood.

(5)

In an article on Böhme's relevance to ecocritical study, Kate Rigby offers terms applicable to Conrad's treatment of natural spaces:

Recognizing our somatic susceptibility to the impressions that something, someone, or someplace make on us, our own emotional affectedness by the atmosphere they generate, we recognize ourselves as sharing with them a physical existence as a body being. Recovering a sense of our own corporeality, we discover that we are ecological selves, existing in environments and with others by whom or which our psycho-somatic disposition is inevitably inflected.

(144)

As may be seen above, the figurative possibilities Rigby raises here are synthesized in *Outcast* such that Conrad's wilderness evocations are never just a backdrop to the human realm, but present the somatic arena in which actions unfold:

the heat poured down from the sky, clung about the steaming earth, rolled among the trees, and wrapped up Willems in the soft and odorous folds of air heavy with the faint scent of blossoms and with the acrid smell of decaying life. And in that atmosphere of Nature's workshop Willems felt soothed and lulled into forgetfulness of his past, into indifference as to his future. The recollections of his triumphs, of his wrongs and of his ambition vanished in that warmth, which seemed to melt all regrets, all hope, all anger, all strength out of his heart.

(74–5)

Here, the "atmospheric" renderings of the text color its moods, offering a mobile aesthetic frame ("Nature's workshop") wherein the moral and cultural failings of the scenario blend seamlessly with the actual clouded or suffocating effusiveness of a Malay wilderness. By such means, the ambient and often meteorological conditionality of the natural scene provides Conrad's character with forums of interaction and reflection. Nature might be by turns ambivalent or inert, but in its embodied aspect it is never unproductive, nor, as Conrad expressed in another of his retrospective author's notes, separate from the need to "envelop" fictional events "in their proper atmosphere of actuality" (*WTT* 6).

In her work on the Malay books, Agnes Yeow suggests that, with Conrad (or as I argue here—his representations of nature), vision "is itself dialogic, *a relation*," one that "takes the form of a conversation between sensory perception, aesthetic illusion, and theatricality" (11, original emphasis).[20] Yeow's brief observations can be pressed toward Conrad's natural settings in a more defiant way, for the issue of representational tactics, what Yeow goes on to call "the subjectivity of vision," does not stop at the aesthetics of interiority, but performs symbiotic connectivities between characters and environments. Nor is such interplay limited to Conrad's affectively charged tropes. As seen above, the atmospheric and concrete phenomena buttressing Conrad's conceits are dynamic to the extent that their author imagines them "falling together, monstrously mixed, upon the stunned earth" (28). It might therefore be observed that the symbolic potential of Conrad's aesthetics of nature, while belonging to his literary apprenticeship, have a generative value across his oeuvre: they do something within his texts. Indeed, they are theatrical in the sense that they infer actions and the play of perspectives by which the personal dynamics of Conrad's characters are performed and witnessed. The drama of nature therefore coexists with that of Conrad's scenarios in a performatively concrete manner, not only by animating the actual wilderness environments by which many of the texts after *Outcast* stage their dramatic highpoints, but by offering, in a fully symbiotic manner, the nexus of human consciousness with a natural scene. That symbiosis is most clearly essayed as a fully realized poetics in *Lord Jim*, where following his jump from the *Patna*, Jim is morally at sea in a swirling oceanic squall, one of several "souls of men floating on an abyss and in touch with immensity" (95). As with *Outcast*, the atmospheric actuality of nature in *Lord Jim* is not merely a mobile scenery "confound[ing] sea and sky into one abyss of obscurity" (81) but one that performs the ambient (because embodied) linkages of human consciousness with a particular surrounding. In this setting, the Arabian Sea is not simply an actual atmospheric sensorium or the interactive locus of his consciousness and existential condition, but a figure for the failure of Western discourses of heroic individuation: the scene is as drama.

In conclusion, where nature is for Conrad both affectively charged and ambivalent, the scenographic poetics whereby he invigorates his settings gives rise to an ecocritical interplay at the point that human consciousness is not only seen to think its surroundings, but, so to speak, to be thought by them. Considering the role of nature in Willems's moral dissolution in *Outcast*, and Jim's interiorizations of natural space in *Lord Jim*, it becomes clear that both novels mine nature in order to animate broader thematic contents. Indeed, it is due to the complexity of Conrad's example and of his attempts to locate his protagonists in spaces of alterity that a performative turn becomes justified when addressing the dynamics of nature in his fictions. At the very least, a case can be made that Conrad's tropical settings operate as a theatricalized literary ecology. Conrad himself appears close to recognizing just how theatricalized his writing could be, hence Willems's attempt to navigate the collusion of his jungle surroundings with an "empty blackness [that] seemed to him impenetrable and enigmatical like a curtain hiding vast spaces full of unexpected surprises" (146). At either end of the human-nature spectrum, Conrad's readers learn that the unfolding ecology of the scene is more actual, and more dynamic, than one's purchase upon it.

Notes

1. See, for instance, 65ff. Guerard 1958: That critic's disinclinations to see *Outcast* as an effective story as compared to *Almayer's Folly* is argued, not very convincingly, on generically narrative terms. He does not, for instance, read the latter as a step up from the wan romanticism of its former's exotic realm. A more amused reading of the Malay settings can be seen in Max Beerbohm's send-up of Conrad's early story, "The Lagoon". See Beerbohm's *A Christmas Garland* (Heinemann, 1912).
2. It is perhaps worth observing that while "theatrical" can infer the play of perspective by which we know objects and states, theater remains no less phenomenal in its effects than nature.
3. Watt is relying upon the 1914 Doubleday edition of *The Nigger of the Narcissus*.
4. Here I would not presume Gregory's reliance upon an hermeneutics built upon absent presences or the productive gappiness of modern fiction, but foreground how Conrad's textual performance, like that of his natural environments, animates their "between" in a manner conversant with ecocritical thinking on humans and the places with which they partake.
5. Space disallows full comment here, but that long simmering early and late novel, *The Rescue* (1920), sets out an order of reality within a particular social and geographic milieu that remains tied to its proper atmosphere in a manner different to the early works.
6. As suggested through the last of my epigraphs above, Conrad's mobile aesthetics of nature, like Merleau-Ponty's thesis concerning Cézanne's canvases, prompt Conrad's readers to suspend those "habits of thought" by which the artifice of the human world proceeds, so to lay bare not just the interactive aesthetic site in which embodied consciousness might make itself at home in the world, but "the base of inhuman nature upon which man has installed himself" (16).
7. Other words are of course available for this dovetailing of energies. The late environmentalist Paul Shepard described the members of an ecosystem "as engaged in a kind of [generative] choreography of materials and energy and information" while calling for "a wider perception of the landscape as a creative, harmonious being where relationships of things are as real as the things" (134). Thinking of the natural "choreography" of a thereby inclusive terrain is certainly relevant to the literary representation of landscapes as a performative scenography, but we need to hold on to Shephard's warning that "English becomes imprecise or mystical – and therefore suspicious – as it struggles with 'process' thought", at any rate, when separated from the divided human world "of static doers separate from the doing" (135).
8. Berns's online article is broken into paragraph sections.
9. Berns is working from the 1909 "Preface to the New York Edition" of Henry James's *The Ambassadors* (Penguin, 1986: 45–51).
10. Buell is citing Lopez's "Landscape and Narrative" (64).
11. To again cite Buell, this chapter aims to underline the stages wherein the natural scene is not "ancillary to the main event," nor provides its figurative vehicle, but is that event. In a related vein, Edward Garnett describes how Conrad "creates dissolving worlds, fading mirages out of the stuff men call reality," while leaving us largely unsatisfied as to where the possible actuality of such "reality" lies (in Sherry, 1973: 107–8).

    Still, even if we are faced with the blind surfaces and illusions of an actuality we can never achieve—the ruins, for instance, of Willems's self-serving "temple of the self" (31)—one still has the concrete profusion and affective

potential of the same nature within which Conrad's characters are so bootlessly immersed.
12 The title character of "Karain," discussed several paragraphs below, is another symbiotic receptor of environment, though one liable to moving from atmospheric theatricalizations of his immediate environment to increasingly abstracted framings of place. In the following passages, Karain moves from psychosomatic investment in a surrounding to a cognitively nuanced description of exposure and loss: "But in front of the steady long barrel the fields, the house, the earth, the sky swayed to and from like shadows in a forest [...] and that strange country seemed so big, the rice-fields so vast, that, as I looked around, my head swam with the fear of space" (39). In the first statement, his interior drama alters the scene; in the second, the changed space he occupies unnerves him.
13 All the same, suppositions concerning the "impalpable" qualities of the environment can appear to run against the grain of Conrad's stated views concerning the material aspects of his art. In a famous 1902 letter to William Blackwood, Conrad defends his own modernity in partly phenomenological terms, claiming that he writes of "nothing but action – action observed, felt and interpreted with an absolute truth to my sensations (which are the basis of art in literature) – action of human beings that will bleed to a prick, and are moving in a visible world" (CL II: 418, emphasis added).
14 Such, for instance, is the case for the increasingly uneasy Almayer in *Outcast*, for whom a dusky riverside forest is transformed into "a straight wall of formless blackness [beneath] the rapid flight of high and invisible vapours" (213).
15 Hampson's excellent book captures something of the difficulty of accommodating postcolonial criticism's insistence on particular tropes, for instance where "the colonial space is figured as female; the colonial landscape is figured as 'nature' rather than 'culture'; and non-Europeans are similarly situated as part of 'nature' rather than as part of 'culture'" (118).
16 As befits a working theatre practitioner and theorist, Howard's work is interdisciplinary: here she is discussing the work of the seventeenth-century painter Jean-Siméon Chardin, though her point extends to all aspects of the scene.
17 As already seen of Willems's unhappy wanderings at Sambir, the stages of Jim's exile are here not only "unstable, fluid, ever changing" as Fischer-Lichte intimates of theatricalized arenas (2009: 180), but Marlow's and Stein's movements partake in their constitution just as an actor responds to the thereby performative environment his thoughts, words and actions are already a part of. More broadly, of course, the theatrical aspect of Conrad's treatment of the Malay wilderness provides tool by which we might better comprehend European fears concerning inability to remain independent from one's surroundings.
18 In "The Lagoon," we read how natural sounds morph into language in an equally scenographic manner as Jim's fellow officers visually emerge from oceanic darkness: "A plaintive murmur rose in the night [...] as if the great solitudes of surrounding woods had tried to whisper into his ear the wisdom of their immense and lofty indifference. Sounds hesitating and vague floated in the air round him, shaped themselves slowly into words; and at last flowed on gently in a murmuring stream of soft and monotonous sentences" (194).
19 As Fischer-Lichte points out in her work with Böhme's ideas, sensory presences belong as much to "aesthetic discourse" as they do that of the environment (2009: 115).

20 But see my "Performance Value: Theatrical Atmospheres & Ethical Space in The Lagoon & Lord Jim." *Époque Conradienne*, No. 38, 2013: 83–101. In this paper I argue that such conversations are essentially ethical, an angle I do not have space to rehearse here.

Works Cited

Armstrong, Paul. *The Challenge of Bewilderment: Understanding and Representation in James, Conrad, and Ford*. Cornell University Press, 1987.

Berns, Ute. "Performativity." Ed. Peter Hühn et al. *The Living Handbook of Narratology*. Hamburg UP. Web. hup.sub.uni-hamburg.de/lhn. [view date: 14 May 2015] Web. http://wikis.sub.uni-hamburg.de/lhn/index.php/Performativity.

Böhme, Gernot. "Atmosphere as the Fundamental Concept of a New Aesthetics." Trans. David Roberts. *Thesis Eleven*, vol. 36, 1993. pp. 13–26.

———. Atmosphäre. Essays zur neuen Ästhetik. Suhrkamp, 1995.

———. "The Space of Bodily Presence and Space as a Medium of Representation." *Transforming Spaces: The Topological Turn in Technology Studies*. Eds. Mikael Hård and Andreas Lösch. Dirk Verdicchio. [Online publication of the international conference held in Darmstadt, Germany, 22–24 March 2002]. Web. 14 September 2011.

Buell, Lawrence. *The Environmental Imagination: Thoreau, Nature Writing, and the Formation of American Culture*. Harvard University Press, 1995.

Conrad, Joseph. *Almayer's Folly & Tales of Unrest*. Dent, 1947.

———. *The Collected Letters of Joseph Conrad. Volume 2. 1861–1897*. Eds. Frederick R. Karl and Lawrence Davies. Cambridge University Press, 1986.

———. *Lord Jim. The Cambridge Edition of the Works of Joseph Conrad*. Eds. John Stape and Ernest Sullivan. Cambridge University Press, 2012.

———. *An Outcast of the Islands*. Doubleday, Page & Company, 1920.

———. *A Personal Record & Notes on Life and Letters*. Doubleday, Doran & Company, 1938.

———. *Within the Tides. The Cambridge Edition of the Works of Joseph Conrad*. Eds. A. Fachard, L. Davies, and A. Purssell. Cambridge University Press, 2012.

Dryden, Linda. "Performing Malaya." *Joseph Conrad and the Performing Arts*. Eds. Baxter, Katherine and Richard Hand. Ashgate, 2009. 11–27.

Fischer-Lichte, Erika. "Performative Spaces and Imagined Spaces: How Bodily Movement Sets the Imagination in Motion." *Dynamics and Performativity of Imagination: The Image between the Visible and the Invisible*. Eds. Bernd Huppauf and Christoph Wulf. Routledge, 2013. pp. 178–187.

———. *The Transformative Power of Performance: A New Aesthetics*. Trans. S. I. Jain. Routledge, 2008.

Gregory, Derek. *The Colonial Present: Afghanistan, Palestine, Iraq*. Blackwell, 2004.

Hampson, Robert. *Cross Cultural Encounters in Joseph Conrad's Malay Fiction*. Palgrave Macmillan, 2000.

Howard, Pamela. *What Is Scenography?* Routledge, 2002.

James, Simon. *The Presence of Nature: A Study in Phenomenology and Environmental Philosophy*. Palgrave Macmillan, 2009.

Lopez, Barry. *Crossing Open Ground*. Vintage, 1988.
Lothe, Jakob. *Conrad's Narrative Method*. Clarendon Press; Oxford University Press, 1989.
Mannheim, Karl. Ideology and Utopia. Collected Works of Kark Mannheim. Volume I. Routledge, 2013 [1936].
McKinney, Joslin and Philip Butterworth, eds. *The Cambridge Introduction to Scenography*. Cambridge University Press, 2009.
Merleau-Ponty, Maurice. "Cézanne's Doubt" (1945), *Sense and Nonsense*. Trans. Hubert Dreyfus and Patricia Allen Dreyfus. Northwestern University Press, 1964.
Rigby, Kate. "Gernot Böhme's Ecological Aesthetics of Atmosphere" Eds. A. Goodbody and K. Rigby. *Ecocritical Theory: New European Approaches*. University of Virginia Press, 2011.
Seel, Martin. *Aesthetics of Appearing*. Trans. John Farrell. Stanford University Press, 2005.
Shepard, Paul. "Ecology and Man – A Viewpoint." *Deep Ecology for the Twenty-First Century*. Ed. George Session. Shambhala Books, 1995. 133–134.
Sherry, Norman. *Conrad: The Critical Heritage*. Routledge and Kegan Paul, 1973.
Wallace, Alfred. "Equatorial Vegetation." *Tropical Nature & Other Essays*. Macmillan & Co., 1878.
Watt, Ian. *Conrad in the Nineteenth Century*. University of California Press, 1979.
Whitehead, Alfred North. *The Concept of Nature* (1920). Cosimo, 2007.
Yeow, Agnes. *Conrad's Eastern Vision: A Vain & Floating Appearance*. Macmillan, 2009.

Part III
Conrad, Ethics and Ecology

8 Conrad and Nature, 1900–1904

Hugh Epstein

Conrad is not a naturalist, naturist or nature writer in the line of George Meredith (whose work he detested),[1] or W. H. Hudson (whom he admired), or Richard Jefferies (whom he nowhere mentions), or even his young friend Edward Thomas. However, what I argue in this essay is that "Nature" remains an essential term in a discussion of Conrad's fictional universe at exactly that crucial point for his writing when he has to find his way forward from what he knows are the major achievements of *Heart of Darkness* and *Lord Jim*. In his favorite book, *Bleak House*, Conrad no doubt read that Sir Leicester Dedlock "would on the whole admit Nature to be a good idea (a little low, perhaps when not enclosed with a park-fence)"; Conrad does not think Nature a good idea, but a necessary one, and the "nature" of his novels and short fiction is definitely not of the park-bench variety. It is the very opposite of the transcendentally restorative nature of Emerson, whose widely read 1836 essay "Nature" seeks to abolish atomizing separation and bring us into unity with God. It belongs rather to the severely disillusioned regard of later nineteenth-century philosophy and science, of which Mill's "Nature" can be taken as a representative statement:

> In sober truth, nearly all the things which men are hanged or imprisoned for doing to one another, are nature's everyday performances...Nature impales men, breaks them as if on the wheel, casts them to be devoured by wild beasts, burns them to death, crushes them with stones like the first Christian martyr, starves them with hunger, freezes them with cold,...All this Nature does with the most supercilious disregard both of mercy and of justice, emptying her shafts upon the best and the noblest indifferently with the meanest and worst...Such are Nature's dealings with life.[2]

The essentially Conradian statement in Mill's essay is that "nature" is "a name for the mode, partly known to us and partly unknown, in which all things take place."[3] Conrad is always interested in the mysteries of this "mode ... in which all things take place" which, in his novels, becomes their never-ending examination of the vibrating medium in which events strike the senses, a conditioning of nature which is the subject of this essay. J. D. Morell, who claimed to have coined the term "sensationalism," in his *An Historical and Critical View of the Speculative Philosophy of Europe in the Nineteenth Century* (1846) links "nature" to the senses in a way which allows us to see Conrad's affinities with mid- and late nineteenth-century investigations in empirical science:

> Now, physical science, being an expansion of the fundamental idea of nature, is one of the most necessary products of a sensational age. ... sensationalism in its cosmological tendencies always evinces a disposition more or less decisive to erect the idea of nature over that of God.[4]

I am not here concerned with extracting from Conrad's novels an "idea" of nature, so much as exploring the sensational encounter with its various manifestations in those works too readily designated as "transitional" between his first great phase, of ontological doubt, and his second—the political novels. Not ignoring Conrad's idealist temperament, it is the empirical spirit of the physical sciences which provides the most illuminating guide when considering the depictions of nature in Conrad's fiction: as his friend Arthur Symons commented in *Notes on Joseph Conrad* (1925), "The rarest subtlety in prose is its physiological quality; for prose listens at the doors of all the senses, and repeats their speech almost in their own tones."[5]

In his outstanding essay, "The Future of Conrad's Beginnings,"[6] Geoffrey Galt Harpham proposes a "charmed interval" (23) for Conrad's prose, a "brief period of linguistic mastery" (24) in which language is "forced to yield something unsuspected" (24) by the effort to depict man's place in nature. Before 1897, Harpham suggests, nature in Conrad's works is often "a heaving rhythm of mindless generation and death, in which human beings are embedded and from which they distinguish themselves only fitfully and with great difficulty" (25). Then, "beginning with *The Nigger*, nature becomes in his work a reduced, merely physical phenomenon ... no longer a metaphysical threat" (25). In this greatest creative period, "nature becomes secondary to human concerns, a background and a trial but not a matrix of inhumanity, a challenge to one's very being" (25). The charged and arresting strangeness of *Heart of Darkness* is Harpham's exemplary text. "And then, passing through this period – passing the test – Conrad seems to lose interest in nature: in *Nostromo* (1904), nature is a setting, if an imposing one" (25). Harpham des not examine his distinction between creative "background" and inert "setting"; so here I explore the lacuna, "passing through this period," from 1900 to 1904 to see whether "nature" ebbs away for Conrad as a site of existential bewilderment as Harpham claims, or remains potent in ways that reward enquiry.

If not quite so "charmed" as the previous three years, it is an immensely creative period. Conrad finished *Lord Jim* in July 1900 and begins writing "Typhoon" two months thereafter. Ten days after completing the story in January 1901 he begins writing "Falk", and in May he begins "Amy Foster" which he finishes a month later. Throughout this period, he is working with Ford Madox Ford on *Romance*, completed in March 1902, and early in that year he completes "To-morrow" and starts work on "The End of the Tether", part of the manuscript of which is burnt in an accident with an oil lamp on 23rd June. On 23rd October is the first mention of *Nostromo* (CL 2:448), the first part of which Conrad finishes in August 1903, at the same time as revising the proofs of *Romance*, which is published in October. In January 1904, T. P.'s Weekly begins the serialization of *Nostromo*, by which time Conrad has written the play *One Day More*. By the end of March, he has completed six of the essays that will become *The Mirror of the Sea*, in August completes *Nostromo*, by mid-October has completed "Henry James: An Appreciation," and by the end of the year has completed four more essays for the *Mirror of the Sea*, is planning "Autocracy and War," and is even contemplating returning to the deeply mired *The Rescue*. By any standards, this is a period in Conrad's writing life worth discussing for its integrity or diversity. My particular question is whether there is a trajectory, from the stately bamboo grove where Marlow catches his final glimpse of Jewel and Stein to the absorbent airs of the Placid Gulf which dissolve Decoud, that makes nature visible in these works as a set of phenomena with active agency, not quite background nor setting, as Harpham has proposed.

Conrad's journey is certainly remarkable. From the imaginist Jim, who avoids the facts of circumstance thrust upon him by nature, he takes us to the literalist MacWhirr, who faces nature's decomposing and atomizing power with human resolution, and then yet further to his deepest encounter with what is anti-humane (yet most human in its nature) in "Falk". The extinction of providential trust in nature's beneficence is written in "The End of the Tether", requiring of Conrad's characters that they ironically acknowledge their detachment from nature's processes (though so few achieve this!), which is so extensively examined in *Nostromo*. And throughout there is a deep anxiety, alternately hopeful and despairing, about what we can know of what encompasses and inhabits us. This epistemological questioning is what makes the Conrad section of *Romance* worth reading; it fuels the counter-voice of Jukes's terror in "Typhoon" and migrates to other forms of sublime encounter in the bewilderment and sudden revelations of "The End of the Tether" and the night scenes of *Nostromo*. Such groundless forms—though full of sea and air—make up the "nature" whose written form I now more closely examine. Resistant and invasive, indifferent and demanding, nature in this period of Conrad's writing is protean, unconciliable, and not to be evaded.

*****

In 1922 Conrad gave an interview to the Japanese academic Tadaichi Hidaka, in which he responded to Hidaka's query about Hardy's works differing from his with the reply, "They must do. In facing nature, Mr Hardy faces static nature, whereas I face dynamic, active nature, so we are naturally different."[7] Leaving Hardy aside (I don't agree with Conrad), all of Conrad's narratives inscribe in one way or another humanity's compelled participation in a cosmic dynamic that confers no sense of natural belonging. Unrequired by nature, humanity requires, for a full idea of itself, a sense that the struggle to exist within the conditions of nature makes human endeavor necessary to the unfolding cosmic spectacle.[8] This is a conflict most succinctly expressed at the opening of Chapter 5 of *The Nigger of the "Narcissus"*: "On men reprieved by its disdainful mercy, the immortal sea confers in its justice the full privilege of desired unrest" (67). At the same time as seeking domestic tranquility in the Kentish countryside Conrad himself is continually exercised by such "desired unrest," and the three short stories this essay examines each portray how the unruliness of nature is kept severely separate from the tidy domestic arrangements which it economically supports. In the midst of rewriting *Romance* in August 1901, Conrad characterizes himself to William Blackwood as "wearied by all the unrealities of a writing life, discouraged by a sunless, starless sort of mental solitude, having lost its reckoning in a grey sea of words, words, words" (*CL* 2:354). Cloistered from elemental nature by his chosen vocation, he declares in contrast that "A wrestle with wind and weather has a moral value ... men engaged in such contests have been my spiritual fathers too long for me to change my convictions" (ibid.), and one view of the Conrad of this period might well be, like the Marlow of "Youth," as a prematurely aged spinner of adventure stories whose function is to compensate for the adventures he can no longer have.[9] But "nature" is composed of more serious matter and emerges a more equivocal entity than a mere procurer of scenes in which man can be victim or hero. The reviewer of "Typhoon" *and Other Stories* for the *Daily News* (April 22, 1903) recognizes this without relinquishing the simplicities of "the test": "With him Nature has once more become alive and the old 'panic' returns, the home of animated, unseen Presences engaged in conflict with man".[10] *The Glasgow Evening News* reviewer, eight days later, in an article headed "Mr Conrad's Philosophy," comes nearer to a sense of modernity in these encounters:

> he has felt – possibly felt more than perceived – the essential loneliness of the human soul, face to face with the universe.
>
> In all his writing one feels that his problem has been the revelation of the soul wrestling with, or sinking beneath, its own weakness, the elemental forces of Nature, or the mysterious force of circumstances – struggling, yielding, suffering, but always solitary, individual, isolated.[11]

Nature in "Typhoon" itself is conveyed with such intensity that a responsive reading of the tale projects the reader into sympathetic physical extremities belied by silent cerebration in an armchair. Atmosphere is not background nor setting; it invades consciousness, reordering dimensions:

> At its setting the sun had a diminished diameter and an expiring, brown, rayless glow, as if millions of centuries elapsing since the morning had brought it near its end. A dense bank of cloud became visible to the northward; it had a sinister dark olive tint, and lay low and motionless on the sea, resembling a solid obstacle in the path of the ship. She went floundering towards it like an exhausted creature driven to its death. The coppery twilight retired slowly, and the darkness brought out overhead a swarm of unsteady, big stars, that, as if blown upon, flickered exceedingly and seemed to hang very near the earth.
>
> (26)

Time and space, vision and texture, are manipulated by the four similes here to move away from the surfaces of things perceived in order to find veracity in sensations. The rhetoric of simile enables a fugitive sense of the end of things to remain haunting, substantial though composed of air. In this respect, Conrad's art of writing nature is consistently physiological, but addressed to the human participation in the physics of the external scene. It is akin to that of his contemporary, the physicist Ernst Mach, who writes, "my epistemological standpoint is based on a study of the physiology of the senses ... in so far as it concerns physics."[12] In this apprehension, the impersonal processes of indifferent nature, which define the truth of our condition, can only be known in the truths of individual sensation; it follows that Conrad is a great writer of fragmentary isolation but one whose aim is to seek the conviction of an indissoluble bond with fellow creatures.

In this attempt to "hang together,"[13] at times in "Typhoon" it is only language—"a few words" (69) the narrator will later say of MacWhirr—that the characters have to hold onto. Yet, as in *Heart of Darkness* and *Nostromo*, official and written language comes in for scrutiny, not here for institutional mendacity but for their inadequacy in representing the experience of the senses. Immediately after the evocation of the oncoming storm, Jukes goes to the chart room to write up the ship's log: "'Ship rolling heavily in a high cross swell,' he began again, and commented to himself, 'Heavily is no word for it'" (26). Finding words for it, Conrad has Jukes glance out through the door, and writes,

> in that frame of his vision he saw all the stars flying upwards between the teakwood jambs on a black sky. The whole lot took flight together and disappeared, leaving only a blackness flecked with

white flashes, for the sea was as black as the sky and speckled with foam afar. The stars that had flown to the roll came back on the return swing of the ship, rushing downwards in their glittering multitude, not of fiery points, but enlarged to tiny discs brilliant with a clear wet sheen.

(26/7)

There is no pretense that we meet nature unconditioned in Conrad; here, the double frame of Jukes's retinal vision and that of the doorway are the specified conditions of contact, and a further frame of his duties and his sensibility (and MacWhirr's) always mediate encounter. Encompassing this again is the written report of sensational events; but, as opposed to the sober log, the narrator's account—initially focalized through Jukes and later MacWhirr—strives to do away with protective armature and allow perception of nature's terrifying presence. With an extraordinary precision of observation, the reader is whirled away from familiar terrestrial inhabitation to be given the impression of "raw" seeing. Yet while the vestibular system recovers equilibrium, Jukes "closed resolutely his entries: 'Every appearance of a typhoon coming on'" (27). Customary written forms have their calming effect, and sometimes an enabling one. For Conrad is not simple in his treatment of the place of language in bringing nonhuman forms and forces in some way within man's compass. In the engine room, where the machines of Solomon Rout wage their heroic struggle with the elements, it is the "grouped letters ... emphatically symbolic of loud exclamations: Ahead, Astern, Slow, Half, Stand by," and, above all, "Full," which "captured the eye as a sharp cry secures attention" (55). In the end, words are what we go by: penetrated by the storm, orders see Jukes through, as well as the "frail and indomitable sound" of his captain's voice, "as if from very, very far – 'All right'" (38).[14]

"The darkness palpitated down upon all this, and then the real thing came at last" (36). For all the strength the tale accords to words, the reader is left in no doubt that there is a "real thing" beyond all reckoning, verbal or otherwise. When the dial-hand in the engine room jumps from "Full" to "Stop":

Nobody – not even Captain MacWhirr, who alone on deck had caught sight of a white line of foam coming on at such a height that he couldn't believe his eyes – nobody was to know the steepness of that sea and the awful depth of the hollow the hurricane had scooped out behind the running wall of water.

(58)

"Nobody was to *know*"—nature in "Typhoon" wields forces beyond empirical knowledge, beyond verification by the senses, rendering the colloquial phrase "couldn't believe his eyes" literal and oddly moving. MacWhirr's wish to "know" where the hands had got to after the hurricane first falls on the ship distresses Jukes as, "Under the circumstances they were nowhere, for all the use that could be made of them" (40). To Jukes, the "humane intention" (65) in this futile knowledge is obliterated by forces that cannot be temporized with on the *Nan-Shan*, "while the whole atmosphere, as it seemed, streamed furiously past her, roaring away from the tenebrous earth" (40). But finally, what human beings can, and should, know about their fellow beings (there is a profoundly moral imperative at the heart of this story of comic incomprehension) becomes the scene of events, not the overwhelming of the human by indifferent nature. At the end of "Typhoon" the humane intention in MacWhirr's appreciation of the immediate condition of the Chinese passengers/coolies takes over from intimations of an existential condition, glimpsed through the extremities undergone by the *Nan-Shan* at the hands of wind and water. However, the encounter with the *in*human in nature is never dispelled, though it is of an order barely communicable between the characters in the tale. In Solomon Rout's letter home at the end of the tale, he writes "just a word or two of the typhoon; but *something* had moved him to express an increased longing for the companionship" (73) of his wife (*emphasis added*).

"Falk", on the other hand, is very precisely about the encounter with what is "human" in nature. Both tales portray the irruptive power of nature though both, unusually for Conrad, have a conventionally "happy ending." But in siting nature, in "Falk", not only in the mysterious Antarctic but primarily within the more mysterious and impenetrable interior of the human organism, the tale that Conrad goes on to write is more disturbing in its implications than "Typhoon's" quietly ironic encomium for the man who faces the test of external nature's extremity. In 1898 Conrad writes to Cunninghame Graham, "fidelity to nature would be the best of all ... if we could only get rid of consciousness. ... We can't return to nature, since we can't change our place in it" (*CL* 2:30). Falk's consciousness of what he has done, of what it is in human nature to do, and Hermann's refusal to countenance what nature requires of us for survival, mean that an uncomplicated "return to nature" is not what the tale advocates. Like "Typhoon", the issue is knowledge of our fellows and also of the capacities of our own natures, the acknowledgment of drives, to use the psychological term contemporary with Conrad's story. But the difference is that, rather than observe an admirable "humane intention," the narrator of "Falk" must digest the account of a murderous necessity. Driven inwards, it would seem, after recording the heroic struggle to remain steady amid external forces, Conrad finds in nature-within demands that civilized life would rather not recognize.

Unlike "Typhoon", in which external nature assaults early and obviously, in "Falk" the stealthy approach of nature—so uncompromising in its final declaration—is subdued or deflected for much of the tale, repressed by the thick wadding of family decencies aboard the "world-proof" *Diana*. As opposed to its "roaring lusts" (88), the sea visits the *Diana* with what, to the narrator, "looked like reticence" (88), giving the clue to the largely sensationally subdued style of "Falk" in comparison to "Typhoon". Neither the narrator nor the convention-bound Hermann is actively to "know" the repressed truths of human nature, the unwelcome gift of extreme circumstances from which they both, though not equally, shelter themselves:

> The ruthless disclosure was, in the end, left for a man to make; a man strong and elemental enough and driven to unveil some secrets of the sea by the power of a simple and elemental desire.
>
> (88/9)

And thus "nature," like so much in "Falk" for so much of its length, is approached indirectly, for, as the narrator says of the eponymous central figure, "Natural forces are not quarrelsome" (117). Meanwhile, nature's presence in the tale is merely ironic, displaced into the purely linguistic register. Confronted as to why he had paid off Johnson so that he wouldn't pilot the narrator downriver, Falk protests: "Never bribed. He knew the man wouldn't work as long as he had a few cents in his pocket to get drunk on, and, naturally (he said – 'naturally') he let him have a dollar or two" (120). As the narrator ponders Falk's declaration, "I have been unfortunate once" (123), he wonders whether this misfortune was "indistinguishable from a breach of trust. Could it be something of that nature?" (124). When the narrator conveys Falk's offer of marriage to Hermann, he has to hear a diatribe in which "there was nothing of any nature said or done by Falk ... that did not seem to have been a cause of offence" (125). The retrospective ironies in each of these instances are only increased by their incidental, normal-manner-of-speech quality.

Thus, when we finally read of the voyage of the *Borgmester Dahl*, delivered by a man whose face "was immovably set and hungry, dominated like the whole man by the singleness of one instinct" (133), but largely paraphrased by the narrator into a direct, forward-moving, unadorned account, we have been defended by every facet of the narrative from the expectation of direct revelation. In contrast, "He wanted to live" (133) announces the very different mode that will hold as "from question to question I got the whole story" (136) through six pages. The prelude to this narration is a direct exchange, crucial to the picture of nature that emerges within "Falk" as a complete tale:

> And with my head full of preconceived notions as to how a case of 'cannibalism and suffering at sea' should be managed I said – 'You were then so lucky in the drawing of lots?'

'Drawing of lots?' he said. 'What lots? Do you think I would have allowed my life to go for the drawing of lots?'

Not if he could help it, I perceived, no matter what other life went. 'It was a great misfortune. Terrible. Awful,' he said. 'Many heads went wrong, but the best men would live.'

'The toughest, you mean,' I said. He considered the word. Perhaps it was strange to him, though his English was so good.

'Yes,' he asserted at last. 'The best.'

(135)

"The toughest" and "the best" recall Herbert Spencer's restatement of Darwin's "struggle for existence" as "the survival of the fittest," but more particularly and fruitfully can be seen to be in dialogue with T. H. Huxley's celebrated *Evolution and Ethics Romanes Lecture of 1893*. Huxley's essay sketches the relations between nature and human ethics in various civilizations up to the present day. He is resolutely opposed to the way in which, in modern times, the notion of goodness has become attached to "nature." With evident relevance to the passage from "Falk" just quoted, Huxley writes,

> I suspect this fallacy has arisen out of the unfortunate ambiguity of the phrase 'survival of the fittest'. 'Fittest' has a connotation of 'best'; and about 'best' there hangs a moral flavour. In cosmic nature, however, what is 'fittest' depends upon the conditions. ... Social progress means a checking of the cosmic process at every step and the substitution for it of another, which may be called the ethical process; the end of which is not the survival of those who may happen to be the fittest, in respect of the whole of the conditions which obtain, but of those who are ethically the best.[15]

"Falk" does not have a social program equivalent to Huxley's polemical essay: while corresponding to Huxley's reading in its unsentimental depiction of nature,[16] it ruthlessly subjects Huxley's ethical "best" to discomforting interrogation. Falk himself is not a sympathetic figure inviting the reader's identification, and *his* "best" does not necessarily command assent. However, within the tale it does command the authority of firsthand experience, one that knows a great deal more than the narrator does when ironically he adjures Falk, "but you must do your best yourself" (123), in the courtship of Hermann's niece.

The experience aboard the *Borgmester Dahl*, so tersely recounted, faces both narrator and reader directly with the means whereby "to get in touch with the real actuality at our elbow" (135); but "getting in touch" with the lived dynamics enjoined by unaccommodating nature is something very different in "Falk" from the assault upon the senses which is the experience of reading "Typhoon". "Falk's" contrasting stylistic quietude indeed contributes to the gain in intensity in the closing pages of the tale,[17] but scarcely leaves the reader knowing what to do with the "actuality." When, quite late in the story, the narrator achieves "the first of (his) knowledge of Falk" (116), the language casts Falk as a specimen in an anthropological study:

> This desire of respectability, of being like everybody else, was the only recognition he vouchsafed to the organisation of mankind. For the rest he might have been the member of a herd, not of a society. Self-preservation was his only concern. Not selfishness, but mere self-preservation. Selfishness presupposes consciousness, choice, the presence of other men; but his instinct acted as though he were the last of mankind nursing that law like the only spark of a sacred fire. (116/7)

Held at an analytical distance, this dispassionate view of the Falk-animal, the centaur, sees him acting upon pre-social impulse and necessity, his affinities belonging to animal heat not to the solidarity (so famously appealed to by his creator, Conrad) born of the consciousness of a common condition. Although this language explains him, it does not invite the reader to share his sensory experience. The exterior view of Falk is maintained right to the end of the tale, to the narrator's last glimpse of him with Hermann's silent niece provoking the surmise, "It seemed to me they had come together as if attracted, drawn and guided to each other by a mysterious influence" (144). The narrator can only fall back, diminished, upon his own sense of Falk's superior energy: "From afar I seemed to feel the masculine strength with which he grasped those hands she had extended to him with a womanly swiftness" (144). His history heard and compassionately understood, Falk departs intact from the tale which bears his name, essentially as untouched and mysterious as when he entered, and it is in this irreducible quality of his being that Conrad's vision of nature in this tale is located.

Without straining the issue too far, MacWhirr's "Face it," and his action in the equitable division of the dollars, is compatible with Huxley's well-known conclusion to the Romanes Lecture: "Let us understand, once for all, that the ethical progress of society depends, not on imitating the cosmic process, still less in running away from it, but in combatting it."[18] But the same cannot be said of "Falk", where the remorseless energies of "a natural force" pursue their goal and are accorded an honorable place within the bounds of respectable society. Falk is impelled by the claim of a biological imperative whose achievement does nothing to dis-ennoble him in the tale. But if this is read as a celebration merely of appetite, rather than a realization of being, then the tale has failed. It would be to equate necessity with a thoroughly un-Conradian materialism, while in the narrator's most powerful statement about "this appalling navigator" the idealism is explicit: "He evidently wanted to live his whole conception of life. Nothing else would do" (142).[19] Stephen Reynolds wrote in 1912 that Conrad's tales "bring(s) civilization to the judgment of nature"[20]; but an understanding of nature at this stage of Conrad's career must comprehend man's participation in the cosmic process as something other than the binary of being either set over against it or being defeated by it. Man's ideal conception of himself, whether as an individual or as a species, is always a condition for the encounter with nature, but this subjectivity of apprehension does not thereby eliminate the reality of nature's independent existence, of which man forms a minute, discomforted, part.[21]

****

In the thoroughly mapped and charted world of "The End of the Tether", a world in which even for Mr van Wyk in upriver Batu Beru "the wilderness, once his adversary, [was] now his vanquished companion" (209), in which commerce is the overriding consideration and the urbanization of Singapore its primary manifestation, the presence of anything we could call "nature" seems incidental and anachronistic. The writing has none of the nightmarish and febrile quality of *Heart of Darkness*, the story that it follows in the *Youth* volume, and proceeds, rather, with the lugubrious smoothness of Captain Whalley's own deliberate tread. In "Typhoon" we are told early on, and with absolute conviction, "and then the real thing came at last" (36), while in "The End of the Tether", "Nothing very real had ever troubled Ned Eliott" (155), and Captain Whalley feels that "the testimony of his whole life" would now seem "a screed traced in obsolete words – in a half forgotten language" (144). Harbor-masters' documents and legal transactions have superseded "nature." And yet, at its very center, "The End of the Tether" contains Conrad's longest uninterrupted descriptive evocation of a progress through a natural environment, one in which man succeeds in maintaining only the barest foothold.

This great sequence is, initially, focalized through the first mate Sterne: "Always ... on the lookout for an opening to get on," constantly watching "for something 'that one could lay hold of'" (180), he is the tale's arch-empiricist. But as he watches from the rail of the *Sofala* the surface of the water amid the reefs of Pangu Bay, the description escapes from his utilitarian scrutiny to become a meditation—not Sterne's—upon natural forms and how life inhabits them, until it returns to the "revelation" that comes to Sterne from his indifferent gazing upon the scene, and then his "discovery" about Captain Whalley, which comes from an entirely different quarter. The issue impressed upon the reader is not, as in the previous two stories, the struggle for existence exacted by nature, but a more fundamentally epistemological one of the contentions

184 *Hugh Epstein*

of physiology and psychology in the processes of perception. After the absolutes of "Falk", the feeling that pervades almost every paragraph of "The End of the Tether" is doubt, and uncertainty about what the eye sees provides the sensational experience which underlies the story's enquiry into man's place in nature. The power of natural forms throughout the story to provoke equivocal mental representations reveals "nature" to be no mere adjunct or background setting, even though its role in "The End of the Tether" is of a different order of agency than in the previous stories. The effort of apprehension through the glare of light is the conditioning of nature that the writing insists upon: the insignificant rocks which, far ahead, will prove so significant to the tale, are

> crumbs of the earth's crust resembling a squadron of dismasted hulks run in disorder upon a foul ground of rocks and shoals... like anchored rafts, like ponderous, black rafts of stone ... squat domes of deep green foliage that shuddered darkly all over to the flying touch of cloud shadows....
>
> (182)

Despite the wealth of language seeking to convey the impression upon the senses, this is a place of such desolation that "the lives of uncounted generations had passed it by" (182) to become the haunt of seabirds "emitting a strident and cruel uproar ... the living part of the broken land beneath" (183). How this little portion of the earth's surface is inhabited, the relation between organic life and inorganic forms, becomes increasingly a domain of the imagination even in the registration of its visible outline. The birds' wings

> soared and stooped over the pinnacles of the rocks, over the rocks slender like spires, squat like Martello towers; over the pyramidal heaps like fallen ruins, over the lines of bald boulders showing like a wall of stones battered to pieces.
>
> (183)

All these similes! Pangu Bay, brought within the compass of such scrutiny, dissolves into figurative language while remaining irreducibly, materially itself and there, as the tale's dénouement in the impact upon "the sheer ridge of a stone reef" (244) surely tells us. The commerce between the real and the ideal is what is made of nature in this mercantile story and will indeed become the explicit subject of Conrad's great examination of the material world and its idealized exploitation, *Nostromo*.

The verisimilitude which Conrad strives for in "The End of the Tether" is closer to the observational sensationalism of "Typhoon" than to the tale told by a narrator which is the procedure of "Falk". A method which resolves descriptive accuracy into likenesses tends to displace the fixed identity conferred by maps and charts in favor of indeterminate spaces which are filled by the imagination. As all of Conrad's writing declares, this is what encounter with our surrounding world feels like. The preoccupation with between-ness, with the conditioning medium through which things are seen and heard, is of a piece with much of nineteenth-century scientific enquiry, and particularly the physics of electromagnetic fields, as developed out of Faraday's fields of force by Clerk Maxwell in the 1860s, and aphoristically summed up by the fine Conrad critic Donald Benson as "dematerializing substance while substantiating the immaterial."[22] This is vividly enacted in the modality with which the passage through Pangu Bay in calmer weather is conceived:

> On such days the luminous sea would give no sign of the dangers lurking on both sides of her path. Everything remained still, crushed by the overwhelming power of the light; and the whole group, opaque in the sunshine – the rocks resembling pinnacles, the rocks resembling spires, the rocks resembling ruins; the forms of islets resembling beehives, resembling mole-hills; the islets recalling the shapes of haystacks, the contours of ivy-clad towers – would stand reflected together upside down in the unwrinkled water, like carved toys of ebony disposed on the silvered plate-glass of a mirror.
> (184/5)

As so often in Conrad, light transforms substance—successively imaged as "the rocks," "the forms of islets," "the islets"—into shapes conceived by eyes squinting into the fierce sunlight: pinnacles, spires, ruins, beehives, mole-hills, haystacks and ivy-clad towers. The English landscape that materializes from a reef in the Malacca Strait is formed from inland scenes in the imagination of homesick British seamen, the immaterial made substantial—yet the effect of this "resembling" and "recalling" is not to invite a reader into a conceptualizing mental space, but to place her in that vibrating space between the eye and the rocks as they shift their forms in an insistence upon an exchange in the realms of physiology and physics. A multiplicity of resemblances is finally stilled to a single image that renders the islets remote and strange in form and texture. Although pictorial, the effect is not like that of looking at a picture in its frame, but of being drawn out to an encounter in an indeterminate space with forms that seem to have come adrift from their referents as known and plotted on charts and maps. The part, then, played by nature in "The End of the Tether" is not to offer a contrast to "civilized" modern Singapore, as the Arctic does to the comfortable "Diana" in "Falk", but rather to provide the site where calculations based upon visual perception are cast into a realm of proliferating similitude rather than resolved into single certainty.

Evidence in "The End of the Tether" is inconclusive and belongs to the realm of suggestion. When the *Sofala* traverses Pangu Bay at night,

> All would be still, dumb, almost invisible – but for the blotting out of the low constellations occulted in turns behind the vague masses of the islets whose true outlines eluded the eye amongst the dark spaces of the heaven [*sic*].
>
> (183)

"What the eye has seen is truth!" declares Arsat passionately in *The Lagoon*, but in "The End of the Tether" the eye is inadequate, and "vague masses" only give an impression of their dimensions by what is "occulted," the astronomical term carrying with it a suggestion of the mysterious and unexplained, secreted in "the heaven." It is at this point, too, that other eyes than those on board the *Sofala* radically change the sightlines of the story: the "few miserable, half-naked families" that "strove for their living in this lonely wilderness of islets" (183) gaze back briefly at the "monthly apparition" (184) of the passing steamer. The activities of their lives, visually imagined with such beautiful precision, leave the reader quite uncertain about the medium within which they are conducted: "and the men seemed to hang in the air, they seemed to hang enclosed within the fibres of a dark, sodden log, fishing patiently in a strange, unsteady, pellucid, green air above the shoals" (184). These figures visit a story in which they are not required, briefly to transform the reader's sense of where life is carried on, and what it can be known to be:

> their lives ran out silently; the homes where they were born went to rest and died ... were hidden out of sight from the open sea.... the unbreathing, concentrated calms like the deep introspection of a passionate nature, brooded awfully for days and weeks together over the unchangeable inheritance of their children....
>
> (184)

"The End of the Tether" is exactly about lives running out and the inheritance of children; "the brown figures stooping on the tiny beaches" (184), so incidental to the tale and to the great world of commerce in the Far East, bear the burden of nature and the "unchangeable inheritance" that it visits upon their children in a manner which requires the reader to adjust his sense of where the center of this story lies.

In "The End of the Tether" the importance of the natural world, far from providing a locus of authenticity and human integration in "the cosmic process," is that it produces scenes of uncertainty, of ambiguities that must be interpreted. The ambiguity, however, is not only epistemological; it extends itself back into the concept of nature itself which, in this story, is never granted beauty or charm. As the *Sofala* proceeds upriver toward Batu Beru,

> Where the earth had been crumbled by the floods it showed a steep brown cut, denuding a mass of roots intertwined as if wrestling underground; and in the air, the interlaced boughs, bound and loaded with creepers, carried on the struggle for life, mingled their foliage in one solid wall of leaves, with here and there the shape of an enormous dark pillar soaring, or a ragged opening, as if torn by the flight of a canon-ball.
>
> (193)

This competition along the banks of the river is simultaneously mirrored onboard the *Sofala* by Sterne's struggle to get on in life, seeking to displace Whalley as captain by revealing his blindness to the unsavory shipowner Massy. After Massy has brusquely rebuffed Sterne,

> The ship had in that place to shave the bank so close that the gigantic wall of leaves came gliding like a shutter against the port; the darkness of the primeval forest seemed to flow into that bare cabin with the odour of rotting leaves, of sodden soil – the strong muddy smell of the living earth steaming uncovered after the passing of a deluge.
>
> (198)

Such images of wrestling and invasion are continuous with Conrad's early Malay fiction; whether they convey the fresh and healthy vigor of natural growth to contrast with the fetid moral atmosphere aboard the *Sofala*, or whether they suggest that a comparably ruthless, unproportioned and malodorous cycle is "natural," will probably depend upon the disposition of the reader to believe in the goodness of nature. But the ambiguity of nature—how human beings should respond to the instinctive drives within that seem to be our connection to the natural world that precedes, surrounds and will postdate us—becomes the point at issue in the closing stages of the story. While for Falk there was no debate upon the subject, Mr van Wyk, made privy to Whalley's deception about his fitness to captain a ship, finds himself contending with the rhetorical question, "How could I forsake my child, feeling my vigour all the time – the blood warm within me?" (224). Despite the "ghost of justification" that Conrad raised in a letter to David Meldrum (*CL* 2:441), the tale does not advocate that the claim of such natural bonds should sanction criminal deception—that is close to the sentimentalist reading which Conrad explicitly rejected in his exclamation to Edward Garnett, "Touching, tender noble, moving ... Let us spit!" (*CL* 2:468).[23] But van Wyk's reaction does not reduce the contesting claims of nature, obligation and legality to a single, unquestionable line of conduct:

> And Mr van Wyk, whose feeling of outraged love had been translated into a form of struggle with nature, understood very well that, for that man whose whole life had been conditioned by action, there could exist no other expression for all the emotions; that, to voluntarily cease venturing, doing, enduring, for his child's sake, would have been exactly like plucking his warm love for her out of his living heart.
>
> (224)

This is not quite Marlow's choice of nightmares; yet van Wyk feeling "outraged love" (on Whalley's behalf?) as "a form of struggle with nature" (his own? that of collective mankind? of the indifferent cosmic process?) confirms powerfully, if thoroughly ambiguously, the ineradicable place of nature in Conrad's picture of human relations. In his "illuminating moments of suffering" Whalley, who had conceived of his life as "necessary," sees "the whole earth with all her burden of created nature" (240) anew, and not as the gift of Providence. If life is not God's love, can it be known simply as the exercise of human love? In "The End of the Tether" intimations of nature, without or within, leave man bewildered. The story brings Captain Whalley face to face with the imperious demands of his own nature but declines to confirm his desire that his promptings be recognized as belonging to a surrounding scheme of things embodying benevolence, shape and order.

*****

A concern for the spatial dimension of human life in the surrounding scheme of things extends from "The End of the Tether" to the portrayal of nature in the much grander work to follow. In *Nostromo*, it is noisy contemporary Sulaco, "where the military band plays sometimes in the evenings between the revolutions" (11), rather than the august immobility of Higuerota or the Placid Gulf, that excites Conrad's most innovative writing, which would seem to support Harpham's contention that by this time nature has exhausted its power to generate the vital mystery of his style that aroused so much early excited comment. Yet if its role in the novel is seen to be simply that of a silent backdrop against which man's efforts at governance of all sorts appear puny and self-important—"a violent game played upon the plain by dwarves mounted and on foot" (27)—then the likelihood is that *Nostromo* will be read only as satire, with nothing of any tragic dimension. But the more active agency of nature, not merely as a belittling presence but as an extinguishing force with which man must contend, gives haunting life to several of the novel's memorable scenes.

It is in the feeling of sensory envelopment by surrounding space that the novel conveys the presence of nature as potentially invasive, as more than a static setting. Punctuating the long letter written by Decoud to his sister in the Albergo d'Italia Una, the encroachment of night is an offshore action drawing the talkative journalist toward a dissolution in silence that he does not have the resources to withstand:

> Looking out of the window, Decoud was met by a darkness so impenetrable that he could see neither the mountains nor the town, nor yet the buildings near the harbour; and there was not a sound, as if the tremendous obscurity of the Placid Gulf, spreading from the waters over the land, had made it dumb as well as blind.
>
> (229)

The encounter of the senses with apparent vacancy manipulates near and far in Conrad's typical manner to reorder habitual awareness of the dimensions that surround us:

> Decoud lifted his head to listen. But there were no sounds, neither in the room nor in the house, except the drip of the water from the filter into the vast earthenware jar under the wooden stand. And outside the house there was a great silence.
>
> (244)

The concentration of the ear upon something close at hand extends that silence infinitely. Indeed later, when with Nostromo in the black Gulf night he is listening for Sotillo's steamer, "the stillness was so profound that Decoud felt as if the slightest sound conceivable must travel unchecked and audible to the end of the world" (284). When it comes, that sense of envelopment by an unfamiliar and potentially infinite dimension as the lighter pushes off into the extinguishing night is accomplished with extraordinary swiftness as "the effect was that of being launched into space": "It was a new experience for Decoud, this mysteriousness of the great waters spread out strangely smooth, as if their restlessness had been crushed by the weight of that dense night" (261). In practice, throughout the episode, more prominent than these firm unhurried rhythms is the crepitation of the constant whispering between Decoud and Nostromo and of the surprise occasioned by Decoud's own thoughts, which has the effect of reserving for the night and the Gulf a great latent power sensed through human reaction rather than direct description.

But this is not the jungle of *Heart of Darkness* before whose immensities European "pilgrims" hollow out a small space for their rapacity, and of which Marlow says, "And outside, the silent wilderness surrounding this cleared speck on the earth struck me as something great and invincible, like evil or truth, waiting patiently for the passing away of this fantastic invasion" (65). J. Hillis Miller is right to observe of *Nostromo*, in the Introduction to the volume that opens with Harpham's essay, "the complete absence of the 'metaphysical' dimension so important in 'Heart of Darkness' … all the 'metaphysics of darkness' seem to have vanished from Conrad's work in the few short years between 'Heart of Darkness' and *Nostromo*."[24] But my argument is that, even in so political a novel as *Nostromo*, "nature," divested of metaphysical freight, retains potency in describing Conrad's portrayal of the human relationship to the circumambient universe. It is Nostromo and Decoud, their vastly different capacities for response functioning analogously to MacWhirr and Jukes, who suffer this exposure. Ezra Pound, of all people, frames the point very well when he says in 1914,

> firstly you may think of him [a man] as that toward which perception moves, as the toy of circumstance, as the plastic substance *receiving* impressions; secondly, you may think of him as directing a certain fluid force against circumstance, as *conceiving* instead of merely reflecting and observing.[25]

Conrad floods his characters with impressions, an epistemology which excites Pound's scorn because (he is thinking specifically of Ford Madox Ford's poetry and its "origins" in Gautier and Flaubert) "This school tends to lapse into description."[26] However, the brilliant phrase "directing a certain fluid force against circumstance" memorably depicts how Conrad's characters, caught up in the cosmic process, in various ways seek to resist their plight. Dr. Monygham, in his need to idealize in Nostromo those capacities he feels he lacks himself, offers the novel's most heroic vision of man, "precipitated suddenly into an abyss of waters and darkness, without earth or sky, and confronting it not only with an undismayed mind, but with sensible success" (433). He invests the illustrious Capataz with the fortitude to contend with "the crushing, paralyzing sense of human littleness, which is what really defeats a man struggling with natural forces, alone, far from the eyes of his fellows" (433). This ideal picture of the mind's capacity to counter the disintegrating formlessness of nature is later made actual in the silent moment out in the Gulf in which Nostromo's soulless body is re-tenanted: "The Capataz frowned: and in the immense stillness of sea, islands, and coast, of cloud forms on the sky and trails of light upon the water, the knitting of that brow had the emphasis of a powerful gesture" (494). Human consciousness opposes itself to the infinite recession of silence and light. The mere frown of a new awareness is "a powerful gesture," an imposition of definition upon the forms and immaterial formlessness within which human activity is cast. It is what human beings must do: "In our activity alone do we find the sustaining illusion of an independent existence as against the whole scheme of things of which we form a helpless part" (497). And yet the magisterial statement is implacable, for we are no more than "a helpless part" of "the whole scheme of things," and all our activity creates only an "illusion." Nature is ready to invade at any moment in which the necessary illusion demanded by human nature can no longer be maintained.

Unlike Nostromo, the journalist, boulevadier and sceptic Decoud fails entirely in the task of self-maintenance. Circumstance finds him to be a fundamentally uninhabited figure, requiring the stimulus of some outward sensation to assure himself of his own existence:

> After three days of waiting for the sight of some human face, Decoud caught himself entertaining a doubt of his own individuality. It had merged into the world of cloud and water, of natural forces and forms of nature.
>
> (497)

"Swallowed up in the immense indifference of things" (501), this is the absorption and dissolution of an organism which can no longer raise a gesture to resist its own defeasibility. Decoud's merging contrasts explicitly with that of Nostromo's knitting of his brow three pages previously: Nostromo had been able to compel "cloud forms on the sky and trails of light upon the water" (494) into a picture serving his understanding of the dimensions of life to come, while "the world of cloud and water" is met with no such shaping power in Decoud, and overwhelms him. As has frequently been remarked, Decoud is a figure whose skepticism makes him peculiarly close to Conrad himself. Writing to John Galsworthy in 1901, Conrad insists upon skepticism as "the tonic of minds, the tonic of life, the agent of truth – the way of art and salvation" (CL 2:359), a tonic—though certainly not a salvation—that Decoud provides in the novel of 1904. But at the end of *Nostromo* Conrad finds such "intellectual audacity" (501), "the affectations of irony and scepticism" (497), insufficient to withstand enforced solitude and the demands of "facing nature." It requires "a deliberate belief," as Marlow had put it in *Heart of Darkness*, while the skeptic can see only illusion upon illusion. Whatever Conrad's own beliefs, his fiction exacts from its protagonists an encounter with natural forces which necessitates the imposing of a conception of human existence upon worlds both material and immaterial that know nothing of our conceptions nor our existence.

*****

"Nature" is still an essential term in Conrad's vocabulary in *Nostromo*, but the novel proves a tipping point in this respect. For Robert Penn Warren, in his justly renowned Introduction to the 1951 Modern

Library *Nostromo*, "Man is lost in this overwhelming scene. ... lost in the blankness of nature" (xxxv). Yet perhaps this does not allow enough scope to man's activity in the face of nature, illusory though it may be in establishing an independent existence outside nature's processes. If we return to Edward Garnett's important essay, "Mr. Conrad's Art," his review of *Nostromo* for *The Speaker*, November 12, 1904, we come somewhat closer to the Conradian strife than Penn Warren's 'lost'. He says of Conrad,

> that he has a special poetic sense for *the psychology of scene*, by which the human drama brought before us is seen in its just relation to the whole enveloping drama of Nature around, forming both the immediate environment and the distant background. In Mr. Conrad's vision we may image Nature as a ceaselessly-flowing infinite river of life, out of which the tiny atom of each man's individual life emerges into sight, stands out in the surrounding atmosphere, and is lost again in the infinite succession of the fresh waves of life into which it dissolves.[27]

"Lost again," and again, certainly; but how an individual life "stands out in the surrounding atmosphere" seems to me to catch perfectly the fleetingness, the attempt at permanence, the desired unrest and the wished-for repose, with which Conrad invests his psychological scenes of man in Nature.

Galsworthy, the recipient of Conrad's enduring friendship as well as his adjurations about skepticism, twice characterized the fundamental impulse behind Conrad's art, and in so doing indicated how fluctuating and how less-than-formulated into fixed "views" are the relations to nature depicted in Conrad's novels. In "Joseph Conrad: A Disquisition" (1910), exploring the "cosmic spirit" in Conrad, Galsworthy writes, "In the novels of Turgenev the characters are bathed in light. Nature with her many moods is all around them, but man is first. In the novels of Joseph Conrad, Nature is first, Man second." Fourteen years later, in "Reminiscences," he modifies this to "First and last he was interested in men, fascinated by the terrific spectacle of their struggles in a cosmos about which he had no illusions."[28] Galsworthy's first reading conceives of Conrad as a nineteenth-century materialist influenced by late Victorian science; his second sees Conrad as more interested in the mental construction of worlds than their physical constitution, and brings his vision closer to that of a heroic version of twentieth-century absurdity.[29] Examining Conrad's writing between 1900 and 1904 yields a powerful sense of his unique integration of both of these forms of skepticism, rendering simultaneously the material otherness of the universe we inhabit and the human perceptual processes to which any knowledge of it is subject. In such an enterprise, a concept of nature remains fundamental to Conrad's capacity to write this world. It is not fortuitous, then, that in 1904 he pictures the power of nature as an inescapable condition in his inspiring vision of writing as an act of retrieval:

> Action in its essence, the creative art of a writer of fiction may be compared to rescue work carried out in darkness against cross gusts of wind swaying the action of a great multitude. It is rescue work, this snatching of vanishing phases of turbulence, disguised in fair words, out of the native obscurity into a light where the struggling forms may be seen, seized upon, endowed with the only possible form of permanence in this world of relative values – the permanence of memory.[30]

Notes

1 In conversation with H.-R. Lenormand, Conrad "praised Kipling, Hardy and Bennett, but detested Meredith" (rpt. in Martin Ray, *Joseph Conrad: Memories and Impressions*, 2007, 87). Roger Ebbatson claims "The tradition of the Nature-novel begins with Meredith as its only begetter" (*Lawrence and the Nature Tradition*, 1980, 72).
2 "Nature" (1858, published 1874), *"On Liberty" and Other Essays* (1926), 159. In her chapter, "Narrative and Nature" Elizabeth Ermarth shows how "As the nineteenth century wears on, 'nature' ceases to support the demands of faith" (*The English Novel in History 1840–1895*, 1997, 44).
3 *Ibid.*, 143.
4 Morell, Vol. 2, 448/450.
5 *Notes on Joseph Conrad* (1925) 37.
6 In Kaplan, Mallios, White eds., *Conrad in the Twenty First Century* (2005), 17–58.
7 I take this from Yoko Okuda, who translated and introduced Hidaka's piece for *The Conradian* 23:2 (Autumn 1998), 73–87, under the title "East Meets West."
8 Cf. "I have come to suspect that the aim of creation cannot be ethical at all. I would fondly believe that its object is purely spectacular" (*A Personal Record*, 92).
9 Much earlier, and before the invention of Marlow, Conrad writes to Edward Garnett, "The opportunities do not last long enough. / Unless in a boy's book of adventures. Mine were never finished. They fizzled out before I had a chance to do more than another man would" (*CL* 1:321).
10 John Peters ed., *Joseph Conrad, the Contemporary Reviews* (2014), Vol. 2, 20.
11 *Ibid.*, 30.
12 Ernst Mach, *History and Root of the Principle of the Conservation of Energy* (1911, originally 1872), 9.
13 *Lord Jim*, 170.
14 According to his friend Stephen Reynolds, "All right" was "a favourite phrase of Conrad's too, in letters and conversation" ("Joseph Conrad and Sea Fiction," *Quarterly Review* 217, July 1912, reproduced in Carabine, *Joseph Conrad Critical Assessments*, 1992, Vol. 1, 499).
15 *The Collected Essays of T. H. Huxley* (2001), Vol. 9, 80/81.

194 Hugh Epstein

16 Contrast the uncharacteristically sentimental reading given by Virginia Woolf, in her *Times Literary Supplement* obituary (14 August 1924), of Conrad's early characters: "Nature was their antagonist; it was she who drew forth honour, magnanimity, loyalty ... Above all, it was Nature who turned out such gnarled and tested characters as Captain Whalley and old Singleton."
17 Michael Lucas, in *Aspects of Conrad's Literary Language* (2000), identifies "Falk" as a fault-line in the "normalisation" of Conrad's literary English. See also my slightly different account in "'The Fitness of Things': Conrad's English Irony in 'Typhoon' and *The Secret Agent*," *The Conradian* 33:1 (Spring 2008), 1–30.
18 *Ibid.*, 83.
19 It is to the point that Huxley was not a straightforward materialist either. He argues, in "Bishop Berkeley on the Metaphysics of Sensation" (1871), "if I were obliged to choose between absolute materialism and absolute idealism, I should feel compelled to accept the latter alternative" (*op. cit.*, Vol. 6, 279).
20 *Op. cit.*, 505.
21 See Kate Soper, *What Is Nature?* (1995), 8: "I recognize, that is, that there is no reference to that which is independent of discourse except in discourse, but dissent from any position which appeals to this truth as a basis for denying the extra-discursive reality of nature."
22 Donald R. Benson, "Constructing an Ethereal Cosmos: Late Classical Physics and *Lord Jim*," *Conradiana* 23:2 (Summer 1991), 135.
23 See footnote 16.
24 *Op. cit.*, 14.
25 "Vorticism," in *Gaudier-Brzeska: A Memoir* (1916), 85, quoted in Martin Kayman, *The Modernism of Ezra Pound: The Science of Poetry* (1986), 37.
26 "Status Rerum," *Poetry* 1:4 (Jan 1913), 125, quoted in Kayman, 38.
27 In Norman Sherry, *Joseph Conrad: The Critical Heritage* (1997), 175.
28 John Galsworthy, *Two Essays on Conrad* (1930), 66, 46.
29 Elizabeth Ermarth: "The step towards seeing nature as neither meaningful nor meaningless, but simply absurd, takes Conrad one giant step away from the tradition of English narrative" (*op. cit.* 64).
30 "Henry James: An Appreciation, 1905," *Notes on Life and Letters* (1949), 13.

Works Cited

Benson, Donald R. 'Constructing an Ethereal Cosmos: Late Classical Physics and *Lord Jim*', *Conradiana* 23:2 (Summer 1991), 133–49.
Carabine, Keith. *Joseph Conrad Critical Assessments.* 4 vols. Helm Information, 1992.
Conrad, Joseph. *Lord Jim.* Eds. H. H. Stape and Ernest W. Sullivan II. Cambridge University Press, 2012.
———. *The Mirror of the Sea & A Personal Record.* Ed. Zdzisław Najder. Oxford University Press, 1988.
———. *The Nigger of the "Narcissus."* Ed. Allan H. Simmons. Everyman, J. M. Dent, 1997.
———. *Nostromo.* J. M. Dent and Sons Ltd., 1947.
———. *Nostromo.* The Modern Library (Random House), 1951.

———. *Notes on Life and Letters.* J. M. Dent and Sons Ltd., 1949.

———. *Sea Stories:* 'Typhoon', 'Falk' *and the Shadow-Line.* Ed. Keith Carabine. Wordsworth Editions, 1998.

———. *Youth, Heart of Darkness,* "The End of the Tether". Ed. Owen Knowles. Cambridge University Press, 2010.

Ebbatson, Roger. *Lawrence and the Nature Tradition: A Theme in English Fiction 1859–1914.* Harvester Press, 1980.

Epstein, Hugh. '"The Fitness of Things": Conrad's English Irony in 'Typhoon' and *The Secret Agent*', *The Conradian* 33:1 (Spring 2008), 1–30.

Ermarth, Elizabeth Deeds. *The English Novel in History 1840–1895.* Routledge, 1997.

Galsworthy, John. *Two Essays on Conrad.* W. T. H. Howe, 1930.

Huxley, Thomas Henry. *Collected Essays.* Volumes 6 & 9. Thoemmes Press, 2001.

Kaplan, Carola, Peter Mallios, and Andrea White, eds. *Conrad in the Twenty First Century: Contemporary Approaches and Perspectives.* Routledge, 2005.

Karl, Frederick R., and Davies, Laurence et al. *The Collected Letters of Joseph Conrad.* Cambridge University Press, 1983–2007.

Kayman, Martin A. *The Modernism of Ezra Pound: The Science of Poetry.* Macmillan, 1986.

Lucas, Michael. *Aspects of Conrad's Literary Language.* Columbia University Press, 2000.

Mach, Ernst. *History and Root of the Principle of the Conservation of Energy.* Open Court Publishing, 1911.

Mill, John Stuart. *On Liberty and Other Essays.* Macmillan, 1926.

Morell, John Daniel. *An Historical and Critical View of the Speculative Philosophy of Europe in the Nineteenth Century.* 2 vols. William Pickering, 1846.

Okuda, Yoko. 'East Meets West: Tadaichi Hidaka's "A Visit to Conrad", translated and introduced By Yoko Okuda', *The Conradian* 23:2 (Autumn 1998), 73–87.

Peters, John G., ed. *Joseph Conrad: The Contemporary Reviews.* Volume 2. Cambridge University Press, 2014.

Ray, Martin. *Joseph Conrad: Memories and Impressions, an Annotated Bibliography* (Conrad Studies 1). Editions Rodopi, 2007.

Sherry, Norman, ed. *Joseph Conrad, the Critical Heritage.* Routledge, 1997.

Soper, Kate. *What is Nature? Culture, Politics and the Non-Human.* Blackwell, 1995.

Symons, Arthur. *Notes on Joseph Conrad.* Myers & Co., 1925.

Woolf Virginia. *Collected Essays.* 4 vols. Ed. Leonard Woolf. Chatto & Windus, 19.

9 "A Paradise of Snakes"
Conrad's Ecological Ambivalence

J. A. Bernstein

One of the currents of Conradian criticism in recent years has been the question of where Conrad's work can be placed on the spectrum of environmental ethics. Jeffrey Meyers, for example, drawing on the writings of Aldo Leopold, notes that Kurtz in *Heart of Darkness* (1899) develops an "ecological consciousness" (107). Jeffrey Mathes McCarthy expands that reading to suggest that *Heart of Darkness* falls largely within the ethical scheme of deep ecology, Arne Næss's philosophical vision, wherein humankind and the natural world are inherently "interrelated" and thus of equal value (635). Aaron Clayton, looking at Conrad's *Victory* (1915), also argues that Conrad "erodes the distinction between man and nature, and reimagines man's relationship to nature by establishing the conditions for the possibility of a radically different ontology," an ontology that is important, in Clayton's reading, for linking Marxism with tenets of ecology (123). These readings place Conrad's characters within a deanthropocentrized universe and thus attribute to him some element of environmental conviction.

I will argue that such readings downplay the contradictions of Conrad's work and the extent to which humankind does, at times, dominate the natural world, both metaphysically and morally. Specifically, I will look at *The Nigger of the "Narcissus"* (1897), *Heart of Darkness* and *Nostromo* (1904), all of which suggest that while Conrad does embrace elements of environmentalism, particularly deep ecology, there are also moments in each work that express his skepticism toward what has come to be known as deep ecology, as well as social reform movements generally. This skepticism is important, because it underscores not only the complexity of Conrad's writings—and the difficulty of assigning labels to his texts—but also the problems inherent in fielding an environmental movement when that movement's most basic tenet, holistic ontology, questions the capacity for ethics, or the human ability to somehow transcend nature and implement a moral framework. This is a problem that troubles the deep ecology movement and one that Conrad anticipates.

Art of Darkness: The Obscurity of Næss's Vision

Before delving into Conrad, it is useful to delineate some of the major approaches to environmental ethics. While the field draws on a variety of historical writings and philosophies, it only emerged, as Andrew Brennan and Yeuk-Sze Lo point out, as an academic discipline in the early 1970's, particularly with Næss's coining of the phrase "deep ecology" in a 1973 article in *Inquiry*. Although Næss later revised his conception,[1] his original definition of deep ecology entailed two key elements: the rejection of anthropocentrism, or the human-centered view of the universe; and the promotion of "biospheric egalitarianism," or the principle that all organisms have an "equal right to live and blossom" ("The shallow" 95–6). Thus, while deep ecology shares with other environmental movements a belief in ecological protection, it differs radically in that it embraces a holistic ontology and ascribes an inherent set of rights to the natural world. In both respects, it seeks to go "deeper" than previous environmental outlooks, such as the traditional, stewardship approach, wherein the natural world is seen as fundamentally separate from humankind and only valuable insofar as it serves human interests.

One aspect of deep ecology that is especially pertinent to Conrad studies is the element of self-realization that it allows. Næss explains that by abandoning the anthropocentric worldview and accepting one's place in the biosphere, one "reaches an understanding from within" ("The shallow" 95). He adds that "this quality depends in part upon the deep pleasure and satisfaction we receive from close partnership with other forms of life" ("The shallow" 96). The approach is almost mystical, and it certainly calls to mind earlier thinkers like Wordsworth and Rousseau, if not the Polish Romantics of whom Conrad himself was quite fond.

Clearly, there are also strong overlaps between deep ecology and other recent environmental approaches, such as: feminist ecology, which traditionally opposes the ethics of "domination" (over both women and nonhumans); the new animism, which generally finds value in the close affinities that people have with the living world; and social ecology, which generally ascribes the world's ecological problems to capitalism. There are also fierce debates about what the living world entails (e.g., mountains or soil), what the root cause of environmental destruction is (e.g., patriarchy, capitalism or anthropocentrism), and where moral consideration should end (e.g., sea kelp).

As all these nuances demonstrate, environmental ethics is a variegated field in the midst of productive redefinition. Hence, there is considerable difficulty in assigning any writer, let alone Conrad, a particular ecological outlook. Yet, Conrad anticipates the perils of modern colonialism and its impacts on the earth—both ecologically and politically.

Another difficulty inherent in approaching Conrad ecocritically is the question of whether any social vision, ecological or otherwise, can be gleaned from his writings. Robert P. Marzec characterizes Conrad's concern with environmental spaces as problems of knowing and representation. As Marzec explains, Conrad foregrounds the limitations of representation—especially in relation to colonial spaces and environments—in each of his narratives. The inability of Marlow to find an adequate means of representation lies at the center of the narrative of *Heart of Darkness*, *Lord Jim* and *Victory*. Interestingly enough the environment itself serves as the key vehicle for foregrounding this impossibility of representation in each of these works. In *Heart of Darkness* Marlow describes the land as "featureless," "empty," and a "wilderness" that contributes to Kurtz's madness (420). Thus the environment, in Marzec's view, has an occluding effect in Conrad's writings. The issue is primarily epistemic, rather than ethical, insofar as the "unfamiliar environments in Conrad…take on significance of a kind that calls into question the very ontological grounds of comprehension for the narrators, characters, and texts" (421).

Paul Armstrong voices a similar concern in reading *Nostromo*. As he explains, "Conrad is ambivalent about social change," and "his attitude towards politics oscillates between hope and despair" ("Conrad's Contradictory Politics" 19). According to Armstrong, this oscillation stems not just from Conrad, but from fundamental problems in metaphysics, specifically those uncovered by Heidegger and later Derrida. Armstrong even likens Conrad's outlook to Derrida's concept of "play" (19), a view that in many ways echoes Marzec's characterization of Conrad's "contradictory engagements" (421) and raises the question of how one can ascribe to him any standing vision. In *The Challenge of Bewilderment* (1987), Armstrong highlights these "ontological contradictions," particularly as they apply to the natural world (157). He points out the dueling role of nature in *Nostromo*, for example, noting that it "transcends humanity and defies assimilation but…is also a social construct and a hermeneutic variable" (157).

Yet what that uncertainty over meaning in Conrad overlooks is the degree to which he was at times clear-cut in his vision, particularly in disparaging his colonial-minded contemporaries. In 1903, several years after completing "An Outpost of Progress" (1897) and *Heart of Darkness*, for instance, he famously wrote to R. B. Cunninghame Graham, describing the "modern Conquistadors":

> Their achievement is monstrous enough in all conscience—but not as a great human force let loose, but rather like that of a gigantic and obscene beast. Leopold is their Pizarro, Thys their Cortez and their 'lances' are recruited amongst the [pimps, non-coms, bullies, and failures] of all sorts on the pavement of Brussels and Antwerp.
>
> (*Collected Letters* 3: 101)

Indeed, the letter ends with Conrad imploring Graham to meet Roger Casement (Conrad's friend and a critic of colonial abuses in the Congo) and, as Zdzisław Najder points out (163), employs wording that directly recalls that of the harlequin in *Heart of Darkness*: "He could tell you things! Things I've tried to forget; things I never did know." Thus, for all the epistemic quandaries his writing presents, Conrad does sound a clear note about the horrors of colonial oppression and, importantly, ascribes to the colonialists—Leopold and Thys in particular—a "beast"-like quality, rather than a "human" one. In doing so, Conrad upends not only the traditional assumption that colonialists are enlightened, or innately superior to those they oppress, but also the assumption that humans are fundamentally distinct from animals, both themes that his writings, as we shall see, reiterate.

Narcissus and the Powers of the Sea

The last of Conrad's early sea novels, *The Nigger of the "Narcissus,"* establishes many of the themes that would predominate in Conrad's middle works, most notably an ambiguous narrator and the overwhelming power of the natural world, in this case, the unruly sea. The moment in the text that comes closest to paralleling Kurtz's epiphany in the jungle, and, in fact, asserts the dominance of the natural world, is the night of the storm, where the *Narcissus* nearly sinks:

> Most seamen remember in their life one or two such nights of a culminating gale. Nothing seems left of the whole universe but darkness, clamour, fury—and the ship. And like the last vestige of a shattered creation she drifts, bearing an anguished remnant of sinful mankind, through the distress, tumult, and pain of an avenging terror.
> (54)

As in Næss's vision, human individuality becomes subsumed by a "total-field image" ("The shallow" 95). Indeed, the personalities of the ship are lumped together under the collective frame of the ship, which becomes its own vital organism:

> She had her own future; she was alive with the lives of those beings who trod her decks; like that earth which had given her up to the sea, she had an intolerable load of regrets and hopes. On her lived timid truth and audacious lies; and, like the earth, she was unconscious, fair to see—and condemned by men to an ignoble fate.
> (29–30)

In this case, the "ignoble fate" of "the earth" parallels that of the crew, and Conrad sounds the first of many ecological critiques (although the exact nature of the earth's condemning and what causes it remain unclear in this account). Yet there is no doubt that the sea is alive, at least in the crewman's account:

> The problem of life seemed too voluminous for the narrow limits of human speech, and by common consent it was abandoned to the great sea that had from the beginning enfolded it in its immense grip; to the sea that knew all, and would in time infallibly unveil to each the wisdom hidden in all the errors, the certitude that lurks in doubts, the realm of safety and peace beyond the frontiers of sorrow and fear.
> (138)

It is also unclear whether the sea represents an actual organism in this case as much as an elemental force, perhaps even a mythological one. But the deep ecological reading is apt insofar as humans are invariably linked to the planet, in this case, a surging sea, and one that assumes not only value, in their eyes, but commanding power over them.

Of course, the men's reactions to their immersion are characterized less by "deep pleasure and satisfaction," as Næss prescribes ("The shallow" 96), than "sorrow and fear"—at least in the moment. At the end, the unnamed narrator, who turns from a "we" to "I," reflects nostalgically:

> Haven't we, together and upon the immortal sea, wrung out a meaning from our sinful lives? Good-bye, brothers! You were a good crowd. As good a crowd as ever fisted with wild cries the beating canvas of a heavy foresail; or tossing aloft, invisible in the night, gave back yell for yell to a westerly gale.
> (173)

The Nigger of the "Narcissus" represents, more than anything, Conrad's triumphal farewell to the sea and his valorization of the kind of camaraderie it engenders among sailors—a camaraderie that is very much lacking on land, in his view. Zdzisław Najder sums up this contradiction nicely when he explains that "'land affairs' are a suspect and dubious medley of events, contradictory desires, low motives, false ideas, and illusory beliefs. The sea represents a realm ruled by simple duties, a clearly defined hierarchy of values, comradeship, and honest good work" (164). In that sense, seafaring, for Conrad, like mountaineering for Næss, takes on a fundamental ecological dimension insofar as sailors are immersed in an overwhelming natural world. Less clear, however, is whether the sea—or even the suspect land—can be said to possess any innate value in Conrad's account, and whether humans should be regarded as fundamentally part of those domains, or merely fundamentally tested by them. At bottom, the novel presents a metaphysical quandary in that the sailors are ontically connected to the sea and yet expected to overcome it or survive it. The issue is also one of agency: if the sailors are "enfolded" in "the immense grip of the sea," as the narrator proclaims, is it even possible for them to steer themselves—physically or morally? Of course, this issue, as we will see, afflicts Næss's theory of deep ecology as much as it does Conrad's sailors.

The "Wilderness" of Kurtz

In fact, *Heart of Darkness*, Conrad's subsequent work, touches on all of these themes. A more skeptical work in character and tone, it also questions to an even greater degree whether Conrad's vision can lend itself to any particular ethical framework, such as Næss's conception of deep ecology. Certainly, there are moments in the novella, as McCarthy points out, that reflect a holistic vision of nature, as well as the self-realization that, in Næss's eyes, comes with it. Marlow, for example, explains how

> watching a coast as it slips by the ship is like thinking about an enigma. There it is before you—smiling, frowning, inviting, grand, mean, insipid, or savage, and always mute with an air of whispering—Come and find out. This one was almost featureless, as if still in the making....
>
> (54)

Marzec points out that the "unfamiliar environment" has a bewildering effect on Kurtz and "contributes to his madness" (421, 420). Of course, it is questionable whether it is the environment itself or simply the unrestrained pursuit of ivory and other pleasures—what Marlow calls the "gratification of his various lusts" (104)—that leads to his madness. It is also possible that introspection itself becomes the main catalyst, as when Marlow explains that Kurtz's "soul was mad—being alone in the wilderness, it had looked within itself and by Heavens! I tell you it had gone mad" (113–14). It is not clear that the "wilderness" represents "nature" as much as human isolation and the moral introspection or unchecked greed that that allows.

Certainly, the "whispering" of the coast in the above passage (54) likely corresponds with Kurtz's transformation, where the "wilderness" takes hold of him, even whispering to him, in Marlow's account:

> But the wilderness had found him out early and had taken on him a terrible vengeance for the fantastic invasion. I think it had whispered to him things about himself which he did not know, things of which he had no conception till he took counsel with this great

> solitude—and the whisper had proved irresistibly fascinating. It echoed loudly within him because he was hollow at the core.... I put down the glass, and the head that had appeared near enough to be spoken to seemed at once to have leaped away from me into inaccessible distance.
>
> (104)

McCarthy reads this passage as indicating that "Kurtz saw and feared the 'complete knowledge' his immersion in nature delivered" (642). That immersion is amplified by Marlow's characterization of Kurtz's final revelation, a revelation that Marlow himself nearly shares:

> The vision seemed to enter the house with me, the stretcher, the phantom bearers, the wild crowd of obedient worshippers, the gloom of the forests, the glitter of the reach between the murky bends, the beat of the drum, regular and muffled like the beating of a heart, the heart of a conquering darkness. It was a moment of triumph for the wilderness, an invading and vengeful rush which it seemed to me I would have to keep back alone for the salvation of another soul. And the memory of what I had heard him say afar there, with the horned shapes stirring at my back in the glow of fires within the patient woods, those broken phrases came back to me, were heard again in their ominous and terrifying simplicity.
>
> (121)

As in deep ecology, the biosphere takes on a soul of its own, replete with a "beating heart," and it subsumes all forms, even nonliving ones, like the stretcher (which perhaps expands Næss's holistic vision into something closer to pantheism). Again, where Næss attributes "deep pleasure and satisfaction" to this immersion ("The shallow" 96), Kurtz finds "horror" (179). Importantly, Marlow also finds in Kurtz's face "the expression of sombre pride, of ruthless power, of craven terror—of an intense and hopeless despair" (177). If it were simply pride coupled with terror, one might liken the experience to that of the Kantian Sublime. Yet the produced effect is much wider, at least in Marlow's account, insofar as Kurtz's perceived reaction to "the wilderness" ranges from one of sheer "power" to helplessness, thereby demonstrating, above all, the complexity of nature's subsuming and the varying roles it assumes in Marlow's telling. The power that Kurtz assumes from this interaction is equally important because it represents less of a "close partnership with other forms of life," as Næss's vision entails, than the use or dominance of them, resulting, in this case, in staked heads and detusked animals.

Furthermore, it is far from clear that Marlow's vision is Conrad's. Indeed, Marlow's reliability as a narrator, or as a purveyor of Kurtz's revelation, has been amply questioned by critics,[2] especially given Conrad's choice to have Marlow's story related by an anonymous narrator. The narrator freely acknowledges Marlow's propensity to "spin yarns" (45), which also calls into question the veracity of the account and adds another layer of mystery to it. In some ways, the narrative detachment may even correspond to the message. As the unnamed narrator explains, to Marlow

> the meaning of an episode was not inside like a kernel but outside, enveloping the tale which brought it out only as a glow brings out a haze, in the likeness of one of these misty halos that sometimes are made visible by the spectral illumination of moonshine.
>
> (45)

Although Næss never precisely defines his epistemology in framing deep ecology, his conception of knowledge acquisition is similarly obscure. He explained that he conceived his philosophy less as a set of rules than a series of gestures, or what he calls "norms" that "should be freely used and elaborated" ("The shallow" 99). Reading Kurtz's message through Næss's conception of "complexity," or the "systems theory" on which it draws, helps explains Marlow's convoluted interpretations. Indeed, "spinning yarns" is precisely the point of a philosophy, be it Marlow's or Næss's, that involves entanglement and individual self-discovery.

My own view is that *Heart of Darkness* corresponds less to deep ecology than to two of its original precepts: self-realization and a de-anthropocentrized universe. Certainly, Kurtz undergoes a revelation at the hands of the jungle and all of its concomitant ills. And certainly humans, even Kurtz, occupy a rather fleeting place in this "wilderness," as Marlow calls it. Marlow muses, in a line that foreshadows his later description of the "conquering heart of darkness" and "the triumph for the wilderness," that "the silent wilderness surrounding this cleared speck on the earth struck me as something great and invincible, like evil or truth, waiting patiently for the passing away of this fantastic invasion" (65). Marlow's description of the wilderness as "great and invincible" echoes the belief of Næss that nature is all-encompassing. Yet what that "evil or truth" precisely is in Marlow's account remains obscure to both him and the reader and forms a shaky ground for ascribing any sort of ethical imperative to Conrad. Moreover, unlike in deep ecology, and perhaps even *The Nigger of the "Narcissus,"* it is not entirely clear that humans and the natural world are ontologically linked. Humans clear whole sections of the jungle—"paths...through burnt grass" (61), for example—and hoard tons of ivory. Even the characterization of the "wilderness" as "waiting patiently" for the colonists to disappear suggests more of an inherent disconnect, as does the very notion of a "conquering darkness." After all, if the wilderness and humankind are ontologically linked, of what need is a conquest?

That said, since these descriptions come near the beginning and middle of the story, they assume less importance than the description near the end of Marlow's vision of Kurtz, where the natural world and humankind, or at least Kurtz himself, are firmly intertwined. There, Kurtz is greeted with the wilderness's "invading and vengeful rush." Of course, the question remains how Kurtz could act morally, or independently choose a non-"evil" path, if the "darkness" is indeed "conquering," as Marlow proclaims. Kurtz's immersion in nature prompts readers to wonder where morality comes from, whether it requires human agency, and whether it necessitates a metaphysical separation from one's surroundings, all questions that likewise surround deep ecology itself.

Nostromo and "the immense indifference of things"

Nostromo was published five years after *Heart of Darkness*, in a time of tempestuous marriage, mounting debts and severe gout. Conrad considered it his most difficult book to write, and Ford Madox Ford assisted him in the effort, either producing himself or taking down from Conrad's dictation about 30,000 words. The result was Conrad's most massive and, in many estimations, most ambitious novel.

Nostromo presents no less than nineteen main characters, any number of whose perspectives are given. Unlike in *The Nigger of the "Narcissus"* and *Heart of Darkness*, where one character narrates from a more or less consistent vantage point, *Nostromo* presents an ambiguous narrator who manages to slip inside characters' heads at times, at other times offering a semi-omniscient viewpoint. The timeframe is even more warped, and, as Jakob Lothe points out, offers an incredibly complicated narrative structure (175). Much has been written about the effects of these devices, but little has been said about the novel's particular view of ecology, and how these devices might cloud it.

The most startling example of a character's immersion in nature, and one that bears the most comparison to Kurtz's revelation, is when Decoud find himself stranded on the Isabels and succumbs to the isolation by sinking himself in suicide:

> After three days of waiting for the sight of some human face, Decoud caught himself entertaining a doubt of his own individuality. It had merged into the world of cloud and water, of natural forces and forms of nature. In our activity alone do we find the sustaining illusion of an independent existence as against the whole scheme of things of which we form a helpless part. Decoud lost all belief in the reality of his action past and to come. On the fifth day an immense

melancholy descended upon him palpably. He resolved not to give himself up to these people in Sulaco, who had beset him, unreal and terrible, like jibbering and obscene spectres. He saw himself struggling feebly in their midst, and Antonia, gigantic and lovely like an allegorical statue, looking on with scornful eyes at his weakness.

(497–8)

As in Kurtz's revelation and as with the crew of the *Narcissus* during the storm, Decoud "merges" with the life forms around him ("the world of cloud and water, of natural forces and forms of nature"), and in so doing, loses his individuality. The image is entirely de-anthropocentric insofar as it emphasizes human nothingness. To call it "biotic," however, as would be required for Næss's conception of holistic ontology, would be to ignore the desolation of the place. Even "the sea-birds of the gulf shun the Isabels" (496), the narrator reminds us, as if to heighten the isolation. In fact, it is this solitude, not the natural world, that ultimately engulfs Decoud:

A victim of the disillusioned weariness which is the retribution meted out to intellectual audacity, the brilliant Don Martin Decoud, weighted by the bars of San Tomé silver, disappeared without a trace, swallowed up in the immense indifference of things.

(501)

Perhaps the only identifiable object in this surrounding, apart from the sea and clouds, is the silver, which is fitting, given that the silver becomes both the central motif of the novel and the source of each character's undoing, including Decoud. Certainly, he longs to return to Antonia, his love interest, and uphold the reputation of his family, but he remains so committed to his strategy that he ends up dying on account of it, literally "weighted by the bars of San Tomé silver" (501).

Clearly this scene, if not the whole of the book, emphasizes the silver's predominance, and indeed the role of materialism generally. In that sense, it shares deep ecology's critique of capitalism. It also emphasizes the ultimate power of the nonhuman world—personified most aptly by the silver. But silver, importantly, is not a living organism and cannot easily be conceived as part of what Næss calls the "biospheric net" ("The shallow" 95). When Decoud is "swallowed up in the immense indifference of things," his immersion is with "things," and in particular the "merciless solitude" (500), not "life forms," and it would be mistaken to construe his envelopment as entirely analogous to that which Næss depicts. That said, insofar as the silver mine takes on a life of its own—"there was no mistaking the growling mutter of the mountain pouring its stream of treasure under the stamps" (105)—there is room for a pantheistic interpretation, as in Kurtz's revelation, where the stretcher is also "swallowed up." After all, Decoud rightly admits to Mrs. Gould that "everything turns upon the San Tomé mine" (214), raising the possibility that the mine does assume a theistic or divine role. It is also possible to read the living force of the silver as linking economics with ecology, as Clayton does in interpreting *Victory*. Likewise, in *The Challenge of Bewilderment*, Armstrong argues that "much of the mystery and fascination surrounding the silver of the San Tomé mine is due to the ambiguous position it occupies" between "culture and nature," representing both a "natural resource" and a "sign" whose "capacity for representation is infinitely variable" (158). Either way, it seems clear that the narrator's central concern in describing "the immense indifference of things" is with the metaphysical quandary of being, not just ecology.

More broadly, *Nostromo* is rife with moments of ecological importance, even if they do not involve the same level of immersion in nature. An example comes in the middle of Book Two, depicting Mrs. Gould's short train ride:

> The carriage rolled noiselessly on the soft track, the shadows fell long on the dusty little plain interspersed with dark bushes, mounds of turned-up earth, low wooden buildings with iron roofs of the Railway Company; the sparse row of telegraph poles strode obliquely clear of the town, bearing a single, almost invisible wire far into the great campo—like a slender, vibrating feeler of that progress waiting outside for a moment of peace to enter and twine itself about the weary heart of the land.
>
> (166)

As in *Heart of Darkness*, *Nostromo* presents a recurrent dichotomy between the untapped terrain of the jungle and the encroaching technology of colonists, symbolized most trenchantly by the ever-expanding railway tracks and telegraph lines. This passage directly echoes the earlier description at the beginning of Book Two, where

> the telegraph line [did not] cross the mountains yet; its poles, like slender beacons on the plain, penetrated into the forest fringe of the foot-hills cut by the deep avenue of the track; and its wire ended abruptly in the construction camp at a white deal table supporting a Morse apparatus, in a long hut of planks with a corrugated iron roof overshadowed by gigantic cedar trees—the quarters of the engineer in charge of the advance section.
>
> (135)

It would be a mistake to view the conflict as solely about technology versus nature, however. The technological emblems—telegraph poles and railways—also become a recurrent symbol of feigned progress in the book. Early on, Sir John, the head of the railway, assures Mrs. Gould that she "shall have more steamers, a railway, a telegraph-cable—a future in the great world which is worth infinitely more than any amount of ecclesiastical past" (36). In fact, all of these inventions, particularly the telegraph, become the catalyst for the revolution's unfolding: "The initial moves were the seizure of the cable telegraph office and the securing of the Government steamer lying in the narrow creek which is the harbour of Esmeralda" (287). The grand irony of the telegraph line, then, is that, hardly the purveyor of riches that are promised to her, it becomes the source of Mrs. Gould's undoing insofar as it secures her husband's mining concession and thus furthers his habitual neglect of her. When Mrs. Gould jealously tells Giselle at the end, "I have been loved, too" (561), she reveals the extent of her own solitude and in many ways epitomizes the emptiness of her husband's whole venture, if not the colonial enterprise and its promise of civilizational advancement. Thus, culture, in *Nostromo*, becomes as isolating and impoverishing as the very jungle it has sought to replace.

For his part, Charles Gould, the proprietor of the mine, remembers how, accompanied by his wife, "he had gazed for the first time upon the jungle-grown solitude of the gorge" (105). The passage echoes Marlow's first glimpse of the coastline, as well as Conrad's preface to *The Nigger of the "Narcissus,"* where he declares the goal of art to be to "compel men entranced by the sight of distant goals to glance for a moment at the surrounding vision of form and colour, of sunshine and shadows; to make them pause for a look, for a sigh, for a smile" (xxviii). On its face, Conrad's message espouses an environmental ethic, wherein humans find beauty and solace in the majesty of nature, perhaps even akin to Næss's vision of the "deep pleasure and satisfaction we receive from close partnership with other forms of life" ("The shallow" 96). Yet Conrad's passage in *Nostromo* continues with a musing from Don Pépé, the mine manager, who "rode up, and, stretching his arm up the gorge, had declared with mock solemnity, 'Behold the very paradise of snakes, señora'" (105). Don Pépé, obviously wary of the rebels, evinces his distrust of the populace. His cynicism contrasts not only with the initial idealism of Charles Gould and other colonists; this construing of the jungle's inhabitants as snake-like, and presumably treacherous, contradicts Naess's vision of a natural immersion characterized by "close partnership with other forms of life."

As in the jungle of *Heart of Darkness*, nature is very much present in the gorge, and probably even coextensive with humans, especially insofar as the inhabitants are perceived as "snakes." It is a gorge where, for example, Hirsch "crouched, crept, crawled, made dashes, guided by a sort of animal instinct, keeping away from every light and from every sound of voices" (272); where "Don Pépé, descending the path from the upper plateau, appeared no bigger than a large beetle" (394–5); and where even Nostromo "stretched himself with a slow twist of the waist and a leisurely growling yawn of white teeth, as natural and free from evil in the moment of waking as a magnificent and unconscious wild beast" (412). As in Næss's holistic vision, there are clear linkages, if not direct overlaps, between humans and animals, particularly in the narrator's eyes. Certainly, these depictions of humans as animals, and especially "beasts" and "snakes," are ironic insofar as the characters—Hirsch, Don Pépé and Nostromo—all represent figures of perceived civility in Sulaco. More than this, however, these animal images undercut the notion of civilizational progress or the idea that humans, through technology or advancement, could somehow transcend their animal backgrounds and evade the realm of nature.

Clearly, Jeffrey Meyers is right in that Conrad allows for an "ecological consciousness" (107). What is not clear, however, is whether Conrad himself is advocating Gould's naive embrace of nature ("the jungle-grown solitude"), or Don Pépé's more cynical vision ("a paradise of snakes"). Indeed, Conrad is presenting both views and mocking them equally.

That mockery is important, if only because it reflects a broader problem in deep ecology: the movement's ambiguous conception of morality. Næss conceived his movement as a pluralist "platform," rather than as a doctrine of any sort ("The Basics" 61). Yet, as Andrew Brennan and Yeuk-Sze Lo point out,

> Næss failed to explain in any detail how to make sense of the idea that oysters or barnacles, termites or bacteria could have interests of any morally relevant sort at all. Without an account of this, Næss's early "biospheric egalitarianism"—that all living things whatsoever had a similar right to live and flourish—was an indeterminate principle in practical terms.

In practical terms, the natives of Sulaco, chiefly the "Indios," welcome the running of the mine and the exploitation of the earth insofar as it secures them from poverty. Even though, in the distant past, "whole tribes of Indians had perished in the exploitation" of the mine (91), *Nostromo*'s narrator also explains, however ironically, that "whole families had been moving from the first towards the spot in the Higuerota range, whence the rumour of work and safety had spread over the pastoral Campo" (101). Likewise, members of the developing world question whether an ecological framework that imparts mutual value to the non-human world is not in some way elitist or discounting of the historical injustice meted out by colonialism.

Ramachandra Guha is especially blunt, comparing deep ecology's proponents, whom he terms "missionaries," with Woodrow Wilson and other Americans "who have sought to impose their vision of the good life on the rest of the world" (272). Guha even asks whether deep ecology does not mask an underlying colonial intent. He adds that "specious nonsense about the equal rights of all species cannot hide the plain fact that green imperialists are possibly as dangerous and certainly more hypocritical than their economic or religious counterparts" (276). The deep ecologists, in his account, celebrate the natural world at the expense of the impoverished and historically oppressed, for whom it forms a livelihood, rather than a form of spiritual awakening. Sulaco's "indios" are likewise an afterthought for dreams of Costaguana's independence.

Certainly, these questions transcend Conrad and pertain more to environmentalism itself. Yet it is plausible that Conrad would share Guha's critique, or at the very least question the motives of those advocating environmentalism. When Don Pépé describes the gorge as a "paradise of snakes," Conrad expresses his skepticism toward schemes of moral progress, colonial ventures and ecological visions marked by benevolent "partnerships," as Næss calls them. Conrad's characters endorse the crude exploitation of the jungle and then fall comically victim. Yet Conrad's novel questions how humans with a propensity to act like "snakes," "beetles," and "beasts" could somehow rise to a level of morality, or enact the sort of "progress" to which the colonists, and, by analogy, ecologists like Næss, aspire.

Thus, while Conrad often shares Næss's distrust of human exceptionalism, it is not fair to conclude that he embraces environmental holism. Rather, Conrad's approach is deep skepticism that problematizes any ecological reading or narrative of green progress.

Notes

1 Næss later claimed that a holistic vision of ontology was unnecessary for deep ecology, maintaining that "you may or may not have your principal loyalty focussed on the biosphere as an organic whole" ("The Basics" 65). In fact, in composing a new list of principles for the movement, which he admitted were "in need of clarification, collaboration, and comments" ("The Basics" 68), he omitted any direction mention of anthropocentrism or other metaphysical aspects. He also modified the principle of "biospheric egalitarianism" to one of assigning equal value to ecology, not equal rights. Thus deep ecology became less a doctrine than a grouping of ideas, or a "platform," as Næss called it ("The Basics" 61). For the sake of clarity, I am going to limit my discussion to Næss's original conception.
2 Ian Watt, for example, points out that "Marlow is in effect his own author, and so there is no reliable and comprehensive perspective on him or his experience," a facet that Watt attributes to Conrad's "skepticism about understanding character" and finds employed for the first time in *Heart of Darkness* (169).

Works Cited

Anker, Peder and Nina Witoszek. "The Dream of the Biocentric Community and the Structure of Utopias." *Worldviews: Global Religions, Culture, and Ecology*, vol. 2, no. 3, 1998. pp. 239–256.

Armstrong, Paul B. *The Challenge of Bewilderment: Understanding and Representation in James, Conrad, and Ford*. Cornell, 1987.

———. "Conrad's Contradictory Politics: The Ontology of Society in *Nostromo*." *Twentieth Century Literature*, vol. 31, no. 1, Spring 1985. pp. 1–21.

Brennan, Andrew and Yeuk-Sze Lo. "Environmental Ethics." *The Stanford Encyclopedia of Philosophy*. Edited by Edward N. Zalta. Fall 2011 Edition. http://plato.stanford.edu/archives/fall2011/entries/ethics-environmental/

Clayton, Aaron. "*Victory* in Nature: An Ecocritical Reading of Joseph Conrad's Novel." *Conradiana*, vol. 42, no. 1, 2010. pp. 129–139.

Conrad, Joseph. *The Collected Letters of Joseph Conrad*. Edited by Frederick R. Karl and Laurence Davies. Cambridge, 1988. vol. 3.

———. *Heart of Darkness and Other Tales*. Edited by Owen Knowles. Cambridge, 2010.

———. *The Nigger of the "Narcissus."* John Grant, 1925.

———. *Nostromo*. Edited by Norman Sherry. Dent, 1974.

———. *Notes on Life and Letters. The Cambridge Edition of the Works of Joseph Conrad*. Edited by J. H. Stape and Andrew Busza. Cambridge, 2004.

Guha, Ramachandra. "Deep Ecology Revisited." *The Great New Wilderness Debate*. Edited by J. Baird Callicott and Michael Nelson. University of Georgia, 1998. pp. 271–279.

Hochschild, Adam. *King Leopold's Ghosts: A Story of Greed, Terror, and Heroism in Colonial Africa*. Mariner Books, 1998.

Lothe, Jakob. *Conrad's Narrative Method*. Clarendon, 1991.

Marzec, Robert P. "Speaking Before the Environment: Modern Fiction and the Ecological." *Modern Fiction Studies*, vol. 55, no. 3, Fall 2009. pp. 419–442.

McCarthy, Jeffrey Mathes. "'A Choice of Nightmares': The Ecology of *Heart of Darkness*." *Modern Fiction Studies*, vol. 55, no. 3, Fall 2009. pp. 620–648.

Meyers, Jeffrey. "The Anxiety of Confluence: Evolution, Ecology, and Imperialism in Conrad's *Heart of Darkness*." *ISLE*, vol. 8, no. 2, 2001. pp. 97–108.

Næss, Arne. "The Basics of Deep Ecology." *The Trumpeter*, vol. 21, no. 1, 2005. pp. 61–71.

———. "The Shallow and the Deep, Long-Range Ecology Movement. A summary." *Inquiry*, vol. 16, no. 1, 1973. pp. 95–100.

Watt, Ian. "Marlow, Henry James, and *Heart of Darkness*." *Nineteenth-Century Fiction*, vol. 33, no. 2, September 1978. pp. 159–174.

Zdzisław, Najder. *Joseph Conrad: A Life*. Camden, 2007.

10 "What Could His Object Be?" Form and Materiality in Conrad's "The Tale"

Jarica Linn Watts

Joseph Conrad begins his 1917 short fiction "The Tale" with the image of a "large single window" which neatly frames "a long room" equipped with a "deep, shadowy couch" and a "low ceiling" (93). The scene here depicts the first of two settings in which the story takes place and is parallel, in all of its materiality, to the sea and its fierce waters, its "rocky, dangerous coast," its "wall of fog," its "great convolutions of vapours" (100). To begin his work by showcasing "the order of material appearances" ("Typhoon" 3) is not uncommon for Conrad, though I hope these lines establish the ways Conrad's war story foregrounds discussions of the modernist encounter with the object as a nonhuman entity. The purpose is to claim for this little-studied text a seminal importance in Conrad's oeuvre; a secondary purpose is to illustrate for Conrad studies, and for scholars interested in the relation between nature and new materialism more specifically, how Conrad uses "The Tale" to rethink his representation of the natural world. The new relation presented in "The Tale" is a shift from Conrad's previous attention to the materiality of the natural world as symbol or uncaring backdrop. Here, the material world is both presence and actant, and Conrad uses "The Tale" to wrestle with the best ways to present that world in narrative form.

Paul March-Russell asserts that of the various interpretations of "The Tale" plied by readers and critics, an emphasis on narrative form stands out. The meticulous scholarship of William Bonney, Jakob Lothe and Jeremy Hawthorn, among others, draws attention to the story's multilayered structure and the metaphoric, compositional, rhetorical, narratorial and aesthetic contributions that structure makes to the moral relativism of the story itself. From the work of these narrative theorists, readers are able to chart not only Conrad's complicated concentric narratives but also the deceptions and omissions that highlight the story's subtext of deceit. The problem, as March-Russell sees it, is that such interpretations effectively shut down more nuanced readings of "The Tale" while simultaneously "devalue[ing] the story's ethical imperative" (March-Russell 267).

While I am sympathetic to March-Russell's insistence that readers must move readings of "The Tale" beyond a simple recitation of narrative structure, such decisive—and divisive—distinctions between the poetic and the political are deductive, and, in the case of this particular story, detrimental. Conrad's fiction, after all, shows the many ways in which Conrad himself wrestles equally with the material reality of the world and the formal presentation of that world—he is one, as both sailor and writer, who is forever experimenting with formal device in an attempt to iconicize the back-and-forth relationship between the world as such and the human structures that exist alongside it.

Recent strides in neo-formalism and neo-materialism illuminate Conrad's attempts to navigate the ontological fields of both human and nonhuman. The suppositional foundation of this discussion is Bruno Latour's claim that the advent of modernity (or the modern) led to a "Great Divide," which placed the power, interests and politics of humans at one end of the spectrum, while knowledge about objects and the nonhuman was placed at the other (39). Conrad, I will show, actually ties these material forms together and shifts focus from the human experience of things to the network relationship of things themselves. Conrad's fiction anticipates and complicates Latour's approach because it overcomes the rift between object and subject, and in so doing spurs thinking about the ways in which the nonhuman, as an agentic force, exerts a powerful hold over the human mind and imagination.

Form and Narrative

Form is Conrad's road to objects and things. As the critical commentary confirms, there is no question that Conrad very much intended "The Tale" to be a story about narrative structure. Depending on which theoretical approach one takes, "The Tale" is either a three-pronged narrative (Lothe, 74) or a four-pronged narrative (Bonney, 208–14), both of which carry a subtext of lies and deceit (Hawthorn, 263). Though Bonney, Hawthorn, and Lothe all emphasize what Paul March-Russell calls "the paranoic and delusional beliefs of the commanding officer," the picture they paint places an undue emphasis on the processes of readability "for the reader" of Conrad's tale (269). In contrast, my own reading summons the framed narrative for its ability to incorporate both listener and speaker in a structural complexity that shows meaning as derived from a variety of configurations. In this way, and unlike the narrative theorists previously mentioned, I intend to shift the scholarly discussion away from the reader of Conrad's text in favor of the nameless woman—the listener—who brings the commander's tale into being.[1]

The narrator launches into the account of the Commanding Officer and the Northman—the second in the concentric structure—with a line that self-reflects on narrative openings. He takes playful but perverse license with the traditional phrase for getting under way in fairy and folk tales: "Once upon a time," he begins, there was a "Commanding Officer and a Northman" (95). The assumption here is that the commanding officer, now taking on the narrative voice, will not only deliver a "tale," as the title suggests, but that he will deliver a *fairy*tale.[2] But rather than following the familiar sing-song cadence of that form—as we see in, say, the opening lines of Joyce's *A Portrait of the Artist as a Young Man* ("Once upon a time and a very good time it was there was a moocow coming down along the road" [3]) and Lawrence's "The Rocking Horse Winner" ("There was a woman who was beautiful, who started with all the advantages, yet she had no luck" [269])—the commanding officer instead follows with an injunction about characterization. He insists that the names and the titles of those involved in his story be "put in the capitals...because they had no other names" (95). Here, the could-be fairytale is thwarted before it can even be fractured (as with Lawrence) or dissolved into a state of nonsense (as we see with Joyce); instead, the commanding officer draws attention to the formal and functional aspects of language, even down to that all-important capital letter. This leaves readers to conclude that the outset is both an upset enacted specifically through narrative form and a distancing device since the commanding officer is, as we later discover, telling his own tale and desires to remain objective so that the woman will ultimately declare either his guilt or innocence.

Given that her expectations as listener have been thwarted, it is no surprise that the mistress is intent on discerning which form the officer's tale will ultimately take. As such, she prods and he parses: "It's going to be a comic story"; "there was love in it, too"; "it will be human... and it won't be a noisy story"; and finally, "all the long guns in it will be dumb" (95). At last, she knows: it will be a war story. And here is where we must necessarily return to the title. For while the mistress begins the second narrative account with the demand, "tell me something...why not tell me a tale?" the commanding officer changes the register from "tale" to "story" ("it won't be a noisy story" [95]) once he begins to detail the account of the Commanding Officer and the Northman. The change in formal registers here is important for readers of "The Tale" because it places us and the unnamed mistress in the same position of expectancy. While the mistress demands that her formal expectations be met in terms of genre (love story, war story, comedy), we, too, demand much the same from the text: Is it a tale? Is it a story? Is it a confession? And what, really, is the difference?

The word "tale" is a loaded choice for Conrad in wartime.[3] Gaetano D'Elia explains that Conrad reserved the word "tale" for this, one of his last stories, in order to "consecrate" the oral delivery upon which so much of his prose is based (51). D'Elia insists that after penning "The Tale," Conrad's use of the word "tale" took on a different meaning "as an archaic term or as a rhetorical and poetic noun" (51). He continues:

> [A]fter writing ["The Tale"], when Conrad employs [the word 'tale'] again in "The Dover Patrol," it will mean "number," "total": "The tale of the Dover Patrol is the tale of a small nucleus of ships and crews of the Royal Navy; It was their conception of their honour and they carried it out of this war unblemished by a single display of weakness by the slightest moment of hesitation in the long tale of dangerous service." In a very indirect way these two examples, in which "tale when referred to the war loses its current meaning, show the greatest mistrust in the possibility of telling a tale...of the war.
> (51)

If D'Elia is correct in assuming that Conrad found the word "tale"—and its associations with falsehood and deceit—ineffective in detailing an account of war, then we can easily understand why the commanding officer makes the shift in his own narrative account. What is more, the move from "tale" to "story" helps explain the biographical nature of the events and the slippage of pronouns that occurs as the commanding officer reveals himself culpable in the plot points: "There was comedy in it, and slaughter...And since I could find in the universe only what was deeply rooted in the fibres of my being there was love in it too" (95). To put it simply, when the commanding officer shifts from "tale" to "story," he does so to help manage the formal expectations of both mistress/listener and reader and to make clear that he is about to embark on a personal account of war: He is not going to "tell" a "tale" or spin a yarn, his word choice insists; instead, he will relate "his" story, a history of sorts.

While March-Russell sees the exchange between the commanding officer and his mistress as a representation of "the potential void within any communicative act," and lambasts the woman for her hesitancy and constant interruption (275), I instead see her litany of questions as a dependence on the various narrative techniques that readers use to symbolize knowledge and to synthesize, arrive at, and represent understanding. This is why, in addition to working through the conventions of genre, the mistress also questions the officer about setting:

> 'It could be a tale not of this world,' she explained.
> 'You want a tale of the other, the better world?' he asked...
> 'No. I don't mean that. I mean another—some other—world. In the universe—not in heaven...
> ... 'But as to this "another world"—who's going to look for it and for the tale that is in it?
> (95)

We learn from this passage that the story the commanding officer will recite is above all about a material world—"it [i]s a world of seas and continents and islands" (95); tellingly, it is also a world that contains its own essence ("whose going to look...for the tale that is in it?" [95]). In short, it is a world, which flattens the binary between human and nonhuman and allows readers to experience that relationship more horizontally.

There is much to unpack from any discussion of Conrad's sea, but I wish here to focus only on Celia Kingsbury's insistence that the sea "becomes the dominant metaphor" in "The Tale," a configuration that ties all of the other formal elements together in its ability to conceal or deceive. According to Kingsbury, "what the sea hides becomes more important than what its depths bring up" (159). I am particularly drawn to Kingsbury's discussion because she all but names the sea as a material force. The sea has a life, Kingsbury seems to insist, reduced though it is by its association with metaphor, but an "existence" nonetheless. But that is not the complete story, for Kingsbury also tells us that the sea is a site of concealment, a word replete with notions of visibility, invisibility and perception.

The commanding officer speaks of the sea as a "matter of visual first-impression" which "had to be watched; watched by acute minds and also by actual sharp eyes" (96). His task, we are told, is to chart certain courses "too see—what he could see" (96).[4] The processes of visualization are central to the commanding officer's enterprises of conceptualization and become the site upon which Conrad is able to launch the moral invigoration of the story. It is somewhat curious that in a story so heavily focused on the material force of "things," one of Conrad's most reliable phrases—"the fitness of things"—is conspicuously absent.

Conrad has enlisted the line "the fitness of things" in various texts to various ends. In *Chance*, Conrad uses the phrase to call attention to cultural and political constructions that not only dominate but ultimately supplant individual thought processes and consciousness.[5] Hugh Epstein suggests to readers that in *The Secret Agent*, the phrase is a "sour joke," "a specious term...nakedly exposed as one that conveys the unruffled ease of the establishment in preserving its power by appeal to providential arrangement" (24).[6] But it is the use of the line in "Typhoon" that has applicability here, particularly in light of the material realities revealed in the following stanza:

> The still air moaned. Above Jukes' head a few stars shone into the pit of black vapours. The inky edge of the cloud-disc frowned upon the ship under the patch of glittering sky. The stars too seemed to look at her intently, as if for the last time, and the cluster of their splendour sat like a diadem on a lowering brow.

> Captain MacWhirr had gone into the chart-room. There was no light here; but he could feel the disorder of that place where he used to live tidily. His armchair was upset. The books had tumbled out on the floor: he scrunched a piece of glass under his boot.
>
> (83)

In these lines, the stillness of the air, the stars and the sky are overturned abruptly and immediately by the discord of darkness and chaos and the disarray of everyday objects. Epstein comments that

> in its tremendous evocation of the forces of the typhoon, what the novella...impress[es] upon the reader is that there is no ordained fitness of things, no providence, no design. Yet what it also shows us is that the MacWhirrs of the world...impose upon the shapelessness of things an order
>
> (23)

This is a world not far removed from that of "The Tale." For like "Typhoon," the fitness of things finds its assurance in the stable hierarchies of human construction—and for the commanding officers, maritime conventions, chains of command, and codes of warfare foster and, ultimately, sponsor his assurances and realities. Yet it is the processes of visualization and the compulsive need to see—it is the secrecy, the espionage and the threat beneath the surface—that mocks the fitness of things in this story. The commanding officer will be subject through the remainder of the story to a more searching examination of what is "fit" in his encounter with both the barrel at sea and the Northman.

When the commanding officer thus speaks of the "unchanged face of the waters," which belie neither hostility nor friendship, we must read it as especially influential:

> On fine days the sun strikes sparks upon the blue; here and there a peaceful smudge of smoke hangs in the distance, and it is impossible to believe that the familiar clear horizon traces the limit of one great circular ambush.
>
> Yes, it is impossible to believe, till some day you see a ship not your own ship..., but some ship in company, blow up all of a sudden and plop under almost before you know what has happened to her. Then you begin to believe. Henceforth you go out for the work to see—what you can see, and you keep on at it with the conviction that some day you will die from something you have not seen.
>
> (97)[7]

In passages such as this, the commanding officer articulates not only the deceitful nature of the sea but also the elemental force of the water;

in so doing, the sea emerges as semantic support in the story which scaffolds the twin notions of human and nonhuman with Conrad's own concerns about the material world and the formal presentation of that world.

Form and Materiality

How do literary forms influence material forms, and how do material forms influence literary forms? In her recent work *Forms*, Caroline Levine explains the many ways in which form propagates widely over human cognition. Levine notes that "form and materiality are inextricable," though her discussion falls short of theorizing the various forms of the material (9); as such, it is necessary to complicate her tidy reading in order to ask more elemental questions about what forms materiality may take and the extent to which human being and object interpolate one another. What do we do, for example, with the obvious interconnections between human and nonhuman elements in a story like Conrad's? And, more specifically, what are the various forms that facilitate the active participation of material forces in a plotline like "The Tale"?

In order to answer this last question, we must begin, as the commanding officer states, with the "unusual object...floating at sea" (107). The commanding officer pacifies the now-silent female listener by explaining, "I may tell you at once that the object was not dangerous in itself. No use in describing it. It may have been nothing more remarkable than, say, a barrel of a certain shape and colour" (98). What follows is then an account of the conversation between the commanding officer and his second-in-command, wherein an association emerges between the barrel (as material object) and human thought:

> It appeared to them to be not so much a proof of the sagacity as of the activity of certain neutrals. This activity had in many cases taken the form of replenishing the stores of certain submarines at sea. This was generally believed, if not absolutely known.... The object, looked at closely and turned away from with apparent indifference put it beyond doubt that something of the sort had been done somewhere in the neighborhood.
>
> (98)

"Generally believed," "something," "somewhere"—the certainty of the officers' experience is, as Rundle bluntly states, "rendered ludicrously inadequate by this tidal wave of qualification" (22). Such uncertainty is not new for Conrad. In his *The Limits of Metaphor*, James Guetti turns to *Heart of Darkness* to show how Marlow's conception of the wilderness is paradoxical—grounded in confidence, on the one hand (at the center of the wilderness lies "the amazing reality of its concealed life" [35]), and shrouded in abstraction on the other (Marlow becomes aware of a "general sense of vague and oppressive wonder" [20]). Megan Quigley's notable study *Modernist Fiction and Vagueness* can go a long way in helping readers to determine precisely why Conrad may have included such imprecise language. She writes: "vagueness, unlike ambiguity or multiplicity, fails to provide clear, if multiple, ways to read a text... vagueness, therefore, brings up a range of issues for fiction, of which two are salient and related: On the one hand, an author who seems to be vague may in fact be writing with precision about an atmosphere or situation that is itself vague; on the other hand, another writer may be vague about a precise situation in order to make the reader think" (7). Quigley singles out "atmosphere" as a medium not just conducive to literary vagueness but also a form unrivaled in its resourcefulness to human thinking and knowing. It is within this very atmosphere that fog clamors for position in Conrad's text—but just like the sea that sees and the tale that tells, the fog here signals much more than a cloud of water droplets or ice crystals suspended in the air.

In 1832 Prussian military analyst Carl von Clausewitz used the word "cloud" in reference to the uncertainty brought on by wartime experiences: "War is the province of uncertainty: three-fourths of those things upon which action in War must be calculated, are hidden more or less in the clouds of great uncertainty. Here, then, above all a fine and penetrating mind is called for, to search out the truth by the tact of its judgment" (Clausewitz). At the end of the nineteenth century, Col. Lonsdale Hale, of the Royal Engineers, went beyond Von Clausewitz's metaphorizing of uncertainty and directly used the phrase "fog of war" to describe "the state of ignorance in which commanders frequently find themselves as regards the real strength and position, not only of their foes, but also of their friends" (Hale). Working through the metaphor it provides, fog scaffolds uncertainty especially in conflicts and times of war, and it precisely this image that Conrad plays with when he describes the fog in "The Tale":

> Great convulsions of vapours flew over, swirling about masts and funnel, which looked as if they were beginning to melt...The ship was stopped, all sounds ceased, and the very fog became motionless, growing denser and as if solid in its amazing dumb mobility. The men at their stations lost sight of each other. Footsteps sounded stealthy; rare voices, impersonal and remote, died out without resonance. A blind white stillness took possession of the world.
>
> (100)

The fog here settles in, and in obliterating the sea itself (the commanding officer and his crew can literally see less and less), it serves both as a metaphor for the confusion the commanding officer experiences and as an atmospheric presence facilitating that very confusion (97). The commanding officer suspects that "something is in the air," as it were, and it is the fog—both of the wartime and water vapor variety—which facilitates his belief that an unstipulated, basically indeterminate "something" will materialize.

Put more directly, in Conrad's story, atmosphere functions as an agentic force capable of distributing its energy mutually to people and things. It is a structure that structures; it is that which facilitates the commanding officer's perceptual and psychological enthrallment with the potentially benign barrel, and it is that which governs the direction of things to come in the narrative. As readers, then, we have little choice but to interpret the vagueness in the commanding officer's account as a mimesis of reflection which emphasizes that the relation between human and non-human is not one between an "internal" self and an "external place" but rather a complex and unitary field of existence. Nidesh Lawtoo, writing on *Lord Jim* and "Typhoon" elsewhere in this volume, believes that such a strategy encourages readers to trace how nonhuman forces in the background have the physical and affective power to decenter human actions in the foreground. This nonbinary perspective encompasses typhoons and terrific storms, sailors and seaman, each of which shapes and conditions the other through a game of social and natural forces.[8]

All this to say that because Rundle interprets the commanding officer's qualifications through the linguistic turn toward deconstruction—the floating object is a "literal floating signifier," which is ultimately "not adequate to generate meaning" (22)—she falls into the all-too-common trap of overlooking the world of objects and things. Douglas Mao, outlining modernism's broad turn to the object world in his work *Solid Objects*, believes that this tendency to signify stems "from an older tradition in which the object appears principally as a signifier of something else or a component of scenic plentitude"; in contrast, modernity demands a measure of vibrancy by way of a "new order in which [the object's] value depends neither on metaphoricity nor on marginality" (13).

In the barrel, we thus have an object that is gaining supreme agency—and each time the object is discussed, it begins to exercise more force upon the commanding officer and his crew, until, ultimately, it becomes vital to the officers' certitude, a force stronger than human speculation (108). In this way, the barrel ultimately becomes what Bruno Latour calls an actant/operator. Jane Bennett parses Latour's definition:

> [An] actant ... is ... a source of action; an actant can be human or not, or, most likely, a combination of both. Latour defines it as "something that acts or to which activity is granted by others. It implies no special motivation of human individual actors, nor of humans in general." An actant is neither an object nor a subject but an

"intervener," akin to the Deleuzean "quasi-causal operator." An operator is that which, by virtue of its particular location in an assemblage and the fortuity of being in the right place at the right time, makes the difference, makes things happen, becomes the decisive force catalyzing an event. Actant and operator are substitute words for what in a more subject-centered vocabulary are called agents.

(9)

Much of the puissance of Conrad's barrel is that it is, in fact, the "decisive force catalyzing" the tragic events which play out at the end of the story, and much of this is seen in the way the barrel accentuates and orients the commanding officer's perception. In an almost syllogistic progression, the commanding officer thinks over the floating object—it is "evidence of what we were pretty certain of" (99)—and from there his thoughts begin to swirl around the "atmosphere of gratuitous treachery" (103): there must be "certain neutrals...replenishing the stores of certain submarines," and these neutrals must be engaged in "some deep and devilish purpose" based on "the murderous stealthiness" of their methods and "the atrocious callousness of complicities," all manifest in the barrel itself. In this progressiveness of step leading to illogical step, the barrel more than administers to the commanding officer's thinking; it is a criticality over all of his enterprises of conceptualization. Imbued with such productivity—and indeed, such independence—the barrel qualifies as more than a simple object (as the commanding officer continually insists); more broadly, it is a means to provoke affects in the commanding officer, which renders it, at least according to Bill Brown's definition, a "thing." According to Brown, "We begin to confront the thingness of objects when they stop working for us: when the drill breaks, when the car stalls, when the windows get filthy, when their flow within the circuits of production and distribution, consumption and exhibition, has been arrested, however momentarily" (*Thing Theory* 4). In short, things come into visibility when the thought of them ruptures or ebbs.

W.J.T. Mitchell supplies evidence that both human and nonhuman materials have long had a reciprocal association in which each has influenced the other. Setting the stage for Graham Harman, Levi Bryant and the other object-oriented ontologists, Mitchell overturns the entrenched notion that human beings are the subjects acting on the passive objects of the nonhuman world. By replacing this hegemonic view with the contention that we, in turn, are the recipients of the activities of nonhuman materials, Mitchell sees the necessity to demarcate between the world of "objects" and the world of "things." He writes: "objects are the way things appear to a subject—that is, with a name, an identity, a gestalt or stereotypical template.... Things, on the other hand...[signal] the moment when the object becomes the Other, when the sardine can looks back, when the mute idol speaks, when the subject experiences the object as uncanny and feels the need for what Foucault calls 'a metaphysics of that never objectifiable depth from which objects rise up toward our superficial knowledge'" (Mitchell qtd. in Bennett, 2).[9]

If Conrad's barrel is an actant imbued with what Bennett terms "thing-power" (2), and if, as such, it becomes the premier appliance through which the commanding officer's thoughts are churned, then we must examine the ways it manifests its presence once he encounters the Northman and his stranded vessel. With his "very faint, very elusive" suspicions about the floating barrel encircling his mind, the commanding officer considers all facts relating to the ship as evidence of espionage activity. Initially he questions why "the ship so suddenly discovered had not manifested her presence by ringing her bell" (101). This leads to more certainty-filled vagueness: "they must have heard our leadsmen," "they may even have made us out," and "the fellows on board must have been holding their breath" (101). Next he questions the Northman's "complicated story of engine troubles" and wonders why the vessel did not "sneak out unnoticed" before the commanding officer and his crew arrived in the ill-fated cove (102).

The commanding officer, of course, is very much aware that his reservations are inclined to snag—"such suspicions as the [type] which had entered his head are not easily defended" (102)—though he is disinclined to let them go: "what if she were the very ship which had been feeding some infernal submarine or other?" (103). In this way, once the Northman begins his tale, the commanding officer listens to an "inward voice" and a "grave murmur" that gratifies his suspicions "as if on purpose to keep alive in him his indignation" (104). If we attend to the new materialism, the "voice" and the "murmur" is actually the barrel itself; for, "the object, looked at closely..., put it beyond doubt that something...had been done somewhere in the neighborhood" (98). And just as the commanding officer continues to look beyond the surface of the barrel to its latent potentiality of spy games and secrecy, once on the Northman's boat, he again privileges what he cannot see over what is openly visible. When the Northman mentions that the vessel provides "bare living for my family," the commanding officer responds that "out of this war...you will be making a fortune yet for your family with this old ship" (103). When the Northman mentions the logbook and papers, which are "in perfect order," the commanding officer insists that "a log-book may be cooked. Nothing easier" (102, 105). And finally, when the Northman calls the commanding officer on his suspicions ("But you can't suspect me of anything" [105]), the commanding officer thinks to himself, "Why should he say that?" before returning to the string of doubts that have sustained his suspicions thus far: "why was he lying with steam up in this fog? ... why didn't he give some sign of life?" (106).

It is clear in this moment that the officer's reservations are taking a rewarding shape and a distinctive outline before him: "He felt alarmed at catching himself thinking as if his vaguest suspicions were turning into a certitude" (106). "Nothing could be trusted," he declares, at which point he again returns to the barrel in order to unfold and finally fulfill his own (un)certainty:

> "I don't know where I am," the Northman ejaculated, earnestly, "I really don't."
> He looked around as if the very chart room fittings were strange to him. The Commanding Officer asked him whether he had not seen any unusual objects floating about while he was at sea.
> "Objects! What objects? We were groping blind in the fog for days."
> "We had a few clear intervals," said the Commanding Officer. "And I'll tell you what I've seen and the conclusion I've come to about it."
>
> (107)

In this passage, the commanding officer explicitly references the barrel as the actant that puts the remainder of the plot events in motion, and it is thinking about it again that allows him to feel—unhesitatingly—the rightness and "certitude" of his decision to send the Northman's vessel and its crew to their death (108).

The barrel's existence points to aspects of a vital materialism that Conrad scholarship has failed to gauge. "The Tale" shows one avid listener that the floating object legitimately qualifies as an actant, just as it warns all readers of the many ways nature is a volatile mix of other actants all working together in an agentic constellation. Indeed, when the materiality of the barrel grabs the attention of the second-in-command, it is in part because of the arrangement it has formed with other elements, including maritime codes and warfare rules, the atmosphere, the fog, the sea, the ship, the sailors, the hierarchy of the officers and even the relationship between the commanding officer and his mistress. For had the war not "been carried on...over the water [and] under the water," had the weather not given a "nasty" sign of foreboding, had the fog not deceived, had the ship not turned, the second-in-command might not have given a second thought to the barrel (96, 97). Such a configuring is managed by what Bennett names an "assemblage" and is, in turn, what I consider the most influential form in Conrad's story (12). Bennett notes that

> Assemblages are not governed by any central head: no one materiality or type of material has sufficient competence to determine consistently the trajectory or impact of the group. The effects generated

by an assemblage are, rather, emergent properties, emergent in that their ability to make something happen (a newly inflected materialism, a blackout, a hurricane, a war on terror) is distinct from the sum of the vital force of each materiality considered alone. Each member and proto-member of the assemblage has a certain vital force, but there is also an effectivity proper to the grouping as such: an agency of the assemblage.

(12–13)

If we follow the urging of Mao and turn away from metaphor and marginality in favor of what is really a human/nonhuman assemblage, it becomes apparent that perhaps the most dominant form of materialism—and by extension the dominant form in Conrad's story—is that which draws on both the collaboration and cooperation of bodies and forces. Indeed, we can look to Conrad's text to see a viable example of Bennett's assemblage; here, after all, we have a variety of human elements (maritime code, rules of warfare, hierarchy between ships and officers) and nonhuman elements (sea, ship, fog, atmosphere, barrel), all working together to produce the commanding officer's deadly belief in the Northman's deceit while also deflecting culpability away from the commanding officer by placing responsibility on the material actants themselves.

Ultimately I am suggesting that there is not so much an agent behind the Northman's unfortunate death as an effecting by a human/nonhuman assemblage. Indeed, what the swerve toward mutualism and materialism has shown us is that agentic capacity must be seen as differentially distributed across a wider range of ontological types. For Jane Bennett, such an idea is expressed in the notion of "deodand," a figure of English law from about 1200 until it was abolished in 1846. Bennett explains that "in cases of accidental death or injury to a human, the nonhuman actant, for example, the carving knife that fell into human flesh or the carriage that trampled the leg of a pedestrian—became deodand (literally, 'that which must be given to God'). In recognition of its peculiar efficacy (a power that is less masterful than agency but more active than recalcitrance), the deodand, a materiality 'suspended between human and thing,' was surrendered to the crown to be used (or sold) to compensate for the harm done" (9). According to William Pietz, "any culture must establish some procedure of compensation, expiation, or punishment to settle the debt created by unintended human deaths whose direct cause is not a morally accountable person, but a nonhuman material object" (97).

As Bennett notes, "there are of course differences between the knife that impales and the man impaled," between the barrel floating out at sea and the commanding officer, the narrator of its vitality. But I think Bennett has it right when she insists that these differences "need to be flattened, read horizontally as a juxtaposition rather than vertically as a hierarchy of being" (9–10). Indeed, Conrad's story does tantalize readers with such flattening, as the narrative channels an impressive roster of moments that cross and conflate. The opening paragraphs are illustrative and typical. As the narrator describes the scene—"it was a long room" where a man's voice, "passionately interrupted and passionately renewed," ebbs and flows like a tide—the "crepuscular light" reveals him: "tall under the low ceiling, and somber all over except for the crude discord of the white collar under the shape of his head and the faint, minute spark of a brass button here and there on his uniform" (91). If the figure presented here, presumably the commanding officer, is little more than collar and brass button, Conrad fashions the mistress by his side as the perfect nursemaid for his material form, as she is nothing more than oval, dress, and hands: "he could see only the faint oval of her upturned face and, extended on her black dress, her pale hands" (91).

By its transformative and overturning nature, the dissolution of the human/nonhuman binary is suited to transfigure agency, an impressive feat Conrad is able to suggest by not only looking at the human actants in the story but also at their nonhuman counterparts. Thus, the commanding officer's ship was "like a pretty woman who had suddenly put on a suit of sackcloth and stuck revolvers in her belt," and the sea carries with it an "unchanged face…with [a] familiar expression"; it is a sea which "pretend[s] that there [i] s nothing the matter with the world," a hypocrisy that resonates with the night that "hides" and the mist that "deceives" (96–7).

Ultimately these visual and verbal depictions from the annals of anthropomorphism serve to minimize the difference between subject and object and elevate the shared materiality of all things. The ethical imperative of Conrad's story thus becomes not so much a politics of militarism and sexual conflict, as Erdinast-Vulcan insists, but rather a desire to distribute value more generously as we attend to matter and its power. I proposed earlier that "The Tale" works to reconfigure modernist encounters with materiality by blurring and blending, confounding and conflating human and nonhuman agency. Not only does this reading enliven what is arguably one of Conrad's most overlooked texts, but it forces Conrad scholarship to begin to think about "things" and "objects" as actors working alongside entire networks that, up to this point, have been largely ignored. A bonus is that such an approach inevitably puts Conrad's works in conversation with those of his modernist counterparts—and here I am thinking specifically of Forster's *Howards End* or Virginia Woolf's *To the Lighthouse*—wherein houses (to say nothing of bowls of fruit or sacred swords) enjoy an overlapping agency with their characters and demonstrate the neo-materialist notion that the world of things exists, in a simultaneous juggling of similarities and differences, with the world of human actants.

The about-face comes as the narrative recedes from the tale about the commanding officer and the Northman and cycles back to the account of the commanding officer and his mistress. Uncertainty garners a unique prominence in the mind of the commanding officer—the phrases "I don't know" and "I don't believe" are repeated four times in seven short sentences—as he questions his own actions and moral responsibility as commander of a wartime vessel. Noortje Marres rightly notes that "it is often hard to grasp just what the sources of agency are that make a particular event happen" and that this "ungraspability may be a [necessary] aspect of agency" (216). The commanding officer seeks confirmation and assurance; he desires to return to a prescribed fitness of things where structure and order mitigate conflict. Yet this a story where the fitness of things is in disarray, in part because of the workings of both the human and the nonhuman, the seen and the unseen.

The commanding officer's compulsion toward his own guilt is strong—"I gave that course to him. It seemed to me a supreme test"—yet he also seems to be aware of the ways in which elemental forces influence his own thinking. This is why he is able to immediately chase statements about his own culpability with pauses and dashes and uncertainty: "I believe—no, I don't believe. I don't know" (110). The push and pull here promotes discussions of literary impressionism as a device for exploring consciousness, for it is the commanding officer's lingering in both uncertainty and contingency that allows readers to see how the crystallization of each of the points that put the murder in motion can only be revealed retroactively. Thus, on the one hand, the weighty fall of the monosyllable "I," "I," "I," contributes to the heavy, somber mood of the commanding officer's mental state and reveals the Northman's death as a product of human intentionality ("I don't know whether I have done stern retribution or murder"); on the other hand, the quality of his conflicted mind as well as his frustration and its intensity trace equally to material form and function: the Northman "seems to have been driven out by a menacing stare—nothing more" (110).

It is the inseparability between human action and nonhuman agency that renders Conrad's story not only ambiguous in terms of its moral despair but also marks the new ground between this story and other works in Conrad's oeuvre. Nidesh Lawtoo and Jeffrey McCarthy have both argued that a deeper understanding of nature in Conrad's works—of how weather, catastrophe and atmosphere—can expose a structural interplay between the human and the nonhuman. These critics turn toward the material to develop an ecology of agency that is grounded in nature, space, and place, while I would pursue an assessment of the agentic capacity carried forth by the "things" in that ecology. My argument is that as Conrad scholarship begins to think through materiality in environmental terms, it must also begin to account for the nonhuman and post-human realm of the material sources of action—those objects and actants so central to a work like "The Tale." No longer is Conrad interested in presenting the natural word as a symbol; here, he reconfigures the material world as a vibrant force deeply embedded with questions of causality. In this way, Conrad celebrates the materiality of nature, objects and things as entities profoundly 'Other' while offering the basis for a new understanding of—and relationship with—the natural world.

If McCarthy and Lawtoo are correct, then we must question why "The Tale" seems to be engaged in a project analogous to, but distanced from, the material focus on nature that appears so prevalent in Conrad's early works. What I am asking, I suppose, is what transpires from the time Conrad publishes *Heart of Darkness* in 1899 (or *Lord Jim* in 1900, "Typhoon" in 1903, and *The Secret Agent* in 1907) to his penning of "The Tale" in 1917 that dramatically alters the gaze with which he looks at the material? The short and obvious answer is the Great War,[10] where suddenly humanity is forced to recognize the permanence—and indeed the thing-power, the staying-power—of objects in relation to the transience and ephemerality of man. Bill Brown's "The Secret Life of Things" turns to Woolf's "Solid Objects" to describe the reciprocating relation between material objects and World War I particularly in light of wartime scarcity (16). Most apposite to this discussion, however, is his discussion of *Jacob's Room* and the absolute presence of "things"—"all the unburied remains, those possessions no longer possessed" (14)—despite Jacob's literal absence following his death in the war.

At a time when "things" (letters, belongings, clothes, military identification tags) were returning home, but men were not, Conrad, much like Jacob's mother, must have had a sharp awareness of the ways in which these nonhuman materialities became vivid entities not entirely reducible to the wartime context in which they had been set: "What am I to do with these?" Jacob's mother asks, holding out a pair of his old shoes (*Jacob's Room* 143). The commanding officer of Conrad's "The Tale" consequently sums up his vision of the purported spy games by acknowledging: "The last reported submarined ships were sunk a long way to the westward. But one never knows. There may have been others since then not reported nor seen. Gone with all hands" (98). All that remains, of course, is "something on the water," "small wreckage," "a barrel of a certain shape and colour" (98). The most obvious feature here is how the things of the world have become the materials of war, how the commanding officer's descent into a state of moral opaqueness is decidedly less spiritual or psychological than it is material.

The fact that Conrad shifts his focus from the agency of "nature" to the agency of "things" casts and certifies more fully his desire to show the back-and-forth influence between human and nonhuman elements. In fact, it is fair to say that these dual materialisms conform and complete each other in a way that forces them—and, by extension, Conrad scholarship—to engage with the mammoth cognitive machinery of new materialism. Thus, while my own reading of "The Tale" grows out of a more object-oriented approach, focusing on the relation of "all" objects in the world, it is still very much in line with the ways things exist beyond the consciousness—and, according to McCarthy, "that makes object-oriented ontology a key player in the new materialism's conversations about nature's relation to humanity" (6). As such, McCarthy continues, "these [new materialist and object-oriented] readings need not contradict each other but can operate in parallel" (6); in this vein, my own reading of "The Tale" adds another voice to the conversation delineating the ways that Conrad articulates materiality in relation to human experience. But by shifting the focus from nature to thing, this argument brings to Conrad scholarship the object-oriented notions that we see played out in current theoretical discussions of the new modernist studies and which have been kept of the critical Conradian stage until now.

Silently strung through and loomed deep within this discussion is again the perplexing nature of the story's title. As indicated earlier but worth repeating, Gaetano D'Elia suggests that Conrad finds the word "tale" unfitting for stories of warfare (51), which leaves readers to assume that the "tale" the title refers to is not, in fact, the story the commanding officer delivers to his mistress, but rather the account the Northman conveys to the Commanding Officer. We are told that "the commanding officer listened to the [Northman's] tale," but perhaps more significant is the association with the "tale" of deceit and the ways in which the commanding officer believes himself "faced by an enormous lie, solid like a wall, with no way round to get at the truth" (107).

But still I wonder if there is more to the mistress's opening charge—"Why not *tell* me a *tale*?" (94, emphasis added)—particularly in a narrative that plays so heavily on the side-by-side arrangement of "see" and "sea." I will conclude by suggesting that a proper reading of "The Tale" depends, primarily and unequivocally, on a few denotations of the word "tale."

In its noun form, the primary definition of "tale" has to do, of course, with conversation or discourse. It is "the action of telling" in both written and spoken forms. When we hearken back to the beginning of Conrad's story and consider the displacement felt by the narrator's mistress as she attempts to parse the form of the story she is about to hear, we see both the secondary and tertiary definitions of "tale" emerge. Beyond its scope of narrative and discourse, "tale," according the *Oxford English Dictionary*, also denotes "a report of private matters not to be divulged," "a story, true or fictitious, drawn up so as to amuse," "a history [attempting] to preserve the....fact of an incident," "a falsehood" and finally, "an account or a reckoning." The tremendous utility of this single word—as conversation, fiction, report, secret, story, entertainment, history, preserver of fact, lie and confession—was a natural choice for

Conrad to title a story so heavily predicated on narrative form. Drawing on Conrad's *The Return*, we are reminded that "words mean something" (qtd. in Schneider 31). Lissa Schneider-Rebozo discusses Conrad's use of exceedingly potent words as structuring devices—she is interested in "how, where, and with what effect [such words] are made manifest in Conrad's writings" (33). Looking specifically at the word "trick" (taken from an oft-quoted remark Conrad made about *The Secret Sharer*—"No damned tricks with girls there"), Schneider-Rebozo claims that when in it comes to Conrad's word choice, readers must attune themselves to the ways in which the words are illimitably mutable—intentional, on the one hand, and capable of "escaping or exceeding their implied limitations," on the other (35). When read as a noun, Conrad's title is intentional; it is self-referential in terms of the complicated and conflicting narrative forms the story itself engages. Yet, as an adjective it fascinates in its ability to escape its own limitation. In this sense, it is an object, "a thing set to reveal something." It is designated further as an entity "that reveals or betrays what is not intended to be known"; it "provides warning of something" else ("Tale").

As both noun and adjective, capable of turning both inward and outward, we see the word "tale" possess two essential components which are necessary and sufficient to my interpretation of Conrad's story: First, a "tale" is "a thing." And second, it functions, both in its material and narrative forms, to either reveal or disclose; in short, its purpose is to "tell." Such language suggests that in order to read Conrad properly, one must acknowledge Conrad's own awareness of the material reality of the world—those objects and things—and his wrestling with the best ways to present that world in narrative form. These definitions also help to parse whether Conrad's story is primarily an account of "the tale" or whether it is an account of the barrel floating at sea. The answer, as should now be obvious, is that it is both—for a "tale" is equally a "thing" that reveals and provides warning (i.e., the barrel), but it also a narrative story that is imaginatively recounted. In what is perhaps Conrad's most prodigious feat, he masterfully selects a title—and a single word, at that—which underscores the relation between the formal and the material by putting such forms on equal footing.

Notes

1 Vivienne Rundle's claims are closer to my own, yet in her account of both the physical and dialogical relationships between the officer and his mistress, Rundle overlooks the woman's desire to understand the formal conventions of the story she requests to hear (18).

2 For a more detailed look at the fairytale motif in Conrad's work, see Jeremy Hawthorne's chapter "*Nostromo*: Adventurers and Fairy Tales" in which he discusses "The Princess and the Page," a fairytale "Conrad either wrote or translated…some time near the beginning of his writing career" (212).

Form & Materiality in Conrad's "The Tale" 229

3 Conveniently, for Conrad our sailor-turned-writer, the secondary and tertiary definitions of the word "tale" are drawn from sailing: "an indicator showing the position of a ship's rudder", or, "[on a sailboat] a feather, string, or similar device, often attached to the port and starboard shrouds and to the backstay, to indicate the relative direction of the wind" ["Tale"].)

4 Unmentioned in the criticism is the special side-by-side symmetry between "see" and "sea," a wordplay that is paramount to the standard by which the commanding officer instinctively judges both the human and nonhuman forces in the story. The repetition of this line—"to see—what you can see" (96, 97, 98)—shifts, at least for contemporary readers, the formal register of the story from could-be fairytale to nursery rhyme: "A sailor went to sea, sea, sea/To see what he could see, see, see. /But all that he could see, see, see, /Was the bottom of the deep blue sea/sea/sea (McMorland, Song 33). While there is no evidence to suggest that Conrad would have had access to this rhyme while penning *The Tale*—by all accounts it sprung up in response to a joke between Fred Astaire and Ginger Rogers in the 1936 film "Follow the Fleet" (Mavis 426)—it's significant in that the rhyme hauntingly depicts the fate of many soldiers, who, looking into the sea, see only their own death, the bottom of the sea where their fleets and bodies will rest, reflected back.

5 Marlow ruminates: "You understand that nothing is more disturbing than the upsetting of a preconceived idea. Each of us arranges the world according to his own notion of the fitness of things" (*Chance* 242).

6 The following lines pick up in Chapter 5, following the introduction of Chief Inspector Heat of the Special Crime Department:

"He had gone even so far as to utter words which true wisdom would have kept back. But Chief Inspector Heat was not very wise – at least not truly so. True wisdom, which is not certain of anything in this world of contradictions, would have prevented him from attaining his present position. It would have alarmed his superiors, and done away with his chances of promotion. His promotion had been very rapid.

"There isn't one of them, sir, that we couldn't lay our hands on at any time of night and day. We know what each of them is doing hour by hour," he had declared. And the high official had deigned to smile. This was so obviously the right thing to say for an officer of Chief Inspector Heat's reputation that it was perfectly delightful. The high official believed the declaration, which chimed in with his idea of *the fitness of things*. His wisdom was of an official kind or else he might have reflected upon a matter not of theory but of experience that in the close-woven stuff of the relations between conspirator and police there occur unexpected solutions of continuity, sudden holes in space and time. A given anarchist may be watched inch by inch and minute by minute, but a moment always comes when somehow all sight and touch of him are lost for a few hours, during which something (generally an explosion) more or less deplorable does happen. But the high official, carried away by his sense of *the fitness of things*, had smiled, and now the recollection of that smile was very annoying to Chief Inspector Heat, principal expert in anarchist procedure."

(173; emphasis added)

7 Conrad must have been aware of this troubling dialectic not only as a sailor but also as a civilian. Wollaeger reminds us that Conrad wrote *The Tale* after a trip to Scotland where he toured naval bases, went out on a mine sweeper, and flew on a patrol flight. He had intended, while on this journey north, to join the Admiralty on a Q-ship, a well-armed anti-submarine vessel that was disguised to look like a harmless Norwegian merchant (*Modernism*

32–33). And while Conrad did not board the Q-ship until after he wrote *The Tale*, Kingsbury insists "he arranged for the trip earlier and knew what the Q-ships were" (161). This small detail accounts for the ways in which the commanding officer bewails a state of frenzied, wide-eyed paranoia, for Conrad himself understood how vulnerable the Q-ships were to submarine attack. It is in this atmosphere of paranoia and moral outrage that the correspondence between Conrad and J.B. Pinker becomes particularly apposite. According to Kingsbury, "Before setting out on this second journey north, Conrad wrote to Pinker asking him to take care of his affairs if he should not return. Explaining that he did not have 'gloomy forebodings,' Conrad tells Pinker, 'Should the ship fail to report herself for more than ten days after the time fixed for her return [...] there will be no use hoping for her return,' that is, the ship would likely have been torpedoed by a submarine" (161–162).

8 See Lawtoo, "Conrad in the Anthropocene: Steps to an Ecology of Catastrophe."

9 Jane Bennett borrows from Mitchell's concept in order to advance a vital materialist theory of "thing-power," which "gestures toward the strange ability of ordinary, man-made items to exceed their status as objects and to manifest traces of independence or aliveness" (xvi). I appreciate Bennett's theorization, for above all, it deprivileges humans as knowing bodies while aiming to attend to things as actants.

10 For useful commentary on Conrad's response to the Great War, see Cedric Watts's "Joseph Conrad and World War" and John G. Peters's "Conrad's Literary Response to the First World War."

Works Cited

Bennett, Jane. *Vibrant Matter: A Political Ecology of Things*. Duke UP, 2010.

Bonney, William. *Thorns & Arabesques: Contexts for Conrad's Fiction*. Johns Hopkins UP, 1980.

Brown, Bill. "The Secret Life of Things: Virginia Woolf and the Matter of Modernism." *Modernism/Modernity*, vol. 6, no. 2, 1999, pp. 1–28.

———. *A Sense of Things: The Object Matter of American Literature*. U of Chicago P, 2003.

———. "Thing Theory." *Critical Inquiry*, vol. 28, no. 1, 2001, pp. 1–22.

Clausewitz, Carl von. *On War*. Library of Congress, 1998. *eBook Collection (ProQuest)*. Web. 26 January 2016.

Conrad, Joseph. *Chance*. Penguin, 1974.

———. *Heart of Darkness and The Secret Agent*. Doubleday, 1997.

———. "The Tale." *The Penguin Book of First World War Stories*. Edited by Barbara Korte and Ann-Marie Einhaus. Penguin, 2007.

———. *Typhoon*. Doubleday, 1902.

D'Elia, Gaetano. "Let us make Tales, not Love." *The Conradian*, vol. 12, no. 1, 1987, pp. 50–58.

Epstein, Hugh. "'The Fitness of Things': Conrad's English Irony in 'Typhoon and The Secret Agent." *The Conradian*, vol. 33, no. 1, 2008, pp. 1–30.

Erdinast-Vulcan, Daphna. *The Strange Short Fiction of Joseph Conrad*. Oxford UP, 1999.

Guetti, James. *The Limits of Metaphor*. Cornell UP, 1967.

Hale, Lowdale. "The Fog of War." *Journal of the Military Service Institution of the United States*, vol. 19, 1896, pp. 522–37. *Google Book Search*. Web. 26 January 2016.

Hawthorn, Jeremy. *Joseph Conrad: Narrative Technique and Ideological Commitment*. Routledge, 1990.

Kingsbury, Celia. *The Peculiar Sanity of War: Hysteria in the Literature of WWI*. Texas Tech UP, 2002.

Latour, Bruno. *We Have Never Been Modern*. Harvard UP, 2012.

Lawtoo, Nidesh. "Conrad in the Anthropocene: Steps to an Ecology of Catastrophe." *Conrad in Nature*, Edited by Lissa Schneider-Rebozo et al. Routledge, 2018.

Levine, Caroline. *Forms: Whole, Rhythm, Hierarchy, Network*. Princeton UP, 2015.

Lothe, Jakob. *Conrad's Narrative Method*. Clarendon, 1989. Print.

Mao, Douglas. *Solid Objects: Modernism and the Test of Production*. Princeton UP, 1998.

March-Russell, Paul. "Close, but Without Touching: Hearing, Seeing and Believing in Conrad's 'The Tale'." *Conradiana*, vol. 28, no. 3, 2006, pp. 267–82.

Marres, Noortje. "Issues Spark a Public into Being: A Key But Often Forgotten Point of the Lippmann-Dewey Debate." *Making Things Public*, Edited by Bruno Latour and Peter Weibel, MIT P, 2005. 208–17.

Mavis, Curtis. "A Sailor Went to Sea: Theme and Variations." *Folk Music Journal*, vol. 8, no. 4, 2000, pp. 421–37.

McCarthy, Jeffrey Mathes. *Green Modernism: Nature and the English Novel, 1900–1930*. Palgrave, 2015.

McMorland, Alison. *The Funny Family*. Ward Lock, 1978. Song 33.

Mitchell, W.J.T. *What do Pictures Want? The Lives and Loves of Images*. U of Chicago P, 2005.

Peters, John G. "Conrad's Literary Response to the First World War." *College Literature*, vol. 39, no. 4, 2012, pp. 35–45.

Pietz, William. "Death of the Deodand: Accursed Objects and the Money Value of Human Life." "The Abject," Edited by Francesco Pellizzi, special issue, *Res: Anthropology and Aesthetics*, vol. 31, 1997, pp. 97–108.

Quigley, Megan. *Modernist Fiction and Vagueness*. Cambridge UP, 2015.

Rundle, Vivienne. "The Tale and the Ethics of Interpretation." *The Conradian*, vol. 17, no. 1, 1992, pp. 17–36.

Schneider, Lissa. *Conrad's Narratives of Difference: Not Exactly Tales for Boys*. Routledge, 2003.

"Tale, n.1." *OED Online*. Oxford UP, March 2017. Web. 20 March 2017.

Watts, Cedric. "Joseph Conrad and World War I." *Critical Survey*, vol. 2, no. 2, pp. 203–7.

Woolf, Virginia. *Jacob's Room*. 1922. Edited by Suzanne Raitt. Norton Critical Editions. Norton, 2010.

Part IV
Nature, Empire and Commerce

11 *Nostromo* and World-Ecology

Jay Parker

> The supreme importance of material interests.
> —*Nostromo* and world-ecology[1]

> Seen indistinctly through the dust of my collapsed universe, the good lady glanced about the room.
> —Joseph Conrad, *A Personal Record* (1912)[2]

It is with this apocalyptic tone that Joseph Conrad humorously describes being interrupted while writing, and the dust through which he peers is no less than the molecules of Costaguana, the setting for his political novel *Nostromo* (1904). While it is a commonplace that novelists create worlds, the terms in which Conrad describes this interruption indicate the depth and intricacy of his imaginative effort:

> I had, like the prophet of old, "wrestled with the Lord" for my creation, for the headlands of the coast, for the darkness of the Placid Gulf, the light on the snows, the clouds in the sky, and for the breath of life that had to be blown into the shapes of men and women [...] there was not a single brick, stone, or grain of sand in its soil I had not placed in position with my own hands.
> (*A Personal Record* 187–8)

Nature is central in this account and in the novel itself, which emphasizes repeatedly the impact of the natural world on history and politics. Yet *Nostromo* depicts various different "natures," working through ideas of the natural world alongside notions of nature in terms of character, and mobilizing concerns with representation and point of view that occupy the novel as a medium, Conrad's novel challenges the notion of an authoritative representation of "nature." "The supreme importance of material interests" (*Nostromo* 260) emerges as a deeply ironic statement, at once affirming the power of capital in shaping the world, while also destabilizing our sense of its ability to determine events.

These qualities allow *Nostromo* to speak constructively and critically both to eco-critical modes of literary analysis and broadly Marxist methods that combine examinations of the interrelations between history, politics and environment. In particular, it visits the kind of theoretical terrain mapped by Jason W. Moore, which combines these two modes and theorizes "capitalism as *world-ecology*, a perspective that joins the accumulation of capital and the production of nature in dialectical unity" ("Transcending the Metabolic Rift" 2, original emphasis). More specifically, literary critics, such as Michael Niblett and Sharae Deckard, deploy Moore's thought to frame an engagement with world-literature—for Niblett capitalist by definition—as "the literature of the capitalist world-ecology (Niblett, "Specters in the Forest" 55).[3]

Like world-ecological criticism, *Nostromo* is also critical of capitalism, which is ironized through the novel's depiction of the history and agency of a prodigious silver mine. It asks whether capital can plausibly be seen to drive all aspects of life, "as if the silver of the mine had been the emblem of a common cause, the symbol of the supreme importance of material interests" (*Nostromo* 260). My reading here of "a common cause" finds alongside the overt reference to political causes, a covert querying of capital as "a common cause" in relation to causation as well as politics—a view of capital that drives Marxist theories.[4] *Nostromo* undermines (forgive the pun) singular and coherent narratives such as Moore's—which makes capitalism the prime agent in the production of nature—suggesting that these kinds of stories depend upon myths and illusions. This is not to discredit such views completely, however, since in Conrad's writing in general, the imaginary is not idle fantasy—fictions have force in the creation and recreation of the world. Nevertheless, Conrad's imaginative project works through the limits of what *Nostromo* terms "sustaining illusion" (*Nostromo* 497)—values that give life meaning and worth—and throughout his oeuvre, Conrad focuses on the limits of these values and their tendency toward self-destruction.

Nostromo stages a conversation between mythic modes of knowledge and identity production and a modernity influenced rather than determined by capital. It asserts the power of various "natures" in these interactions (particularly in relation to the significance of individual character), which broad-brush theories such as Moore's inevitably elide. While *Nostromo* supports many elements in world-ecological theory and Marxist theory in general, it also offers an important critique of both their realist bias and privileging of capitalism over other natures in the totality of productive activity. Yet Conrad's novel also points to ways in which fiction—through its abilities to express and ironize conflicting points of view, and map intellectual terrain using diverse scales—can begin to realize Moore's goal to "implicate the widest range of meta-processes in the modern world as socio-ecological, from family formation to racial orders to industrialization, imperialism, and proletarianization"

("Ecology, Capital" 110), without granting unchallenged primacy to particular myths or subjecting individual agencies to erasure.

Nostromo's Ecology

Nostromo's opening reads like a case study of the interrelation of economy and ecology advanced by Moore: it presents a becalmed gulf waiting for the technology of steam to open up the territory to the exploitation of "material interests," and in particular to provide the means of transportation of the interior's formidable silver reserves to satisfy the voracious appetite of global capitalism:

> Perhaps the very atmospheric conditions which had kept away the merchant fleets of bygone ages induced the O.S.N. Company to violate the sanctuary of peace sheltering the calm existence of Sulaco. The variable airs sporting lightly with the vast semicircle of waters within the head of Azuera could not baffle the steam power of their excellent fleet. Year after year the black hulls of their ships had gone up and down the coast, in and out, past Azuera, past the Isabels, past Punta Mala—disregarding everything but the tyranny of time.
> (*Nostromo* 9)

This describes an ongoing relation between ecology and economy: Sulaco's coastal weather and terrain form a placid barrier to global capitalism until the developments in the technology of trade open up its interior. The San Tomé silver mine itself is the hub of a conversation with nature, tragic and absurd in equal measure, mediated by the political will of a succession of cynical governments.

An early stage of the mine's history highlights the interdependence of nature and politics. Rediscovered by an English company "after the War of Independence," the mine is returned to profitability, until a miners' revolt turned on "their English chiefs and murdered them to a man" (*Nostromo* 52), enabling the government to confiscate the mine. Eventually, the mine is granted as a concession to the Gould family, whose patriarch is a naturalized Costaguanan capitalist of English origin with close ties to his homeland and its culture. The concession is a curse, however, because Gould senior is ignorant of the business and technology of mining:

> He knew nothing of mining; he had no means to put his concession on the European market; the mine as a working concern did not exist. The buildings had been burnt down, the mining plant had been destroyed, the mining population had disappeared from the neighbourhood years and years ago; the very road had vanished under a flood of tropical vegetation as effectually as if swallowed by the sea.
> (*Nostromo* 54)

As well as connecting the mine explicitly to the sea, whose conditions in the opening of the novel are framed as the limiting factor in early capitalist expansion, nature is figured as a flood, which interacts with the politics of the region to render the mine inaccessible to capitalist development. Sharae Deckard provides an account of this tidal trope, which evolves from "green imperialism" in the late eighteenth and early twentieth centuries into a contemporary "emergent postcolonial ecocriticism that is unabashedly positioned against the continuing processes of imperialistic exploitation and authoritarian abuse that result in ecological crisis" ("Jungle Tide, Devouring Reef" 47–8). Although Conrad does not express himself in terms of an "ecological crisis," he certainly expresses a sense of individual and political crisis as inextricable from and channeled by wider natures, and although he does not strictly write in a postcolonial context, *Nostromo*'s setting is at once neocolonial and postcolonial. Even though it is partly a story of British and US imperialism (through business and political intervention rather than conquest), it deals with the aftermath of Costaguanan independence from the Spanish empire. Furthermore, Conrad's anti-imperialist stance[5] cements his writing in general as an important precursor to the postcolonial strand in world-ecological literary criticism represented by Deckard and Niblett.

Nostromo, Marxism and Capitalism as World-Ecology

If *Nostromo* anticipates some current trends in ecologically minded Marxist theory, it has an equally strong heritage in Marxist literary criticism. Fredric Jameson has famously accounted for the novel as undermining "the categories of storytelling in order to project, beyond the stories it must continue to tell, the concept of a process beyond storytelling" (279), namely, the impact of capitalism in "its imperialist stage" (273). For Benita Parry, it is a text focused on contradictions, presenting antagonistic views of history as testimony, on the one hand, to the "depravity of human nature and the futility of politics [while] the other registers anger at the foulness of the present condition and offers a prospect on the regenerative dimension to politics" (118). She concludes that *Nostromo*'s hopefulness exists in the ability of Nostromo himself to live on after his death as a heroic exemplar to the poor of Costaguana in spite of his moral fall, and by "intimations of a transfigured future" in its closing lines (127).

Yet as Conrad scholar Allan Simmons suggests, while *Nostromo* provides "a broadly Marxist vision of Costaguana's history as the product of economic forces," as he also observes, its fragmented chronology and "shifting viewpoints emphasize the impossibility of ever seeing the whole picture of Costaguana, while simultaneously calling attention to the limitation of any one interpretation" (128). Character and event in

Nostromo are refracted through a range of perspectives, and the histories of the nation itself cannot be disentangled from vested interests. Likewise, Ursula Lord suggests that although *Nostromo* resonates with Marxist understandings of the alienation of labor, its staging of ideologies is too fragmented and conflicting to grant it an affinity with a single political stance (252). Christopher GoGwilt's *The Invention of the West* argues that though "*Nostromo* follows Marx's critique of republicanism" (204), as a whole it "illustrates the profoundly fictive structure of political history" (219). GoGwilt's connection between the narrative fictions of *Nostromo* and guiding fictions that have shaped the history of the West resonates with the argument I will develop later regarding Conrad's sense of the force of fiction. If *Nostromo* were to be anachronistically aligned with a current in twentieth-century theory, it would potentially have more in common with post-structuralism. The novel's emphasis on perspective and fragmentation might emphasize the construction and histories of knowledge embedded in the notion of ecology itself, where ironically, a term emphasizing the study of environment and ecosystems has come to stand for the very subject terrain it once only purported to describe.[6]

This is the very issue that threatens Moore's theory. There are a two key senses that Moore gives to "world-ecology": first and foremost it is a system—another is feudalism—developing through the matrix of relations that constitute the *actuality* of human-natural processes ("Transcending the Metabolic Rift" 5–6, my emphasis). Moore terms this the "oikeios" ("Ecology Capital" 113), "a way of naming the creative, historical, and dialectical relation between, and also always within, *human and extra-human natures*" (Capitalism in the Web of Life 35, my emphasis). Nature itself is largely synonymous with "the web of life" (see, e.g., "Transcending the Metabolic Rift" 22; Capitalism in the Web of Life 13).[7] The second sense of "world-ecology" is as a "world-historical process" ("Ecology Capital" 112), and in the case of the capitalist world-ecology, it involves the production and organization of the natural (including human) world ("Ecology Capital" 107).[8]

From these senses and slippages,[9] capitalism emerges as a relation in nature that both produces knowledge about nature and produces the natural world itself, and which has during the capitalist period of history succeeded in dominating natural relations so as to become the world-ecology, where "ecology" means not knowledge about the world, but the world-system. For Moore, capitalism as the world-ecology operates historically along various "commodity frontiers," which shift according to value relations between natural resources. In a particular location, a resource is extracted so long as the combination of these factors makes it cheap to do so. When something tips the balance, the commodity frontier moves to a new location ("This lofty mountain of silver" 60–1).[10]

Nostromo and Nature

According to this summary (Moore's interest in South American silver production aside), Conrad writing about nature is at first glance dealing with something very different. *Nostromo* also appears to differ from world-ecological theory when it describes "the accumulation of capital and the production of all nature (humans included!) as dialectically constituted" (Moore, "Ecology Capital" 108).[11] Most commonly in *Nostromo*, when the words "nature" or "natural" are used, the novel is referring to character and personality, whether of persons, things or events. Yet though this distinction is important, it is equally important to acknowledge that descriptions of wider nature are not entirely different to nature as character; both senses imply a kind of determinism, even in a paradigm which regards the human and the natural as separate—the laws of nature, on the one hand, or a core of personality or being that changes either with great difficulty or not at all, on the other. Crucially, in discussing "human [...] natures," Moore himself plays upon this equivocation, blurring the boundary between concepts of the natural world, human nature and individual character. This multiplication of ideas of nature in world-ecological theory invites an examination of its resonances with Conrad's own ironic duplications of nature in *Nostromo*.

A key feature of irony's duplicity, as Linda Hutcheon observes in *Irony's Edge*, is that it both affirms and negates simultaneously (27)—a potentially ironic statement can either be read with irony in mind, in which case it is self-undermining, or without consciousness of that irony, in which case it becomes a simple affirmation. Conradian irony expands upon this feature, creating what Ian Watt describes as a paradoxical alienation and commitment (1–19). Thus, *Nostromo* heaps its most crushing irony upon the heads of the Costaguana aristocrats whose values reflect Conrad's own most closely. For example, when Don Jose Avellanos expatiates "upon the patriotic nature of the San Tomé Mine" (*Nostromo* 51), he is referring to the ways in which it supports the cause of stability and security in Costaguana and also its role in preserving the rule of the aristocratic Ribierist party. His statement, however, prompts reflection by Emilia Gould on its dubious history:

> Worked in the early days mostly by means of lashes on the backs of slaves, its yield had been paid for in its own weight of human bones. Whole tribes of Indians had perished in the exploitation; and then the mine was abandoned, since with this primitive method it had ceased to make a profitable return, no matter how many corpses were thrown into its maw'.
>
> (*Nostromo* 52)

Mrs. Gould is aware that behind Don Jose's patriotism is a history of cruelty and exploitation that his representation of the mine erases, reminding us of how frequently appeals to nature mask attempts to reduce the complexity of a narrative to focus on a single perspective. Yet Emilia Gould is herself unaware at this point that by the end of the novel, her own husband will have recapitulated the Spanish colonial dynamic in a new form. The silver whose power Charles Gould leverages to create stability and security for those who work the mine as well as their masters (notably through the arguably unpatriotic action of seceding the Occidental Republic from Costaguana) threatens to embody the very things it was used to destroy: "the time approaches when all that the Gould Concession stands for shall weigh as heavily upon the people as the barbarism, cruelty, and misrule of a few years back" (*Nostromo* 511).

When read alongside world-ecological readings of nature, this takes on an additional ironic resonance. The mine is a natural resource used for nation-building (and destroying), a "patriotic nature" that captures the interconnection of human and nonhuman. Yet in Emilia Gould's perception of the mine, this relation gives birth to something terrible. The mine is figured as a bizarre fusion of business concern and genocidal worship: "whole tribes of Indians [...] thrown into its maw" conjure an image of human sacrifice, with the mine as a deity or idol. The "patriotic" mine becomes mythologized and abstracted, and its patriotism depends on its consumption of other nations, namely, the "whole tribes of Indians." The mine becomes a space in which patriotism eats itself. Yet this worship is also a transaction, and the origins of the mine lie in the almost literal commodification of labor—the transformation of "human bones" into a form of currency, with the limitations of terrain and technology determining the value and efficacy of this exchange. If the mine is an idol or religious icon, it can stand for capitalism itself, as something monstrous—a grotesque nature fed by humans on human life.

So far, Conrad's depiction of a South American silver mine appears to be a historicization in miniature of relations between capitalism and natural resources. Yet the mine is never only a mythologization of capitalism. Nor is it simply a material reality through which capitalism operates. It is a site in which capitalist and patriotic myths coalesce. These myths conflict and conjoin both in the description of the mine and its impact on Costaguanan history. On the one hand, Don Jose's narrative of a "patriotic" mine conflicts with Emilia Gould's focus on its destructive commodification of human life, while, on the other, both stories combine within the novel's wider narrative, evoking the ways in which patriotism and capitalism feed and feed off one another in the history of Costaguana. Where world-ecology grounds itself in metaphors drawn from geography—frontiers, extraction, exhaustion—*Nostromo*'s monstrous mine reminds us that nature depends upon feeding and that consumption is a metaphor with implications far beyond its sense in relation to economics.

Yet the San Tomé mine also shows us another side of nature, where the natural is not simply a category describing the nonhuman world, or alternatively in Moore's analysis the world of human and nonhuman natures, but rather a moral category that might be opposed, on the one hand, to the unnatural, the monstrous, and, on the other, the human and the divine. In the first of these parings, nature is elevated above the base or terrible (often inhuman), and in the second, it is the nature that is debased in relation to mankind under God. This dichotomy is complicated by traditions that conjoin the monstrous and the divine, but what is shared by all these views is the sense that neither wider nature nor human nature is a morally neutral category. *Nostromo*'s nature is also the nature of myth and legend, where moral lessons are intertwined with just-so stories. It could be argued that considering so many different natures together strains Moore's equivocation on "nature" beyond its breaking point; that though they share a name, these actually relate to separate or incompatible modes. Yet in bringing together wider and human natures, world-ecological theory itself aims at breaking down the limits around the concept of nature and must be prepared to absorb the implications of this logic.

Nostromo's historicization in miniature of "capitalism-in-nature" asks us to think about the historicization of the concept of nature itself, and in particular the ways in which our thinking about nature is routed in various directions by nature's own conflicting conceptual history. The ironic contradiction in which *Nostromo* entangles ideas of nature reminds us that coherent stories aiming to make sense of complex realities involve more selection than synthesis. In particular, it suggests that capitalism is one system of value among many value systems and that "capitalism-in-nature" bears a similarity to pantheistic conceptions, which locate divinity in the natural world. Following this train of thought, world-ecology narratives might emerge appearing less like science and more functionally similar to religious traditions as foci for communities and their values.

The sense of capitalism as a religion in which human life is sacrificed to feed "material interests" is complicated by the decidedly religious aspect of the novel's foremost capitalist, Mr Holroyd. His name evokes "holy rood," and the man himself directs a "Protestant invasion of Sulaco organized by the Holroyd Missionary Fund" (*Nostromo* 509), suggesting how capitalism and religion can become intertwined. Religion blends narrative and values, enabling Holroyd's sense of a destiny that is at once his own and his entire nation's—he states, "We shall run the world's business whether the world likes it or not. The world can't help it – and neither can we, I guess" (77). Yet Holroyd seems unaware of the contradiction between his "material interests" and immaterial, spiritual concerns, despite the images of idolatry that define the history of the hungry San Tomé mine. Ironically, his faith is hollowed out by capital, while capitalism itself becomes a religious creed. Capitalism in *Nostromo* fits a vision of religions as systems of value defined by faith, and indeed both Holroyd and Charles Gould place excessive faith in the power of capital as a means to achieve positive progress. This is not the only hollowing of faith, however: if religion is a force in Costaguana, the divine itself is decidedly absent. Instead, religious interests intersect with class, ethnic and gender divisions, and it is notable that the two sides in religious conflict by the end of the novel, namely, Protestants and Catholics, are nevertheless both also aligned with a concentration of power around intertwined aristocratic and capitalist interests. Religion itself feeds and feeds off the inequalities that permeate *Nostromo*, even while (or perhaps because) it offers consolation to the powerless.

Nostromo and Nature's Power

Nonhuman agencies like the silver mine can support or challenge entrenched power, but their effects are unpredictable and outside human control. These "natures," like the humans with whom they interact, are parts of a wider nature as an overarching system. This is an important distinction, whose implications are explored in a pivotal moment in the novel. This episode involves Martin Decoud, a Europeanized Costaguanero who having returned to his homeland becomes embroiled in a fight against its latest revolution—a military coup which overthrows the Ribierist party. This revolution sweeps through Costaguana, but is resisted in Sulaco, leading to the succession fomented by Charles Gould and the Ribierists. A purportedly crucial factor in the revolution is the fate of a large consignment of silver from the Gould concession. If the silver falls into the hands of the Monterists, who oppose Sulacan independence, the Sulacan cause will be fatally undermined. So Decoud hatches the daring plan of spiriting away the silver in secret, to be hidden and returned once the revolution is over. But the boat in which he and the titular Nostromo are moving the silver is struck and damaged by a ship transporting Sotillo (a former Ribierist commander and turncoat to the Monterist cause) and his forces into Sulaco. Decoud and Nostromo are not discovered, but manage to pilot the silver to a nearby island. Nostromo, in a feat of prodigious heroism, swims to shore, leaving Decoud to guard the silver. Left alone, he loses his mind, eventually killing himself.

The section on which I will focus involves the depiction of Decoud's isolation, the development of his insanity and his eventual suicide. It begins with an astounding maneuver of self-erasure, which at once asserts the narrator's absolute omniscience and renders the narrative voice paradoxically incorporeal. Nostromo, having ridden heroically over the mountains surrounding Sulaco to summon a sympathetic general and his troops to the region, is returning by steamer with the soldiers. He sees the boat used to transport the silver abandoned in the bay. Diving overboard, he searches the vessel, finding nothing but an old bloodstain. So he returns to the island in an attempt to discover Decoud's fate. He finds nothing but a mystery—Decoud is gone along with four bars of silver. Nostromo is struck by the impossibility of ever knowing the answer to this conundrum:

> He could not know. Nobody was to know. As might have been supposed, the end of Don Martin Decoud never became a subject of speculation for anyone except Nostromo. Had the truth of the facts been known, there would always have remained the question, Why? Whereas the version of his death at the sinking of the lighter had no uncertainty of motive. The young apostle of Separation had died striving for his idea by an ever-lamented accident. But the truth was that he died from solitude, the enemy known but to few on this earth, and whom only the simplest of us are fit to withstand. The brilliant Costaguanero of the boulevards had died from solitude and want of faith in himself and others.
>
> (*Nostromo* 496)

Nostromo later allows public opinion to maintain that the boat of silver sank after it had been struck, taking Decoud with it. This is the "ever-lamented accident" referred to above. But though Nostromo knows of the truth of the silver, he never discovers Decoud's fate. Thus, when the narrator announces, "Nobody was to know," as well as voicing Nostromo's own imperative to secrecy—because he becomes rich by concealing the silver and over a course of years transporting it back to the mainland—this statement also announces the fictionality of the novel.

But the narrative elsewhere makes clear that fictions have force in reality. Alongside the very real hidden treasure that is the source of Nostromo's later wealth, is the legend of another buried trove, a legend which ironically exerts as much impact upon the outcome of the revolution as the actual silver buried on the Isabels. This treasure purportedly resides in another remote region of the Costaguana seaboard:

> On the other side, what seems to be an isolated patch of blue mist floats lightly on the glare of the horizon. This is the peninsula of Azuera, a wild chaos of sharp rocks and stony levels cut about by vertical ravines. It lies far out to sea like a rough head of stone stretched from a green-clad coast at the end of a slender neck of sand covered with thickets of thorny scrub. Utterly waterless, for the rainfall runs off at once on all sides into the sea, it has not soil

enough – it is said – to grow a single blade of grass, as if it were blighted by a curse. The poor, associating by an obscure instinct of consolation the ideas of evil and wealth, will tell you that it is deadly because of its forbidden treasures.

(*Nostromo* 3–4)

From a distance, the poetically named Azuera seems an insubstantial mist on the horizon, before closer inspection resolves it into a jagged and harsh landscape, flagging perhaps the dangers of viewing locales from too wide a perspective. Yet inscribed upon this landscape is a legend of cursed wealth. The narrative goes on to describe this legend in more detail, telling of two sailors, "gringos of some sort for certain," who hunted for the treasure and never returned. They haunt it, "now rich and hungry and thirsty" (*Nostromo* 4). This inhospitable landscape is linked to an idea of evil, the realities of its terrain and topography are parsed by a simile, "as if it were blighted by a curse." Evil is connected to infertility, a lack of the means to sustain life, highlighting a connection between human values and ecological productivity that is radically disconnected from the treasure. These riches cannot provide sustenance—the "rich" are eternally "hungry and thirsty." This location is filtered through the lens of culture and myth, in the association of "the ideas of evil and wealth" by the poor. It gives rise to a legend, speaking to the appropriation of terrain by Marxist grand narratives, but rendered more deeply ironic because of the subsequent relationship established between the legend and the revolution itself.

Sotillo, the commander allied with the Monterist cause whose steamer collided with boat full of silver, occupies the harbor and lingers there, determined to seize the treasure for himself. He is told that it is lost, but thinks the story is a ruse, and becomes obsessed with finding the silver. As the revolution progresses, the other Monterist forces arrive in the plains outside the town. If Sotillo abandons his search and joins them, the Sulacan cause will be lost, so Nostromo and Dr Monygham, an English doctor and veteran of Costaguana's political turmoil, hatch a plan. Inspired by the story of the "miserable gringos on Azuera" (*Nostromo* 460), Nostromo suggests leading Sotillo to believe that the treasure is concealed in the shallow waters of the harbor waiting to be recovered by divers. Sotillo then spends the remainder of the conflict dredging the harbor, until he is killed by one of his own officers.

Ironies abound in this episode. Monygham believes the treasure to have sunk in the deep waters of the gulf, where it is irretrievable. His original plan is to tell Sotillo that the silver is buried on the Isabels, but Nostromo persuades him that this is implausible in order to preserve the secret location of the silver, which of course was actually buried by Decoud on these islands. So the fictional treasure of the Azuera becomes a counterpoint for the real treasure on the Isabels and also inspires a fictional account from Monygham and Nostromo, which plays a decisive role in the outcome of the Sulaco conflict. Each character in this episode is trapped in a web of deceit. Sotillo is unable to discern the strands of reality and succumbs to Nostromo's and Monygham's deception, whose plausibility depends upon both Sotillo's greed and the wider atmosphere of conspiracy. Sotillo disbelieves those who tell him the truth, mistaking honesty for intrigue and vice versa. In reality, the silver was being taken away from Sulaco, and it is a chance collision with Sotillo's own ship that has prevented its removal, and it resides now on the Isabels. Sotillo is coincidentally right that the treasure is not lost, but his belief that events are playing out according to some grand design only renders him susceptible to the machinations of Monygham and Nostromo. Likewise, Monygham when he lies to Sotillo that the silver is not lost, is himself also mislead, because his lie depends itself upon Nostromo's dishonesty regarding the true fate of the silver. But Nostromo himself becomes trapped in his own web in a different way. He is not deceived, but instead falls into a moral snare, compromising his heroic integrity in order to possess the treasure himself: "neither dead nor alive, like the Gringos on Azuera, he belonged body and soul to the unlawfulness of his audacity" (*Nostromo* 531). He becomes paradoxical "master and slave of the San Tomé treasure" (*Nostromo* 554), ironically doubling the slaves thrown into the maw of the mine under Spanish rule.

Terrain in *Nostromo* thus has multiple valencies: it is positioned in a dialectical relationship with politics and economics. It also acts as a repository of legend, representing a wider cultural imaginary that has real impact on the world, but also ironically represents the dangers of a myth-making propensity to find coherent intention in a world shaped by chance and contingency. As part of this landscape, the Isabels become the ironic double of the fabled Azuera in the topographical imaginary of both Nostromo the title character and the novel itself. If we return to Decoud's lonely death, we find this doubling asserted distinctly. Decoud becomes conscious of his isolation and begins to tread the path toward insanity and suicide, when he realizes there are no birds on the islands:

> For some good and valid reasons beyond mere human comprehension, the sea-birds of the gulf shun the Isabels. The rocky head of Azuera is their haunt, whose stony levels and chasms resound with their wild and tumultuous clamour as if they were forever quarrelling over the legendary treasure.
> At the end of his first day on the Great Isabel, Decoud, turning in his lair of coarse grass, under the shade of a tree, said to himself – "I have not seen as much as one single bird all day."
>
> (*Nostromo* 496)

The novel asserts the doubling of Azuera and the Isabels as an introduction to its deconstruction of Decoud's sense of self. At the same time, it places the complexity and mystery of the natural world in dialogue with legends of treasure. This does not have the effect of suggesting, however, a dialectical relationship between ecology and economy, but rather highlights that there are elements of the natural world that remain incomprehensible. The narrator situates them in relation to anthropocentric narrative, "as if they were forever quarrelling over the legendary treasure," but this simile is absurd, an aestheticization of the aforementioned "good and valid" reasons that defy human understanding. Furthermore, *Nostromo*'s omniscient narrator, despite possessing knowledge of the unknowable details of Decoud's own death, does not attempt to parse this nonhuman conundrum beyond the whimsical absurdity of its fleeting incorporation into the myth of Azuera.

Regarding the unknowable details of Decoud's death, the narrator's omniscience, however, swells from the ability to look into the depths of his psyche to encompass a diagnosis of a syndrome in the human condition itself. As I have already discussed, having told us Decoud "died from solitude and want of faith in himself and others," we are informed that

> Solitude from mere outward condition of existence becomes very swiftly a state of soul in which the affectations of irony and scepticism have no place. It takes possession of the mind, and drives forth the thought into the exile of utter unbelief. After three days of waiting for the sight of some human face, Decoud caught himself entertaining a doubt of his own individuality. It had merged into the world of cloud and water, of natural forces and forms of nature. In our activity alone do we find the sustaining illusion of an independent existence as against the whole scheme of things of which we form a helpless part. Decoud lost all belief in the reality of his action past and to come.
>
> (*Nostromo* 497)

Decoud's immersion into "the world of cloud and water, of natural forces and forms of nature" does not result in their subjugation to human considerations, but instead in the dissolution of his identity and ultimately his suicide. His death resonates throughout Nostromo as a counterpoint to the novel's own representation of the relentless dominance of "material interests." Far from presenting a dialectic between human and natural, their synthesis dissolves meaning and identity. In Conrad particularly, this is dense material, suffocating under the weight of conceptual significance. "The affectations of irony and scepticism," are in many ways the definitive attribute of Conradian narrative. Yet in Conrad as a whole and in the modernity that he anticipated, irony and skepticism are the signs of an alienation which paradoxically mark the epistemological parallel to Decoud's radical isolation on the Isabels. Indeed in so much of Conrad's work, irony and skepticism challenge the possibility of solidarity, the "faith in himself and others," which Decoud loses. But here, "irony" and "skepticism" are counterpointed against "utter unbelief." The narrator suggests that doubt itself becomes meaningless in the face of an absolute lack of faith. Decoud has up to this point himself been an ironist and a skeptic, and here it is revealed that it is these very qualities, which earlier in the novel marked him apart from his peers, that actually constitute his bond to both humanity, and also the threads from which his "sustaining illusion" is woven.

Conclusions

So as far as *Nostromo* is concerned, the world can be apprehended as a "whole scheme of things of which we form a helpless part," but this scheme has two distinct characteristics which are incompatible with Marxist thought. First, capitalism, like other ideologies, is a fiction projected onto the world by human beings, actualized in its shaping of human action and interaction with a nature, which operates largely "beyond mere human comprehension." It is a "world-ecology" only in ecology's most limited sense—a framework that defines knowledge production about the world but which if we totalize into a "world-ecology" (or other world-system) subjects the complexity of reality to erasure, regardless of how complex we try to make this capitalist system itself. Second, the world-view itself is an iteration toward meaninglessness.

Thus, the extent to which a theorization of a world-system is successful, insofar as it genuinely looks at the whole world, is also the extent to which it can say nothing. Alternatively, to claim a view of the world in a meaningful way is to exert a rhetoric that effaces this world in proportion to the extent that the view of the world created has coherence. I want to end with the description of Decoud's suicide, which captures these problems almost aphoristically:

> A victim of the disillusioned weariness which is the retribution meted out to intellectual audacity, the brilliant Don Martin Decoud, weighted by the bars of San Tomé silver, disappeared without a trace, swallowed up in the immense indifference of things.
> (*Nostromo* 501)

Decoud's fate is a cautionary tale to us all. The full extent of totalizing narratives of nature is a sense of our own insignificance that politically unravels us—our values are revealed as illusions and our lives are dwarfed by the vast scale of nature in time and space. Even the mighty San Tomé silver, with all its material value, is simply dead weight, although as such it maintains its physical capacity to drag Decoud down to his death.[12] Theoretical frameworks based on notions of world-systems and world-ecologies cannot engage with the whole of nature, and the extent to which they claim to do so is also the extent to which they efface the world. There is something hubristic about capitalism as world-ecology: as the monstrous San Tomé mine suggests, it engages in a bizarre deification of capital, granting it prime agency in a narrative that places the whole world in its grasp. *Nostromo* confers "material interests" immense power and suggests they operate beyond the control of most mere mortals and only partially under the influence of great capitalists like Holroyd. Yet "material interests" do not possess the kind of singular agency Moore's work implies. Alternatively, capitalism as world-ecology threatens to become a misleading synecdoche, increasingly encompassing human activity and the whole of nature itself. Capitalism is an ecology, insofar as it produces knowledge about nature, and its narratives of production, exhaustion and degradation exist only in relation to its own values or other human values.

Moore's theory of capitalism as world-ecology, though it marks a useful conceptual evolution of Marxist theory, like other systems of value depends upon myths and illusions. Furthermore, such critiques of capitalism depend upon the specific notions of economic value they aim to undermine. *Nostromo* is also suffused with mythic imagination, but it adds to this a dialogic dramatization of competing myths, a self-conscious awareness of its own fictionality and an ironic undermining of narrative authority. Furthermore, as Decoud's suicide implies, stripped of all sustaining illusions, *life* itself loses its value. Moore's sense of nature as the "web of life" depends upon this value for its force, and without this potency, the threat that life might disappear from nature loses any meaning. Capitalism endangers certain kinds of life—and most worryingly, forms valuable to humanity—but it cannot threaten "natural forces" and can do no more than alter "forms of nature" in ways whose benefits or disadvantages are again always defined in relation to human values. The extreme extent of *Nostromo*'s logic is that life itself is merely another "sustaining illusion," but also that illusions come at a cost: sustenance after all requires some kind of consumption. Yet these economies of sustenance themselves hinge on fictional values: they feed cannibalistically—even on life itself.

Notes

1 I would like to thank Graham Huggan for his continuing advice and suggestions. Additionally, a version of this essay was presented at the Postcolonial Studies Association Conference at the University of York, 2014. I am

grateful to the association for the valuable comments and feedback, and in particular to Jennifer Wenzel, whose conversation helped me clarify key issues.
2 *A Personal Record* (193).
3 For more detail, see Michael Niblett, "World-Economy" and Sharae Deckard, "Mapping the World-Ecology."
4 It is worth noting that *Nostromo*'s token Marxist receives unsympathetic treatment: "an indigent, sickly, somewhat hunchbacked little photographer, with a white face and a magnanimous soul dyed crimson by a bloodthirsty hate of all capitalists" (528).
5 See Patrick Brantlinger's epilogue to *Rule of Darkness*, Kurtz's *Darkness* and Conrad's *Heart of Darkness* for a discussion of the ways in which Conrad combined conscious anti-imperialism while remaining complicit with modes of knowledge production that served imperial ends. What Brantlinger neglects, however, is to observe how Conrad undermines even the values he holds most dear. Though Conrad does maintain a nostalgia for "the traditional ideals of honour, glory, conscience" (259), as I have argued elsewhere, this is counterpointed by his awareness that "heroic adventure" and chivalric ideals have historically been a mask for plunder (Parker).
6 This sense of ecology is present in Moore's thought, particularly when he writes about the ways in which capitalism produces nature as a separate knowledge category from the human ("Ecology Capital" 126, 135n), but this is only one, uncommon, way in which Moore uses the term.
7 For Moore, capitalism is one of many possible consecutive or concurrent world-ecologies ("Ecology Capital" 110), although at times he slips into capitalism as the whole oikeios ("Ecology Capital" 112), or more commonly suggests that capitalism is the whole of the oikeios during a particular historical period ("Ecology Capital" 123–5, 128; "Cheap Food" 227; "Transcending the metabolic rift" 12, 22).
8 See also "Ecology Capital" (110, 117, 134), "Amsterdam" (34, 41), "Cheap Food" (227) and "Transcending the Metabolic Rift."
9 To be fair to Moore, he explicitly states that "the search for unified theory of crisis in historical capitalism [...] does not entail the collapsing of distinctions [...] Capital-centrism is not by nature capital-reductionism" ("Transcending the Metabolic Rift" 16). Moore also displays a passing awareness that his project is the telling of a story ("Transcending the Metabolic Rift" 17), but these examples represent a handful of relatively isolated qualifications amid a narrative, which as I have suggested, promotes the very errors Moore here warns against.
10 At the base of Moore's theory of capitalism is its ability to produce cheap food. When this ability is sufficiently diminished, a system-wide crisis occurs. Capitalism has historically overcome these through frontier movement and technological change, but Moore suggests that we are involved in a contemporary crisis that may (and he thinks it will) provoke an epochal change (like the move from feudalism to capitalism) in the fundamental mode of production, namely, the end of capitalism itself.
11 Closer to *Nostromo* is Moore's references to the "human natures of the capitalist labor process, household reproduction and family formation [...] and much more" ("Transcending the Metabolic Rift" 39).
12 Sam Perks, elsewhere in this collection, describes a parallel situation, in which the material of capital, this time in the form of coal, performs a similar function in the drowning of Jones in *Victory*.

Works Cited

Brantlinger, Patrick. *Rule of Darkness: British Literature and Imperialism, 1830–1914.* Cornell University Press, 1988, pp. 255–74.

Conrad, Joseph. *A Personal Record.* J. M. Dent & Sons, 1919.

———. *Nostromo: A Tale of the Seaboard.* Doubleday, Page & Company, 1924.

Deckard, Sharae. "Jungle Tide, Devouring Reef." *Postcolonial Green: Environment Politics and World Narratives,* edited by Bonnie Roos and Alex Hunt. University of Virginia Press, 2010, pp. 32–48.

———. *Mapping the World-Ecology: Conjectures on World-Ecological Literature.* N.p., 2012, www.academia.edu/2083255/Mapping_the_World-Ecology_Conjectures_on_World-Ecological_Literature

GoGwilt, Christopher. *The Invention of the West: Joseph Conrad and the Double-Mapping of Europe and Empire.* Stanford University Press, 1995.

Hutcheon, Linda. *Irony's Edge: The Theory and Politics of Irony.* Routledge, 1994.

Jameson, Fredric. *The Political Unconscious.* Cornell University Press, 1981.

Lord, Ursula. *Solidarity versus Solitude in the Novels of Joseph Conrad: Political and Epistemological Implications of Narrative Innovation.* McGill-Queen's University Press, 1998.

Moore, Jason W. "'Amsterdam Is Standing on Norway' Part I: The Alchemy of Capital, Empire and Nature in the Diaspora of Silver, 1545–1648." *Journal of Agrarian Change,* vol. 10, no. 1, 2010, pp. 33–68.

———. *Capitalism in the Web of Life.* Verso, 2015.

———. "Cheap Food & Bad Money: Food, Frontiers, and Financialization in the Rise and Demise of Neoliberalism." *Review,* vol. 33, no. 2–3, 2011, pp. 225–61.

———. "Ecology, Capital and the Nature of Our Times: Accumulation and Crisis in the Capitalism World-Ecology." *Journal of World-Systems Research,* vol. 17, no. 1, 2011, pp. 107–46.

———. "'This Lofty Mountain of Silver Could Conquer the Whole World': Potosí and the Political Ecology of Underdevelopment, 1545–1800." *The Journal of Philosophical Economics,* vol. 4, no. 1, 2010, pp. 58–103.

———. "Transcending the Metabolic Rift: A Theory of Crises in the Capitalist World-Ecology." *Journal of Peasant Studies,* vol. 38, no. 1, 2011, pp. 1–46.

Niblett, Michael. "Specters in the Forest: Gothic Form and World-Ecology in Edgar Mittelholzer's *My Bones and My Flute.*" *Small Axe: A Caribbean Journal of Criticism,* vol. 18, no. 2, 2014, pp. 53–68.

———. "World-Economy, World-Ecology, World Literature." *Green Letters,* vol. 16, no. 1, 2012, pp. 15–30.

Parker, Jay. "'He Was One of Us': Rortyian Liberal Ethnocentrism and Ironic Narrative Voice in Joseph Conrad's Lord Jim." *Textual Practice,* 2016, doi: 10.1080/0950236X.2016.1237993.

Parry, Benita. *Conrad and Imperialism.* Macmillan, 1983.

Simmons, Allan H. *Joseph Conrad.* Palgrave Macmillan, 2006.

Watt, Ian. *Essays on Conrad.* Cambridge University Press, 2000.

12 "He Can't Throw Any of His Coal-Dust in My Eyes"
Adventurers and Entrepreneurs in *Victory*'s Coal Empire

Samuel Perks

Joseph Conrad's discomfort with the mission and the methods of empire has long been remarked upon by literary critics (Parry 12). His lamentation for the increasing redundancy of the romantic adventurer figure has also become a well-worn topic within Conrad studies (Brantlinger, Dryden, Parry and White). However, little scholarship to date has recognized that the articulation of this lamentation is embedded in the aesthetics of coal. Coal is central to many of Conrad's novels and short stories. The narrative progress of such canonical texts as *Heart of Darkness* (1898) and *Lord Jim* (1900), for example, depends upon the burning of coal, while "Youth" (1898) and "Typhoon" (1902) are more explicit in their representations of coal's integral part in Britain's imperial infrastructure. Just as "imperialism had been naturalised by fiction" at the time of Conrad's writing, in Benita Parry's words (128), the use of coal, too, had been naturalized—albeit with a mixture of anxiety and fascination (MacDuffie). Conrad's fiction, however, rendered imperialism an altogether alienating and uncomfortable experience, and he renders the empire's shift to coal in a similarly subversive manner. This chapter analyzes *Victory* (1915), one of Conrad's keenly coal-conscious novels, to show how the ecological revolution entailed by this shift to coal is denaturalized. It is through the adventurer figure (an archetype that Conrad frequently undermines) that a critique emerges in *Victory*. The purported heroism of the adventure hero is shown to be fundamentally at odds with the new, coal-fired energy regime, as the novel tracks Heyst's transformation from adventurer to entrepreneur in the interests of coal empire, before finally killing himself by setting fire to his colonial bungalow. This final act takes on new meaning in this interpretation, as Heyst symbolically—and perhaps heroically—self-combusts in a refusal of coal-fired colonial capitalism's new dynamics.

Coal dictated the dynamics of the empire during Conrad's merchant career, and most of his writing career. *In The Coal Question* (1865), W.S. Jevons explained that "with coal, almost any feat is possible," and he linked the British Empire's unparalleled exploitation of coal reserves to its global civilizing mission (2, 374). The exploitation of coal across the empire intensified, and by 1898, public commentators could declare that "[c]oal is the first requisite of empire" (Hurd 718). Conrad's society and culture were fueled by coal, and coal seems to have fueled his disenchantment with the imperial project, too. Allen MacDuffie has referred to Conrad's critique of coal-fascination as exhibited in "Youth" and suggests that the narrative represents "an early story of disillusionment" (221). Framed this way, "Youth" marks the early stages of a writing career that laments the decline of imperial heroism and adventure (Brantlinger 42). To elucidate the relation between energy and empire with greater clarity, theorization of the imperial system is required, and this theorization must tie together ecological, economic and energy concerns.

This system has been theorized by Jason Moore in world-systemic terms. Moore outlines a capitalist world-ecology in which "nature" is put at capital's disposal, in order for capital to annex "natural" "free gifts," which include minerals, unpaid labor and sources of energy (109). Moore cites David Harvey's work on the concept of the "spatial fix" to discuss the expansion of this "fundamentally socioecological" system, as it attempts to resolve its internal contradictions (Harvey 284–311; Moore 110). Historically, a complex network of coaling stations was required to link and resupply commodity frontiers in this world-ecology in its colonial phase and to accelerate the circulation of raw materials to core sites from peripheral zones. Colonial capitalism was able to expand these frontiers using steam power. Moore describes this transition in methods and relationships as an "ecological revolution," which depends as much upon "system-making organizational revolutions" as "technological innovation" in order to expand commodity frontiers (130). The "ecological revolution," then, was constituted by the transition from an array of energy sources which include wind propulsion and wood burning to coal. The transition was not simply one of energy source, however. It was organizational as well as technological, which means that the ecological dynamics were reconfigured. Social, economic and ecological dimensions to the world-system (across its history) coproduced each other and were, therefore, transformed at the same time as part of the same processes. As a result, "[c]oal and steampower linked up with capital and empire to radically extend frontiers of appropriation, and thereby secure a radically augmented ecological surplus (cheap food, labor, and inputs)" in Moore's words (128). The capitalist and colonial relations that made up the world-ecology in its colonial phase were fundamentally underpinned by dependence on coal.

To analyze texts' mediation of this dependence on coal, engagement with the emerging field of the energy humanities is required. The energy humanities build toward "an energy-driven literary theory," in the words of Patricia Yaeger, to interrogate texts'—and by extension, cultures'—ways of seeing the world, as they are inflected by particular energy regimes (306–8). Imre Szeman suggests that this new discipline allows us to "think about the history of capital not exclusively in geopolitical terms, but in terms of the forms of energy available to it" ("System Failure" 806). This field has often taken "petrofictions," "petrocultures" and "petromodernity" as its objects of analysis,[1] thus foregrounding scrutiny of the aesthetic logic of oil. The field also provides a framework for engagement with coal. Just as "[n]eoliberalism is an oil system" (MacDonald, "The Resources of Culture" 10), in the sense that its organization maximizes the output that oil can deliver, capitalism in its colonial phase was a coal system. The British Empire was organized in such a way as to optimize the use of coal, and as such, it was a coal empire. Coal empire's literary output was inflected by its dependence upon coal. Graeme MacDonald observes that "[a]ll modern writing is premised on both the promise and the hidden costs and benefits of hydrocarbon culture" ("Oil and World Literature" 31), and by extension, it follows that coal empire's cultural production was that of a coal culture, insofar as it emerged from a coal-dependent set of relations. A subset of cultural production of an energy culture deals explicitly with energy. In petromodernity, there is a body of works that deals explicitly with oil encounters—petrofictions. Szeman shows that petrofictions can "understand oil not as a social problem to be (somehow, miraculously) ameliorated, but as a core element of our societies" (Introduction to "Petrofictions" 3). We might think of Emile Zola's *Germinal* (1885) as a canonical example of a coal fiction, in which coal is shown to be central to its contemporary national society. *Victory*, a coal fiction which narrates the activities of a coal mine-owning European aristocrat in Southeast Asia, narrates the unfolding of an ecological revolution. This depiction of a transition from one energy regime to another (in all of its spatial unevenness) can enrich our understanding of the relation between energy and fiction and prompt a rereading of the coal-fired fictions of empire.

Mapping Coal Empire for Adventurers and Entrepreneurs

Victory was finished in 1914 and published in 1915, at the height of the British Empire, and at a moment when oil became of strategic importance. Anxieties over oil security had been put forward in London-based publications over the preceding few years, as British military infrastructure adopted oil as the chief energy source in key areas (such as fueling warships).[2] An energy transition was on the horizon, but coal remained integral to infrastructure in the metropole. *Victory* is set at the historical moment of the arrival of steamers in maritime Southeast Asia, and at a time when coal mining remains small-scale, open-cast and localized—that is, in the second half of the nineteenth century (Boomgaard 171, 263; Tarling 22–3). Conrad thus narrates the unfolding of one ecological revolution at the historical dawning of another, with all of its attendant anxieties. The most pressing problem posed by the transition to coal, for Conrad, is the rendering obsolete of the adventurer character in the reconfigured coal empire—a figure that features somewhat heroically in imperial literature. The protagonists of the fictions of H. Rider Haggard, R.M. Ballantyne, G.A. Henty and W.H.G. Kingston, to name just a handful of Victorian-era writers, tended to be courageous, principled and modest. As Linda Dryden and Andrea White have shown, Conrad's protagonists are more complex, and they struggle to reconcile their ideals with the practice as colonial officers or traders. Conrad writes against the template in which "[a]dventure, wealth, and return to English 'civilization' for the white hero" are celebrated, and opts to show that those "who strive for a romantic ideal find only disillusionment, and death becomes a welcome escape from a world in which the idealist has no place" (Dryden 8, 198). Heyst's ideals have been discussed by many critics, and I do not mean to recount them here. It is important to note, however, that Heyst briefly embraces the commercialism of his contemporary moment, only for it to cast him aside. His mode of "escape" becomes all the more symbolic of the romantic adventure hero's incompatibility with coal empire, in this light.

He may not be a typical romantic adventurer, but Heyst's patterns of behavior overlap with those of many such heroes. He discovers coal seams during his wanderings, proving his explorer credentials (*Victory* 5–6), and dutifully aids Morrison in his unprofitable version of trade: distributing rice to hungry populations and "preach[ing] to them energy and industry"—a small-scale "improving" project (*Victory* 15–16, 10–11). None of these characteristics led him to great profit, however. This mirrors the situation Andrea White observes in *Almayer's Folly* (1895), where "[a]dventure has been severely reduced [...] to [...] promises of gold and diamonds that never materialize." In this sense, Almayer is "most unheroic" (121). Almayer opts to wander the world when prompted by "discontent at home" (124), and Heyst is in a parallel situation, having "lit out into the wide world" after the death of his father, who was known as "something of a crank" (*Victory* 33). The Conradian adventure hero is more complicated than the heroes of Victorian adventure fiction writers, as White shows. His role as an adventurer is complicated even further, however, by his reinvention of himself as an entrepreneur, when he acquires finance for the company and having prospectuses issued (*Victory* 23–4). *Victory*'s representation of the fraught relationship between adventurers, entrepreneurs and investors is developed through the map that Heyst commissions.

The map in the prospectus is designed solely to lure investment into the company, and Conrad ironizes this process having the unnamed narrator of the novel register surprise at its initial success.

> From the first he had selected Samburan, or Round Island, for the central station. Some copies of the prospectus issued in Europe, having found their way out East, were passed from hand to hand. We greatly admired the map which accompanied them for the edification of the shareholders. On it Samburan was represented as the central spot of the Eastern Hemisphere with its name engraved in enormous capitals. Heavy lines radiated from it in all directions through the tropics, figuring a mysterious and effective star – lines of influence or lines of distance, or something of that sort. Company promoters have an imagination of their own. There's no more romantic temperament on earth than the temperament of a company promoter. Engineers came out, coolies were imported, bungalows were put up on Samburan, a gallery driven into the hillside, and actually some coal got out.
>
> (*Victory* 23–4)

The narrator's surprise is understandable: the shareholders' "edification" involves a representation of the space of Samburan that elides the inhabitants, terrain, flora and fauna of the island—all of which must be dealt with by Heyst once he arrives to supervise the extraction process. The prospectus situates Samburan in an imaginary network, in which Samburan is the central station, implying that a whole new network of coaling-stations was to be established. Just as empire was "a potent force in the British imagination" in the adventure tradition (Dryden 4), coal's place in the colonial capitalist imaginary became more central. As Andreas Malm observes, a burgeoning "coal fetishism" cast coal as innately powerful and miraculous (220). Conrad does not simply register or naturalize this centralization of coal, however. He shows the role of coal, or rather, the empire-wide transformations that lead to the optimal use of coal, in rendering the adventurer an entrepreneur. To put it another way, he shows coal's part in the adventurer's downfall.

The narrative focalizes the singular character who prompts this industrialization and then sits idle, replicating the model entrepreneur rather than the glamorized adventurer. Heyst has performed the adventurer role, having identified the coal outcrops, but he then lapses from the adventurer lifestyle and allows the map, which is in no way commensurate to the geography of Samburan, to circulate, in order to tempt investors. The map does not show that Samburan's surrounding ocean is "a tepid, shallow sea," and perhaps unsuitable for navigation by large steamships (*Victory* 4).[3] It fails to represent the Indigenous Alfuro community, rendering the Java Sea a field for only European activity (*Victory* 179).

It fails to represent the mosquitoes, whose presence makes some areas uninhabitable for the colonizers (*Victory* 4). It fails to depict the vegetation that eventually "invaded" the settlement (*Victory* 5). The map's duplicity is necessary to garner the largest possible investment and accelerate the extraction process. The navigator-adventurer is placed in a double bind: being at the mercy of unpredictable movements of financial capital, he must accommodate himself to its preferences and language, even as this means compromising his position as an adventurer. It is the ecological revolution that optimizes the use of coal that creates this double bind.

The flight of financial capital from Samburan dooms Heyst's company. Within two pages of the account of the establishment of the Tropical Belt Coal Company, the narrator reports that the company fails (*Victory* 25). *Victory* registers unease at the financial processes which lead to Heyst's failure.

> The Tropical Belt Coal Company went into liquidation. The world of finance is a mysterious world in which, incredible as the fact may appear, evaporation precedes liquidation. First the capital evaporates, then the company goes into liquidation. These are very unnatural physics.
>
> (*Victory* 3)

These "unnatural physics" can be contrasted with "the black piles" and "the mound of derelict coal" that build up on Samburan (*Victory* 231, 284), which are visible and tangible to the narrator. The high finance that governs the direction of empire is incommensurate with the tangible results of mining, and indeed the adventurism of the individuals who work in empire's name. The coal, which is substantial, inert and exploitable, is figured as "natural," to be contrasted with the "unnatural" dynamics that governs its exploitation and distribution. Financial capital's "evaporation" proceeds in accordance with the logic of colonial capitalism: regardless of how much more coal could potentially be mined from Samburan, it is the efficiency and profitability of an enterprise that determines whether financial capital remains invested. Far from moving in "mysterious" ways, financial capital moves to new and prospectively more profitable sites of extraction, in a thoroughly rational manner. The failure of the Tropical Belt Coal Company, therefore, represents the success of imperial expansion, because capital only leaves if a more profitable site is brought into the colonial capitalist world-ecology and made accessible to investors through such phenomena as prospectus maps. The empire expands and incorporates more profitable sites of resource extraction, in accordance with the best interests of investors, rather than the adventuring spirit of Heyst.

This map elides information that might endanger investment. Adhering to the cartographic conventions that give power to the colonizer and following the trope of the navigator-adventurer who names the places he "discovers," Heyst and Morrison name the bay on Samburan. "Till Heyst and Morrison had landed in Black Diamond Bay, and named it, that side of Samburan had hardly ever heard the sound of human speech," claims the narrator (*Victory* 180). The Alfuro presence is rhetorically eliminated by this act of naming, while the historically—and culturally—specific metaphor also closes the site to alternative interpretations of the space. It binds together the commodification of coal and diamond with their similarity in chemical properties, rather than marking the presence of an adventurer who might inscribe himself on the site through the place-name. The absurdity of the naming gesture is compounded by Davidson's later encounter with the landform, as he steams near "the slight indentation which for a time was known officially as Black Diamond Bay" (*Victory* 28). By describing the landform as an "indentation" rather than as a bay, Conrad implies that the site was named to stake a claim to the island as the pair's property and source of energy. The indentation's only known characteristic is having hosted the pair's landing, but the name anticipates coal mining. The name is simply not commensurate with the physical space of that area of Samburan. As far as Heyst and Morrison are concerned, however, the necessity of garnering investment is paramount. They have seen that steamers are arriving in Southeast Asia, and they stake an early claim in the coal market accordingly. To enhance this claim, the site is named to magnify coal's presence. Heyst and Morrison begin to perform the roles of "navigator-explorer-traveller[s]" by naming the landform (White 9), but they are locked into naming it at finance's convenience, rather than to match the physical features or self-aggrandize like conventional colonial adventurers. This new set of priorities is ushered in by the ecological revolution of steam power. The overarching systemic change alters individuals' behavior, making them more amenable to exploiting the new source of energy which will power imperial infrastructure in the region.

Once there is "actually some coal got out," coal-fueled colonial capitalism exerts greater pressure on the individual merchant-adventurers. By way of contrast with the cynical representation of space in the prospectus, Conrad describes "the trader's special lore which is transmitted by word of mouth, without ostentation, and forms the stock of mysterious local knowledge," which extends beyond the bounds of conventional geographical knowledge (*Victory* 11). This suggests that there is great expertise and a sense of community among the traders in Southeast Asia, who consider themselves sharing in "the world of hazard and adventure" (*Victory* 23). These are the archetypal romanticized traders, but their community does not welcome steam power to the region.

> [E]ven those who smiled quietly to themselves were only hiding their uneasiness. Oh yes; it had come, and anybody could see what

would be the consequences – the end of the individual trader, smothered under a great invasion of steamers. We could not afford to buy steamers. Not we.

(24)

The narrating voice emphasizes the collective aspect of the commercial struggle ahead. It is the community of traders who will be "smothered" together. Heyst is recast as a threat to the community with which he had been affiliated and becomes "the destroyer of our little industry" (24)—a phrase that suggests valiance on the part of the humble traders and monopolistic might on the part of Heyst. The introduction of steam power to the region and its attendant ecological revolution alter the social relations for these merchants. Their adventuring spirit has become a hindrance in coal-fired colonial capitalism. Large companies have expanded and intensified methods of extraction and distribution at their disposal, while individual traders do not have the requisite economies of scale to compete. Heyst had been a part of the group of traders before taking full advantage of the discovery he makes in his capacity as an adventurer, and it is the adventuring ethos of this individual trader that leads him to set up the Tropical Belt Coal Company. The adventurer hero type that was lionized by some Victorian novelists is drawn into complicity with the world-ecology that renders him obsolete in *Victory*. His adventuring practices become linked to wider imperial and colonial capitalist pursuit of commodities and energy security between commodity frontiers. The newly enhanced scale of extraction permitted by coal causes the merchants' unease, because they are rendered uncompetitive and redundant in the new industrialization of Southeast Asian trade.

If the adventurer figure is compromised by the introduction of steam power to Southeast Asia, what relation did the adventurer have to colonial capitalism in previous energy regimes? Conrad offers examples of "gentlemen" who do not depend on steam power and rely on alternative methods of colonial capitalism. Besides Heyst, the son of a baron (*Victory* 159), Davidson (*Victory* 42) and Mr. Jones (*Victory* 103) lay claim to the title of gentleman, as do Jim (*Lord Jim* 8) and the pirate, Gentleman Brown (*Lord Jim* 253) elsewhere in Conrad's fiction. The Conradian "gentleman" holds together several contradictory characteristics. Conrad critiques the adventure genre's lionization of "gentlemanly" explorers who must be seen as curious, rather than greedy, and who must subscribe to a "gentlemanly code insist[ing] on honour and the protection of weaker souls" (Dryden 19, 150). In contrast to convention, Conradian "gentlemen" are often motivated by greed and expropriate from one another frequently and with varying degrees of honesty. Ricardo outlines a political position that distances himself from wage labor and draws him closer to a sort of loot relation, which he institutes by collaborating with Mr. Jones and Pedro, under the banner of "plain Mr. Jones & co.," before invading Samburan in search of riches (*Victory* 145, 118). It is this combined company and gentlemanly status that allows the group to expropriate rather than perform wage labor, and a similar structure exists with Gentleman Brown and his comrades in *Lord Jim*, as well as Heyst's Tropical Belt Coal Company in *Victory*. The groups of protagonists and antagonists in each narrative identify as gentlemen, pursue a loot relation and eschew steam-powered transport. By presenting these features together in these characters, Conrad disbars nostalgic interpretations of his representation of energy. As coal-fired colonial capitalism redirects the adventure ethic of early capitalism, Conrad highlights the plight of individual traders. His sympathy for the traders is tempered with a recognition that the same logics dictated both coal-fired, entrepreneur-led and earlier, adventurer-led phases of colonial expansion. *Victory* undercuts the romance and gentlemanliness of imperial heroes from across the phases of empire's expansion, but Conrad shows the individual trader under coal-driven colonial capitalism to be a particularly compromised figure, whose contradictions finally render him obsolete. MacDuffie argues that coal permits "a global-scaled instantiation of appetites that have always been with us" (221), and it is indeed the scale of extraction and expropriation methods that are transformed to accord with the dominant energy source as part of the ecological revolution. The logic of colonial capitalism itself remains unchanged. These examples recall Peter Cain and Antony Hopkins' description of an era of "gentlemanly capitalism," which was characterized by aristocratic investment overseas, "[leaving] its imprint on the reorganization and formal extension of empire after 1850" (18). Cain and Hopkins point out that "gentlemanly capitalism" does not persist beyond the First World War—the "first great carbon-fueled conflict" that breaks out before Conrad publishes *Victory*—suggesting that coal-fired methods render aristocratic intervention irrelevant (Cain and Hopkins 18; Mitchell 66). Instead, the financial world's "unnatural physics" and logic of profitability prevail. Simultaneously, the imperial adventurer is rendered obsolete, "smothered" by coal-fired methods of extraction and transportation. Coal-fired colonial capitalism captures the practices of the merchant-adventurer and the aristocratic adventurer and redirects their energies toward the securing of the coal-station network, the expansion of commodity frontiers and the global circulation of commodities at an accelerated pace, compared with previous energy regimes. *Victory* registers this process and renders it an unnatural, uncomfortable experience, in which the last pretenses to imperial glamour are stripped away. Schomberg, for one, is wary of the transformation of Heyst, from aristocrat to adventurer to entrepreneur, and he rightly highlights the role of coal in these transformations. When he claims that Heyst "can't throw any of his coal-dust in my eyes. There's nothing in it. A fellow like that for manager? Phoo!" (*Victory* 25), he is exhibiting his characteristic cynicism, but with startling prescience.

The idea of this aristocratic figure "rushing all over the Archipelago" to perform the role of entrepreneur appears false to Schomberg (*Victory* 25). The landlord's dismissal of "coal-dust" spotlights coal's role in these false and failing transformations. Conrad does not allow the transition to coal be represented as natural or inevitable, but rather, he penetrates past its "mystical" qualities (*Victory* 3) to highlight the consequences of the social and ecological transformations that maximize coal's usefulness to empire. That it should be Schomberg, one of Conrad's most rapaciously commercial characters—"the archetypal capitalist" in Daniel Schwartz's words (76)—to draw attention to this, suggests that it is his qualities of cynicism and self-interest which will persist through this ecological revolution. Heyst's gentlemanly, adventuring aristocrat attributes will be redundant. *Victory*'s dramatization of this process undercuts Victorian representations of heroic imperial adventurers from across the history of capitalism and demythologizes the individual trader figure in particular, as outdated in an era of financialized coal-fired expansion. The harnessing of steam power makes the last vestiges of imperial adventure untenable.

From Harnessing "Purposeful Energy" to Burnout

Heyst commits his bodily energy to the exploitation of coal, and thus he joins the ranks of the "historically located protagonists" that Parry observes in Conrad's fiction, "whose autonomy is curtailed by their roles as agents of imperialist's purpose, who are doomed to deformation and defeat" (15). The deformation that he undergoes involves his loss of his short-lived adventurer role: he is rendered irrelevant as an adventurer, sapped of energy, and eventually loses his corporeal form by burning to ashes in the final section of the novel (*Victory* 410). Heyst's energy levels in *Victory* match his levels of usefulness in the coal enterprise: he moves through phases of "purposeful energy" to aimless "drifting" (*Victory* 25, 92). As Heyst's energy is depleted to the point of inefficiency and exhaustion, his business fails. By juxtaposing and conflating definitions of energy, both as human and as a specific world resource, Conrad shows how colonial capitalism harnesses and repurposes both categories of energy with the same mechanisms. The pressures brought to bear on Heyst's body, for example, direct his energy toward empire-building, in his capacity both as adventurer and entrepreneur, just as they direct coal's energy through the imperial distributional network.

The mechanisms of colonial capitalism pressure bodies to act in its interests. Heyst's energy is harnessed and exhausted. In addition, the coal that is mobilized by capital during this phase of colonial capitalism is composed of millions of ancient plant bodies, compressed by geological forces. Colonial capitalist forces then compel these bodies to release their energy to propel and expand empire. The novel's opening discussion of the "close chemical relation" between diamonds and coal (*Victory* 3) serves to obscure this fact by relating the substance to its chemical category, rather than its historic (or prehistoric) origin. The name Black Diamond Bay also mystifies the fact that the island will host the extraction of an energy source that is a repository of millions of mineralized bodies. Diamond is carbon, like coal, but it is not the product of compressed ancient bodies. This colonial act of naming obscures the fact that coal is mostly biological matter. Thus, coal's corporeality is concealed. This is not a primary motivation for the bay's name, of course, but the name highlights the ideological shaping of thought patterns that coal-fired colonial capitalism instills: Exchange value is celebrated, while the nature of the commodity being exploited is obscured, deflecting potential reflexivity regarding the adventurer-entrepreneur's own role in this system.

Heyst's suicide suggests that there remains a degree of reflexivity regarding his own role in the advancing coal capitalism in Southeast Asia, however. Critics have read his suicide variously as the resolution of Heyst's philosophical impasse, as "self-recognition," as "an act of nature that returns him to nature" or as an expression of despair after a tragically curtailed romance (Clayton 137; Jones 53; Kaplan 84; Leavis and Wagenaar 499). These interpretations do not pay sufficient attention to the manner of the suicide or the novel's fascination with coal. Heyst kills himself, Davidson reports, by setting fire to the principle bungalow, and two further bungalows also catch fire in the process. Davidson investigates the site the following day and says that "[w]e found enough to be sure" that Heyst had died in the blaze (*Victory* 409–10). What might the self-immolation of this failed coal magnate mean, in the emergent coal-inflected colonial capitalist imaginary?

His act can be read as a protest suicide, occurring in the wake of the extinguishing of the last parts of his life which have given him meaning. The death of his lover, Lena, compounds the loss of his coal enterprise and his friend Morrison, and as a result, there are no remaining purposeful ways for Heyst to expend his energy. In this reading, he kills himself in one final purposeful action. By self-immolating, he joins the multitude of fossilized bodies that have been combusted in form of coal, but he does not combust in the interests of colonial capitalism. His combustion does not propel coal empire's expansion. This is a moment in which he distinguishes himself, as a subject of coal empire, from the fossilized bodies in the coal, even as he enacts a dark sort of solidarity with them. His combustion is recast as resistance, rather than service, and he succeeds in setting light to some of the wooden bungalows on Samburan too—rendering the coal-mining project less easily recoverable should it become profitable once more. Heyst creates a symbolic spectacle of the combustion of the subject of coal empire, rejecting any easy naturalization of the transition to a coal-dominated energy regime. In this sense, the cost of this transition is measured in traditions and values, as the adventurer figure, with all of his attendant complexities, destroys himself. This is a new instantiation of the earlier process in which the steamers (which Heyst, it is implied, helped to fuel) render the adventurer-trader obsolete. This resonance creates a greater sense of closure, not just for the novel, but for the adventurer figure in a more abstract sense. *Victory* illustrates the burnout of this figure as a consequence of the advancing coal empire and thus destabilizes any straightforward cultural consecration of the organizational logic of coal.

Heyst's suicide becomes a final act of heroism in an age which does not accommodate the heroic. Consideration of his suicide as heroic or romantic sits uncomfortably with Conrad's modernist style, but if we consider *Victory* a later attempt by Conrad to grapple with modernity's predations upon the romantic conception of society (and of the adventurer figure in particular), further readings become available. In "The Paris of the Second Empire in Baudelaire," Walter Benjamin describes the social and literary function of suicide in the wake of modernity.

> Modernity must stand under the sign of suicide, an act which seals a heroic will that makes no concessions to a mentality inimical toward this will. Such a suicide is not resignation. It is *the* achievement of modernity in the realm of the passions. [...] Someone like Baudelaire could very well have viewed suicide as the only heroic act available to the *multitudes maladives* [...].
> (47–8)

Regardless of whether Heyst is *maladive* (sickly)—and he may well be, as he drifts inconsolably around maritime Southeast Asia—Benjamin's description suggests that heroism is modified in modernity, and consequently we should reread Heyst's suicide as an heroic achievement *in the face of modernity*. *Victory*'s representation of modernity is coal-inflected, since it is on the basis of the exploitation of coal that the individual trader is rendered obsolete and a new age is ushered in. Heyst's suicide protests coal modernity and is a heroic act. This final act of heroism may well be the "victory" of the novel's title. Rather than an "ironical victory for life," in F.R. Leavis' words (208), it is a victory for the heroic adventurer as he destroys himself in the face of rapacious coal imperial logic. Suresh Ravel, however, argues that we ought to consider the novel's "victory" as being located outside the novel's characters (163), and it may be the case that coal empire also emerges victorious at the novel's end as well, since it advances (albeit unevenly) into Southeast Asia. Heyst's suicide is a dark and desperate form of victory in that his final act as adventurer-turned-entrepreneur is a heroic gesture and thus a return to the heroic adventurer type. Even as the conditions for heroism are quashed by coal empire, Heyst manages to carry out an heroic act. He bids to reclaim his adventure hero status by self-combusting in a wooden structure, in a gesture that frustrates future exploitation of coal on Samburan.

Comparison with Mr. Jones' suicide makes this clearer. Mr. Jones, too, kills himself at the end of the novel and is discovered by Davidson.

> I suppose he tumbled into the water by accident – or perhaps not by accident. The boat and the man were gone, and the scoundrel saw himself all alone, his game clearly up, and fairly trapped. Who knows? The water's very clear there, and I could see him huddled up on the bottom between two piles, like a heap of bones in a silk blue bag, with only the head and feet sticking out.
>
> (*Victory* 411)

This suicide, by contrast, is not heroic. Jones never acts in a heroic manner, even if he holds together the contradictions typical of a Conradian "gentleman." His final act here is one of resignation at his "game," as he repeatedly describes his scurrilous activities (Schwarz 75–6), being over. His suicide does not make a gesture in relation to his life, other than to end it. Davidson finds this suicide impenetrable and can only speculate about what has happened. The symbolic potential and chemical potential energy of the coal are squandered in this scene, since the coal is used as dead weight with which to drown. Jones has simply weighed himself down and drifted to the seafloor, largely out of sight. Heyst's suicide is far more spectacular. His self-immolation, an act of combustion, embraces of the imagery of coal empire and stands in contrast to Jones' drifting to the seabed. The "great stride forward for these regions" that Heyst claims to partake in (6) inevitably involves the mystifying language of "progress," which Parry describes as entailing "the increased domination of the material environment" (13). Neither Heyst nor Jones dominates the material environment in their deaths, although Heyst attempted to do so in his entrepreneur guise. Both men use the material environment to kill themselves—Heyst with the wood of the bungalows and Jones with the piles of coal. Having hastened the "progress" of coal empire in Southeast Asia, Heyst ceases to take part in the "stride forward." He thus refuses to continue propagating coal capitalist "progress," in a final heroic gesture that uses his material environment, but which does not dominate it.

Rereading *Victory* as a Fiction of Coal Empire

Some of the critical interpretations of *Victory* require revision in light of this rereading of coal's role in Heyst's adventurer career and suicide. F.R. Leavis' claim that *Victory*'s ending is a "victory over skepticism, a victory of life" (202), albeit one that comes too late for Heyst, gains further weight in light of this reinterpretation that argues for the (limited) agency of Heyst's suicide. His is an active, rather than passive, refusal of coal capitalism's obsolescence of the adventurer figure. In addition, it demonstrates a keen "self-recognition," although not necessarily in a philosophical sense, or in relation to an abstracted notion of "nature." Rather, Heyst sees himself in the grander scheme of coal capitalist expansion and then refuses to continue to aid this expansion or accept its post-adventurer values. His suicide can also be seen as an expression of despair that encompasses the imagery of the funeral pyre of his tragic romance, as well as the romance-turned-tragedy of the adventurer figure. Heyst repurposes the image of the furnace, too. The furnace does not connote coal capitalist industry and propulsion here ("the great stride forward" in Heyst's words), but rather, it signifies a violent act of agency against coal empire.

There are ramifications, in this reinterpretation, for Conrad studies more generally. Critics are well aware of Conrad's contradictory relationship with imperialism in his fiction, as well as his ambivalence toward the adventurer figure. His relationship with coal, however, is less clear. *Victory* registers the ecological revolution that is entailed in the transition to coal, but it does not naturalize it. The novel shows how these transformations, which optimize the use of coal, also serve to empty colonialism of even its dubious "improving" ethic and thus permit new levels of rapacity and commercialism. The adventurer was always a complicated figure in Conrad's fiction, but in this late novel, even this figure's fig leaf of moral justification for colonialism is rendered obsolete in the wake of coal-fired colonial capitalism. *Victory*'s narration of the process by which the adventurer hero is made redundant does not constitute a lament for the passing of the adventurer figure (whom it recognizes was always a compromised, ambivalent figure in colonial capitalism), but it testifies to coal empire's dynamics at the moment of the adventurer's obsolescence. The organizational revolution that destroys the adventurer figure is represented as destructive, amoral and incompatible with adventurer heroism. Heyst's last heroic act—the *only* heroic act available to him in coal modernity—means that the traditions and values of pre-coal capitalism literally go up in flames. Coal's discovery compels the adventurer to transform himself beyond a capacity for heroism, and Heyst's final gesture constitutes a refusal to be complicit in this ecological revolution.

If we consider *Victory* to be a fiction of coal empire, it is a fiction that manipulates the symbolism of coal-fired industry and infrastructure to critique the new and enhanced modes of extraction that coal permits. It is a coal fiction that does not presume to see the world through the prism of the dominant energy source, but rather, it problematizes the increasing use of this energy source as a deeply discomfiting phenomenon. The unnamed narrator describes coal as "the supreme commodity of the age in which we are camped like bewildered travellers in a garish, unrestful hotel" (*Victory* 3), and bewilderment and unrestfulness come to characterize Conrad's representation of coal empire. It is an empire which is distinctly uneven, unheroic and ungentlemanly, and the novel's end recapitulates the victory of coal empire in Southeast Asia together with the final victory of the lone remaining adventurer, who stakes one last claim to heroic status.

Acknowledgments

I am indebted to the late Anthony Carrigan for alerting me to this edited collection. I would also like to thank Arunima Bhattacharya, Sourit Bhattacharya, Graham Huggan, Jeffrey McCarthy, Jay Parker, John Peters, Lissa Schneider-Rebozo, Imre Szeman, Claire Westall and Angus Young for their advice and suggestions.

Notes

1. This terminology is found in the work of Stephanie LeMenager, Timothy Mitchell, Imre Szeman and Patricia Yaeger, among others.
2. See, for example, "Oil Fields of the Empire" in the *Financial Times* and "Oil and the Empire" in the *Daily Mail* in 1910 and "Empire Oil Supplies" in the *Financial Times* and "The Lack of British Oil" in the *Daily Mail* in 1911.
3. Davidson's routine of "tak[ing] his steamer past Samburan wharf (at an average distance of a mile) every twenty-three days" after the liquidation of the Tropical Belt Coal Company suggests that Samburan cannot operate as a coal-station. Even though Davidson has strong personal ties to Heyst and there is excess coal lying about the island (*Victory* 183, 225), he does not venture closer to Samburan until the end of the novel. When he does "grope [his] way dead slow into Diamond Bay," it is to assess the situation after Jones and his team arrive (*Victory* 409). Davidson's caution implies that it is difficult to reach the island in a steamer and thus that the island is useless as a coal-station.

Works Cited

Benjamin, Walter. "The Paris of the Second Empire in Baudelaire." 1938. *Walter Benjamin: Selected Writings*. Edited by Howard Eiland and Michael W. Jennings, translated by Edmund Jephcott et al., vol. 4. The Belknap Press of Harvard University Press, 2006. 3–92.

Boomgaard, Peter. *Southeast Asia: An Environmental History*. ABC-CLIO, 2007.

Brantlinger, Patrick. *Rule of Darkness: British Literature and Imperialism, 1830–1914*. Cornell University Press, 1988.

Cain, P J. and Anthony G. Hopkins. "Gentlemanly Capitalism and British Expansion Overseas II: New Imperialism, 1850–1945." *The Economic History Review*, vol. 40, no. 1, 1987, pp. 1–26.

Clayton, Aaron. "*Victory* in Nature: An Ecocritical Reading of Joseph Conrad's Novel." *Conradiana*, vol. 42, no. 1–2, Spring/Summer 2010, pp. 123–39.

Conrad, Joseph. "Heart of Darkness." 1898. Introduction and Notes by Gene M. Moore, Universiteit van Amsterdam. *Heart of Darkness and Other Stories*. Wordsworth Editions Ltd., 1999. 29–106.

———. *Lord Jim*. 1900. Penguin Books, 1994.

———. "Typhoon". 1902. Doubleday, Page and Company, 1918.

———. *Victory: An Island Tale*. 1915. Dent, 1967.

———. "Youth". 1902. *Heart of Darkness and Other Stories*. Introduction and Notes by Gene M. Moore. Wordsworth Editions Ltd., 1999. 1–28.

Dryden, Linda. *Joseph Conrad and the Imperial Romance*. Palgrave, 2000.

"Empire Oil Supplies." *Financial Times*, 24 July 1911. 3.

Harvey, David. *Spaces of Capital: Towards a Critical Geography*. Routledge, 2001.

Hurd, Archibald S. "Coal, Trade, and the Empire." *The Nineteenth Century*, vol. 44, no. 257, July-December 1898, pp. 718–23.

Jevons, William Stanley. *The Coal Question: An Inquiry Concerning the Progress of the Nation, and the Probable Exhaustion of our Coal Mines*. Macmillan, 1865.

Jones, Susan. *Conrad and Women*. Clarendon Press, 1999.

Kaplan, Carola M. "Navigating Trauma in Conrad's *Victory*: A Voyage from Sigmund Freud to Phillip Bromberg." *Conradiana*, vol. 43, no. 2–3, Fall/Winter 2011, pp. 81–92.

Leavis, F. R. *The Great Tradition: George Eliot, Henry James, Joseph Conrad*. 1948. Chatto and Windus, 1973.

Leavis, F. R. and Detlef Wagenaar. "Conrad's *Victory* and the English Tradition." *Neophilologus*, vol. 87, no. 3, 2003, pp. 487–99.

LeMenager, Stephanie. *Living Oil: Petroleum Culture in the American Century*. Oxford and Oxford University Press, 2014.

MacDonald, Graeme. "Oil and World Literature." *American Book Review*, vol. 33, no. 3, Spring 2012, p. 7, 31.

———. "The Resources of Culture." *Reviews in Cultural Theory*, vol. 4, no. 2, Summer 2013, pp. 1–24.

MacDuffie, Allen. *Victorian Literature, Energy, and the Ecological Imagination*. Cambridge University Press, 2014.

Malm, Andreas. *Fossil Capital: The Rise of Steam Power and the Roots of Global Warming*. Verso, 2016.

Mitchell, Timothy. *Carbon Democracy: Political Power in the Age of Oil*. Verso, 2011.

Moore, Jason W. "Ecology, Capital and the Nature of Our Times: Accumulation and Crisis in the Capitalist World-Ecology." *Journal of World-Systems Research*, vol. 17, no. 1, 2011, pp. 108–47.

"Oil and the Empire." *Daily Mail*, 11 June 1910. 8.

"Oil Fields of the Empire." *Financial Times*, 4 June 1910. 2.

Parry, Benita. *Conrad and Imperialism: Ideological Boundaries and Visionary Frontiers*. Macmillan Press, 1983.

Raval, Suresh. *The Art of Failure: Conrad's Fiction*. Allen and Unwin, 1986.

Schwarz, Daniel R. *Conrad: The Later Fiction*. Macmillan, 1982.

Szeman, Imre. Introduction to "Petrofictions." *American Book Review*, vol. 33, no. 3, March/April 2012, p. 3.

———. "System Failure: Oil, Futurity, and the Anticipation of Disaster." *South Atlantic Quarterly*, vol. 106, no. 4, Fall 2007, pp. 805–23.

Tarling, Nicholas. "The Establishment of the Colonial Regimes." *The Cambridge History of Southeast Asia*. Edited by Nicholas Tarling, vol. 2. Cambridge University Press, 1992. 5–78.

"The Lack of British Oil." *Daily Mail*, 24 January 1911. 4.

White, Andrea. *Joseph Conrad and the Adventure Tradition: Constructing and Deconstructing the Imperial Subject*. Cambridge University Press, 1993.

Yaeger, Patricia. "Editor's Column: Literature in the Ages of Wood, Tallow, Coal, Whale Oil, Gasoline, Atomic Power, and Other Energy Sources." *PMLA*, vol. 126, no. 2, March 2011, pp. 305–10.

13 Guano, Globalization and Ecosystem Change in *Lord Jim*

Mark D. Larabee

What exactly is the guano island episode doing in *Lord Jim* (1900)? Marlow's vision of Jim partly buried in bird waste seems worthy of more attention than it has received, at least given the oddity of the image. The scholarship that has considered this passage at any length has focused primarily on biographical sources. Other critics dealing with the guano island episode have tended to do so only in passing, reading it as symbolizing Jim's punishment or a life of greed, corruption or material interests, leaving the guano itself unexamined. However, such readings lack the historical context of guano as an endangered natural resource in Conrad's time. Restoring the novel to those neglected ecological circumstances allows us to reread the episode as pivotal to Conrad's extended portrayal of Jim's relation to the natural world. The result reveals essential ties between landscape and character in Lord Jim, as well as the critically unexplored but crucial role that ecosystem changes played in the novel's composition and reception.

We learn about the guano island immediately following the end of the *Patna* inquiry, when a West Australian named Chester approaches Marlow just after Jim leaves the courtroom and disappears down the street. Marlow describes how Chester "had discovered—so he said—a guano island somewhere, but its approaches were dangerous, and the anchorage, such as it was, could not be considered safe" (123). This island, "[r]ight bang in the middle of the Walpole Reefs," beset by hurricanes and surrounded by deep water, was nevertheless "[a]s good as a gold-mine" (124), in Chester's words, for one could make a fortune shipping the material as fertilizer to "Queensland sugar-planters" who would "fight for [it] on the quay" (126). Unfortunately, he could not yet "get a skipper or shipowner to go near the place" (124). A man he had approached in Auckland had demurred: "Rocks, currents, no anchorage, sheer cliff to lay to" (125). Chester explains, "So I made up my mind to cart the blessed stuff myself" (124), seeking his own ship and proposing that Jim supervise operations on the island. Chester mentions the need to catch rainwater, and an "amazed" Marlow points out, "There are whole years when not a drop of rain falls on Walpole" (127). Chester promises to "fix up something for them—or land a supply" (127), but Marlow, falling silent, then tells us:

> I had a rapid vision of Jim perched on a shadowless rock, up to his knees in guano with the screams of sea-birds in his ears, the incandescent ball of the sun over his head; the empty sky and the empty ocean all a-quiver, simmering together in the heat as far as the eye could reach.
>
> (128)

Marlow refuses to pass the offer along to Jim—fortuitously, it turns out, as Chester and his crew bound for the guano island are never heard from again, presumably lost in a hurricane a month later (135).

In a biographical study, David Gill has provided the most detailed accounting of the episode's possible origins, connecting it to William Paramor's 1885 shipwreck on the *Lorenzo* while gathering guano at Sydney Island (in the Phoenix Islands group, nearly 3,000 miles northeast of Australia). Paramor and Conrad met in 1893 on the *Adowa*; according to Gill, Paramor may have told Conrad of his ordeal when the two exchanged stories (Gill 17–23). For Gill, "The Chester-Robinson project is a burlesque commentary on one of Conrad's favourite themes: material interests," and guano, like the ivory in *Heart of Darkness* and the silver in *Nostromo*, figures in how "the obsessive focus on material resources leads to corruption and disaster" (25). Other critics dealing with the episode have done so incidentally, as various early studies of the novel established readings focusing on the character of Chester or on the supposed infamy of the situation. For example, Albert Guerard interprets Marlow's vision of Jim on the island as "[t]he classic Promethean image of unending punishment" and a reminder of Jim's "moral isolation" (161). Ian Watt emphasizes the threat posed by "[t]he unscrupulous adventurer Chester, together with his villainous associate Holy-Terror Robinson," as their "unsavoury scheme" offers Jim "so squalid a fate" (304). Ross C. Murfin stresses the parallels between the unworthiness of this fate and of Jim (in Chester's eyes). Jim could potentially "devote the rest of his years to living in a place—and trading in a commodity—reflective of society's view of his worth," for "there would have been nothing ennobling about becoming a guano exporter" (80). While Gill emphasizes the grotesque materialism that guano seems to represent, in the other critical instances the physical foulness of the guano comes to the forefront, paired with Chester's lack of scruples and decency. Why the guano would be on the island, why Chester would go to such pains to get it and why it would be worth so much are questions that scarcely enter into the picture.

Meanwhile, the most comprehensive studies of geography in the novel do not examine the guano island at all.[1] Those scholars who have looked deeper for a historical source for Chester's island point to what they term the Walpole Reefs in the Loyalty Islands (near New Caledonia, 1,300 miles northeast of Brisbane) (Conrad 540n124.2; Gill 24). However, while there are in fact no reefs with that specific name in that area, there is a Walpole Island—but not yet noted by critics. Walpole Island had already been discovered and described in nautical references in Conrad's time, and it could plausibly have inspired his creation of Chester's island, particularly given its striking similarities to what Chester describes. In *Lord Jim*, Conrad is largely faithful to the details of the real Walpole Island. Like Chester's discovery, Walpole Island is a small (1½ miles by ¼ mile) coral table island, uninhabited at the time, and "very difficult of access" (according to a contemporary nautical reference), having "perpendicular cliffs" and "no anchorage," as it was surrounded by deep water (Findlay 554). The only differences between the real and fictional islands are that Chester's island has sea birds (in Marlow's imagination) and is arid (and therefore has little or no vegetation), while Walpole Island had "but few sea birds" in midsummer, and although "without any prominent trees," it was "covered with herbage" (554). Although this 1884 guide mentions no guano deposits, the island did in fact have high-quality guano. Additionally, while mining did not begin until 1914, it was as early as 1879 that a French company had leased Walpole from the French government in order to harvest the guano.[2] In the essentials of its navigational dangers, however, the fictional island corresponds remarkably closely to its factual counterpart.

Furthermore, Chester accurately points to the considerable economic worth of guano, which is the accumulated droppings and remains of sea birds, seals and bats. Rich in nitrogen and phosphorus, guano makes an excellent fertilizer and was a highly valuable, internationally traded commodity in Conrad's time. Guano is found primarily in South America, as Alexander von Humboldt discovered in his 1802 exploration of Peru. For millennia, huge flocks of the guanay cormorant, as well as pelicans, gannets, gulls and other sea birds, had found the Chincha Islands off the Peruvian coast to be ideal for nesting, and their waste had been used as manure for farming since at least the sixth century (Skaggs 4). Europeans had indirectly known about guano before the nineteenth century, but they considered it a South American curiosity (Cushman 26). Humboldt observed previously unknown quantities of the material, though, and when he brought samples back to Europe, chemists confirmed their extraordinarily powerful properties as a fertilizer. This momentous discovery touched off the great age of the guano trade as European farmers became dependent on the foreign material, in a process of globalization that expanded dramatically in the 1840s thanks to preexisting worldwide nautical networks of whaling and sealing (Cushman 27).

However, by the middle of the nineteenth century, it appeared that the prized Peruvian guano deposits were running out. While early estimates had calculated that the Chincha Islands held 117 million tons of the substance, an alarming 1853 study indicated that only 6 million tons remained (Cushman 59). In the late 1860s, consequently, the center of guano mining moved from the Chincha Islands to nearby islands to the north and south—where the guano was of lower quality—and while Peruvian guano exports reached their peak at over 700,000 tons in 1870, exports sank to less than 100,000 tons by 1879 and virtually collapsed by 1890 (Cushman 47). In Britain, the Royal Agricultural Society recognized how indispensable this revolutionary new fertilizer had become, and they established a prize in 1852 for identifying a manure equivalent in potency but less expensive for British farmers (Green 89)—a prize that would never be claimed.

"The final exhaustion of guano"

The 1850s was also the decade in which Conrad began his sea career, and while none of his ships evidently carried guano as cargo, he would have known of the vital importance of this material and the shifting patterns of the worldwide guano trade, for several reasons. First, he sailed from the Pacific to the Atlantic via Cape Horn in 1879 during the War of the Pacific (1879–84) between Peru and Chile over guano and other nitrates in disputed territory—the first war of the industrial age fought principally over competition for natural resources (Cushman 19). Additionally, a series of articles in the London *Times* in this period explained to the British public the significance of this war and of the changes that the guano trade was undergoing in the latter half of the century. An article that appeared on May 30, 1879, for instance, detailed the complexities of the three-way disputes between Peru, Bolivia and Chile over territory and resources ("The War in South America").

A lengthy article entitled "Peruvian Wealth" appeared the following year, in 1880, describing how the value of Peru's fabled gold and silver mines was "simply contemptible when placed by the side of the amount reached by the figures representing the annual export of guano in recent times." The correspondent noted, however, that while even "as late as 1873" new guano deposits were claimed to be discovered in Peru,

> it seems, however, a settled point that the richest guano beds of the Chincha Islands [...] have yielded all they had to give, while the guano that may still be found in the Lobos Islands [and elsewhere] is said to be of inferior quality.

Even there, "its total exhaustion within a few years was naturally predicted," and "[t]he rapid diminution and even the final exhaustion of guano" throughout the country was only a matter of time ("Peruvian Wealth").

More articles in the 1880s gave the British public further information about guano and its vital importance to British farming. For example, in 1882, a 6-year legal dispute between the government of Peru and the Peruvian Guano Company was finally resolved, as chronicled in additional *Times* coverage ("Our law reports"). Two years later, an 1884 letter to the editors of the *Times* remarked on the peace treaty between Peru and Chile ending the War of the Pacific. As that author also observes, "The famous Chincha Island guano has all been shipped off long ago. The deposits which remain are of a comparatively worthless character," notwithstanding the well-known court case, recently concluded, over their value and sale (Williamson 4).

Soon afterward, the discovery of a major new guano deposit took place in the East Indies—just when Conrad began his 1885 voyage on the *Tilkhurst*, bound for Singapore. An article in the *Times* that year describes a report that the Royal Colonial Institute received regarding conditions in British North Borneo. Among the "considerable deposit[s] of natural riches" found, there were "the mammoth caves of Gormanton," full of "innumerable swifts" and bats. As the *Times* correspondent relates, "Together they have occupied the locality for untold generations, and the floor is covered with a guano deposit so thick that a twenty-foot testing pole has failed to reach the bottom." While "British North Borneo abounds in natural riches and in the means of creating riches," only "[l]abour is wanted," and Chinese workers under "European masters" would be ideal ("Sir Walter Medhurst")—providing the situation that would be echoed in Chester's vow to "dump forty coolies there" in order to harvest the material under Jim's supervision (127).

This fortunate discovery near the waters Conrad was then sailing came at a crucial moment, because as Peruvian guano stocks became exhausted in the last two decades of the century, British developers had been searching farther afield for new fertilizer sources, particularly in the Indian and Pacific Oceans. Many bird-rich atolls in the Central Pacific, such as in the Line Islands and Phoenix Islands groups, had become centers of guano production in the 1870s (Cushman 96). Yet even these supplies too were giving out toward the end of the century. For instance, Baker, Jarvis and Howland Islands were abandoned around 1891 after being stripped of phosphate deposits (Skaggs 216). In the 1890s, then, just as known guano sources seemed to have reached exhaustion, and Borneo gave tantalizing indications of possible new stockpiles, the stage was set for yet another extraordinary discovery: "rock guano," or phosphate rock, on Christmas Island (south of Java), and Banaba and Nauru Islands (northeast of the Solomon Islands) (Cushman 117). In 1899, the same year that Conrad began writing *Lord Jim*, commercial mining of high-grade phosphate rock was in progress on Christmas Island, and samples from Banaba and Nauru confirmed the presence of vast quantities of tricalcium phosphate–rich deposits on both islands, potentially mitigating the loss of bird guano in supplying the insatiable European demand for fertilizer (Cushman 117–18).[3]

In this context, therefore, Chester does not exaggerate in his twice-stated declaration having made the momentous discovery of a guano island "[a]s good as a gold-mine" (124). Conrad's readers would have recognized the import of this remark, having been made sensitive to how vital guano was to British agriculture, through extensive newspaper coverage. Furthermore, Conrad effectively manipulates factual topography to make Chester's guano island so evocative as a portrayal of natural resources in demand. The fictional location effectively combines specific geological features of Walpole Island (its size, plateau shape, sheer cliffs and lack of an anchorage) with the thick deposits of places such as Banaba, Nauru and North Borneo, with teeming bird life such as that at the Gormanton caves, with the rocky barren aridity of the Chincha Islands and with the need for imported laborers, as on other uninhabited guano islands in the Pacific. Conrad's creation of the guano island thereby indicates an awareness, on the part of both the author and his readers, of important changes to global resource networks—changes that critics have not yet fully considered. For example, when Gill concludes that the Lorenzo's owner "fit into the guano trade [...] right at the very end" because "Supplies were running out, and farmers were turning to other fertilizers" (25); this assessment positions guano as a substance no longer in demand. As we have seen, however, guano was in such high demand that new sources were eagerly sought—thereby rendering Chester's discovery so vitally important, beyond what today's readers of the novel may imagine.

The value of the guano does allow Conrad to emphasize Chester's greed, making him someone from whom Marlow ought to protect Jim, yet Marlow's curious reticence in explaining exactly why he does not pass Chester's offer along to Jim hints at something more than an aversion to materialism or to the ignoble status of a guano merchant, as scholars have argued. The most obvious problem with Chester's offer is simply the physical matter of survival, given that the island has no drinking water. Yet the offer evidently has a metaphysical dimension as well, having to do with Jim's relation to the natural world. Marlow considers how "On all the round earth, which to some seems so big and that others affect to consider as rather smaller than a mustard-seed, [Jim] had no place [...] where he could withdraw" and "be alone with his loneliness" (130). When Marlow brings Jim into his room, he considers it "the only place in the world (unless, perhaps, the Walpole Reef—but that was not so handy) where [Jim] could have it out with himself without being bothered by the rest of the universe" (131). By characterizing the "round earth" as either "so big" or "smaller than a mustard-seed," Marlow attends to the paradoxical qualities of the world as an integrated whole, while the "inaccessible guano deposit" (132) makes the island an emblem of the solitude that Jim needs—which would seem to make the offer attractive.

However, while being on Chester's island would sever Jim's connections to "the rest of the universe," it does not provide any opportunity for Jim to work out his reintegration with that universe, which may be implicit in Marlow's image of Jim on the island: that of merely passive presence in the natural world. To be "up to his knees in guano" (128) puts Jim in (repelling) physical contact with natural riches but does not include him in the larger web of processes that created those riches in the first place. As we have seen, apart from the guano and the birds Chester's island is oddly barren, and made so specifically through Conrad's manipulation of geographical facts. To make better sense of this island's unusual characteristics, and of Jim's relation to the natural world, requires attending next to the contrasting natural setting of Patusan—by way of a much larger ecological problem occupying environmental thinking in Conrad's time.

"The earth is losing her primal fertility"

The search for guano went beyond a matter of monetary wealth, for it took place within a larger anxiety about a dying world. The changes in global patterns of guano exploitation were evidently merely a symptom of this greater problem, as public voices began to declare in the decade leading up to Conrad's composition of *Lord Jim*. Studies published in England as early as 1860 had identified the chemical makeup of various guanos from around the world, as well as their relative power as fertilizers (Skaggs 142–3). Because of the exceptional concentration of nitrogen and phosphates in bird guano (as opposed to bat or other animal droppings), and the unusual aridity of the Chincha Islands (which concentrated and preserved the material), guano from that particular location was clearly superior as an agricultural fertilizer to known deposits from anywhere else (Skaggs 140). It became common knowledge, then, that as Chincha Island stocks gave out, the planet's guano reserves became less potent as a whole.

In England, assessments of these environmental changes demonstrated an understanding of the world as an ecosystem in which human intervention was inexorably altering the agricultural basis of human existence. Charles Stanton Devas described in his influential book *Political Economy* (first edition, 1892) how *exhaustive farming* (italics in the original) was injuring the earth by "taking more from [the soil] than is restored to it, and thus lessening its fertility" (79). Furthermore, he continues, the effects of this "earth-butchery" would be even worse and more noticeable in England "had we not for years past been ransacking the world for fertilizers: guano, coprolites, bone-dust, and bones" (79). Not only were the soils of the world being exhausted, he explains, but also minerals were being depleted, with "mine after mine, and deposit after deposit" giving out (80); forests worldwide were being destroyed, while he decried the "[e]xtermination or diminution of useful plants and animals," such as sea mammals and birds, and the "spread, often a corresponding spread, of noxious ones" (80). Thus, he writes, "No wonder we have alarmists who tell us the earth is losing her primal fertility" (79), a reaction that Devas considers fully justified.

One such "alarmist" was Henry Kains-Jackson, author of the introduction to the agricultural textbook *Fields of Great Britain* (1881). In an 1890 letter to the editors of the *Times*, printed under the headline "The Earth Losing Primal Fertility"—a phrase that would reappear in Devas's *Political Economy*—he wrote publicly of a matter that he had been bringing before the Council of the Royal Agricultural Society: "namely, that yearly, with every harvest, the earth is declining from its primal fertility. The world is poorer to-day than it was yesterday, and it will be poorer to-morrow than it is to-day." With regard to food,

> our great mother earth is a waning planet. The force taken away day by day is greater than the force given day by day in the way of restoration. The world is living partly on its primal capital of fertility, and not upon the interest of such capital.

In this assessment, the riches of technological progress cannot make up for the inexorable loss of biological riches resulting from "the wasting process" associated with cultivation and human presence on the earth (Kains-Jackson 13). Kains-Jackson's claims caused some controversy, with replies—and his counterreplies—posted in more letters to the *Times*.

Had Conrad possibly noticed and remembered the exchange and Kains-Jackson's first letter? Kains-Jackson begins by quoting American author Charles Dudley Warner that England was "originally an 'infertile island'"; in Warner's words, "agricultural production could scarcely exist there until fortunes made in India and in foreign adventure enabled the owners of the land *to pile it knee-deep with fertilizers from Peru and elsewhere*" (italics added by Kains-Jackson). Here, remarkably, we have in the italicized passage the very same language Conrad uses to have Marlow imagine Jim, "up to his knees in guano" (128) on Chester's island. Kains-Jackson concludes that the balance of agricultural fertility can be maintained only "through fresh discoveries in the sub-strata of the earth's unknown mines of fertilizers that can be transmuted into agricultural gold." However, "The known and old mines are giving out. At present the world is spending rapidly its fertility capital." As Kains-Jackson explains, "Phosphoric acid, the life-blood of fertility, and of which guano is the great contributory stream, is no longer in flood, but relatively a trickling stream," and "Several sources of supply are already exhausted." While prospectors were "navigating the world on voyages of discovery" in search of new fertilizer sources, "the world is losing its fertility, and therefore the present sources of fertility are, like gold, becoming appreciated and should continue to rise in value." Kains-Jackson's repeated description of natural fertilizers as "agricultural gold," rising in value "like gold" and found in "mines," has its echoes in Chester's repeated comparison of his guano island to "a goldmine," and even "better" than one (124).

Concerns about the earth's waning overall fertility, expressed in terms of Nature's capital, were heard from even more prominent voices in England. Sir William Crookes, incoming president of the British Academy of Sciences, delivered an inaugural address in 1898 that expounded at length on the danger. Farming had depleted the world's soils of natural nitrogen, he explained, and the use of fertilizers for replenishment only postponed the inevitable: "When we apply to the land nitrate of soda, sulphate of ammonia, or guano, we are drawing on the earth's capital, and our drafts will not perpetually be honoured."[4] He electrified his audience by forecasting the exhaustion of South American nitrates within a few decades, leading to mass starvation. As Thomas Hager has noted,

> Word of mouth turned his presentation into a sensation. News of the impending doom [...] rippled out from Bristol through England, then to newspapers around the world. His words were read not only by scientists but economists, politicians, intellectuals, and businessmen.

Crookes's address proved controversial as well, but the "publicity" caused his speech to become one "of the most influential public addresses of the day," and Crookes published an extended version as "a popular book" (11): *The Wheat Problem*, which first appeared in 1899 and was in its second edition by 1905. Thus, beyond the specific words of Kains-Jackson's letter, the larger sentiment of alarm regarding the depletion of the world's fertility—brought to the widespread public knowledge through such figures as Crookes—forms an inescapable larger cultural surround within which the novel was written and read.

Such discussions of the impoverishment of the world's natural resources, clearly current in the popular imagination, deployed a language of scarcity that manifests also in Conrad's portrayal of the guano island. Significantly, Conrad repeatedly describes the island's features in terms of absence, lack or insufficiency, for guano is all the island has. Conrad first seemingly erases the real Walpole Island's vegetation in creating its fictional counterpart. Then, Chester's island is given "no anchorage" (125), no fresh water, no rain and not even any shadows. It is set in an "empty sky" and an "empty ocean" (128). Even the language describing people and ideas associated with the island emphasizes negation and scarcity. When Chester tries to recruit the Auckland man in the scheme, the latter protests that he "wouldn't do it if there was no other place on earth to send a ship to" (125). In Chester's retelling, "no insurance company would take the risk" (125); Robinson is "an emaciated patriarch" (125); Jim on the island would have "nothing to do" but watch over the laborers (128); for Chester, the problem of water supply is "not the question" (127); even Marlow, confronted with Chester's offer, relates, "I said nothing" (128). Later, Chester and his crew appear to have died without a trace; "not a vestige of the Argonauts ever turned up; not a sound came out of the waste" (135). The entire guano island episode, then, comes to us through a description in which the only wealth is the guano—riches that cannot redeem Jim's lost honor—and all else appears in terms of negation, of absence and impoverishment, especially in the scarcity of other features of the natural world on the island, in its lack of water and vegetation.

"In close touch with Nature"

Through the guano island episode, Conrad thus establishes one half of a discourse of scarcity and abundance, tied closely to Jim and the possibility of his moral redemption, that he completes through his description of Patusan. There, not only would Marlow "see him loved, trusted, and admired" (134) but also the landscape would appear in terms emphasizing its lush vegetation and natural fertility. In that fertile landscape, so unlike the "waste" of the guano island and its neighboring seas (135), Jim will have "captured much honour and Arcadian happiness" (134). This key formulation explicitly and tellingly joins honor and Arcady— where Jim will enjoy "felicity" that "is quaffed out of a golden cup" (134), returning to the idea of gold (as in the "gold-mine" of the guano island), but transforming the wealth into a moral one.

The contrasts between Marlow's visions of Jim on the guano island and at Patusan are striking. Whereas the guano island is "[a]s good as a gold-mine," but only for a natural resource that "Queensland sugar-planters would fight for—fight for on the quay" (126), in Patusan, the gold is the "golden cup" of happiness (134), intangible but of greater value. Additionally, on the guano island, the sun is an "incandescent ball [...] over [Jim's] head," which sets the world "a-quiver, simmering" in the heat (128); in Patusan, Jim is in "a strong light" but not a hostile one, and Jim himself shines "in all his brilliance," as if the felicitous luminescence of the natural world has made him give off light as well (134). Most importantly, it is in Patusan that Marlow has his "last view" of Jim, "dominating and yet in complete accord with his surroundings—with the life of forests and the life of men." There, he is not only simultaneously "in close touch with Nature" and "protected by his isolation" (134) but also his unity with the natural world marks—and perhaps even facilitates—his potential moral transformation.

Patusan's lush profusion of natural growth evokes the "primal fertility" whose decline and apparently imminent loss so preoccupied public figures such as Devas, Kains-Jackson and Crookes. At various points in his narrative, Marlow describes the primeval qualities of the "vast forests" and "swampy plains" of the coast, where "[r]ed trails are seen like cataracts of rust streaming under the dark green foliage of bushes and creepers clothing the low cliffs" (184), and "the immovable forests rooted deep in the soil, soaring towards the sunshine, everlasting in the shadowy might of their tradition, like life itself" (185). The way between Patusan and the sea "seem[s] to lead through the very heart of untouched wilderness," where the waterway courses "between the high walls of vegetation" (249); "the smell of mud, of marsh, the primeval smell of fecund earth, seem[s] to sting [their] faces" (250). Arriving at the coast with Jim, Marlow reports, "I breathed deeply. I revelled in the vastness of the open horizon, in the different atmosphere that seemed to vibrate with the toil of life, with the energy of an impeccable world," prompting him to cry, "This is glorious!" The coast, too, teems with life, as Marlow remembers when he notes the "cliff wooded on the brow, draped in creepers to the very foot" (250). In these landscapes, we see the "colossal forces" of nature (in Stein's words) at work (158), where even the dirt is "fecund," launching powerful vegetative forces that cover the land and stretch toward the sky.

As for Jim, unlike Chester (who sees only monetary wealth in the natural world), he instead views nature through images emphasizing the life force within it. When Jim and Marlow watch the moon rise from behind the "cleavage" between a pair of hills—breast-like symbols of fertility—that moon (itself associated with female fertility) rises above the "chasm [...] as if escaping from a yawning grave in gentle triumph." Jim remarks to Marlow, "Wonderful effect [...] Worth seeing. Is it not?" (168). Yet Jim does more than appreciate signs of life in the natural world: He enters into a reciprocal relationship with nature. First, just as Jim responds to the sight of the moon, nature responds to Jim's arrival and death. Marlow reports how "There was already a story that the tide had turned two hours before its time to help [Jim] on his journey up the river," according to village lore (184). The earth even seems to aid Jim's escape from the stockade after his arrival; as he runs away toward the houses in the village, "The earth seemed fairly to fly backwards under his feet" (192). On the day of Jim's death, "the sky over Patusan was blood-red, immense, streaming like an open vein," prefiguring Jim's death by gunshot: "An enormous sun nestled crimson amongst the treetops, and the forest below had a black and forbidding face." Tamb' Itam relates to Marlow "that on that evening the aspect of the heavens was angry and frightful"—which Marlow can corroborate, for as he tells us, "on that very day a cyclone passed within sixty miles of the coast" (310). The setting sun bookends Jim's relationship with the natural world as disclosed by the moonrise viewing, while the cyclone—passing at a safe distance—reminds us of the hurricane that presumably killed Chester and his crew and would have killed Jim too had he joined them. The object of the anger of the heavens is not clear, but nature's responses to Jim seem to point to his integration with it.

In a key feature of this integration, Marlow describes Jim as influencing nature and even enhancing its fertility, in direct contrast to the exploitation of natural resources planned by Chester and also undertaken by Rajah Allang and Sherif Ali—from whom Jim saves the villagers in his defining act of heroism. The Rajah's "idea of trading was indistinguishable from the commonest forms of robbery," Marlow explains, and he was known for "[h]is cruelty and rapacity." Ali, for his part,

> devastated the open country. Whole villages, deserted, rotted on their blackened posts over the banks of clear streams, dropping piecemeal into the water the grass of their walls, the leaves of their roofs, with a curious effect of natural decay as if they had been a form of vegetation stricken by a blight at its very root.
> (195)

Into this scene of primal fertility degraded by human rapaciousness, Jim unexpectedly enters, where he is "received [...] into the heart of the community" whose environmental fortunes, like his own, he will reverse (195).

By the time Marlow reaches Jim after his victory over Sherif Ali, Jim tells the story of the battle while sitting on a tree trunk; "A new growth of grass and bushes was springing up," Marlow observes, and Ali's earthwork fortifications are now but "traces [...] under a mass of thorny twigs" that had quickly covered them (199). When Jim finishes his story, Marlow sees him

> high in the sunshine on the top of that historic hill of his. He dominated the forest, the secular [i.e., continuing from long ages before] gloom, the old mankind. He was like a figure set up on a pedestal, to represent in his persistent youth the power, and perhaps the virtues, of races that never grow old [...] I don't know why he should always have appeared to me symbolic.
> (200)

Perhaps to the novel's first readers, the symbolic importance is clearer: in his "persistent youth," his benevolent domination of the land, and the regeneration of the natural world that takes place after he drives away the rapacious Ali, the figure of Jim may imply a better version of the relations between humans and nature.

"The spirit that dwells within the land"

Jim's enhancement of the landscape's fertility results from his apparently serving as a link between humans and nature. Part of his actions are merely pragmatic, as when he resolves a dispute that had led townspeople to take sides "[i]nstead of attending to their bally crops" (203). When Marlow and Jim watch the moonrise above the cleft hill, though, Jim remarks on the sight "with a note of personal pride [...] as though he had had a hand in regulating that unique spectacle," Marlow observes; "He had regulated so many things in Patusan! Things that would have appeared as much beyond his control as the motions of the moon and the stars" (168). Marlow explains how this relation with nature is not founded so much on control, however, but on a recognition of the unity of all natural things, including humans, within an ecosystem. In Marlow's words, "Each blade of grass has its spot on earth whence it draws its life, its strength; and so is man rooted to the land from which he draws his faith together with his life" (169)—returning to Stein's focus on grass blades as representative of nature's "harmony," "balance of colossal forces" and "perfect equilibrium," as well as the disruptive presence of humans in their usual activities, "disturbing the blades of grass" (158). In contrast, Jim "had achieved greatness" in Patusan (171), a greatness signaled by his regulating the natural world as well as the lives of the natives, restoring nature's fertility by returning farmers to their crops. That Marlow describes Jim more than once as "dominating" the land (134, 200) calls to mind the prelapsarian relation of Adam to the natural world over which he holds dominion—not in a position of exploitation but one of responsible stewardship.[5] In this respect, through the figure of Jim, the novel as a whole symbolically restores to the land its "primal fertility," whose loss had been so anxiously described in Conrad's day.

We learn of these activities all through what Marlow explains in terms of Jim's ties to "the spirit of the land" through his "imagination," how he "understood" or "felt confusedly but powerfully" the association that joins both man and individual blades of grass to the earth for life (169). Jim in Patusan has apparently "[met] the spirit that dwells within the land, under its sky, in its air, in its valleys and on its rises, in its fields, in its waters and its trees—a mute friend, judge and inspirer" (169). Marlow develops this vision of mystical union between human and nature still further, describing the "disembodied, eternal and unchanging spirit" of the land, this "spirit of the land" (a phrase that repeats nearly identically three times) that may be "careless of innumerable lives" but nevertheless provides life force to humans and nature alike (169–70).

Jim's integration with nature's "harmony" (158) parallels an apparent progression toward redeeming his honor. When his actions in Patusan earn him the trust of the natives there, he has at least partially atoned for his betrayal of the professional trust placed in him when he abandoned the pilgrims on the *Patna*. At the end of the novel, when Jim presents himself to Doramin after the death of Dain Waris, a voice is heard to say "He hath taken it upon his own head," and he rejoins "Yes. Upon my head" (312). As J. Hillis Miller has pointed out, for many critics, "The circumstances of Jim's death and his willingness to take responsibility for the death of Dain Waris [...] make up for all Jim has done before" (28).[6] In such a reading, we can add that Jim's redemptive act is illuminated by the appearance of the natural world, with the "blood-red" light of "[t]he sky over Patusan [...] streaming like an open vein" (244) potentially symbolizing blood sacrifice. The fruitfulness of the land, in which "man" is "rooted," as Marlow asserts (169), is also arguably a marker of his moral regeneration in anticipation of this death, as Jim comes into his own as he comes into "the land he was destined to fill with the fame of his virtues" (185). It is in this natural world, after all, that Marlow reports seeing "[a] new growth of grass and bushes [...] springing up" around Jim and "perhaps the virtues" that he "represent[s]" (199–200), as Marlow hears Jim describe how he helped defeat Sherif Ali on behalf of the natives.

In the key passage articulating these connections between nature, character and honor, worth turning to a final time, Marlow speaks in closely paralleled phrases of "the life of forests and the life of men" (134). He elaborates the parallels between natural and ethical worlds by beginning with his witness to Jim being "trusted" in Patusan, where he "captured much honour." Marlow asserts that Jim is "in complete accord with his surroundings" and is "in close touch with Nature" (134). This passage ends with Marlow reminding us of the significantly contrasting "Walpole islet—that most hopelessly forsaken crumb of dry land on the face of the waters," as he reports Chester's disappearance and evident death in pursuit of his guano-harvesting scheme (135).

Marlow's vision of life with, in and through nature at Patusan has thus been prepared for us through the preliminary vision of Jim on the guano island, and the guano island episode thereby serves a crucial structural role in the novel, despite its brevity. The guano island and Patusan constitute a set of paired landscapes that enhance the novel's focus on Jim's transformation. In a larger sense, though, *Lord Jim* portrays a world at the intersection of globalization and environmental concerns by making the setting—the natural landscape—the site for rendering visible both ecosystem changes and shifts in resource networks. Furthermore, by combining landscape and character development, Conrad implicitly argues for the moral dimension of environmental awareness.

Both British and Peruvian officials and entrepreneurs were becoming aware that human intervention was permanently altering the planet. On Central Pacific guano islands, for example, miners had inadvertently introduced the Norway rat; cats, brought in to control the rat population, then eliminated native birds. On Howland Island, guano miners cut down native kou trees (Cushman 99). John T. Arundel, who oversaw production on such islands in the 1870s, soon realized that guano harvesting was threatening future guano production (Cushman 100). He even hoped to mitigate these changes by planting coconut trees, which he believed would create more rainfall.[7] Meanwhile in Peru, in 1896, the government banned sea lion hunting in order to help ailing guano businesses, in the belief that the mammals helped sea birds to feed (Cushman 176, 176n18). Yet these efforts responded to what was characterized as a looming economic problem. In *Lord Jim*, Conrad has Marlow divert Jim from crude commercial exploitation toward a benevolent stewardship of nature, while Jim's undertaking in Patusan has shared moral dimensions in his integration both with other humans and with the natural world. By joining a valorization of nature to an awareness of modern resource networks on a global scale and set in ethical terms, Conrad presciently suggests a way of thinking about nature that will more fully emerge later in the twentieth century.

Both the guano island and the Patusan settings thus present and interpret landscapes as more than backdrops to human activity—instead, as a complex model of ecosystems, species interdependence and nascent principles of conservancy. In this way, Conrad not only records but also responds to an emerging awareness of an ecological imperative in his time, which only a return to the considerable historical and cultural context of guano opens to readers of the novel today. The conclusions that can be drawn from the presence of the guano island in *Lord Jim* demonstrate the unexpected importance of what may seem at first to be a mere aside—an opportunity simply to contrast Jim with an unsavory character and an undesirable job prospect. Indeed, the importance of this episode in the larger portrayal of Jim's relation to nature points to how much more analysis Conrad's ecologically rich writing invites.

Notes

1. See Lippe, Sherry and van Marle and Lefranc, all of which provide much useful information on the basis of Patusan and other locations but do not address the guano island.
2. In the face of international competition—in 1878, both Britain and France had simultaneously laid claim to the nearby Chesterfield Islands for their guano, and the Melbourne-based Austral Guano Company pressed its claim to Walpole Island in 1906 (Chevalier 411–13).
3. Persistent confusion surrounded the origins of different kinds of natural fertilizer. In the nineteenth century, it was commonly thought that guano, nitrates and phosphates all came from bird waste. However, while Peruvian Island guano is bird excrement, Atacama Desert nitrates are apparently the result of atmospheric ion deposition (Cushman 60), and the phosphates on the raised atolls such as Banaba and Nauru are likely the waste products of ocean microorganisms (Cushman 120).
4. Hager 9, Lawes and Gilbert 3. These remarks later appear verbatim in Crookes, *The Wheat Problem* (39).

5 For other elements of the Eden story, see Erdinast-Vulcan 44.
6 Still, as Miller goes on to explain, "Matters are not so simple in this novel" (29) and "The ending is a tissue of unanswered questions" (30). Critics are divided on the extent and value of Jim's heroism, and the significant distance between Jim and the reader created by the features of Marlow's interposed narration leaves the meaning of Jim's final acts markedly open to interpretation (see Miller 26–31).
7 See Arundel, and Fulton and Greenhalgh, both cited in Cushman 100n56.

Works Cited

Arundel, John T. Letter to Secretary of the Pacific Islands Co. 2 December 1897.

Chevalier, Luc. "Walpole, la citadelle du vertige." *Le Mémorial Calédonien*. Vol. IV. Ed. Philippe Godard. Nouméa: Editions d'Art Caledoniénnes, 1979, c1980. 409–37.

Conrad, Joseph. *Lord Jim: A Tale*. Eds. J. H. Stape and Ernest W. Sullivan II. Cambridge UP, 2012.

Crookes, William. *The Wheat Problem: Based on Remarks Made in the Presidential Address to the British Association at Bristol in 1898; Revised with an Answer to Various Critics*. John Murray, 1899.

Cushman, Gregory T. *Guano and the Opening of the Pacific World: A Global Ecological History*. Cambridge UP, 2013.

Devas, Charles S. *Political Economy*. Longmans, Green & Co., 1892.

Erdinast-Vulcan, Daphna. *Joseph Conrad and the Modern Temper*. Oxford UP, 1991.

Findlay, Alexander George. *A Directory for the Navigation of the South Pacific Ocean; with Descriptions of Its Coasts, Islands, etc., from the Strait of Magalhaens to Panama, and Those of New Zealand, Australia, etc.; Its Winds, Currents, and Passages*. 5th ed. London: Richard Holmes Laurie, 1884.

Fulton, and Greenhalgh. "Report on Christmas Island." 6 November 1902. PMB 1139, Joseph Meek Papers Relating to Lever Pacific Plantations Ltd., 1894–1928 (microfilm) reel 2. Pacific Manuscripts Bureau, Australian National University, Canberra, Australia.

Gill, David. "Joseph Conrad, William Paramor, and the Guano Island: Links to *A Personal Record* and *Lord Jim*." *The Conradian*, vol. 23, no. 2, Fall 1998, pp. 17–26.

Green, Horace. "On Pettitt's Fisheries Guano." *Journal of the Society of Arts, and of the Institutions in Union*. Vol II: From November 11, 1853 to November 10, 1854. George Bell, 1854. 87–93.

Guerard, Albert J. *Conrad the Novelist*. Harvard UP, 1958.

Hager, Thomas. *The Alchemy of Air: A Jewish Genius, a Doomed Tycoon, and the Scientific Discovery that Fed the World but Fueled the Rise of Hitler*. Harmony Books, 2008.

Kains-Jackson, Henry. Letter. *Times* 3 February 1890: 13.

"Our law reports to-day give the result of the appeal [...]." *Times* (London) 27 May 1882: 11.

Lawes, John Bennet, and J. Henry Gilbert. "The World's Wheat Supply." *Times* (London) 2 December 1898: 3.

Lippe, Hans. "'Lord Jim': Some Geographic Observations." *The Conradian*, vol. 10, no. 2, November 1985, pp. 135–8.

Marle, Hans van, and Pierre Lefranc. "Ashore and Afloat: New Perspectives on Topography and Geography in *Lord Jim*." *Conradiana*, vol. 20, no. 2, Summer 1988, pp. 109–35.

Miller, J. Hillis. *Fiction and Repetition: Seven English Novels*. Harvard UP, 1982.

Murfin, Ross C. *Lord Jim: After the Truth*. Twayne, 1992.

"Peruvian Wealth." *Times* (London) 3 April 1880: 4.

Sherry, Norman. *Conrad's Eastern World*. Cambridge UP, 1966.

"Sir Walter Medhurst described to the members [...]." *Times* (London) 25 May 1885: 9.

Skaggs, Jimmy M. *The Great Guano Rush: Entrepreneurs and American Overseas Expansion*. St. Martin's, 1994.

"The War in South America." *Times* (London) 30 May 1879: 10.

Watt, Ian. *Conrad in the Nineteenth Century*. U of California P, 1979.

Williamson, S. Letter. *Times* (London) 29 March 1884: 4.

Part V
Earlier Commentary

14 From *The Challenge of Bewilderment*[1]

Paul Armstrong

... The revolutionary situation in Costaguana casts into bold relief three of the basic dimensions of the social world – power, community, and change. These are the key components of politics, society, and history. The grabs for power by Montero and Sotillo as well as the many conflicts among the major interests in Sulaco raise first questions about politics: What gives rise to conflicts over power? Can its disruptive force be defeated and harnessed for constructive ends? The disturbance to the social order, the clash between the ambitions of the various parties and the hope that a separate state might guarantee peace and justice – all of these bring to the foreground the question of whether and how a unified community might be molded out of a multiplicity of factions. Because Sulaco is a cauldron of actual and potential changes, history emerges as a living process. Questions about the workings of historical time acquire a special urgency: What are the causes and consequences of change? Is it determined, accidental, or subject to human will? In all of these ways, Costaguana is a special, extreme case with unusual revelatory value precisely because of its extremity.

The first step in the establishment of a society – and in the creation of Conrad's model – is the separation of culture from nature. The rendering of the immense darkness of the Placid Gulf in the opening chapter of the novel introduces nature as the mute, indifferent background to the doings of man: "Sky, land, and sea disappear together out of the world when the Placido – as the saying is – goes to sleep under its black poncho."[2] The primordial state of nature is, *Nostromo* suggests, a condition of absolute non-differentiation.[3] By deploying a network of distinctions, society may seek to transform and control nature – but can never fully master it. At most, culture can invent myths, metaphors, or personifications (the gulf asleep under its poncho) that divide and structure linguistically what cannot be more effectively controlled. As the expansion of the mine transforms the plantation society and brings the railroad and the telegraph, the story of Costaguana's development is the increasing establishment of differences to measure time and space, govern and chronicle resources, and distribute cultural features over the natural landscape.

Differences do exist in nature, of course, but Conrad's novel suggests that they only take on positive significance when human purposes give them meaning – finding in them an inspiration for social projects, as when Decoud cries: "Look at the mountains! Nature itself seems to cry to us 'Separate!'" (184), or an obstacle to our plans, as in the complaint of the railway's chief engineer: "We can't move mountains!" (41). Nature's pregiven differentiating structures can be constituted in a variety of ways, and this multiplicity suggests that the meaning of the natural world is a matter of interpretation. We have here one of the novel's first ontological contradictions. The paradox of nature in *Nostromo* is that it transcends humanity and defies assimilation but that it is also a social construct and a hermeneutic variable. Nature is simultaneously beyond the contingency of cultural variation and beholden to it for its meaning.[4]

After portraying the appropriation of nature by culture, *Nostromo* shows culture becoming a new kind of nature. Consider, for example, the surprise and sorrow Mrs. Gould feels because "so much that seemed shocking, weird, and grotesque" in Costaguana is "accepted with no indignant comment by people of intelligence, refinement, and character as something inherent in the nature of things" (165, 109). Brutality and oppression which seem absurd to Mrs. Gould are part of "nature" to the local residents – not political, social contingencies – inasmuch as they seem to defy the ability of the community to change them. Tyranny, torture, and corruption seem as much an inalienable feature of the landscape of Costaguana as the Placid Gulf or Mount Higuerota. This mystification upsets Mrs. Gould perhaps even more than the barbarity she sees all around her, because the illusion that injustice is natural reinforces the impotence of the oppressed. Only a transformation of customary consciousness or the perspective of a foreigner can unmask naturalization to disclose the arbitrariness of what it considers inevitable. Even the Gould Concession, a relatively recent development, is soon similarly cloaked in mystification: "It was traditional. It was known. It was said. It was credible. ... It was natural" (402–03). This series of adjectives provides a neat summary of the factors that naturalize cultural institutions: prolonged duration, shared understanding, common belief, assimilation into daily discourse ("traditional" + "known" + "credible" + "said" = "natural"). Whether the phenomenon it masks is beneficial or baneful, however, naturalization is an illusion – most of all because it itself is a cultural process.

The central symbol in the novel exemplifies Conrad's contradictory understanding of the relation between culture and nature. Much of the mystery and fascination surrounding the silver of the San Tomé mine is due to the ambiguous position it occupies between the two realms. It is a natural resource, obviously, and its seeming inexhaustibility suggests not only potentially infinite power and wealth for the owner of the mine but also the boundless extension of nature beyond the limits of the human world. Its extraction is a highly organized cultural activity, however, and its value is social. Although the silver is called "incorruptible" because it seems to have an inherent purity and power that transcend

Costaguana's political machinations, its worth ultimately derives from a convention – the agreement to consider certain metals precious because of their scarcity and to use them as a medium of exchange. Silver seems to carry its value deep within it, inalienable and everlasting, but what its possessor owns is the desire of others to have what he has. Conrad's novel portrays the value of the silver as paradoxically both naturally immanent and culturally contingent.

Although a product of nature, silver also has the status of a sign. Single itself, silver's capacity for representation is infinitely variable. The silver in *Nostromo* thus participates in Conrad's reflections not only about contingency but also about monism and pluralism. When Mrs. Gould "laid her unmercenary hands, with an eagerness that made them tremble, upon the first silver ingot turned out still warm from the mould," she feels "as though it were not a mere fact, but something far-reaching and impalpable, like the true expression of an emotion or the emergence of a principle" (107). Mrs. Gould's attitude owes much, of course, to her husband, for whom the silver means many things: a triumph where his father had failed, a proof of his competence, a defiance of the corruption and disorder in the surrounding land, a fulfillment of his pact with his backer Holroyd. To the reformers the silver stands for the possibility of progress, prosperity, peace, stability, and justice. To government officials it means a steady, guaranteed income of bribes. To the self-seeking leaders of insurrections it makes the mine a prime object of their quest for power. To the various foreign interests the silver is a guarantee that their investments will be safe. To Holroyd it stands for an opportunity to control a man and to extend the reach of his Protestant sect. Subject to an ever-expanding variety of interpretations, the silver is the origin of an open-ended series of meanings – but a particularly mysterious, fascinating origin because it seems to begin deep within the earth, in the bowels of nature....

Notes

1 From Paul B. Armstrong, *The Challenge of Bewilderment: Understanding and Representation in James, Conrad, and Ford* (Ithaca, NY: Cornell University Press, 1987), pp. 156–59. Reprinted with permission of the publisher.
2 Joseph Conrad, *Nostromo: A Tale of the Seaboard* (Garden City, NY: Doubleday, 1926), p. 6. Subsequent references will be given parenthetically in the text.
3 Royal Roussel makes a similar point in *The Metaphysics of Darkness: A Study in the Unity and Development of Conrad's Fiction* (Baltimore, MD: Johns Hopkins University Press, 1971), p. 4.
4 In an atypical moment of oversimplification, Fredric Jameson misses this paradox when he calls *Nostromo* "a virtual textbook working-out of the structuralist dictum that all narrative enacts a passage from Nature to Culture" (*The Political Unconscious* [Ithaca, NY: Cornell University Press, 1981], p. 272). In Conrad's novel, nature refuses to give way to culture even as, paradoxically, culture is the source of nature's meaning.

15 "Too Beautiful Altogether"
Ideologies of Gender and Empire in *Heart of Darkness*[1]

Johanna M. Smith

Like Kurtz's eloquence in support of imperialism, Marlow's narrative is a mystification of power relations that shows that "[men] want to keep woman in the place of mystery, consign her to mystery, as they say, 'keep her in her place, keep her at a distance'" (Cixous 49). As Marlow uses the savage woman to symbolize the enigma of the jungle, his ideological project is to distance and control both mysteries.

The savage woman who appears as Kurtz is being carried onto Marlow's ship is "the nexus where the discourses of imperialism and patriarchy coincide" (Mongia 146–47). As Marlow constructs her, she is the dark continent of both the African jungle and female sexuality. "A wild and gorgeous apparition of a woman" (Conrad *HD* 77), she is "savage and superb, wild-eyed and magnificent," "ominous and stately." When she appears

> The immense wilderness, the colossal body of the fecund and mysterious life seemed to look at her, pensive, as though it had been looking at the image of its own tenebrous and passionate soul.
>
> (77)

In this symbology Marlow distances the woman's body by conflating her with the jungle: as the jungle takes on a body, the woman becomes the "image" and the jungle's "soul."[2] By symbolizing the woman and personifying the jungle, Marlow works to contain and control both; thus stylized and immobilized, a complex of potentially dangerous forces becomes "pensive" and nonthreatening.

Once the woman moves toward the ship, however, those forces again become threatening, and Marlow again works to contain them. As she approaches the ship, "looking at us ... like the wilderness itself" (77) and "brooding over an inscrutable purpose," she represents for Marlow a menacing jungle sexuality. He has already described the jungle's absorption of Kurtz as sexual cannibalism: "it had taken him, loved him, embraced him, got into his veins, consumed his flesh" (64). As that earlier moment had "feminize[d] the relation between the adventurer and topography" (Mongia 139), so too does the savage woman's "brooding" approach to the ship. She throws up her arms "as though in an uncontrollable desire to touch the sky" (78), and at this moment shadows of the jungle "gather the steamer into a shadowy embrace." In this gesture of appropriation by the woman/jungle, "the boundaries of masculinity—knowledge, restraint, and order—are under siege" (Mongia 141). Even if the content of her gesture is not sexuality but the "wild sorrow" and "dumb pain" Marlow sees in her face, this too threaten the boundaries of masculine restraint, for Marlow has already (over)responded to a similar loss of Kurtz. In his earlier fear that Kurtz was dead, the "startling extravagance" of his sorrow was "even such as I had noticed in the howling sorrow of these savages" (63). And his backpedaling from grief in that scene indicated his masculine view that "unrestrained grief should be left to the natives and the women" (Staten 723). Faced in the savage woman with not only the threat of sexuality but the allure of grief, Marlow contains both with his stylized representation of a woman reaching for the sky, the unattainable.

As Marlow turns the savage woman's body into a symbol of the jungle, this process serves both masculinist and imperialist ends. It is an effort to defuse and control the power and sexuality both of the woman who "tread[s] the earth proudly" (77) and of that "fecund" earth itself. As an ideology of gender works to distance and conquer the savage woman's body, so an ideology of empire works to distance and conquer the mysterious life of the jungle. And Marlow successfully silences the savage woman; like the native laundress, she does not speak in his narrative. Like the laundress's silence, however, this one creates a gap in the text, a sign of ideological stress that makes visible the fragility of such containment. Such a gap thus reveals "the truth which ideology represses, its own existence as ideology itself" (Belsey 63).

Further instances of ideology *as* ideology appear when we re-vision Marlow's representation of the savage woman's adornments. After detailing the "barbarous ornaments" she wears (77), he concludes that "[s]he must have had the value of several elephant tusks on her." The woman's body is here commodified to become merely the thing on which "value" is displayed. Although Marlow notes that her hair is shaped like a helmet and that she wears leggings and gauntlets, he dismisses these martial signs as "charms" that have meaning only as proto-ivory. And although he relays the Russian's report that the woman "'talk[s] like a fury'" (78), he does not record her speech. If we reverse Marlow's emphasis and concentrate on the woman's military ornaments and vehement talk, they suggest that she might not be the conventionally feminine (sexually and emotionally dependent on Kurtz) or conventionally native (economically dependent on the ivory trade) figure constructed by Marlow's ideological narrative. She might be a woman warrior whose gestures and speech, remaining unreadable, give her the power that her "*formidable* silence" indicates (emphasis added). If such an interpretation demystifies Marlow's, however, it also runs the risk of forgetting that the savage woman is finally "an inaccessible blankness circumscribed by an interpretable text" (Spivak 264). In other words, to presume to speak for an Other is to follow Marlow's strategy, to produce a representation as ideologically grounded as his.

I have already noted the utility of men's efforts to keep women's mystery, to "'keep her in her place, keep her at a distance'" (Cixous 49). Marlow's third such effort to mask his collusion in imperialism appears in his distancing representation of the two women he encounters at the Company's Brussels office. The mystery of these two women is overdetermined by Marlow's relentless symbolizing. His insistence on their knitting links them with the three Fates of Greek and Roman mythology, who weave the thread of life and thus control human destiny. Furthermore, when Marlow describes the elder knitter "pilot[ing]" (25) young men into the Company, the verb connects her with Charon, the pilot who ferries the dead across the Styx into Hades. These representations are part of the narrative retrospection intended to protect Marlow from the realization his narrative revives, that in this office he had contracted himself to the Company and to its imperialist "conspiracy." Hence, he displaces the responsibility for his decision onto the younger woman "introducing, introducing continuously [young men] to the unknown" and onto the elder woman, "uncanny and fateful" in her "unconcerned wisdom." Marlow crossed the boundary between the self and the other, between individual adventure and Company conspiracy, once he stepped through the office door; hence, he attempts to distance the troubling aspects of his decision behind the apparently solid boundary of gender difference.

Yet this maneuver is only momentarily successful, for the elder woman returns into Marlow's narrative. As he begins his journey into the jungle to retrieve Kurtz, this woman "obtruded herself upon my memory" (81), breached the boundary established by his displacement. Her reappearance serves as a double signal that Marlow's effort to distance the Other—the women of the Company and the troubling imperialism he transferred to them—was bound to fail. When the elder Company woman intrudes in the shape of "the knitting old woman with the cat," the uneasiness Marlow displaced now returns with greater strength for its repression. This silent figure of civilized domesticity only *seems* incongruous in the jungle; her reappearance dramatizes the futility of Marlow's attempt to separate the realm of domesticity from that of colonial adventure, the feminine sphere from the masculine.

Like the ideology of imperialism, the ideology of the separate, gendered spheres was under pressure in the late nineteenth century. Single and financially independent, the New Woman was becoming visible in the stores, offices, and streets of Europe and even in the dark continent; Mary Kingsley was one of several women travelers in Africa. Yet *Heart of Darkness* clings to the older ideology of separate spheres, in an effort to resolve the contradictions of Marlow's position vis-à-vis Kurtz. Marlow's experience of Kurtz places him in a "feminine predicament," a situation of perceived physical and/or social powerlessness (Klein 102–06). On the one hand, Marlow is seduced by the "unbounded power of eloquence" in Kurtz's imperialist ideology; on the other hand, he is also drawn to Kurtz's final summation, "'The horror! The horror!'" (86), because it too is "the expression of some sort of belief" (87). Marlow attempts to escape this feminine predicament by his representations of his aunt and the Intended. Through them he constructs a feminine world of "idea"-belief to stand alongside the masculine world of Kurtz's "horror"-belief; located in separate spheres, these contradictory ideologies can coexist. And so that Marlow can stabilize his masculinity by confronting feminine ideologies of empire, the two European women are not silenced. By mocking the lack of imperial experience that their words convey, he can represent his own experience as a manly encounter with truth; through their echoes of the case Kurtz made for imperialism, he can reverse the powerlessness evinced in his response to Kurtz's eloquence. Marlow's construction of these women dramatizes the point of his story, its manful effort to shore up an ideology of imperialism with an ideology of separate spheres.

The belief that will later be grounded in the aunt and the Intended first emerges in Marlow's preface to his narrative.

> The conquest of the earth, which mostly means the taking it away from those who have a different complexion or slightly flatter noses than ourselves, is not a pretty thing when you look into it too much. What redeems it is the idea only ... not a sentimental pretence but an idea, and an unselfish belief in the idea—something you can set up, and bow down before, and offer a sacrifice to....
>
> (21)

Although this credo precedes the story Marlow tells his hearers, it is important to remember that he has already "looked into" such a "conquest of the earth." Recuperating that experience requires an ideology whereby an ugly exercise of power ("Exterminate all the brutes!") is redeemed by an idea. Like his irony, Marlow's belief in the "idea" behind imperialism is a retrospective attempt to mask his complicity in the Company's imperialism. But Marlow's statement displays all the contradictions he intends to suppress: between the reality and the idea of conquest, between an idea and a "sentimental pretence" (how would one tell the difference?), between an "unselfish belief" and a self-serving hypocrisy. After these framing sentences, Marlow "broke off" before beginning his tale; this gap reveals the contradiction between his need for an imperialist "idea" and his experience of the horror, a contradiction he attempts to resolve by constructing the feminine sphere of his aunt and the Intended.

>Oh, she is out of it—completely. They—the women I mean—are out of it—should be out it. We must help them to stay in that beautiful world of their own, lest ours gets worse. Oh, she had to be out of it.

That an ideology of separate spheres enables masculine imperialism could hardly be more clearly stated. Where Marlow had earlier dismissed this woman's world as "too beautiful altogether," its ideality is now essential: carefully kept "out of it," separated from "our" world of experience, the feminine sphere of "idea" will prevent the masculine sphere of "fact" from deteriorating. Marlow's speech thus suggests how "the masculine production of feminine identity works in the interests of the dominant ideology" (London 238). Specifically, it suggests his need to construct a "beautiful world" around the Intended. There he can order the cacophony of "voices, voices"—Kurt's "eloquence," his "sincerity," and the Intended's "echo of his magnificent eloquence" (88)—by setting her speech off against the others. And there he can contain Kurtzian imperialism, by embodying in the Intended an "unselfish belief" in the now purified "idea."

Like all the women in this story, then, the Intended is Marlow's construct. As he had earlier commodified the savage woman's body, he now reduces the Intended to a "pure brow" (91) "illumined by the unextinguishable light of belief and love" (92). He locates in her a "beautiful generosity" (93) and "a mature capacity for fidelity, for belief, for suffering" (91)—in short, the "unselfish belief" he requires. Most important, her faith in the power of Kurtzian eloquence enables Marlow to contain and transform that eloquence. "Bowing [his] head before the faith that was in her, before that great and saving illusion" (93), Marlow removes the threat of eloquence from the sphere of his own experience and translates it into her "out-of-it" world. A faith in Kurtz's eloquence would have been a delusion in the man's sphere where it was contradicted by Kurtz's belief in the horror. In the Intended's feminine sphere, however, it becomes the "great and saving illusion" with which Marlow orders the "jabber" that would otherwise destroy his belief in the "idea." As Marlow bows before her faith, then, he fulfills his ideological project of creating the redeeming idea—"something you can set up, and bow down before, and offer a sacrifice to" (21). While he appears to be bowing to *her*, he is in fact idolizing his own "idea"—the "something" he has "set up" in her.

To complete his posture of belief, however, Marlow must "offer a sacrifice," and who better than the Intended with her "capacity for suffering"? Hence his lie, telling her that Kurtz's last words were her name. It is true that Marlow feels he has sacrificed *himself*: even though he "hate[s], detest[s], and can't bear a lie" (42), he tells this one out of his "infinite pity" for her suffering (94). But if Marlow conceives himself as a "heroic deliverer" (Strauss 129) rescuing the Intended from grief, with his "chivalric" lie he is in fact "underscoring an ideology that defines a protective lie as a moral act" when performed by a man. And surely the particular lie Marlow chooses is meant to satisfy his "dull anger" (94) with the Intended's naïveté and her insistence that he give her something "to live with." He and his audience—and the reader—know that by substituting the Intended's name for "the horror" he equates the two; her ignorance of this equation becomes a punishing humiliation. Further intimations of assault are the setting—a "place of cruel and absurd mysteries" (92)—and her responding to the lie with "an exulting and terrible cry" (94) of "unspeakable pain" and "inconceivable triumph." With these four obfuscatory adjectives, Marlow suggests that he has sacrificed the Intended to her own "saving illusion," a suggestion that justifies his act: the pain he intended to inflict is validated (like the rape victim, she asked for it) by accompanying triumph (and she liked it).[3]

Marlow's lie also functions to stabilize both the feminine sphere of "saving illusion" and the masculine sphere of "confounded fact." The lie protects the "beautiful world" of women that now enshrines his "deliberate belief"; because Marlow *knows* it is a lie, however, the world in which men experience the truth of horror continues to stand. Thus "Marlow brings truth to men by ... bringing falsehood to women" (Straus 130). When he states that telling the Intended the truth would have been "too dark altogether" (94), the echo of "too beautiful altogether" reverberates with this defensive rationale for cordoning off the woman's world. By creating an alternative women's sphere "lest ours gets worse," men can continue to confront their "own true stuff" in their world. And the violence with which Marlow's lie sacrifices the Intended to this masculine world indicates the strength of its homosocial bonds. As he successfully competes with the Intended for "the status of Kurtz's most enduring conquest" (London 245), the pain he inflicts on her dramatizes how women are used "to deny, distort, and censor men's passionate love for one another" (Straus 134). And not only women: Marlow's description of his helmsman's death becomes "a supreme moment of male bonding" with his hearers (London 248), and his similar reductions of native men to conduits of narrative "delineate the common ground Marlow and his audience occupy" as white men (London 249). Thus, although Marlow consistently browbeats and insults his audience—and, by extension, Conrad's—finally the white bourgeois male reader is included in Marlow's "voice of cultural authority." With all these techniques of "artistic force" (Fogel 20)—the lie to the Intended, Marlow's offhand uses of the word "nigger," Conrad's "insistent, domineering" style (Fogel 21)—*Heart of Darkness* demonstrates the brutality of in discourses of empire and gender.

In my feminist reading of *Heart of Darkness*, I have tried to show the utility for imperialist ideology of a gender ideology that constructs a feminine sphere as "too beautiful altogether."

Notes

1. From Johanna K. Smith, "'Too Beautiful Altogether': Ideologies of Gender and Empire in *Heart of Darkness*." In *Heart of Darkness: A Case Study in Contemporary Criticism*. Ed. Ross C. Murfin. Bedford/St. Martin's, 2nd edition, 1996, pp. 173–7, 180–4. Reprinted by permission of the publisher.
2. In criticism as well as literature, such symbolizing is "particularly sinister" for women (Robinson 7); Jungian "pronouncements about The Masculine and The Feminine," for example, tend to perpetuate "specious generalizations" about both men's and women's psyches. Although Sullivan's reading of the story is Jungian, she points to the ideological uses of such generalizations when she notes that the savage woman, like the Intended, is "recognized, suppressed, and rejected" in the service of masculinist and imperialist aims (79).
3. Staten (736–9) argues that Marlow functions as Kurtz's emissary, thereby fulfilling the latter's sadistic project of forcing the Intended into the total mourning that will confirm his existence. While Staten gives full value to the Intended's cry, his reading nonetheless shares in Marlow's commodification of her: Staten's tendency to reduce her to a cry is not unlike Marlow's tendency to reduce her to a function of himself.

Works Cited

Belsey, Catherine. *Critical Practice*. Methuen, 1980.

Conrad, Joseph. "Heart of Darkness". *Heart of Darkness: A Case Study in Contemporary Criticism*. Ed. Ross C. Murfin. Bedford/St. Martin's, 2nd edition, 1996. 17–95.

Cixous, Hélène. "Castration of Decapatation?" Trans. Annete Kuhn. *Signs* 7 (1981): 41–55.

Fogel, Aaron. *Coercion to Speak: Conrad's Poetics of Dialogue*. Harvard UP, 1985.

Klein, Karen. "The Feminine Predicament in Conrad's *Nostromo*." *Brandeis Essays in Literature*. Ed. John Hazel Smith. Brandeis U English and American Literature Department, 1983. 101–16.

London, Bette. "Reading Race and Gender in Conrad's Dark Continent." *Criticism* 31.3 (Summer 1989): 235–52.

Mongia, Padmini. "Empire, Narrative, and the Feminine in *Lord Jim* and *Heart of Darkness*." *Contexts for Conrad*. Eds. Keith Carabine et al. East European Monographs, 1993. 135–50.

Robinson, Lillian S. *Sex, Class, and Culture*. Methuen, 1978.

Spivak, Gayatri Chakravorty. "Three Women's Texts and a Critique of Imperialism." *"Race," Writing, and Difference*. Ed. Henry Louis Gates, Jr. U of Chicago P, 1985. 262–80.

Staten, Henry. "Conrad's Mortal Word." *Critical Inquiry* 12.4 (1986): 720–40.

Straus, Nina Pelikan. "The Exclusion of the Intended from Secret Sharing in Conrad's *Heart of Darkness*." *Novel: A Forum on Fiction* 20 (1987): 123–37.

Sullivan, Zohreh T. "Enclosure, Darkness, and the Body: Conrad's Landscape." *Centennial Review* 25 (1981): 59–79.

16 From "Beyond Mastery

The Future of Conrad's Beginnings"[1]

Geoffrey Galt Harpham

... Marlow is a man with little investment in his own identity, a man capable of surrendering himself without surrendering much, but he is Conrad's most psychologically crucial figure, for he serves *Heart of Darkness and Lord Jim* as a lightning rod for the kind of ambiguous, passionate, and nonreciprocal relationships that define Conrad's distinctive sensibility. The general idea Marlow "represents" is that boundaries between people are porous and transgressable – that identity is fluid and less crystallized or "mastered" than we generally think. The idea, in other words, is that identity itself – the character we present to the world and to ourselves – is a deeply unstable configuration: it could be otherwise, and in a sense *is* otherwise: we are not as distinct from each other, as integrated in ourselves, as we might like to think, or as it seems we are. It's entirely possible to locate the center of our being outside rather than inside. So, when we read Conrad and feel that he has expressed us somehow, that it describes as well as appeals to us, we replicate the experience of Marlow. In short, we find it easy to identify with Conrad's work because identification is what his work, or some of his work, is all about.

Adoption

The concept of identification dominated his work for only a brief period, from 1897 to 1900. After this, he wrote a number of worthy books and two extraordinary ones, *Nostromo* and *The Secret Agent*, but he never again returned to this idea, or theme, in quite the same spirit. Still, during this time, he wrote three of his very greatest works, *The Nigger of the "Narcissus," Heart of Darkness,* and *Lord Jim*. Moreover, this period also marks the moment when Conrad's language is at its most magical, its most strangely suggestive, its most distinctively "Conradian," and the intriguing question I'd like now to consider concerns the relationship between these two aspects of Conrad's art.

Almost from the very first, Conrad was accounted a "master of the English language," and this phrase has continued to affect our thinking about his remarkable linguistic achievement.[2] Like many compliments, this one seems empty, suggesting that all we need to do to understand Conrad is to admire him. But the idea of linguistic mastery, rightly understood, actually leads us into a new understanding of Conrad's particular genius. Mastery, we should note, is not precisely synonymous with ease or fluency. It refers not to untroubled dominion or uncontested control but rather to a situation where a potentially rebellious force has been contained or managed. Mastery is achieved against resistance and maintained by effort, with the mastered force constantly threatening to reverse positions with the mastering power. Such a situation is described perfectly by Conrad's friend and collaborator Ford Madox Ford, who marveled at the way Conrad "took English, as it were by the throat and, wrestling till the dawn, made it obedient to him as it had been obedient to few other men" (*Remembrance* 109). The great Polish Conrad scholar Zdzisław Najder points out that for every non-native speaker, there is a moment when the new language is "resistant like every object that is strange and newly discovered, and at the same time softly pliable because not hardened in schematic patterns of words and ideas inculcated since childhood" (*Chronicle* 116). This account accurately characterizes Conrad's relationship to English, but equally important, it confines that relationship to a moment – the very moment, I would suggest, when Conrad achieved a mastery of the language, the moment when identification was his primary theme.

Coming to English as an adult, Conrad passed through a period of awkward apprenticeship, and his accent – idiosyncratic even for a Pole – remained a lifelong marker of foreignness. Yet, he later wrote, he sensed that he was somehow destined to be an English writer, if not an English speaker, and even felt himself "adopted by the genius of the language, which directly I came out of the stammering stage made me its own so completely that its very idioms I truly believe had a direct action on my temperament and fashioned my still plastic character" (*PR* v). Most native speakers do not think of themselves as "adopted" by the language they speak, nor do they think of language in this external, quasi-human sense, as a superior being. But Conrad always regarded English as an alien medium; and besides, the concept of adoption was especially resonant for him because he had been effectively adopted on two other critical occasions. The first was by his uncle, who took responsibility for the young orphan after his parents' death, and the second was by a retired sea captain, who examined Conrad for his captain's license. This gentleman, Conrad wrote years later, was a sort of "grandfather in the craft" who made him feel "adopted" into the fellowship of the sea (*PR* 119,118).

Conrad sometimes fixes on particular words, especially those with multiple meanings, which he explores in various contexts, the result being, on occasion, a startling disclosure of a web of odd associations in his mind. In this case, Conrad seems to respond in the first instance to the fact that adoption compensates for the lack of a given or "natural" identity by conferring an external or contingent identity that can still be effective as a principle of psychic organization. But beyond this, when Conrad says he was adopted by the English language, he seems to be exploring, and applying to himself, the fact that adoption gives one the opportunity to find one's identity in an external or non-natural field of possibilities, and forces one to produce oneself by volition and will rather than merely accepting the gifts of genetic determination. Adopted identity may be bestowed, but it requires assent, a kind of seconding of the motion, and can even be refused. Adoption entails, therefore, a certain openness, an experimental freedom, that might represent, for a creative artist, a salutary condition. The son of a failed Polish patriot, young Conrad might well have felt himself limited to few options, none promising; but adoption opened before him a space for innovation and self-invention – even, perhaps, for self-mastery – without the traumas of the Oedipal crisis: the father already dead, no further fathers need die for the son to flourish.

Conrad seems, then, to have intuited a connection between paternity and linguistic facility, and to have discovered a punning way to express this connection through the term "adoption." As a set of preexisting and "inherited" determinants, conditions, and structures, language seems to most native speakers a natural and unproblematic principle of identity, a "mother tongue." Only lawyers and writers, perhaps, regard it as a medium with its own hidden rules, mechanisms, and possibilities; and a native speaker who sets out to master the language always struggles against a prior sense that language requires no conscious effort at all. For Conrad, by contrast, command of the English language, and therefore of a means of self-expression, was attainable only through labor. What was natural for others was alien for him, and the miracle was that he discovered that the foreign language expressed him perfectly, and he rapidly and eagerly became "its own" as a way – his way – of becoming himself.

"Adoption" thus became for Conrad a way of conceptualizing both his struggle to master the English language and his struggle to achieve his own identity. The point on which I want to insist is that these struggles only lasted for a short time, that charmed interval when the still-"resistant" language itself had become, in his powerful grasp, at last "pliable" or "obedient" but had not yet disappeared as a problem. This was, as I have said, the same time when the theme of identification dominated his work and his imagination. We might begin to explain this striking fact by noting that both adoption and identification involve similar principles – the assumption of another's identity, the inner assent to, or assumption of, an external principle of being. The hypothesis, in other words, is that by depicting the identification of one character with another, Conrad was casting into narrative form the very struggle he was experiencing with respect to his medium.

How can mastery be measured, or even observed? Consider a series of passages in which we can track Conrad's astonishingly rapid progress in his use of the I language. The first is from *Almayer's Folly*, begun in 1889 and published in 1895:

> In the middle of a shadowless square of moonlight ... a little shelter-hut perched on high posts, the pile of brushwood near by, and the glowing embers of a fire with a man stretched before it, seemed very small and as if lost in the pale green iridescence reflected from the ground. On three sides of the clearing, the big trees of the forest, lashed together with manifold bonds by a mass of tangled creepers, looked down at the growing young life at their feet with the somber resignation of giants that had lost faith in their strength. And in the midst of them, the merciless creepers clung to the big trunks in cable-like coils, leaped from tree to tree, hung in thorny festoons from the lower boughs, and, sending slender tendrils on high to seek out the smallest branches, carried death to their victims in an exulting riot of silent destruction.
>
> (165)

In reading this, we need to keep reminding ourselves that the subject is, after all, only trees and vines, for these have been given a wild energy, even a sentience – even a malignant intentionality.[3] Conrad, who could see for himself the effect his speech produced on his listeners, seems to reflect their view of his early infelicities or gaucheries when he describes a character in *Lord Jim* whose "flowing English seemed to be derived from a dictionary compiled by a lunatic" (175). The author of *Almayer's Folly* was no longer in the lunatic phase, but could not yet be described as master of anything in the domain of language; indeed, the language in this passage seems to cry out for a principle of control, of responsible management, that the author is unable to provide.

Now consider a passage from *Nostromo*, published in 1904, a few years after the charmed interval when Conrad, I am arguing, had been a master of the English language. Once again, the subject is nature, but note the orderly fluency of the exposition:

> [T]he head of the calm gulf is filled on most days of the year by a great body of motionless and opaque clouds. On the rare clear mornings another shadow is cast upon the sweep of the gulf. The dawn breaks high behind the towering and serrated wall of the Cordillera, a clear-cut vision of dark peaks rearing their steep slopes on a lofty pedestal of forest rising from the very edge of the shore. ... Bare clusters of enormous rocks sprinkle with tiny black dots the smooth dome of snow.
>
> (5–6)

Despite an achieved assurance that contrasts markedly with the first passage's chaos, here, once again, we are not tempted to call the author a master of language. The overexcited lunatic has departed, leaving in his place a fine and accomplished writer, in perfect command: no natural objects are compared to gloomy giants or invested with a wild death-force; no verbal oddities suggest limitations, much less incompetence. Instead, we have an animated but 'clear-cut vision' of clouds, peaks, rocks, snow. At this point, Conrad can make sense, but, despite a high level of verbal energy, can no longer make magic. The referential grip on the world is much firmer, but the language has been tamed to the point where we scarcely experience it as a separate force at all. The first passage could only have been written by an inexperienced genius, but this passage might have been written by anybody with a high order of competence. If, at the beginning of his career, the language had clearly not yet made Conrad "its own" then by the time of *Nostromo*, Conrad has succeeded in making English altogether *his* own.

Now let's take a passage from the dead center of the period on which I'm focusing, a description of Marlow's approach to the mouth of the Congo River:

> We called at some more places with farcical names, where the merry dance of death and trade goes on in a still and earthy atmosphere as of an overheated catacomb; all along the formless coast bordered by dangerous surf, as if Nature herself had tried to ward off intruders; in and out of rivers, streams of death in life, whose banks were rotting into mud, whose waters, thickened into slime, invaded the contorted mangroves, that seemed to writhe at us in the extremity of an impotent despair ... the general sense of vague and oppressive wonder grew upon me. It was like a weary pilgrimage amongst hints for nightmares.
>
> (YOS 62)

It's difficult to describe the feelings imparted by such a strange and memorable passage, with its extravagant metaphors, the meandering elasticity of its syntax, its oscillation between past and present tenses, its almost garish vitality. But it is precisely such passages that give us the sense of a focused command in which the conventions of the language are being twisted or worked to radically unconventional effect. Early readers of Conrad reported that his prose seemed like an excellent translation from some unknown foreign tongue; others felt that the English language had been invaded by some alien energy; still others felt that Conrad had tapped some facet or dimension that no native speaker or writer had yet discovered. In passages of "purer" description, Fredric Jameson says, "Conrad's sensorium virtually remakes its objects," suggesting "forms of libidinal gratification as unimaginable to us as the possession of additional senses, or the presence of nonearthly colors in the spectrum" (*Political* 231).

During his brief period of linguistic mastery, nobody suggested that Conrad was incompetent, nor did they suggest that he was an effortless professional like Ford. They felt, rather, that he was a master of the English language, and they felt this way because they could actually sense the balance of colossal forces – Conrad's overmastering will to express the truth about things and about his thoughts and sensations, and the conventions of the English language, in which such truths had never yet been expressed. They felt that the language, without being violated, had been forced to yield something unsuspected, in the process being exposed as something less like a passive medium, a lexicon with grammar, and more like a dynamic, almost creative agency with a startling capacity to bring new objects into being – the "earthy atmosphere," the "impotent despair" of the "contorted mangroves," and the notion, novel to many readers even today, of a "weary pilgrimage amongst hints for nightmares." Once again, Conrad precisely describes his own style when he has Marlow characterize Kurtz's speech as consisting of "common everyday words" that nevertheless "had behind them ... the terrific suggestiveness of words heard in dreams, of phrases spoken in nightmares" (*YOS* 144).

I've been arguing that Conrad was fascinated by adoption because it represented a way of acquiring an identity that was not "natural" or given, but externally bestowed. Conrad may have been excited by this possibility because nature had given him so little; and adoption, with its opportunity for self-invention, seemed to offer so much. In the passage from *Almayer's Folly* quoted earlier, we can actually see traces of a half-conscious meditation on the concept of nature itself. In this passage, "a man" appears as an inconspicuous and virtually nonsentient speck in a scene of wild natural vitality; indeed, it's surprisingly easy to read this passage without noticing that human form at all. And, in general, in the first movement of Conrad's career, nature, especially in the form of jungles, rivers, and seas, often seems to dominate the human figures, often appearing as an immense matrix, a heaving rhythm of mindless generation and death, in which human beings are embedded and from which they distinguish themselves only fitfully and with great difficulty. What we seem to be witnessing in the works published before 1897 is a struggle in the roots of Conrad's imagination to pry humanity free from nature, to liberate it from the mass of tangled creepers, in, perhaps, the same manner as Michelangelo's giant unfinished sculptures, known as "Slaves," which seem to be twisting free of the unchiseled rock mass itself in which they are immured, to which they are "enslaved." We can – if we abandon all professional scruples against unfounded speculation – imagine that, during this time, Conrad was trying to imagine himself free from the clutches of nature, trying to see how he might advance, through a series of fortuitous adoptions, from the desolate condition of being an orphan in a defeated country, an unrelated person with no worldly prospects, to being a man of culture, an "author," even a "British" author, a man who fabricates lives, including his own.[4]

Eventually, beginning with *The Nigger*, nature becomes in his work a reduced, merely physical phenomenon – an agency that tries, for example, to ward off intruders, a force against whose periodic furies human beings test and measure themselves, but no longer a metaphysical threat. Exemplified by sea storms, nature becomes a trial one must pass to discover "how good a man I was" as the ubiquitous Marlow, having just endured sea difficulties, says in "Youth" (36). In other words, nature becomes secondary to human concerns, a background and a trial but not a matrix of inhumanity, a challenge to one's very being. And then, passing through this period – passing the test – Conrad seems to lose interest in nature: in *Nostromo*, nature is a setting, if an imposing one; and by 1907 and *The Secret Agent*, Conrad's imagination is predominantly urban, and would remain so. The sword has been pulled from the stone, and human beings emerge fully distinct from their natural context.[5]

But if we probe once again the central text, *Heart of Darkness*, we can see the momentary but disturbing appearance of something far more mysterious than we see either before or after. Take the scene where Marlow describes the natives along the shore as possessing "a wild vitality, an intense energy of movement, that was as natural and true as the surf along their coast" (61). This is, of course, a commonplace, that the natives are closer to nature than the Europeans. But this cliché produces striking effects in context by raising the question of whether Kurtz's gesture of disengaging from the imperial project and paddling back upriver to his jungle hut represents a rejection of a culture become criminal in favor of nature and natural law. Many readers have seen the text in this light, but to do so means understanding as "natural" the practices of the natives, including cannibalism, skulls on stakes, and a willingness to worship a crazed European. Reading *Heart of Darkness*, we are forced to wonder – does nature represent a moral standard or the negation of moral standards? Ought we to be more, or less natural? Do Europeans have a different nature from Africans; do men have a different nature from women? Is human nature "natural" or "un-natural?" None of these questions has an immediate answer, which suggests that, at the moment he composed *Heart of Darkness*, Conrad was temporarily between paradigms, with no clear idea of nature at all.

In *Heart of Darkness* we can truly see what it might mean to be "adopted by the language." Marlow is talking, in the passage below, about the final phase of his penetration into the interior, the last leg of the fateful voyage upriver toward the Inner Station and Kurtz. This account qualifies as one of the very greatest descriptive passages in the English language, and an eloquent testament to the author's mastery. The ostensible subject, once again, is foliage.

> Going up that river was like traveling back to the earliest beginnings of the world, when vegetation rioted on the earth and the big trees were kings. An empty stream, a great silence, an impenetrable forest. The air was warm, thick, heavy, sluggish. .... The long stretches of the waterway ran on, deserted, into the gloom of overshadowed distances. On silvery sandbanks hippos and alligators sunned themselves side by side.... You lost your way on that river as you would in a desert and butted all day long against shoals trying to find the channel till you thought yourself bewitched and cut off for ever from everything you had known once – somewhere – far away – in another existence perhaps.
>
> (92–93)

Unlike the passage from *Almayer's Folly*, things are actually described in a way that does not suggest that language has invested them with an inappropriate force or character. Despite the extravagant simile ("Going up that river was like traveling back... you lost your way on that river as you would in a desert. ..."), the language is firmly referential, and we get a clear image of the scene rather than a kind of hallucination.

But unlike the passage from *Nostromo*, the language is not transparent or obedient to the author's will; in fact, language itself almost seems to make suggestions to the author, of the kind that we saw earlier in the Preface to *The Nigger*, when the pain of solitude yielded to its own balm in "solidarity." The whole passage seems built on a silent metaphor, "the river of time"; but even more intriguing is the quiet but decisive force of the word *deserted* that Marlow uses to describe the absence of people on the river. This word seems to generate all by itself the next thought, that "you lost your way on that river as you would in a desert." The description of being alone, unable to orient yourself, in a featureless space hostile to humanity, is often applied to deserts, but rarely to rivers. A native speaker, thinking primarily of concepts, might never have made the connection, but Conrad, with his anxious sensitivity to English words – to him, still strange, newly discovered, almost material things – was attentive to the form of words as well as their meanings, and this sensitivity enabled him to make the connection between a *deserted* river and a *desert*. And so, by way of a hidden pun, the passage proceeds from an account of a lonely boat trip to a meditation on the experience of finding yourself bereft of your past, your identity, your humanity itself, adrift in a strange world indifferent to your existence. Bewitched by the river and by his own language, Marlow achieves and articulates a degree of detachment, or "desertion," that might never have been voiced in these terms by a native speaker.

In this instance, we can observe, or almost observe, the genius of the language adopting the author, suggesting new thoughts. But adoption, as I have argued, also implies the possibility of resistance, where limits in the power or adequacy of language are recognized, and the language is wrestled into submission. The task of recognizing these limits is delegated to Marlow, who registers repeated shocks at certain habitual or mechanistic verbal conventions. He is irritated, for example, by his aunt's talk about "weaning those ignorant millions from their horrid ways" (59); discomfited by reports that he and Kurtz are considered two of a kind, partners in "the new gang – the gang of virtue" (79); appalled by the manager's description of Kurtz's "unsound method" (137); and amazed by various labels attached to the chained, enslaved, or dying Africans he sees. "Rebels!" he exclaims to himself on hearing the description of the dried heads impaled on stakes outside Kurtz's hut. "What would be the next definition I was to hear. There had been enemies, criminals, workers – and these were-rebels" (132). Marlow senses that the linguistic categories provided by the Belgians (translated into English) are somehow inadequate, even demonstrably wrong, but his unease takes largely passive forms until this outburst, when it suddenly seems about to become ethically productive.

That potential had been signaled a few pages earlier, in the continuation of the passage on which we're focusing. As he steams upriver, Marlow passes groups of natives on the shoreline who seem to him to be scarcely human:

> ... a burst of yells, a whirl of black limbs, a mass of hands clapping, of feet stamping, of bodies swaying, of eyes rolling under the droop of heavy and motionless foliage. The steamer toiled along slowly on the edge of the black and incomprehensible frenzy. The prehistoric man was cursing us, praying to us, welcoming us-who could tell? ... we were traveling in the night of first ages, of those ages that are gone, leaving hardly a sign – and no memories.
>
> (96)

Nothing in Marlow's experience has prepared him for this astonishing scene, except perhaps the conventional presumption that Africans were "pre-historic." Marlow borrows this cliché as he had borrowed the notion that Africans were "natural," but we can sense his discontent with the language at his disposal in his very next comment: "The earth seemed unearthly" (96). What could this mean? Marlow seems to have discovered a limitation in the language, a gap in coverage, an insufficiency, a failure to provide the right term. And so, in the interests of recording the truth, he produces a statement that seems nonsensical. Surely, if anything should be "earthly," it is the earth, but in this instance, it is not so: here, if only here, the earth is unearthly – even, we recall, as the "atmosphere" is "earthy."

Having imposed himself on the language in describing the earth, Marlow proceeds to an even more daring innovation. The passage reads,

> The earth seemed unearthly, and the men were – No, they were not inhuman. Well, you know, that was the worst of it – this suspicion of their not being inhuman. They howled and leaped and spun and made horrid faces, but what thrilled you was just the thought of their humanity – like yours – the thought of your remote kinship with this wild and passionate uproar.
>
> (96)

Clearly, Marlow had been about to follow an "automatic" tendency of language to parallelism and say that the earth was unearthly and the men were inhuman, but then, in a moment of spontaneous self-revision marked by a dash, he decided that the men were *not* inhuman, that the statement offered him by language was not, after all, precise.

This moment represents the most radical and disturbing insight of Conrad's literary career, when Marlow concedes that the "savages," on whose inhumanity or subhumanity was predicated an entire imperial enterprise, were not, in fact, inhuman – that no metaphysical difference intruded between the European and the howling figures on the shore – and that the lavish rhetoric of religious and humanitarian altruism by which the entire squalid affair had been justified lacked a factual premise. It was disturbing to many of Conrad's contemporaries that Marlow could assert a common humanity binding themselves and the savage cannibals of the African interior, and it is disturbing to some others, and to the majority of his readers today, that he has to work this assertion out laboriously, as if it were a new, strange, and unsettling thought.[6] But what's recorded is momentous: in refusing the routine statement offered him by the linguistic mechanism, Marlow also refuses the thought behind that mechanism, and asserts, or admits, a kinship that official ideology denied.[7]

Mastery of the language, then, is not merely a matter of technical facility, the discovery of clever new ways of putting things. It entails both a responsiveness to language – a willingness to hear the suggestions of language (desert ... deserted) – and a willingness to question and even refuse a linguistic mechanism whose sufficiency goes largely unquestioned by native speakers, and, more important, to refuse the ideology that goes silently along with it, embedded in its customary phrases and locutions. When Conrad masters the language in the technical sense, he is able to conceive of and even to urge a relinquishing of mastery in the ideological-imperial sense.

Something traumatic happened to Conrad on his own trip up the Congo in 1890. His journals give little clue as to what that might have been, but he later said that his experience converted him from a "perfect animal" with "not a thought in his head" into a "writer" (qtd. in Garnett, *Letters* xii). Perhaps this conversion occurred when Conrad, son of a patriot who had been arrested, shackled, and removed from his homeland, saw Africans described by their European conquerors as workers, enemies, criminals, and rebels. Perhaps Conrad discovered, during this most formative of his travels, that language does not simply record or reflect identity, but, in a brutally pragmatic sense, confers it, and that mastery of language is mastery itself; perhaps he sensed that his own rapidly increasing powers would one day be sufficient to enable him to manipulate language to unravel prejudicial assumptions and to create new truths. By insisting – a decade after the experience itself – that no, they were not workers, enemies, or rebels, and no, they were not inhuman, Conrad took a long step on this arduous path.

Notes

1 From Geoffrey Galt Harpham, "Beyond Mastery: The Future of Conrad's Beginnings," in *Conrad in the Twenty-First Century: Contemporary Approaches and Perspectives*. Eds. Carola Kaplan et al. Routledge, 2005. Reprinted with permission of the publisher.
2 Listening to his peculiar speech in 1913, Lady Ottoline Morrell found it "difficult to believe that this charming gentleman ... was ... a master of English prose" (qtd. in Gathorne-Hardy 233–4). The compliment is also found in, and indeed presumed by, F.R. Leavis, Edward Said, and Fredric Jameson.
3 For discussions of Conrad's linguistic difficulties in *Almayer's Folly*, see Watt, *Almayer* lxviii–lii; see also Pulc.
4 Note that Conrad describes Yanko Gooral, whom readers often identify as Polish, as immured in nature: "lithe, supple, long-limbed, straight as a pine ... his humanity suggested to me the nature of a woodland creature" ("Amy Foster," *TOT* 111).
5 I do not mean to imply that Conrad never again creates powerful images of nature, only that when he does so (as in *The Shadow-Line*) he often seems to retrieve earlier formulae. We can, incidentally, track a comparable diminishment in the concept of paternal authority. Conrad never depicts strong biological fathers, but at first, he tended to depict powerful male authority figures. Tom Lingard, for example, was described by a contemporary "a personage of almost mythical renown, a sort of ubiquitous sea-hero, perhaps at times a sort of terror to evil-doers" (W.G. St. Clair qtd. in Sherry, *Conrad's Eastern* 315–16). In the world of *Nostromo*, authority is no longer mythical, terrible or paternal; rather, in this book and others, Conrad depicts complex webs and skeins of relationships in which no single figure dominates, a network in which the concepts of charisma, paternity and moral authority are relentlessly exposed as mere semblances. In *The Secret Agent*, both paternity and nature have become remote, almost inconceivable concepts.
6 According to Chinua Achebe's notorious argument, Conrad never did work it out and continued to regard Africans as subhuman (see Achebe, "An

Image of Africa"). In African studies, Conrad is also routinely described in these terms. In their influential *The Africa That Never Was: Four Centuries of British Writing about Africa* (1970), Dorothy Hammond and Alta Jablow comment that most European writing about Africa depicts Africans as "stock figures ... never completely human," so that the image of Africa "became and remains the Africa of H. Rider Haggard and Joseph Conrad" (14).

7 One fact readers have difficulty keeping in mind is that the language in which these events occurred, as it were, must have been French. In listening to suggestions arising within English, Conrad-Marlow is actually pitting the resources of English against the Belgian colonial enterprise.

17 The World of Nature[1]
Ian Watt

Both the traditions of fiction which he inherited and his own early work had provided a literary basis for Conrad to realise his aim of "awakening" in the hearts of the beholders "the feeling of solidarity which binds ... all mankind to the visible world." From Walter Scott and Balzac, to Flaubert, Tolstoy, and Hardy, the novel had developed the description of the environment and its human implications into an important and established feature of narrative. In *Almayer's Folly* and the works that followed Conrad had already shown what were to be the characteristic directions both of his descriptive method and of his intellectual attitude towards the natural world. *The Nigger of the "Narcissus"* takes both the method and the attitude much further; visual presentation is used more precisely and consistently, and Conrad's emphasis on the determining power of the natural environment is applied in a much more persistent and symbolic way.

"I aim at stimulating vision in the reader," Conrad wrote in 1897 (B, 10), and this meant basing the narrative on a succession of concrete physical impressions. Such a concentration on sensory particulars was the dominant consideration in Conrad's revision of *The Nigger of the "Narcissus"*. For instance, the manuscript originally opened: "Mr. Baker the chief mate of the ship 'Narcissus' came out of his cabin on to the dark quarterdeck. It was then just nine o'clock" (*JDG*, 136). In the published version this became:

> Mr. Baker, chief mate of the ship 'Narcissus,' stepped in one stride out of his lighted cabin into the darkness of the quarter-deck. Above his head, on the break of the poop, the night watchman rang a double stroke. It was nine o'clock.

This version is almost twice as long, but dull factual summary has been transformed into an active sequence of sensations, mainly visual but also aural, as in "a double stroke," and kinetic, as in "in one stride" and "rang."

Conrad's most significant visual addition is "stepped out of his lighted cabin into the darkness." This also serves to establish the novel's central symbolic contrast between light and darkness. The contrast continues when we look at the forecastle: "in the illuminated doorways, silhouettes of moving men appeared for a moment, very black, without relief"; the first seaman we see clearly, "with his spectacles and a venerable white beard," is "Old Singleton, the oldest able-seaman on the ship, set apart on the deck right under the lamps" (6). Baker has already been connected with the imagery of light when he orders a "good lamp" for the muster (3); and it is through Baker's agency that the men in the forecastle come from the darkness into the lamp's emblematic circle of light, and are there formally transformed into the crew of the *Narcissus*. One man, however, is missing. Then an invisible late arrival sonorously pronounces the word "Wait!" He comes down towards Baker, but is too tall for the lamplight to illuminate his face. The ominous mystery is only dispelled when "the ship's boy, amazed like the rest, raised the light to the man's face. It was black" (17).

The contrast of black and white gathers more and more associations throughout the novel. One of them is particularly important. When the *Narcissus* goes to sea it leaves the tug, which is described as

> an enormous and aquatic black beetle, surprised by the light, overwhelmed by the sunshine, trying to escape with ineffectual effort into the distant gloom of the land. .... On the place where she had stopped a round black patch of soot remained, undulating on the swell.
>
> (27)

This equation of shore life with darkness is part of Conrad's general thematic contrast between land and sea, which is insistently – often over-insistently – present throughout the narrative.

Ever since it was separated from darkness at the Creation, light, as a necessary condition for being able to see, has been a prime example both of how the natural world structures the human, and of how man uses his perception of nature to evoke a community of response. That community begins in the simplest of routines, such as "Good morning" and "Good evening"; but it extends into a larger structuring of antithetical social and moral ideas. Thus light is a symbol of clear understanding and collective order, while night, as the scene of evil deeds and invisible dangers, becomes the symbol of doubt and chaos. These associations are invoked in the way the characters are presented. Thus the two prime representatives of order in the *Narcissus* when she sets out – Baker and Singleton – are both associated with light, as opposed to the darkness of the land, of the ship while she is tied to it, of Donkin's machinations ("Go for them ... it's dark!" he hisses during the mutiny [123]), and of the menacing blackness of James Wait. The series of correlations between physical and moral properties continues until the end; and it exemplifies Conrad's use of particular and concrete details to establish the basic moral polarities.

This larger purpose is no doubt one reason why, as in *Almayer's Folly*, Conrad's natural description is very little concerned with the purely aesthetic qualities of the world of appearances. In *The Nigger of the "Narcissus"*, Conrad's presentation of the sea, for instance, pays little attention to its varying smells, colours, or wave patterns. Instead, the main focus is on the imperative power which the sea, like other forces of nature, exercises on the lives of the men who sail upon it.

These meanings are magnificently evoked when the *Narcissus* sets out to sea:

> The passage had begun, and the ship, a fragment detached from the earth, went on lonely and swift like a small planet. Round her the abysses of sky and sea met in an unattainable frontier. A great circular solitude moved with her, ever changing and ever the same.
>
> (29)

The passage holds the reader with a deepening sense of man's lonely voyaging towards unattainable frontiers until it concludes in a kind of cosmic vertigo at the featureless immensity of time and space: "The smiling greatness of the sea dwarfed the extent of time. The days raced after one another, brilliant and quick like the flashes of a lighthouse, and the nights, eventful and short, resembled fleeting dreams."

None of the meanings of the natural world are intrinsic; they have all been created and named by man; and so natural description inevitably tends to involve attributing human properties, especially feelings, to natural objects – the pathetic fallacy, as Ruskin called it in *Modem Painters*. When Conrad talks of the sea "dwarfing" or the days "racing," however, the use of the pathetic fallacy is inconspicuous. After all, "dwarfing" and "racing" are both established metaphorical usages for scale and speed; they do not really impute any anthropomorphic intention to natural forces; and their use here – even in the veiled threat behind the deceptively benevolent appearance of the "smiling greatness of the sea" – has the positive effect of referring us continually to the human perceivers of the sea-the ship's crew. This focus on the human observer is even more obvious in the boldest, most successful, and most abstract of Conrad's images in the passage: "a great circular solitude moved with her." The words arrest the reader's attention, and fix it on the centre of the moving circle which is both the ship and the eye of someone on it observing the vast circumference of his isolation.

Conrad's attitude to nature is in one sense the opposite of Wordsworth's. He does not feel love for the landscape, or try to persuade himself that his feelings are in any sense reciprocated; man's essential emotional and spiritual bonds to nature are very different, since the ties which most obviously "bind" mankind to the visible universe are really the shackles which the laws of the cosmos impose upon human aspiration, the iron conditions within which men must attempt to live.

This was Conrad's own general attitude. "The sea," he later wrote, "is uncertain, arbitrary, featureless, and violent. Except when helped by the varied majesty of the sky, there is something inane in its serenity and something stupid in its wrath" (*NLL*, 184). The solidarity of seamen, then, is essentially provoked by a common enemy; and the essence of Conrad's literary use of the sea is reverence for the heroism of man's "continuous defiance of what [the sea] can do."

Conrad's attitude to the visible world also reflects the nineteenth century's growing sense of nature's unconscious but absolute tyranny over human affairs; and he expresses this antagonism through the traditional techniques of metaphor, transferred epithet, simile, personification, pathetic fallacy, and, above all, overt authorial commentary.

Conrad's tendency to editorialise, to force the reader to accept his way of seeing things in an obtrusive and insistent way, has been widely attacked.[2] The most frequent target in *The Nigger of the "Narcissus"* is the extended passage of authorial commentary which occurs after the storm has subsided, and the ship is once again underway:

> On men reprieved by its disdainful mercy, the immortal sea confers in its justice the full privilege of desired unrest. Through the perfect wisdom of its grace they are not permitted to meditate at ease upon the complicated and acrid savour of existence [, lest they should remember and, perchance, regret the reward of a cup of inspiring bitterness, tasted so often, and so often withdrawn from before their stiffening but reluctant lips]. They must without pause justify their life to the eternal pity that commands toil to be hard and unceasing, from sunrise to sunset, from sunset to sunrise; till the weary succession of nights and days tainted by the obstinate clamor of sages, demanding bliss and an empty heaven, is redeemed at last by the vast silence of pain and labour, by the dumb fear and the dumb courage of men obscure, forgetful, and enduring.
>
> (90)[3]

Our modern distrust of the purple passage tends to make us very unsympathetic to Conrad's stylistic intention here. Since T.E. Hulme and the Imagists we have demanded in poetry – and, *a fortiori*, in prose – tautness of rhythm, hardness of outline, exactness of diction; and in this paragraph Conrad uses every device of sound and sense for the very opposite purpose of inducing feelings of rather vague exaltation. His aim is clearly to produce a chiaroscuro effect between one detailed picture – the righting of the ship – and another – the resumption of ordinary life aboard the *Narcissus*; in the respite between the two we are given a reflective pause in which the "magic suggestiveness of music" that Conrad praised in the preface induces a general mood of awe at the endless confrontation of man and nature. The passage seemed to Virginia Woolf – herself a supreme exponent of poetic prose – an example of her general assertion that in Conrad's prose "the beauty of surface has always a fibre of morality within."[4]

To make full sense of this particular passage we must, of course, read it with the sort of flexible and cooperative interpretation we normally give only to some kinds of poetry; in particular, we must allow Conrad his steady reliance on ironic, elliptical, and paradoxical personification of an inanimate object. We must, for example, see that the apparent paradox of "desired unrest" depends on the narrator's view that "life" in general, which all men literally "desire" because its only alternative is death, is nevertheless, like the sea, always a condition of "unrest." We must also accept the pathetic fallacy of Conrad's attributing, albeit ironically, "mercy" and "grace" to the sea; this serves to prepare for the final modulation whereby what has been revealed as the in-fact pitiless power of the sea is implicitly equated with God's supposedly merciful attributes; even so, the irony in Conrad's phrase "eternal pity" remains somewhat obscure until we get to the balancing phrase, "an empty heaven," and realise that Conrad wants to juxtapose his rejection of the consoling religious illusions of "the sages" against the only redemptive reality which he will acknowledge, that "vast silence of pain and labor" which the sea forces men to endure.

The gnomic compression, the largeness of reference, the tone of religious elevation, the continuous latent irony, all suggest a familiar literary analogue: the Greek chorus. The Greek chorus's statement of the general theme depends for its distinctive effect on the impact, at the point of rest in the action, of a plurality of voices and an intensified musicality. There must be a plurality of voices, and not an individualized narrator, because the function of a chorus in general, as of the passage here, is to achieve what Yeats called "emotion of multitude"; there must also be an intensified musicality because the hieratic repetition and balance of cadence and rhythm is itself the formal expression of Conrad's controlled exaltation at the prospect of the laborious but triumphant monotony offered by the tradition of unceasing human effort. The moral tenour of the passage is equally choric in nature: it asserts that, contrary to the crew's longings and to the more sentimental hopes consciously promoted by those clamorous sages Donkin and Podmore, the destiny of the successive human generations is not to find any adequate reward either in this life or the next, but only to labour in their unending confrontation of the environment. The confrontation is unsought and yet obligatory; it is the basis of human solidarity; and its most dangerous enemies are those who seek to confuse, defer, or evade its exactions.

In this and other choric passages Conrad is not technically speaking in his own voice, since the whole novel is told by an unnamed and uncharacterised narrator; and when this narrator pauses to generalise about the experience as a whole, it is surely appropriate that his invocation of solidarity should be pronounced in a noticeably more distant and elevated voice. Conrad's intrusive authorial commentary, however, is much more difficult to justify in other passages where it does not stand alone but is more directly linked to concrete events and actions. Thus in the storm, when we are told that "the ship tossed about, shaken furiously, like a toy in the hand of a lunatic" (53), we cannot but feel that the personification is artificial; the pathetic fallacy the simile of the "toy in the hand of a lunatic," which is intended to convey the utter vulnerability of the *Narcissus* and its crew to the senseless malignity of the storm, actually trivialises both the ship and the sea. A similar objection arises when we seek Donkin returning to the deck after precipitating the death of Wait and stealing his possessions. Conrad writes:

> The immortal sea stretched away, immense and hazy, like the image of life, with a glittering surface and lightless depths. Donkin gave it a defiant glance and slunk off noiselessly as if judged and cast out by the august silence of its might.
>
> (155)

We know why Conrad should feel like this; but Donkin seems rather small game for the sea.

There can, then, be different critical judgments on particular examples of Conrad's use of the pathetic fallacy, or of the voice of generalised authorial commentary for this purpose; but in general they are surely successful only to the extent that the imperative power of the natural upon the human world has already been confirmed by concrete impressions and events in the novel; it is only through narrative that Conrad can "awaken in the hearts of the beholders" a full awareness of the crew's pain and labour, fear and courage, forgetfulness and endurance.

Conrad's treatment of the relationship of man and nature in *The Nigger of the "Narcissus"* is certainly consistent with the general aims he expressed in the preface; for instance, we see many ways in which the crew is "bound to the visible world." Whether the crew feels tied by rewarding bonds or constricting shackles, however, is not raised directly, and most of what transpires merely suggests an automatic and unconscious acceptance of their common subjugation to the power of nature.

The most complete acceptance of that power is attributed to Singleton, the most experienced sailor aboard. He is instinctively alert to every stir of the sea and the wind, which are "as much part of his existence as his beating heart" (26); this alertness makes him perform the first nautical action of the novel: when the cable moves and the *Narcissus* comes to "unsuspected life," Singleton is there to tighten the brake of the windlass; and the first chapter ends with him growling the symbolic command: "You ... hold!" It is also Singleton who voices the danger of trying to rebel against the natural forces which oppose man's wishes. The *Narcissus* is nearly lost because Captain Allistoun "would not notice that" he was asking the ship "to do too much" (52); and when Singleton observes this, we are told, he "broke his habitual silence and said with a glance aloft: – 'The old man's in a temper with the weather, but it's no good bein' angry with the winds of heaven.'"

The crew, then, and their symbolic representative Singleton, seem to feel bound to nature only in the negative sense that for the most part they accept their common servitude to its power. The other question, that of whether the visible world binds the men on the *Narcissus* to each other, receives no more inspiring an answer.

Notes

1 From Watt, Ian. *Conrad in the Nineteenth Century.* University of California Press, 1981. pp. 94–100. Reprinted with permission of the publisher.
2 Marvin Murdock, for instance, speaks of the passage's "unctuous thrilling rhetoric" ("The Artist's Conscience and *The Nigger of the 'Narcissus'*," *Nineteenth-Century Fiction* 11 [1957]: 297).
3 Conrad deleted the passage in brackets when revising for the collected edition, which tended in general toward economy and sobriety of expression (*JDG*, 140–1).
4 In "Mr. Conrad: A Conversation," *The Captain's Death Bed* (London, 1950), p. 77.

Notes on Contributors

Paul B. Armstrong is Professor of English at Brown University. He is author of The Phenomenology of Henry James (1983) The Challenge of Bewilderment: Understanding and Representation in James, Conrad, and Ford (1987), Conflicting Readings: Variety and Validity in Interpretation (1990), Play and the Politics of Reading: The Social Uses of Modernist Form (2005), How Literature Plays with the Brain: The Neuroscience of Reading and Art (2013). He is also editor of the Norton Critical Editions of Conrad's Heart of Darkness (2017) and E. M. Forster's Howards End (1998).

J. A. Bernstein is Assistant Professor of English at the University of Southern Mississippi and the fiction editor for Tikkun. His essays have appeared in The Conradian and Western American Literature, as well as Boston Review, Chicago Quarterly Review, Harpur Palate and other journals. His novel, Rachel's Tomb, won the Hackney Award and the Knut House Novel Contest, and his story collection, Stick-Light, is forthcoming from Eyewear Editions, where it was shortlisted for the Beverly Prize.

Troy Boone is Associate Professor of English at the University of Pittsburgh. His first book, *Youth of Darkest England: Working-Class Children at the Heart of Victorian Empire*, was published by Routledge in 2005. He is completing a book titled *The Natural History of the Present: Victorian Ecology, the Brontës, and the North of England*.

Mark Deggan holds lectureship in World Literature at Simon Fraser University Surrey in British Columbia. He has published on modernist fiction, spatial theory, the poetics of the cinema and the performativity of the scene of nature as represented in film, literature and the image. His work can be found in Époque Conradienne, the Stanford Center for the Study of Language and Information (CSLI), D H Lawrence Studies, the Conradian, Conradiana, Revue Trans- (Paris) and Interférences littéraires (Leuven).

Hugh Epstein is currently the secretary of the Joseph Conrad Society (UK). He teaches in adult education in central London and has published widely in academic journals on different aspects of Conrad and Thomas Hardy, and he is a frequent speaker at conferences on both the authors. His book on Hardy, Conrad and the Senses is currently being considered for publication.

Geoffrey Galt Harpham is a Visiting Scholar and Senior Fellow at the Kenan Institute for Ethics at Duke University, and the former director of the National Humanities Center in Research Triangle Park. His books include *One of Us: The Mastery of Joseph Conrad* (1996), Language Alone: The Critical Fetish of Modernity (2002), The Character of Criticism (2006), and The Humanities and the Dream of America (2011).

Brendan Kavanagh recently received his PhD candidate in English literature at the University of Cambridge. His dissertation explores modernist media systems in the works of Joseph Conrad, Virginia Woolf and James Joyce. He has published articles on Conrad, Joyce and Shakespeare.

Mark D. Larabee is formerly a permanent military professor of English at the US Naval Academy. He currently serves as the Executive Editor of *Joseph Conrad Today*. He is the author of *Front Lines of Modernism: Remapping the Great War in British Fiction* (2011) and articles on Joseph Conrad, Ford Madox Ford, Yasunari Kawabata and travel writing.

Nidesh Lawtoo is Assistant Professor for the Institute of Philosphy at KU Leuven in Belgium. He is the editor of Conrad's *Heart of Darkness and Contemporary Thought: Revisiting the Horror with Lacoue-Labarthe* (2012), author of *The Phantom of the Ego: Modernism and the Mimetic Unconscious* (2013) and, more recently, *Conrad's Shadow: Catastrophe, Mimesis, Theory* (2016). His next project is funded by the European Research Council and titled *Homo Mimeticus: Theory and Criticism*.

Robert P. Marzec is Professor of Environmental and Postcolonial Studies in the Department of English at Purdue University. He is the author of *Militarizing the Environment: Climate Change and the Security Society* (University of Minnesota Press 2015), *An Ecological and Postcolonial Study of Literature* (Palgrave 2007), the editor of *Postcolonial Literary Studies: The First 30 Years* (Johns Hopkins 2011) and the associate editor of *Modern Fiction Studies*. He is affiliated with the Purdue Climate Change Research Center and Purdue's Center for the Environment. He has published articles in *boundary 2, Radical History Review, Public Culture, Postmodern Culture, The Global South* and *The Journal of Commonwealth and Postcolonial Studies*.

Jeffrey Mathes McCarthy is the Director of Environmental Humanities at the University of Utah. He is the author of *Contact: Mountain Climbing and Environmental Thinking* (University of Nevada Press 2008) and *Green Modernism: Nature and the English Novel, 1900–1930* (Palgrave Macmillan 2015), as well as numerous academic articles, book chapters and essays for climbing magazines.

Jay Parker is Assistant Professor in English Literature at Hang Seng Management College in Hong Kong. In 2015, he won the Joseph Conrad Society of America's Bruce Harkness Young Conrad Scholar Award and was awarded the Juliet McLauchlan Prize from The Joseph Conrad Society (UK) in 2012. He has published articles on Conrad in *The Conradian* and *Textual Practice*.

Samuel Perks teaches in the School of English at the University of Leeds, UK, where he also earned his PhD in world literature, focusing on Singaporean historical fiction. His research interests currently focus on representations of the ecology of global cities.

John G. Peters, a University Distinguished Research Professor at the University of North Texas and current General Editor of *Conradiana*. His books include *Joseph Conrad's Critical Reception* (Cambridge 2013), *The Cambridge Introduction to Joseph Conrad* (2006), *Conrad and Impressionism* (Cambridge 2001), *A Historical Guide to Joseph Conrad* (2010), volume 2 of *Joseph Conrad: Contemporary Reviews* (Cambridge 2012) and the Norton critical edition of Conrad's *The Secret Sharer and Other Stories* (2015). His articles have appeared in such journals as *Philosophy and Literature*, *College Literature*, *Studies in the Novel*, *Studies in Short Fiction* and *English Language Notes*. He has also translated the Japanese poet Takamura Kōtarō's book *The Chieko Poems* (Green Integer 2007).

Lissa Schneider-Rebozo is Professor of English and Director of Undergraduate Research at the University of Wisconsin-River Falls. Her book, *Conrad's Narratives of Difference* (Routledge 2003) was released in paperback in 2016; she has published essays on Conrad, Djuna Barnes, Alfred Hitchcock, Park Chan-wook and Louise Erdrich, as well as essays on sustainability, East Asian literatures and cinema, international education and undergraduate research.

Johanna M. Smith was until recently Associate Professor at University of Texas at Arlington. Now retired, she has published articles in such journals as *Nineteenth Century Studies*, *Mosaic*, *Eighteenth Century: Theory and Interpretation*, *Victorian Studies*, *Studies in the Novel*, and *Nineteenth-Century Contexts*. She is also author of *Mary Shelley* (1996), editor of the Bedford/St. Martin's edition of Shelley's *Frankenstein* (2000), now in its third edition (2015), and co-editor of *Life-Writings by British Women, 1660–1815: An Anthology* (2000).

Jesse Oak Taylor is Associate Professor of English at the University of Washington. He is the author of *The Sky of Our Manufacture: The London Fog in British Fiction from Dickens to Woolf* (2016) and co-editor of *Anthropocene Reading: Literary History in Geologic Times* (2017) among other writings on empire, conservation and the environmental humanities.

Ian Watt was Professor of English at Stanford University. He is author of Conrad in the Nineteenth Century (1979), Joseph Conrad: Nostromo (1988), Myths of Modern Individualism: Faust, Don Quixote, Don Juan, Robinson Crusoe (1996), Essays on Conrad (2000), and The Rise of the Novel: Studies in Defoe, Richardson, and Fielding (1957). He is also editor of The Secret Agent: A Casebook (1973) and Jane Austen: A Collection of Critical Essays (1963).

Jarica Linn Watts is Assistant Professor of English at Brigham Young University. She is a scholar of early twentieth-century British literature. Her primary research focuses on experimentation with genre and form, particularly evolutions in short fiction; the cultural shock of the Great War; and critical thematics, including spirituality and mysticism, gender studies and object-oriented ontology from 1900 to 1930. She has published essays on Radclyffe Hall, Joseph Conrad, D.H. Lawrence, Katherine Mansfield and James Joyce.

Index

Achebe, Chinua 34, 41, 309–310n6
Actant 45, 50, 52, 58–59, 62, 64n6, 64–65n9, 211, 219–224, 226, 230n9
Adventure, adventurer 11, 33, 42, 72, 176, 193n9, 228n2, 250n5, 252–266, 270, 276, 292, 294
Affect 46–47, 49, 53–55, 60, 64n5, 86, 134, 149–151, 154, 156–161, 163–165, 166,n11, 219–220, 247, 274, 299
Alaimo, Stacy 5, 14n9, 97, 108–109n9
Anthropocene 7–8, 12, 21–30, 32, 34–36, 39–41, 43–46, 48–56, 61–63, 63n1-2, 64n3, 65n10, 68–69, 73, 75–76, 78, 81–82, 85, 87, 107, 125
Anthropocentrism 5, 44–45, 53–54, 57, 59, 60, 64n4, 75, 77, 85, 93, 97, 99, 114, 119–120, 124–125, 129–130, 136, 138, 196–197, 203, 205, 209n1, 247
Anthropology 54, 182, 231
Anthropomorphism 13n2, 51, 53, 65n13, 108–109n9, 224, 313
Anthropos 23–24, 43, 74, 80, 82, 87, 94, 132
Arendt, Hannah 22
Armstrong, Paul 16, 150–151, 155, 198, 206, 289–291, 291n1, 319
Assemblage 24, 45, 64n6, 65n9, 220, 222–223
Atmospherics 26, 28, 34–36, 39–41, 43, 48–49, 59, 113–140, 141n14, 146–165, 166n5, 167n12, 168n20, 177, 179, 187, 192, 218–220, 222–223, 225, 229–230n7, 237, 246, 279, 283n3, 303–304, 308
Author, authorize 8, 9, 39, 44, 64n6, 88, 129, 148, 150, 151, 153, 157, 159, 161, 164–165, 209n2, 218, 235, 238, 274, 302, 303, 305–307, 314, 316
Authority 43, 48, 58, 68, 181, 249, 297, 309n5

Balzac, Honoré de 12, 311
Bennet, Jane 5, 43, 51, 63n1, 97, 108n9, 219, 223, 230n9
Blanford, Henry Francis 115–116, 124–125, 138, 140n3, 140n5
Böhme, Gernot 163, 167n19
Buell, Lawrence 71, 155, 156, 166n10, 166n11
Byron, George Gordon 94, 95, 101, 106–107, 108n3

Capitalism 4, 14n7, 21–23, 25, 32, 35–36, 38–39, 64n3, 69, 72, 75, 83, 85, 197, 205, 236–239, 241–243, 248–249, 250n4, 250n6-11, 252–254, 256–262, 265
Chakrabarty, Dipesh 23, 28, 44, 68
Civilization 2–3 14n7, 21, 27, 31, 34, 40, 71, 129, 181, 183, 207–208, 255
Cixous, Hélène 292, 294
Climate 2, 8, 9–10, 25, 28–29, 35, 40, 55, 94–96, 107, 113–115, 118, 122, 130–131, 135; climate change 1, 7, 9, 11, 27–28, 44, 48–49, 63n2, 64n6, 69, 94–95, 97–98, 101, 104, 108n3, 109n13; climate refugee 1, 13; climatologists 35
Coal 36, 103, 250n12, 252–266, 266n3; coal empire 252, 254–255, 262–266Colonialism 2, 13, 69, 119, 197, 208, 265; colonial capitalism 252–253, 257–262, 265
Commodity 28, 37, 73, 84, 262, 265, 270, 271; commodity frontiers 239, 253, 259–260

Connolly, William 45, 63n1
Connor, Steven 126–127, 135, 141n14
Conrad, Joseph *Almayer's Folly* 22, 166n1, 167n14, 255, 302, 304, 306, 309n3, 311, 313; "Amy Foster" 10, 175, 309n4; "Autocracy and War" 175; *Collected Letters, the* 136, 198, 309; "The End of the Tether" 175, 183–186, 188, "Falk" 175, 179–182, 184–185, 187, 194n17; *Heart of Darkness* 1–4, 5, 10, 22–23, 26–27, 30, 33, 35, 37–39, 53, 64n4, 64n8, 65n11, 69, 71–72, 74–75, 78, 83, 85–89, 109n16, 123, 153, 173–174, 177, 183, 189, 191, 196, 198–199, 201, 203–204, 206–207, 209n2, 217, 226, 250n5, 252, 270, 294, 297, 298n1, 299, 305, 319–320; "The Idiots" 10; "Karain: A Memory" 159, 160, 167n12; "The Lagoon" 149, 166n1, 167n18, 168n20, 186; *Lord Jim* 6–7, 26, 32, 36, 46, 62, 108n8, 109n13, 113–115, 117–120, 122, 124–139, 140n1, 142n18, 142n23, 146–148, 151, 153, 157, 161–162, 165, 168n20, 173, 175, 193n13, 194n22, 198, 219, 226, 252, 259–260, 269, 271, 273, 275, 282, 283, 299, 302; *The Mirror of the Sea* 51, 95, 99, 101, 102, 106, 131, 175; *The Nigger of the "Narcissus"* 9, 12, 45–46, 51, 55, 57, 93, 101–104, 107, 127, 148, 166n3, 176, 196, 199–200, 203–205, 207, 209, 306, 311–314, 315–317, 317n2; *Nostromo* 7, 12, 36, 69, 74–77, 79–83, 85–87, 151, 174–175, 177, 184, 188–192, 196, 198, 204, 206–208, 228n2, 235–249, 250n4, 205n11, 270, 289–291, 291n2, 291n4, 299, 302–303, 305–306, 309n5, 322; *Notes on Life and Letters* 174, 194n30; *One Day More* 175; *An Outcast of the Islands* 146–150, 152–153, 155–157, 161, 163, 164–165, 166n1, 167n14,; "An Outpost of Progress" 2–3, 7, 12, 14n13, 129, 198; *A Personal Record* 102, 106, 157, 193n8, 235, 250n2; *The Rescue* 148, 166n5, 175; *Romance* 175, 176; *The Secret Agent* 2–3, 13n3, 69, 74, 82–87, 121, 124, 194n17, 215, 226, 299, 305, 309n5, 322; "The Secret Sharer" 45, 46, 55, 59, 60, 65n15, 108n1, 228; *The Shadow-Line* 2, 45, 46, 49, 55, 148, 309n5, "To-morrow" 175; *Twixt Land and Sea* 2, 13n5; "Typhoon" 7–9, 36, 43, 45–48, 50, 52–53, 57–61, 93, 95–101, 103–107, 108n8, 109n11, 109n15, 113, 120–122, 124–125, 127, 130–131, 139, 142n16, 142n22, 175–181, 183–184, 194n17, 212, 215–216, 219, 226, 252; *Under Western Eyes* 2, 14n6, 107n1, 124, 142n15, *Victory* 8, 68, 196, 198, 206, 250n12, 252, 254–266, 266n3; "Youth" 1, 8, 10, 13n2, 36, 46, 176, 183, 252–253, 280, 305, 319
Conservation, conservancy 29, 36, 38, 193n12, 283
Consumers, consumption 11, 94, 220, 241–242, 249
Contagion 46, 49, 53–56, 62, 64n5, 64–65n9
Cosmic cosmic balance 118, 120, 132; cosmic dynamic 176; cosmic exteriority 119; cosmic process 181–183, 186, 188, 190; cosmic spectacle 176; cosmic spirit 192
Cronon, William 6–7, 14n8, 21, 31–33, 36
Cunninghame Graham, R. B. 179, 198

Deacon, Terrence 23, 25
Deep ecology 196–197, 200–205, 208–209, 209n1
Deleuze, Gilles 134–135, 220
Dove, Heinrich 113–115, 121–122, 128, 140n2, 141n9–10, 142n21
Dryden, Linda 141n7, 159, 252, 255, 256, 259

Earthquakes 27, 29, 52, 94
Ecocriticism 1, 3–4, 11, 14n8, 27, 43–45, 49, 51, 72, 94, 101, 104, 107, 108n4, 108–109n9, 109n13, 155, 162, 163, 165, 166n4, 197, 238
Ecology 6, 8, 11, 14n9, 21–22, 24–27, 29–37, 39, 41, 41n1, 43–47, 50–51, 53–55, 57–61, 63, 64n7, 68–72, 74, 76, 78, 85, 87, 93–94, 99–100, 104, 109n13, 117, 123–124, 126–127, 129, 131–132,

135, 138–139, 148–149, 152–153, 158–159, 162–165, 196–197, 199–206, 208–209, 209n1, 225, 230n8, 235–242, 247–249, 250n3, 250n6–8, 252–255, 257–261, 265, 269, 275, 283; ecological revolution 252–255, 257–261, 265
Ecophobia 26, 93
Ecosystem 22, 36, 43, 68–72, 74–77, 80, 85–87, 95, 99, 147, 160–161, 166n7, 239, 269, 275, 281–283; "novel ecosystems" 22, 35
Eden, edenic 7, 11, 284n5
Elephants 37–39, 72
Empire 13n4, 21, 23, 25–27, 33, 37, 71, 82, 84, 93, 119, 123, 129, 238, 252–257, 260–266, 266n1–2, 292–293, 295, 297, 298n1
Energy 11, 79, 87, 88n2, 122, 128, 141n11, 154, 160, 166n7, 182, 193n12, 219, 252–255, 258–262, 264–265, 279, 302–303, 305; energy humanities, the 253; energy regime 254, 259–260, 262
Entrepreneur 76, 252, 255–256, 260–264, 282
Environment, environmentalism 1–13, 14n9, 25–26, 31–32, 35–36, 41n1, 43–52, 54, 56, 59, 63, 64n7, 69, 71–79, 85, 93, 96–97, 101, 104, 106, 109n13, 123, 130, 146–147, 149–150, 153–165, 166n4, 166n7, 167n12, 167n13, 167n17, 167n19, 183, 192, 196–198, 201, 207, 209, 225, 236, 239, 264, 275, 280, 282, 311, 315; environmental holism 209
Epistemology 25, 32, 114, 151, 175, 177, 183, 186, 190, 203, 248
Esty, Jed 23, 117, 118, 119, 129, 130, 141n7
Ethics, environmental ethics 8–9, 15n16, 45, 55–63, 70, 74, 65n14, 93, 95–98, 100–101, 104, 107, 107n1, 108n2, 181, 196–197, 201, 207
Exploitation 25–26, 32, 38, 69, 74, 76, 81, 116, 146, 184, 208–209, 237–238, 240–241, 252–253, 257, 261, 263–264, 275, 280–281, 283
Extraction 1, 22–25, 36–37, 75, 78, 82, 241, 256–257, 259–260, 262, 265, 290
Eysteinsson, Astradur 4, 16

Fertility 245, 275–28; infertility 245
Fertilizer 269, 271–275, 277, 283n3
Fetish, fetishism 37, 84, 256
Fictionality 244, 249
Fischer-Lichte, Erika 159–160, 167n17, 167n19
Flaubert, Gustav 190, 311
Fog 155, 211, 218–219, 221–223; "Fog of War" 218
Fogel, Aaron 297
Ford, Ford Maddox 150, 175, 190, 204, 210, 291, 300, 304
Fraser, Gail 109n15
Fussell, Paul 11

Galsworthy, John 12, 191, 192, 194n28
Garnett, Edward 166n11, 187, 192, 193n9, 309
Garrard, Greg 11
Globalization 1, 3–4, 12–13, 13n3, 24, 35–37, 46, 69, 71, 74–76, 78, 82–84, 129, 237, 253, 260, 269, 271, 274–275, 282–283
Guano 36, 269–278, 282–283, 283n1–3
Guha, Ramchandra 6–7, 208–209

Haggard, H. Rider 255, 309–310n6
Halley, Edmund 113, 142n21
Hampson, Robert 127, 129, 141n7, 159, 160, 167n15
Hardy, Thomas 176, 193n1, 311, 320
Harrison, Robert Pogue 30
Hawkins, Hunt 4
Heidegger, Martin 70, 73–74, 76–78, 141n14, 198
Hochschild, Adam 4, 13n4, 16, 210
Houen, Alex 13n3, 88n1, 88n2, 116, 140n6
Hulme, T. E. 314
Humanism 24, 93–95, 98–99, 102, 104–105, 108n1
Humboldt, Alexander Von 114–120, 125–126, 128–132, 138, 140n4–5, 141n8, 271; Humboldtian Science 114, 116–119, 125–126, 128–132, 138, 140n4–5, 141n8
Hurricanes 7, 28, 48, 52, 54, 59, 97, 101, 104, 105, 113, 120, 121, 141n9, 141n11, 178, 179, 223, 269, 270, 280

Idealism 86, 149, 183, 194n19, 207
Identity 45, 83, 185, 220, 236, 247, 260, 296, 299–301, 304, 306, 309, 309n4; identification 25, 78, 109n11, 181, 205, 226, 299–301; identity politics 53
Illusions 155, 160, 166n11, 192, 236, 248–249, 315; sustaining illusion 190, 204, 236, 247–249
Imperialism 4, 5, 13n4, 25, 27, 29, 39, 72–73, 78, 83, 119, 129, 209, 236, 238, 250n5, 252, 261, 265, 292–297; 298n2
Industrialization 6, 22, 23, 25, 32, 34, 35, 40, 64n3, 93, 97, 101–107, 109n13, 236, 256, 259, 272; Industrial Revolution 34, 64n3
Interdependence 237, 283
Irigaray, Luce 123–124, 141n14
Irony 2, 4, 11, 39, 47, 82–83, 104, 137, 175, 179, 180–181, 191, 194n17, 207–208, 235, 239–249, 263, 295, 315
Ivory 2–3, 1, 24–25, 28, 36–39, 70, 72, 74–75, 87, 201, 203, 207, 293

Jablow, Alta 309–310n6
Jameson, Fredric 26, 109n13, 238, 291n4, 303, 309n2

Keats, John 95
Kingsley, Mary 294

Lacoue-Labarthe, Philippe 47, 64n8, 69–71, 80, 84, 86
Landscape 10, 21–22, 27, 29–37, 108n7, 123, 146, 151, 155–156, 159, 161, 166n7, 166n10, 167n15, 185, 245–246, 269, 278–279, 281–283, 289–290, 313
Language 2–3, 11, 13n6, 30, 32, 53, 69–70, 73–74, 76–77, 95, 100, 109n11, 114, 134–135, 137–140, 141n11, 142n24, 154, 167n18, 174, 177–178, 182–184, 194n17, 213, 218, 257, 264, 276–277, 299–304, 306–309, 310n7; linguistic facility, linguistic mastery 53, 59, 77, 83, 151, 174, 180, 219, 289, 299–301, 304, 307–308, 309n3
Latour, Bruno 43, 45, 47, 53, 55, 63–64n2, 64n6, 64–65n9, 65n12, 130, 212, 219

Lawtoo, Nidesh 64n5, 64–65n9, 65n11, 65n14, 72, 114, 219, 225–226, 230n8
Leavis, F. R. 44, 104, 109n15, 262–264, 309n2
London, Betty 296–297

Mapping, maps 4, 21, 32, 37, 72, 152–153, 183, 185, 236, 250n3, 254–257
Marx, Karl 37, 38, 71, 196, 236, 238, 239, 245, 248, 249, 250n4
Marzec, Robert P. 75, 123–124, 141n13, 198, 201
Materialism, materiality 39, 49, 74, 84, 97, 124, 141n14, 205, 211, 217, 222–227, 270, 274
McCarthy, Jeffrey Mathes 14n12, 25, 31, 37, 63n1, 72, 114, 124, 133, 138, 142n15, 196, 201–202, 225–227, 266, 321
McLuhan, Marshall 139, 142n24, 160
Meillassoux, Quentin 119–120, 138
Meldrum, David 136, 187
Mentz, Steve 8, 12, 14n14
Metaphysics 190, 194n19, 198, 221
Meteorology 10, 94, 108n4 113–116, 121, 124–125, 130, 135, 138, 140n3, 140n5, 141n9–11, 142n20, 155–156, 164
Miller, J. Hillis 72, 139, 142n18, 190, 282, 284n6
Mimesis 45–47, 49–59, 61–62, 63n1, 64n5, 65n9, 69n11, 219, 320
Mining, mines 12–13, 36, 74, 76, 78, 87, 165, 193n9, 205, 208, 229n7, 236–238, 240–243, 246, 249, 254, 274, 276, 278, 289–291
Modernism 1, 3–5, 13n3, 14n10–12, 45, 47, 64n5, 141n14; 166n4, 194n25, 211, 219, 227, 229, 263
Modernity 1, 8, 11, 13, 14n10, 14n14, 23, 25–26, 33, 37, 69, 70, 75–77, 81, 83, 109n14, 119, 123, 129, 131, 153, 167n13, 176, 181, 197, 212, 218, 219, 224, 236, 247, 263, 265
Mongia, Padmini 292–293
Moore, Jason 21, 24–25, 236–237, 239–240, 242, 249, 250n6–11, 253
Morality 8, 23, 30, 61–62, 65n14, 107–108n1, 204, 208, 209, 315
Morton, Timothy 28, 41n1
Murfin, Ross C. 270, 298
Muir, John 30, 32

Mulry, David 13n3
Myth 6, 11, 82, 109n15, 151, 162, 200, 236–237, 241–242, 245–247, 249, 261, 289, 294, 309n5

Næss, Arne 196–197, 199–203, 205, 207–209, 209n1
Najder, Zdzisław 199–200, 300
Narrative 6, 13n6, 22, 25, 26, 40, 45–46, 47, 49, 51–55, 57–59, 61–62, 75, 80, 82, 86, 105, 114, 117–119, 122–123, 126, 129–134, 136–140, 141n7, 142n23, 147–148, 154, 158, 161, 166n1, 166n10, 176, 180, 193n2, 194n29, 198, 203–204, 209, 211–214, 219, 224–228, 236, 239, 241–249, 250n9, 252–253, 256, 260, 279, 291n4, 292–295, 301, 311–312, 316; disaster narratives 45–46, 49, 62
Natural resources 3, 74, 76, 78, 206, 239, 241, 269, 272, 274, 277–278, 280, 290
New materialism, materialism 1, 4, 5, 39, 45, 49, 54, 63n1, 182, 184, 192, 194n19, 205, 211, 212, 215, 217, 221–223, 225–228, 230n9, 235–236, 241, 270, 274
Nietzsche, Friedrich 54, 59, 61, 63n1, 64n5, 65n14
Nitrates 272, 277, 283n3
Nitrogen 271, 275, 277
Nonhuman, the 5, 36, 43–47, 49–56, 58–59, 62, 63n2, 64n5, 64n9, 75, 93, 100, 107, 108n1, 109n9, 114, 117, 121, 124, 127–128, 130, 135, 138, 140, 142n17, 178, 197, 205, 208, 211–212, 215, 217, 219–220, 223–226, 229n4, 241–243, 247

Ontology 5, 6, 23, 25, 54, 69, 77, 84, 86, 114, 120, 124, 125, 138–140, 174, 196–198, 203–205, 209n1, 212, 220, 223, 227, 290; object-oriented ontology 5, 6, 114, 220, 227
Oceans 8, 12, 27, 45, 47, 57, 93–94, 97–99, 108n6, 121, 256, 270, 273, 277, 283n3; ocean acidification 27

Parker, Jay 250n5, 266
Parry, Benita 141n7, 238, 252, 261, 264
Pastoral, anti-pastoral 7, 10–13, 208

Pathetic fallacy 51, 100, 108–109n9, 313–316
Perception 40, 52–53, 149, 160, 163–164, 166n7, 178, 184–185, 190, 215, 220, 241, 312
Performativity 5, 14n6, 56, 146–149, 152–165, 166n4, 166n7, 167n17, 168n20, 173, 258, 260, 261, 297, 316, 319
Personification 27, 52, 100, 151, 205, 289, 292, 314–316
Peters, John G 119, 141n7, 193n10, 266
Phosphates 273, 275, 283n3
Physics 88n2, 115, 124, 177, 185
Physiology 177, 184–185
Physis 69–70, 79–80, 82, 87
Pluralism 208, 291
Politics 2, 3–5, 9, 13n6, 14n10–11, 26, 45, 47, 53–56, 63, 63n1, 65n12, 70, 75–76, 78, 80–87, 88n1–2, 94, 107–108n1, 114, 140n5, 174, 190, 197–198, 212, 215, 224, 235–244, 246, 254, 259, 275–277, 289–291, 291n4, 304
Pollution 70, 94, 96, 103–107, 108–109n9, 124, 131, 132
Postcolonial theory, postcolonial ecocriticism 1, 6, 27, 29, 39, 51, 65n10, 68, 69, 167n15, 238

Race 1, 4, 36, 45, 93
Racism 4, 24, 34
Rigby, Kate 45, 97, 163, 164
Romanticism 2, 4–7, 10, 14n9, 31, 93, 95, 115, 118, 127, 129, 252, 255–256, 263
Ruskin, John 313

Said, Edward 13n4, 39, 81, 309n2
Sailors, seamen 8, 40, 49, 52, 95–96, 98–99, 101–107, 107n1, 110n16, 113, 185, 199, 219, 312, 314; seamanship 93, 102, 104, 106, 109–110n16
Scarcity 226, 277–278, 291
Scenography 146, 153, 161–162, 166n7
Skepticism 40, 47, 118, 156, 191, 192, 196, 201, 209, 209n2, 247–248, 264
Schneider, Lissa 13n2, 13–14n6, 63n1, 228, 266
Scott, Walter 311

Seeber, Barbara K 4
Seel, Martin 148
Sensation 167n13, 177, 191, 194n19, 277, 304, 311; sensationalism 174–184
Serres, Michel 9, 43–44, 46–47, 56–61, 96, 101, 104
Sharpe, Alfred 37–38
Sherry, Norman 166n11, 194n27, 283n1, 309n5
Skepticism 40, 48, 118, 156, 191–192, 196, 201, 209, 209n2, 248, 264
Sloterdijk, Peter 119–120, 130
Solidarity 46, 78, 118, 127, 142n17, 182, 248, 262, 306, 311, 314–316
Spivak, Gayatri Chakravorty 294
Staten, Henry 293, 298n3
Steam 101–107, 108n6, 109n13; steam technology 237; steam power 102, 253, 258–261; steamships 5, 13n1, 22, 33, 47, 98, 101–105, 109n15, 131–132, 186, 189, 207, 244–245, 254–255, 258–259, 263, 266n2–3, 293, 307; steamboats 5, 72, 103; steam engines 49
Storms 8–10, 46, 48, 53, 55, 58, 60–62, 65n14, 96–101, 104, 108n8, 109n11, 109n15, 113, 116–117, 120–122, 124–125, 127, 131, 135, 137–139, 142n16, 156, 158, 177–178, 199, 205, 314, 316
Straus, Nina Pelikan 296–297
Suicide 10, 128, 204, 243, 246–249, 262–265

Techne 64n3, 69–71, 73, 76–78, 80, 82, 84, 87
Technology 69–70, 73, 75–78, 82, 102–103, 106–107, 109n12, 206, 208, 237

Terrain 4, 7, 115, 166n7, 206, 236237, 239, 241, 245–246, 256
Thoreau, Henry David 10, 31–32

Volcanoes 27, 29, 94, 95; Mount Tambora eruption 95, 108n3

Wallace, Alfred 146, 150
Warren, Robert Penn 78, 191–192
Watt, Ian 10, 95, 102, 107n1, 108, 148, 166n3, 209n2, 240, 270, 309n3, 311–317, 317n1, 322
Weather 1, 8–9, 14n12, 50, 55, 60–61, 93–99, 105, 107, 108n4, 114–115, 118, 120, 122–125, 129, 131, 137, 139–140, 141n10, 142n15, 176, 185, 222, 225, 237, 317; "dirty weather" 48, 93, 95, 97–98, 101, 104–107, 108n7, 131
White, Andrea 33, 252, 255, 258
Wilderness 2–4, 6–7, 13n6, 14n7–8, 21–22, 24, 26–27, 29–37, 73, 147, 150–151, 153–155, 157, 161, 164–165, 167n17, 183, 186, 189, 198, 201–204, 217, 279, 292
Williams, Raymond 3–4, 11, 28
Wollaeger, Mark 118, 137, 229n7
Woolf, Virginia 7, 14n2, 194n16, 315
Wordsworth, William 6, 10, 31, 151, 197, 313
World-ecology 25, 235–236, 239, 241–242, 248–249, 250n3, 253, 257, 259

Yeats, William Butler 315
Yeow, Agnes 164

Žižek, Slovaj 81, 160